MEXICO'S SPIRITUAL RECONQUEST

University of New Mexico Press
Albuquerque

Matthew

Butler

MEXICO'S SPIRITUAL RECONQUEST

Indigenous Catholics and Father Pérez's Revolutionary Church

© 2023 by the
University of New Mexico Press
All rights reserved. Published 2023
Printed in the United States of America

First paperback printing 2024

ISBN 978-0-8263-4506-6 (cloth)
ISBN 978-0-8263-4507-3 (paper)
ISBN 978-0-8263-4508-0 (PDF)
ISBN 978-0-8263-6726-6 (ePub)

Library of Congress Control Number: 2022945903

Founded in 1889, the University of New Mexico sits on the traditional homelands of the Pueblo of Sandia. The original peoples of New Mexico—Pueblo, Navajo, and Apache—since time immemorial have deep connections to the land and have made significant contributions to the broader community statewide. We honor the land itself and those who remain stewards of this land throughout the generations and also acknowledge our committed relationship to Indigenous peoples. We gratefully recognize our history.

Book epigraph on page vi extracted from *The Cambridge Edition of the Works of D. H. Lawrence: The Plumed Serpent*, by D. H. Lawrence (Cambridge: Cambridge University Press: 1987). Reproduced by permission of Paper Lion Ltd, the Estate of Frieda Lawrence Ravagli, and Cambridge University Press.

Cover photograph courtesy of the Instituto Nacional de Antropología e Historia, Mexico. Fototeca Nacional #174358.
Design by Isaac Morris
Display type Footlight MT
Body type Times New Roman 11 | 14

For Patrick and Patricia

The Quetzalcoatl movement had spread in the country, but sinisterly. The Archbishop had declared against it, Ramón and Cipriano and their adherents were excommunicated. An attempt had been made to assassinate Montes. The adherents of Quetzalcoatl in the Capital had made the Church of San Juan Bautista, which was called the Church of the Black Saviour, their Metropolitan House of Queztalcoatl. The Archbishop, a choleric man, had summoned his fervent followers, to march in procession to this Church of San Juan, now called the House of Queztalcoatl, and seize it and restore it to the Catholic Church. The government, knowing it would have to fight sooner or later, arrested the Archbishop and broke up the procession after some bloodshed.

Then a kind of war began. The Knights of Cortés brought out their famous hidden stores of arms, not very impressive after all, and a clerical mob, headed by a fanatical priest, surged into the Zócalo. Montes had the guns turned on them. But it looked like the beginnings of a religious war. In the streets the white and blue sarapes of Quetzalcoatl and the scarlet and black sarapes of Huitzilopochtli were seen in bands, marching to the sound of tom-toms, and holding up the curious round banners, made of feather-work, of Quetzalcoatl, and the tall scarlet signs of Huitzilopochtli, long poles with the soft club of scarlet feathers at the top, tufted with a black point.—In the churches, the priests were still inflaming the orthodox to a holy war. In the streets, priests who had gone over to Quetzalcoatl were haranguing the crowd.

It was a wild moment.

—D. H. Lawrence, *The Plumed Serpent* (1926)

CONTENTS

LIST OF ILLUSTRATIONS | *VIII*

ACKNOWLEDGMENTS | *XI*

INTRODUCTION | *1*

CHAPTER ONE | *14*
Habemus Pérez, 1925

CHAPTER TWO | *39*
"Mexico's Newest Revolution": ICAM

CHAPTER THREE | *69*
The Other *Cristiada*: Pérez's Second Coming

CHAPTER FOUR | *112*
"Our Beloved Peasants": ICAM on the *Ejido*

CHAPTER FIVE | *141*
"*Acá todo es vida*": ICAM as Local Religion

CHAPTER SIX | *173*
Bronze Priests: Mexican Revolutionary Clergy

CONCLUSION | *204*
Pérez is Dead, *Viva Pérez*

NOTES | *215*

BIBLIOGRAPHY | *259*

INDEX | *275*

ILLUSTRATIONS

MAPS

MAP 1 | *XIV*
Church Registrations from 1925 to 1938

MAP 2 | *XVI*
Revolutionary Church Foundations in Central and Southern Mexico, 1925–1938

MAP 3 | *XVIII*
ICAM Affiliations in México, Puebla, and Veracruz

FIGURES

FIGURE 1 | *103*
José Joaquín Pérez Budar, February 1925

FIGURE 2 | *103*
Adalberto Tejeda

FIGURE 3 | *104*
Ricardo Treviño

FIGURE 4 | *104*
Luis Morones and Calles

FIGURE 5 | *105*
Neoclassical *callista* allegory

FIGURE 6 | *105*
Schoolgirls performing flag ceremony at Calles's inauguration

FIGURE 7 | *106*
A *callista* welcoming committee waiting for caudillo Álvaro Obregón, March 30, 1926

FIGURE 8 | *106*
Bomberos turning their hoses on Roman Catholic rioters, February 1925

FIGURE 9 | *109*
Patriarch Pérez, Ash Wednesday, 1925

FIGURE 10 | *107*
Patriarch Pérez, Ash Wednesday 1925

FIGURE 11 | *108*
1903 broadsheet showing Our Lady of Solitude

FIGURE 12 | *108*
Facade of La Soledad, ca. 1925

FIGURE 13 | *109*
Main altar, parish of Santa Cruz y Soledad, ca. 1900

FIGURE 14 | *109*
Father Manuel Monge, Patriarch Pérez, and Ángel Jiménez Juárez, February 1925

FIGURE 15 | *110*
Father Antonio Benigno López y Sierra

FIGURE 16 | *110*
Father José Cano

FIGURE 17 | *111*
"Bell of the parish church of La Soledad, the first to ring out after the *arreglos*"

TABLES

TABLE 1 | *77*
ICAM Registrations, 1925–1938

TABLE 2 | *176*
Mexican Clergy, 1925–1940

ACKNOWLEDGMENTS

THIS BOOK HAS been a long time coming, like a proverbial rock band's sophomore album, and it wouldn't be here at all without the help and generosity of many people.

It is a pleasure to begin by thanking University of New Mexico Press, which showed saintly patience in waiting for the final manuscript and then moved quickly to review and publish. Special thanks are due to Lyman Johnson, Clark Whitehorn, Sonia Dickey, Michael Millman, and Zubin Meer, and to the insightful and courteous reviewers of the eventual manuscript.

Writing this has also brought home to me on many occasions the importance of collegiality and the fact that it indeed takes a village to produce a book. Given the lack of a central archive on the revolutionary Catholic movement, I am especially grateful to the many friends and colleagues who down the years remembered this project and kindly sent me copies of useful primary sources when they happened to come across them in the course of their own trips to the archives, whether in Rome, Oaxaca, or San Antonio. I hope that I have remembered you all: Cheasty Anderson, Steve Andes, Robert Curley, Lisa Edwards, Ben Fallaw, José Galindo, Hugo García Valencia, Ulisés Iñíguez Mendoza, Renata Keller, Austreberto Martínez Villegas, Madeleine Olson, Servando Ortoll, Ricardo Pérez Monfort, Mario Ramírez Rancaño, Ben Smith, Brian Stauffer, Ed Wright-Rios, Julia Young, and Susan Zakaib.

Many people also helped me to refine the project by reading and commenting on parts or all of the manuscript, including Roberto Blancarte, Margaret Chowning, Jason Dormady, Ben Fallaw, Antonio Escobar Ohmstede, Tanalís Padilla, and Julia Young. Thank you all. I am also grateful to Rob Karl, Emilio Kourí, and Deborah Toner, respectively, for the opportunity to present parts of the manuscript in the Shelby Cullom Davis Center for Historical Studies seminar series at Princeton University, the Katz Center seminar series at the University of Chicago, and the "Liberalism and Religion" series run by the Institute for Study of the Americas at the University of London.

Support, advice, and encouragement over the years has come from so many people, above all those interested in Mexican and religious history, that it is impossible to name them all. But they include, in addition to all the compadres and colleagues already mentioned above: Adrian Bantjes (*qepd*), Cecilia Bautista García, Jürgen Buchenau, Julie Byrne, Barry Carr, Manuel Ceballos (*qepd*), Fiona Clark, Brian Connaughton, Gabriela Cristiani, Michael Ducey, Mariana Gómez Villanueva, Jennifer Graber, Gerardo Gurza, Gema Kloppe-Santamaría, Alan Knight, Jean Meyer, Pablo Mijangos, Andrea Mutolo, Adriana Pacheco, Erika Pani, Yolanda Padilla, Andrew Paxman, Elizabeth Pritchard, Franco Savarino, Yves Solís, Phil Stover, Itzel Toledo García, Isabel Torres, Valentina Torres Septién, and Pamela Voekel. In Texas, I owe special thanks to all my Latin Americanist colleagues, but especially to Susan Deans Smith and Ginny Garrard, and to the graduate students who have taught me more about Mexican history and sometimes life than I have been able to teach them, especially Jian Gao, Diego Godoy, Elizabeth O'Brien, Madeleine Olson, Manuel Salas, Sal Salinas, Brian Stauffer, and Andrew Weiss. John Erard also deserves special mention and thanks for drawing the maps and matching saints' names to toponyms; likewise my brother scribes in UT-Austin's inaugural Vice-Provost's Author's Fellowship cohort: Ken Greene, Scott Stroud, Shanti Kumar, and Zachary Elkins.

I also would like to give sincere and ecumenical thanks to the custodians of the many church archives that I used in the researching of this book, not least because researching a controversial Catholic figure such as Patriarch Pérez has sometimes felt like wrestling with personal religious conscience through the accidental medium of a historical problem. Perhaps it needs a lapsed Anglican to write a book about such an ambivalent figure. Either way, my deep thanks to Father Antonio Celis García of the Mexican Catholic and Apostolic Church, who on numerous occasions opened his home in Iztapalapa and the surviving ICAM archives in his possession to me, and in so doing taught me that there was a humanity and sincerity of purpose about ICAM. Likewise, special thanks must go to Marco Pérez Iturbe, Berenise Bravo Rubio, and Father Gustavo Watson of the Archivo Histórico del Arzobispado de México, which houses the single largest collection of documents on ICAM. This information was made freely available to me in a truly open-minded, never confessional, spirit. In a similar vein, I am grateful to Bishops Carlos Touché-Porter and Martiniano García of the Diócesis Anglicana de México, and to Chris Higgins and Sarah Dana of the Archives of the Episcopal Church in Austin.

Acknowledgments

Funding for this project came from various sources, to which I would like to express my gratitude: the Mellon Foundation, the Arts and Humanities Research Council (UK), the Institute of Historical Studies, and the College of Liberal Arts at the University of Texas at Austin.

Without the love and support of family and friends this book would not only not have been written; it would not have been worth writing. I have leaned on Antonio Escobar Ohmstede and Brian Stauffer many times. Ben Fallaw provided Midlothian wisdom on many occasions and told me when it was time to stop digging. I definitely couldn't have done this without the Torres Meza family in Mexico City or the Butler, Cadinouche, and Emanuel clans in England. *Los quiero*. Desmond and Elías left us along the way, and they are missed every day. Patrick joined us. The book is for him and Patricia, my beloved wife.

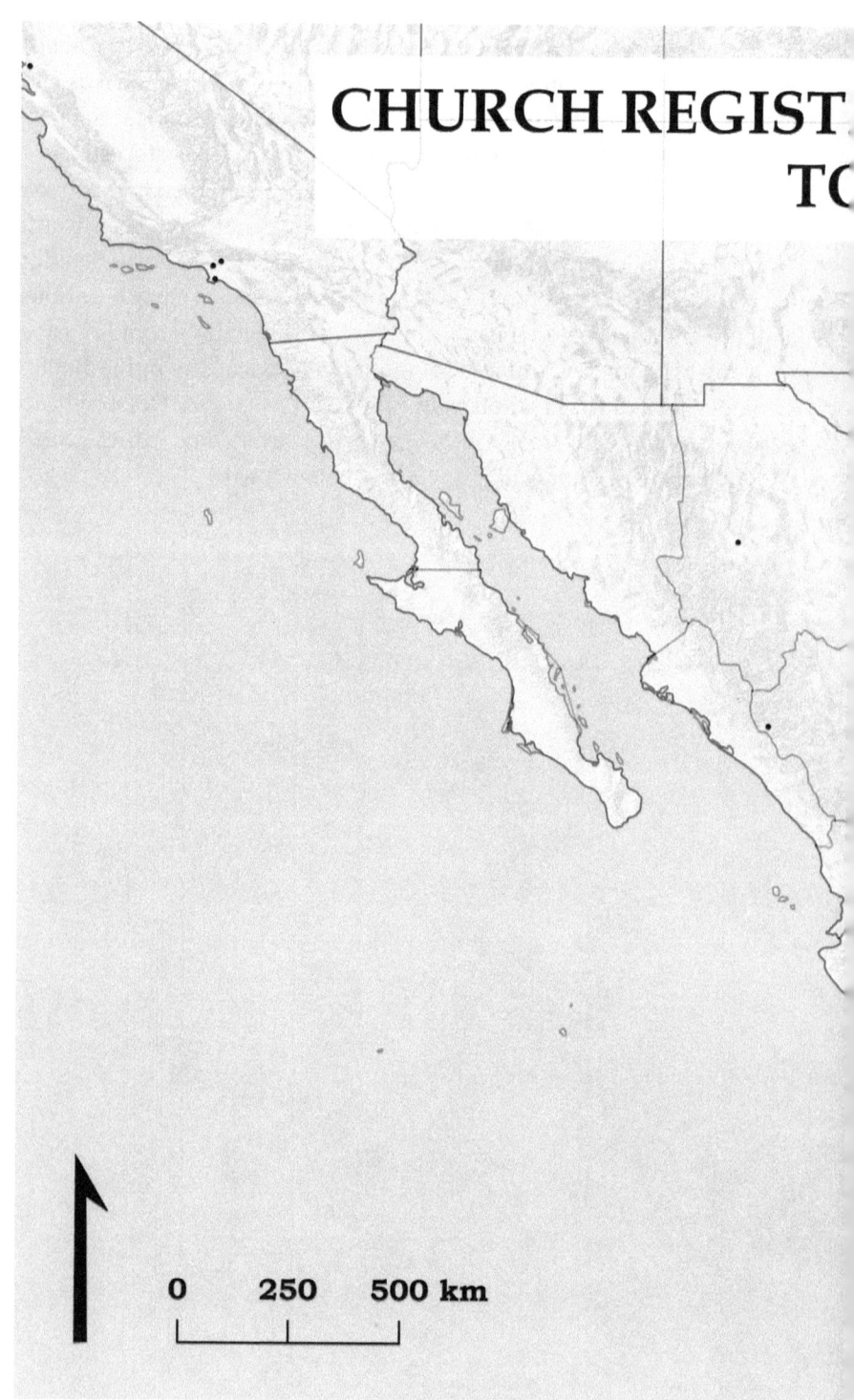

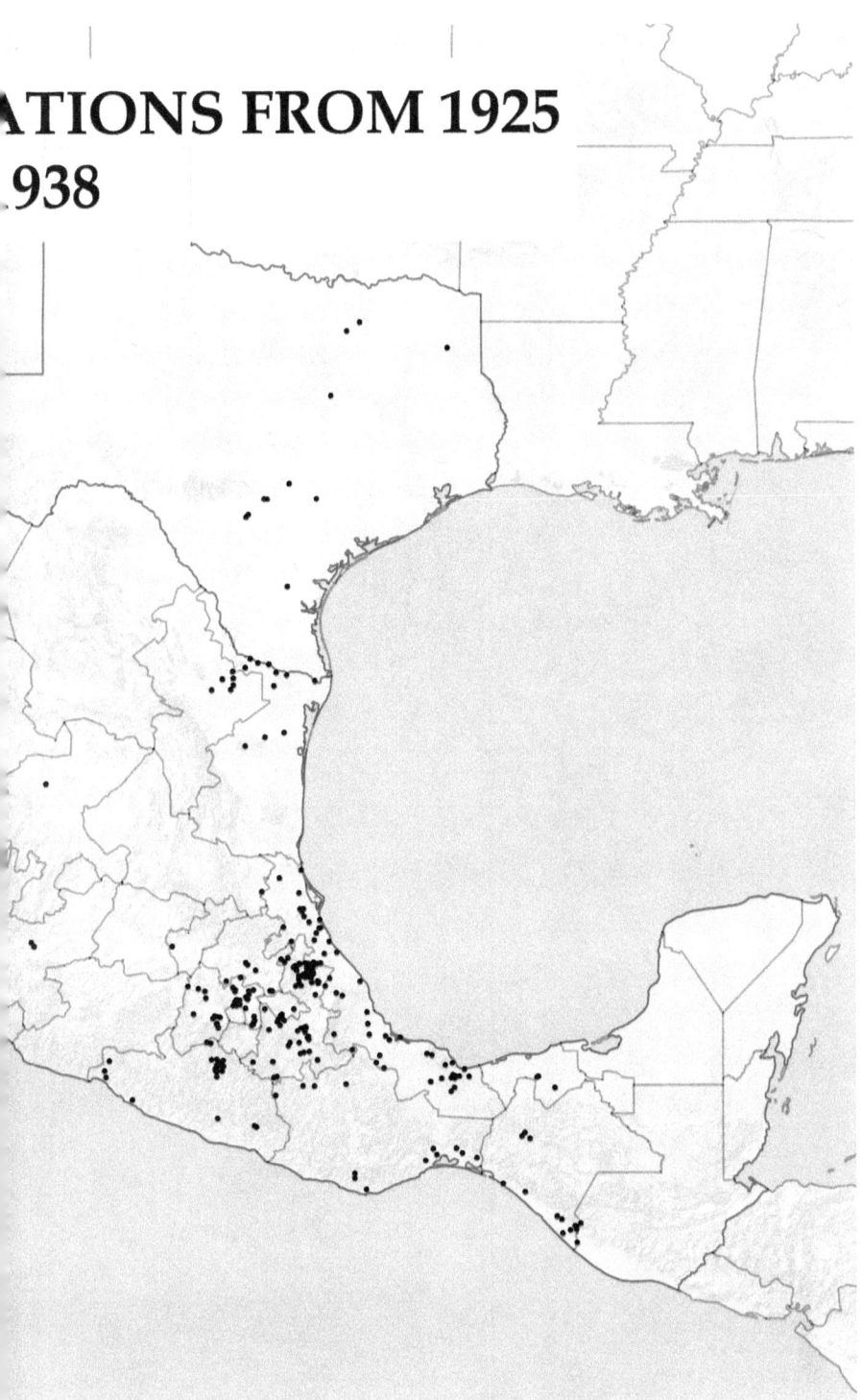

Map 1. Church Registrations from 1925 to 1938. Courtesy of John D. Erard.

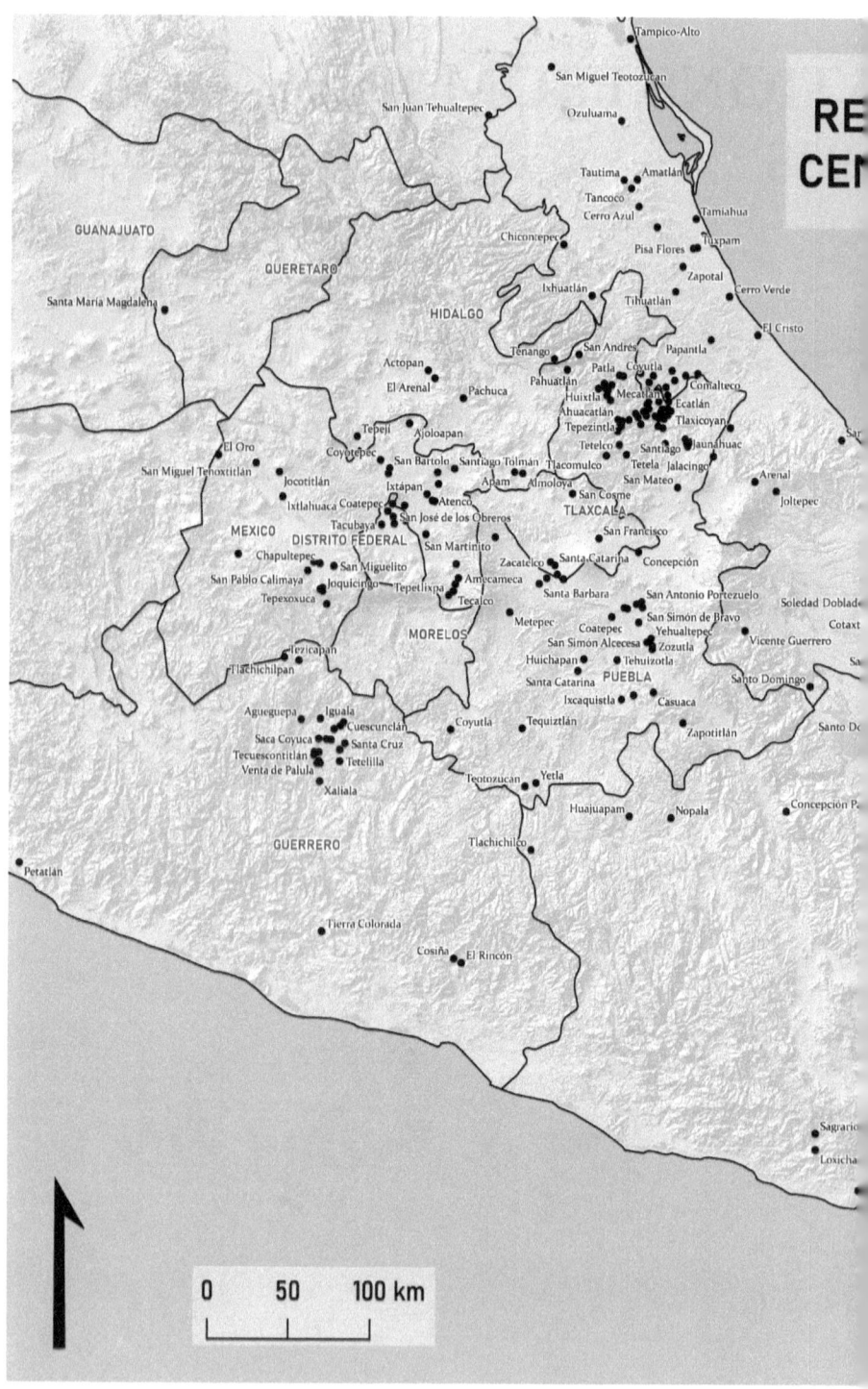

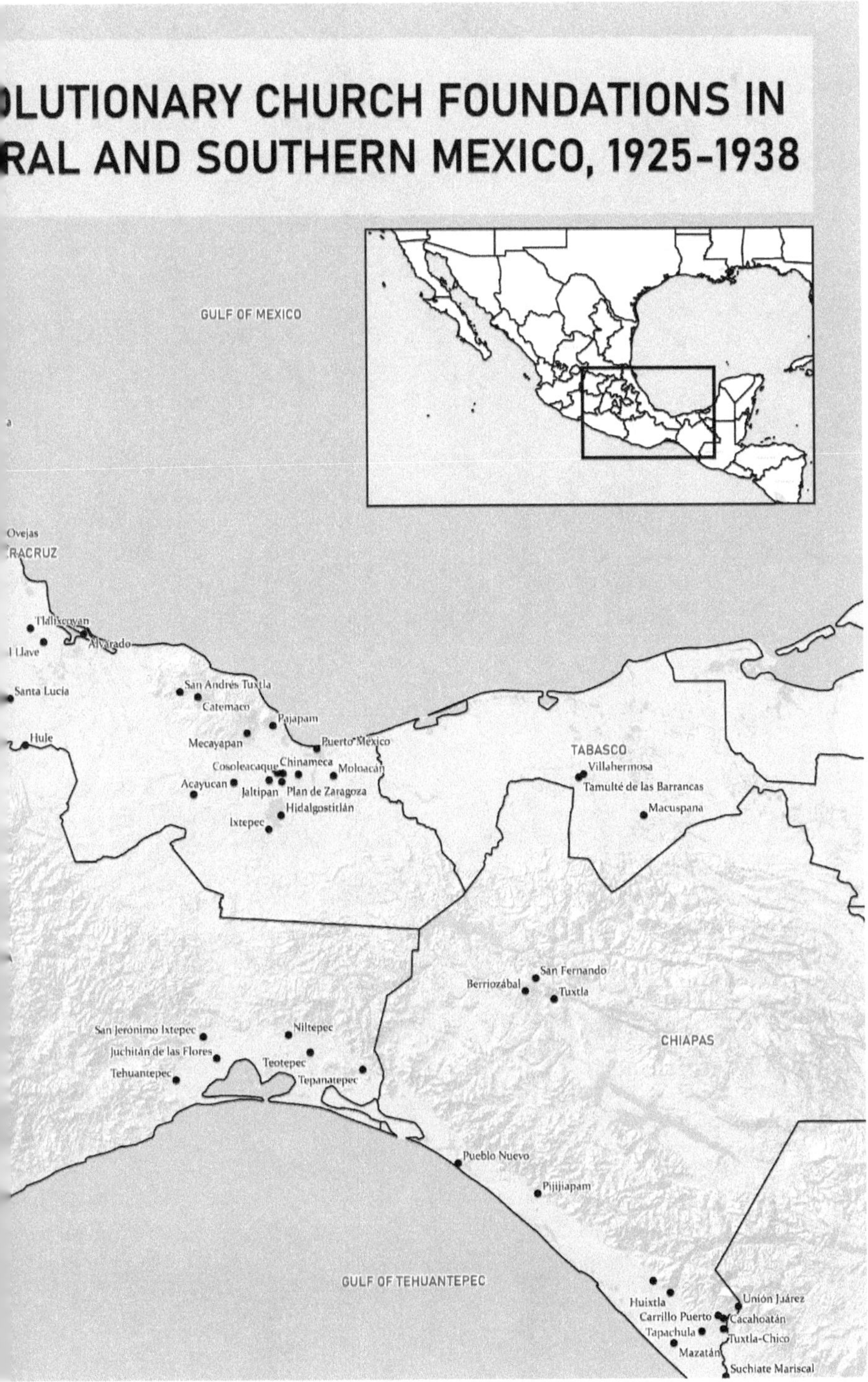

Map 2. Revolutionary Church Foundations in Central and Southern Mexico, 1925–1938. Courtesy of John D. Erard.

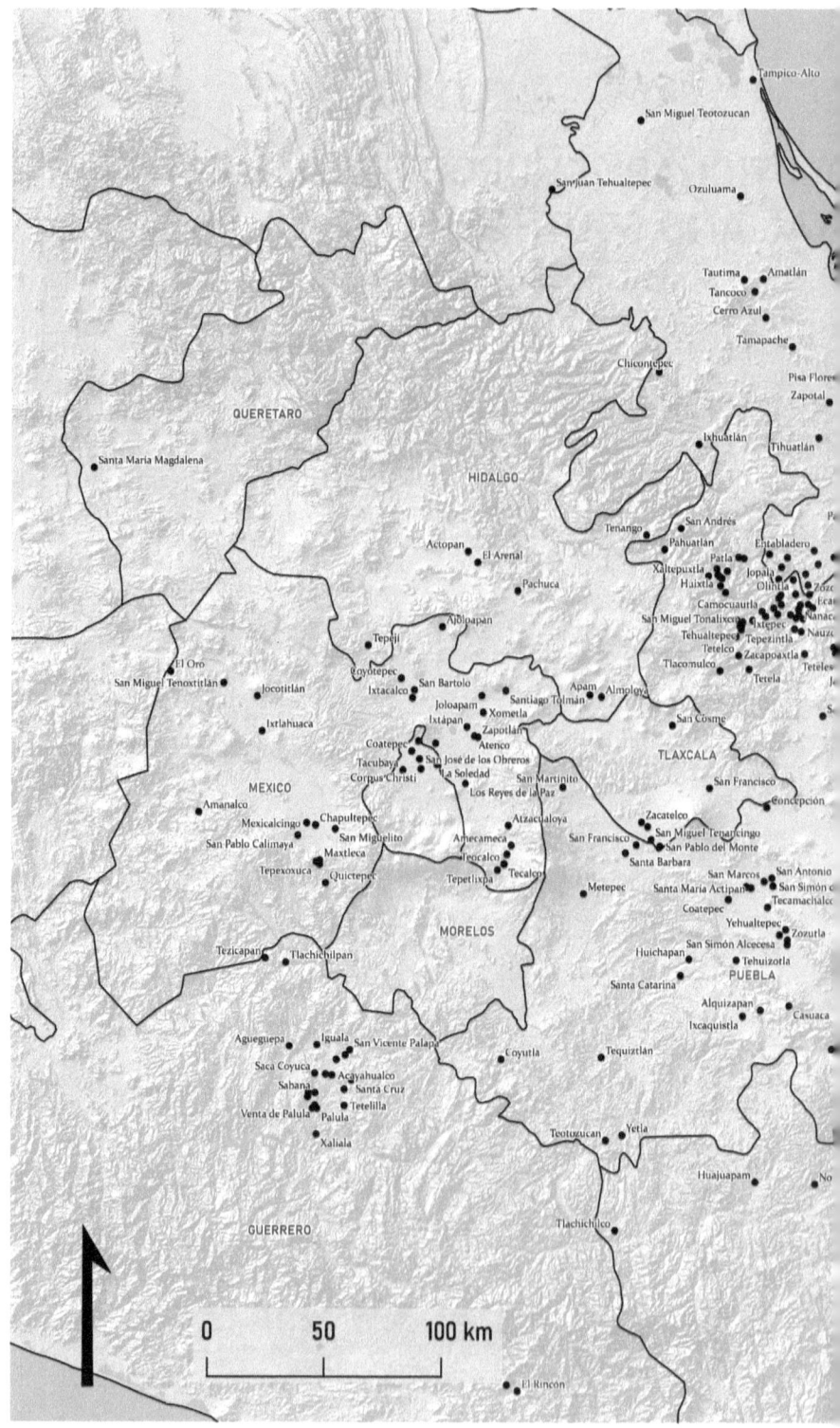

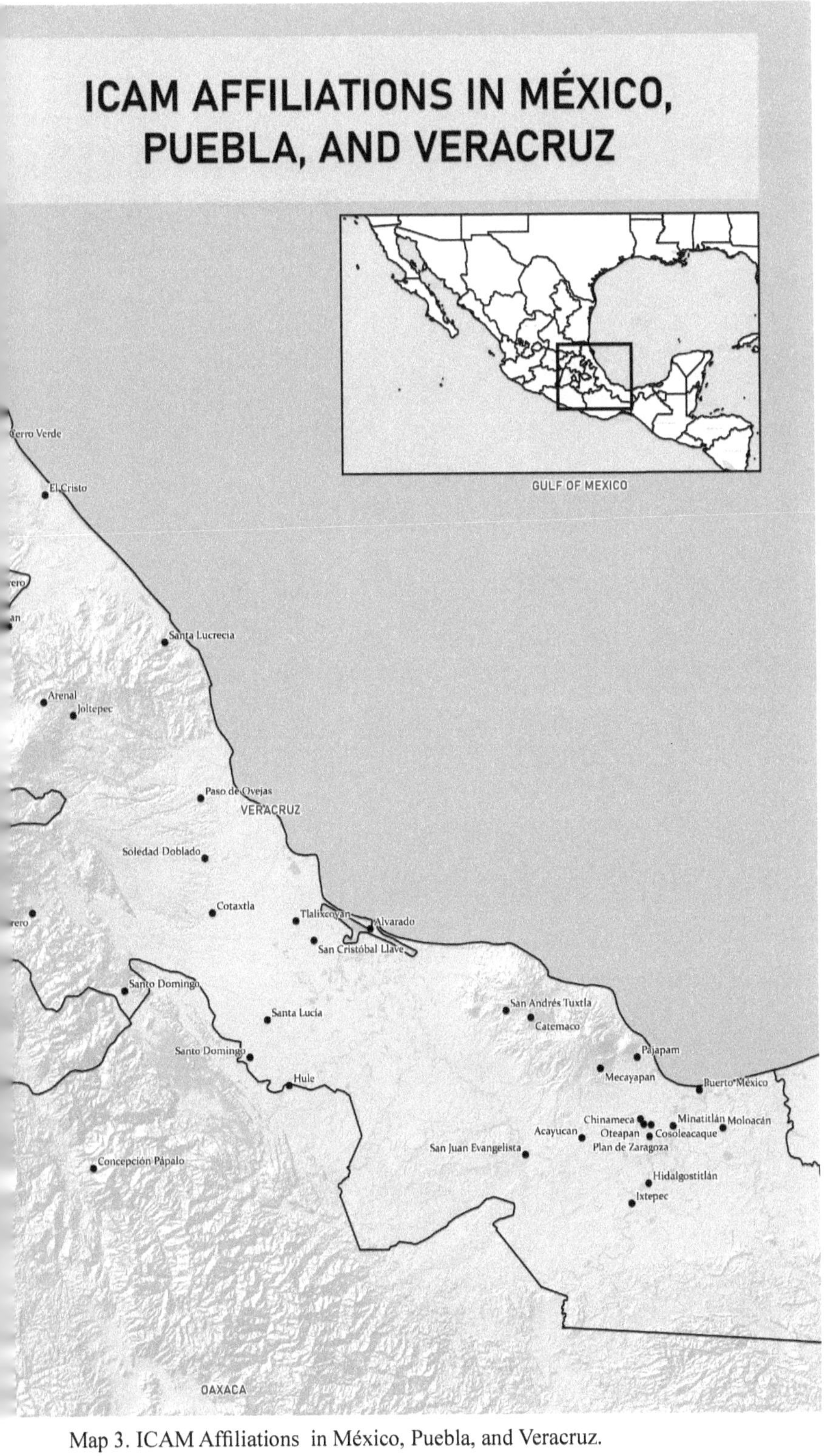

ICAM AFFILIATIONS IN MÉXICO, PUEBLA, AND VERACRUZ

Map 3. ICAM Affiliations in México, Puebla, and Veracruz.
Courtesy of John D. Erard.

INTRODUCTION

FEW FIGURES ASSOCIATED with Mexico's revolution are so reviled as Patriarch José Joaquín Pérez Budar, the wizened soldier-priest who broke with Rome in 1925 and founded the prorevolutionary Mexican Catholic and Apostolic Church (Iglesia Católica Apostólica Mexicana, ICAM).[1] To write about his church is to run a gauntlet of period, mostly Roman Catholic, invective: Pérez was a stooge of the revolution (a "straw patriarch"); a drunken antipope ("Arch-Vinestalk"); or a madman, "perched in a tree, haranguing throngs of invisible faithful."[2] Pérez's nationalism was so crazed, Mexico's curia said, that he despised the donkey, Christ's mount, because the quadruped was imported from Spain. If he had to convert Mexico to Islam to spite Rome, he would do it.[3] What else to expect of a priest who allegedly hocked the Virgin of La Soledad—patroness of the parish where he launched his revolt—in the national pawnshop? Canard of canards, it was said that Pérez recanted on his deathbed in 1931. Even his apostasy was fake.[4]

Unsurprising, many laypeople hated Pérez. In 1925, rioters in Ciudad Hidalgo—a pious Michoacán city—told Pérez to fuck his mother;[5] one *cristero* broadside euphemistically told Pérez to screw himself "along with his reformed church and *jorongo* cassock."[6] Mystics atoned for Pérez with masochistic gusto or wanted him dead: aristocratic Concha Cabrera seared her flesh with a branding iron to cauterize the spiritual wounds Pérez caused; José de León Toral—the avenging angel who shot caudillo Álvaro Obregón in 1928—had Pérez on his hit list.[7]

Mexico City newspapers, meanwhile, mocked Pérez as lowborn and mercenary: "ex-captain Pérez" said "'Martín Garratuza' masses," mocked *Excélsior*, evoking the ecclesiastical masquerades of Vicente Riva Palacio's fictional hero. Others likened him to Lazarillo, the picaresque beggar, or, posthumously, to his drunken fictional namesake, *Pito* ("Prick") Pérez.[8]

Many accounts depicted Pérez's "Mexican" Church as brutish, rum-soaked, and idolatrous—in a word, *Indian*. Pérez was the "Totonac Luther";[9] hence the stubborn myth, oozing colonial prejudice, that he consecrated tortillas and mezcal for Mass, not bread and wine.[10] Hence, too, the corridos and stage tunes. "Everything must be Mexican, made at home / Our devil is the *Nahuál*, not Lucifer from Rome," ran one 1925 song, "National Reformations, Part Two," which mocked Pérez as shaman-in-chief (*nagual*) of a new paganism. The writer claimed Pérez would reinstate human sacrifice to the war god Huitzilopochtli as national cult: "It's our inheritance, which is the reason / Bloodshed at Mass is always in season / We never tire of the goriness / To spill blood well is . . . to progress!" Another song, "Reformist Clergy," mocked Mexico's "new pope" and his "modern friars" as demons leaping from the inferno.[11] To José Vasconcelos, Pérez promoted an atavistic civil religion worthy of Moctezuma.[12]

Pérez's followers, meanwhile, were schismatics (cismáticos), if not, punnishly, "asthmatics" (asmáticos). Alternatively, they were "hungry dogs," "devil's cattle," "sons of darkness," "lepers," "cretins," "skirt-chasers," and "drunken perverts." As "un-poped" Catholics (*despapados*), they were religious bastards (no tuvieron padres).[13] Racialized epithets, again, were common. Pérez wasted his time massing in Spanish, *Excélsior* jeered, because the language that "faithful of the schismatic church" understood "is Nahuatl." Educated Catholics—people who followed the Latin Mass using Nebrija's golden-age lexicon—were not fooled.[14] Perhaps nobody painted a more disgusted, racially tinged picture than another ex-captain, Irishman Francis McCullagh, author of *Red Mexico* (1928). "A more painful and repulsive sight I have seldom witnessed," McCullagh wrote after hearing Pérez say Mass in Corpus Christi, his cathedral on the Avenida Juárez. Pérez was "as evil looking as sin itself," his priests "old and vicious," his church "degraded and superstitious . . . like the Church of Abyssinia."[15]

Perhaps it is as well to get the insults out of the way first. If the sound has been heard once it has been heard a thousand times; this is also a book that tries to understand Pérez, not recrucify him using his haters' words. It is less concerned with rehabilitation than viewing ICAM in proper context—which the book takes to be the history of indigenous Mexico and of reformist Catholicism and the state, not just the Cristero War, with all its passions. To some extent, the question of wider significance poses itself: why the fury, the unbecoming Catholic profanity, if, as everyone maintains, Pérez *had* no followers? Why gift notoriety to a non-entity? Did he *matter*?

The idea of a Catholic priest swearing undying loyalty to the postrevolutionary state and nationalistic hostility to Rome had a certain retro logic. In 1925, the church in Mexico had been separate from the state for what was still less than a biblical threescore years and ten, formal separation having been decreed by liberal president Benito Juárez only in 1859, under the Reform laws. Pérez himself (b. 1851) was older than that; and besides, this traumatic decoupling occurred after well over three centuries of state tutelage, legally enshrined in the royal, latterly the national, patronage.[16] Why, then, as the church flexed its muscles against the regime and the 1917 revolutionary Constitution, should Mexican state and nation builders not think of, or at the very least consider, solving Mexico's "religious question" by reactivating the device of a state church? It is important to capture a sense of historical "ongoingness," and not be fooled by revolutionaries' constant protestations that they were sons of Juárez: church-state separation in Mexico was a work in progress, momentous but reversible, no more an inevitable state of affairs than *Roe v. Wade* or Brexit. The 1917 Constitution itself opened many roads back to the future, even giving officials the power to license priests and fix their numbers, for all that postrevolutionary presidents before the mid-1920s had pragmatically sworn off them.

On the other hand, Catholicism in Mexico had certainly become more "romanized" by the 1920s, as historians like to say: that is, subject to Vatican-centered disciplinary norms and Eurocentric forms of devotionalism. In this context, Pérez was always going to be seen not just as a throwback but also as a religious provocateur, even a traitor. Certainly, his 1925 "liberation" of La Soledad—parodying Miguel Hidalgo's *grito de Dolores*—led to a rapid escalation in church-state tensions. Flanked by goons from the Regional Confederation of Mexican Labor (CROM), the official union, Pérez effected his coup during Carnival, the Roman feast of inversion, only three months into the presidency of Plutarco Elías Calles

(1924–1928). It seemed prophetic—a "grim omen," the archbishop of Morelia said.[17] So it proved: within days, Roman Catholics formed the National League for the Defense of Religious Liberty (LNDLR), which launched an insurrection in mid-1926 after Calles mandated enforcement of the 1917 Constitution's religious articles and the episcopate countered by suspending public worship. Pérez was thus an enabler of the Cristero Revolt (1926–1929), a major Catholic insurrection against the *callista* regime and one of the bloodiest episodes in Mexican history. Historians are merciless. Jean Meyer, speaking for many, condemns *el cisma* as a political ploy devised by labor boss Luis Morones to split Catholic workers and strengthen CROM. Pérez's worker church—part Henry VIII, part Jimmy Hoffa—caused outrage, but in and of itself was meaningless, a religious grotesque.[18]

Again, however, to understand how viscerally Pérez was loathed we must go beyond politics and see him culturally as a projection of Roman Catholic nightmares, an ecclesiastical bête noire. Schismatizing, after all, was an obscure, theological crime—against church unity under the Roman pontiff; it sounded bad, but not everyone knew what it meant, even some who screamed the loudest.[19] One anxiety, which haunted Vatican officials, was that "Catholic" Mexico was less loyal than its bishops admitted; that the old idea of a national church, given encouragement, was not dead, even among priests. Mexican seminaries were awash with "schismatical" ideas, the Josephite superior reported on the eve of the revolution.[20] The appearance of a renegade soldier-priest—Pérez had fought for Porfirio Díaz before taking holy orders—was a ghoulish reminder of state religion. A yet more alarming thought was that the church might never have been won in the first place, not truly. Pérez, with his Everyman name and *mixteco* roots, personified the church's primordial fear of indigenous backsliding. It suited *capitalino* journalists to call him Huitzilopochtli: caste warfare sold newspapers. For Roman clergy, the narcissism of small differences demanded that a *Catholic* competitor be hounded to the ends of the earth. Better, too, to attribute Pérez's revolt to barbarism than admit to any pastoral failings. In postrevolutionary Mexico, as in Willa Cather's *Death Comes for the Archbishop* (1927), Catholic culture was Europeanized; "inculture" was dark-skinned, plebeian. It was ironic, then, that the jibes about Pérez's atavism made him infamous, so helped to create the antipope his opponents feared. Virtually the only people to join Pérez *were* indigenous;

or, failing that, *braceros* in the US-Mexico borderlands or unbeneficed clergy from dead-end Mexican pueblos. The history of braceros' interest in Pérez is worth a study in its own right and will not much preoccupy us here: usually, however, the response mimicked that of other ethnic Catholicisms in the United States, in that groups of migrant Mexican workers in Texas and California consciously sought out a nationalistic church in exile, one that would complement a class and national identity, offer a vernacular liturgy, and counteract what was perceived as neglect by Anglo-Irish clergy.[21]

To *understand* Pérez, therefore—not necessarily forgive—we have to try and see him as his church of untouchables did and remember that, to some people, the idea of being a church inside the state was not the heresy that it was to Rome. This brings us to this book's central claim, which is that ICAM was more than a CROM cut-out but, rather, a popular, prorevolutionary church that, very unusually, connected reformist critiques of Roman Catholicism with an indigenous constituency. That is, the argument is that ICAM was a popular church with its own empirical theology, set of "Mexicanized" Catholic practices, and clergy. Remarkably, too, and in plain sight of Mexico's Cristero War, by the 1930s the Mexican Patriarchate claimed many thousands of rural devotees in indigenous pueblos scattered across central and southern Mexico. In these indigenous redoubts, revolutionary Catholicism signified a third-wave "spiritual reconquest," following the missionary efforts of the sixteenth century and the secularization drives of the eighteenth. There was attendant coercion and violence, as there was with both these earlier churchings. For devotees, however, ICAM meant the right to elect priests and revive exuberant saintly devotions free of clerical surveillance or religious taxes. It moralized indigenous participation in official state projects, added vim to secessionist pueblo politics, and reinforced the political capital of ethnic village elites. At the movement's altars, meanwhile, there stood a clergy of indigenous churchpeople, theological ranters, and liberal or fallen priests. Indigenous Catholics' leveraging of state power for spiritual purposes, and the blowing open of such categories as "Catholic Church" and "priest," the book contends, represented Mexico's "other," forgotten Cristiada, a kind of indigenous reformation.

Not the first study of Pérez, then, it is perhaps the most three-dimensional one, given that most historians who revisit ICAM start by looking in the wrong place—the cities—and then, finding nothing, conclude that ICAM was a state contrivance. Ricardo Pérez Montfort and Víctor Díaz Arciniega—the first historians to take ICAM seriously as part of the regime's ideological apparatus—nonetheless limit themselves to discursive readings of La Soledad.[22] Mario Ramírez Rancaño, in the best study to date, offers a capitalino-based analysis focusing on ICAM's internal politics and oftentimes rakish personalities. Even Miguel Lisbona Guillén and Julio Ríos, noting ICAM's gestation in Chiapas, dismiss this as performative anticlericalism. All it proved was that federal power was growing in the regions.[23]

In contrast, this book argues that ICAM was an example of dialectical church and state formation in which indigenous people animated ICAM, hence Calles's religious policy. It is important, therefore, to distinguish between the CROM-backed putsch of 1925, which was in reality prologue, and ICAM's development thereafter, especially during the Cristero War and 1930s. In these years, ICAM re-emerged as an indigenous constitutional church wherein political, agrarian, and religious factors—local Catholicism, secessionist politics, ethnic resentments, and land disputes—were the drivers.[24] Thus, from 1926, as churches closed and fiestas were canceled, Pérez played host to delegations of indigenous patriarchs (principales) and *agraristas*, not CROM bosses. Like the education ministry (Secretaría de Educación Pública, SEP), ICAM sent out missionaries by train or car, on horse or foot, until, by 1929, Pérez controlled some three hundred parishes and *vicarías* in an area from the Huasteca to the Soconusco. ICAM also had followers in the southern United States, in California and Texas. All in, Pérez had about as many churches as the sixteenth-century religious orders had *doctrinas* (convent parishes).[25] I also estimate that Pérez had two hundred thousand congregants distributed in Nahua, Totonac, Tepehua, Zapotec, Cuicateco, Mam, and Zoque pueblos and highland ejidos. This approximated the contemporary sum of all Protestant congregations, making ICAM the second religious denomination of its day. Though Rome insisted that the regime dismantle ICAM as a condition for peace in 1929, spin-offs still exist.[26]

An indigeneity thesis was planted long ago by nobody less than Robert Ricard. In the final footnote on the final page of his 1933 magnum opus, indeed, Ricard wondered if Pérez's appearance might not reflect the secular or diocesan clergy's historic failure to church indigenous Mexico or create an indigenous clergy, as well as its tolerance of class divisions in ecclesiastical ranks.²⁷ Ricard was right, especially on the first two counts, though he would hardly have sympathized with Pérez theologically.²⁸ ICAM did fan out in indigenous zones: parts of the Huasteca; Puebla's drizzly Sierra Norte; the Totonocapan, which embraced the Puebla-Veracruz piedmont in the 1920s–1930s; the Tehuantepec isthmus joining Mexico's Pacific and Gulf coasts; the Soconusco; and the central plateau (México, Tlaxcala, Puebla), in García Martínez's "pueblos of the sierra." There *was* something historical, and unfulfilled, about this: in terms of ecclesiastical geography, ICAM followed the contours of the Franciscans' Totonocapan mission and the sixteenth-century isthmian see of Coatzacoalcos.²⁹ Indigenous Catholics here sometimes found that ICAM gave them power to appoint priests, worship as they pleased, pay fewer religious taxes, resurrect fiestas, and make their villages new religious centers. It provided cover for land reform (agrarismo). That is, Pérez had support because he mediated between indigenous Catholicism and the bureaucracy: ICAM allowed people to leverage federal power in church affairs and renegotiate the terms of local religion. That was the reality of revolutionary-indigenous religion, not the pre-Columbian revivalism about which D. H. Lawrence fantasized while writing *The Plumed Serpent* in callista Mexico.³⁰

Why is this not remembered? If indigenous Catholics practiced the same romanesque pieties as the *cristeros*, with the fierce certainty that allows historians of a postreligious academy to admire their verve and independence, they would be. But indigenous Catholicism feels ambivalent. We insist it must come to us, and we call it "syncretic" (or similar) when these terms denote a "metasyncretic" power to name and establish hierarchies as much as anything else, as Stewart argues. Here, then, it will be categorized as local religion, which seems sufficiently lived and specific to place/"ethnie."³¹ At the same time, we must be wary of other master narratives, namely, the Catholic-style modernity that historians dub "romanization" and state secularization. Wasn't Catholicism meant to become standardized and pious, following European usage? Weren't revolutions supposed to put the church in its place? A state church was on the wrong side of history twice over, hence people rushed to declare ICAM dead almost on arrival. His Holiness could forget about the "disgraziato apostata Gioacchino Perez," the exiled archbishop of Mexico reassured Pius XI in 1927. But what did he know, reading newspapers in San Antonio?³² "For us, the Roman clergy as well as *los cismáticos* are noxious elements representing a serious threat to the formation of future mentalities," wrote Tomás Garrido Canabal in 1932 (this from the boss who pushed ICAM in his socialist banana republic of Tabasco).[33] Less justifiably, historians of modern Mexico have also been remiss, until recently, in nuancing indigenous Catholicisms, which some still theorize as conservative obstacles to revolutionary state formation.[34]

The first step to writing ICAM's history is therefore to accept its essential messiness, overlaps, and contradictions, not wish them away. If we do this, Pérez's movement has several instructive lessons. The first, as stated, concerns the persistently disruptive power in Mexico of reformist Catholic ideas.[35] These went back, at least, to the 1820s, when Mexican insurgent Fray Servando—a participant in the French Revolution's Constitutional Church—urged congress to create an independent, republican church, in imitation of the democratic, primitive church of the New Testament. Through Pérez, the revolution retied a broken thread with such nation-centered, constitutional (ultimately jansenistic) ecclesiologies, which are usually held to have expired in the nineteenth century as the church became vaticanized. In fact, their persistence should remind us that the Catholic Church's hegemonic Roman status in Mexico was hard-won, only achieved via the suppression of alternative concepts of Catholicism and churchness.[36] Even if ICAM was a lo-fi, street-fighting version of this constitutional ecclesiology, that was its matrix.

Second, the secularization telos of liberal-revolutionary Mexico also looks fuzzier, and the religious motives of revolutionary anticlericals brighter, if we grant more credence to Pérez's prorevolutionary take on Catholicism.[37] Revolutionaries often said as much, even hardcore callistas. Luis León, Calles's agriculture minister, recalled visiting the catacombs on a 1921 trip to Rome and imagined walking with "the revolutionary Christ." Visiting the Latin American College, he was delighted when a Oaxacan intern "of indigenous type" declared that the revolution was gospel incarnate. Interior minister Adalberto Tejeda was nephew of Father Miguel Tejeda, a classic enlightened priest: as *cura* of Altatonga (Ver.), he penned tracts on astronomy and mathematics. Calles himself, two eighteenth-century priests in his lineage, said he would not "de-catholicize" Mexico, just make clergy tend to "Catholic consciences." This in interview to the *New York Times*: but such sentiments characterized callistas' private transcripts, suggesting they brought emotionally complex understandings of Catholicism into politics.[38] As

Riccardo Cannelli calls it, the "logic of the *patronato*"—a statist urge to direct, manage, and improve the church—lasted long after formal separation in 1859.[39] Revolutionaries were often less anticlerical, in the sense of being opposed to priests as a class, than we assume. They had a positive ecclesiastical other in mind—humble, patriotic, self-sacrificing—that was born of their disappointment as to how priests actually were, or seemed to be at any rate. Revolutionaries were often frustrated Catholics, would-be believers more than a band of godless iconoclasts.

If the revolution was surprisingly Catholic, this is not to say revolutionaries entertained naïve illusions about ICAM, only that the idea of *reforming* the church fitted their worldview on religious, not just political, grounds. This gave rise, third, to a contradictory mode of state formation that was often decidedly less than secularist. Callistas exalted official *laicismo* yet talked endlessly of "purifying" the church, as if that fell to them somehow. Roman clergy said the church was sovereign, free of the state; yet howled if religious competitors invaded their turf, as though their spiritual monopoly were natural, not a legacy of historic state protections. Even if secularization is always unfinished, it is surprising that so anticlerical a government as Calles's was *so* indebted to religion.[40] Callistas dabbled in what Anthony B. Smith calls "neo-traditional" nationalism, in the sense that a nationalist project received support from traditional religions, notoriously ICAM but also evangelicals. The callista model of land reform was conceived in corporatist terms derived from Christian social thought; and the regime developed French-style bureaucratic mechanisms—registration of priests under article 130—to engineer a kind of lay, constitutional church. These were not afterthoughts; they showed religious, even Catholic, preferences, not laicist blindness.[41] Using Johnson, Klassen, and Sullivan's idea of churchstateness—denoting an isomorphic church-state relationship in which there is not linear differentiation but simultaneous "pulling away" and "drawing from"—perhaps we should talk of a postrevolutionary *churchstate*. As these authors put it, echoing James Scott, the postrevolutionary state was one that continued "seeing" like a church.[42]

Though the point can be overdone, fourth, Mexico's religious conflict was in a real sense a culture war between Catholicisms.[43] At the grassroots, this should make us reappraise the history of the cristero conflict as a popular rejection of secular statism by reflecting more on the weight of indigenous participation therein. ICAM's growth in central-southern latitudes ensured that the 1920s and 1930s resembled colonial-era secularization, that is, the systematic, and often violent, replacement of missionary clergy with "secular" (diocesan, "in the world") priests under state control.[44] Many pueblos, like Yonne villages in revolutionary France, responded to the incitement to remake their churches politically, economically, and even spiritually.[45] A common pattern was that indigenous principales formed citizens' committees and registered "Mexican" priests as parish incumbents. This was especially true in places where the 1926 suspension of public worship caused a festive neurosis. Where a festive observance in honor of a patron saint was a religious, agricultural, and economic necessity, it was sometimes ICAM, not its Roman antagonist, that guaranteed a pueblo's existential survival. The real agents were indigenous people: town-hall officials, churchwardens, and the like. Pérez knew many such people from his circuit-riding days, and his movement at large recalled the Porfirian veterans' network studied by Patrick McNamara, not some revolutionary central. In Mexico City, Pérez was the point of articulation between a grassroots indigenized churchstate and Gobernación. For the same reason, *secretario* Adalberto Tejeda, not Luis Morones, was Pérez's real consigliere.[46]

This clash between Catholicisms had important ramifications, fifth, even at the level of high politics and the religious diplomacy conducted between the Holy See and the Mexican revolutionary forces.[47] It was one thing for Rome to confront a hostile, generically anticlerical, regime; but quite another to confront a regime that was busy rechurching itself and reassigning hundreds of churches to its own constitutional clergy. As we shall see, the 1929 *arreglos*—Mexico's Lateran Pact—made specific but oblique reference to this question and resulted in the regime's tactical and public decision to abandon Pérez and his peasant followers in order to secure a deal with Rome, just as Rome sacrificed its armed militants (the cristeros). ICAM's unexpected growth was therefore one significant factor in Rome's willingness to sign a truce with new president Emilio Portes Gil in 1929, if not in its decision to elevate more conciliatory members of the episcopate who could more effectively play the role of faithful national episcopate.

Sixth, Pérez is suggestive in a comparative sense. Many revolutions—France, Russia, and China provide obvious examples—create a counterchurch, whether for utopian reasons or sheer political expediency, to place religion within the state's purview or to cow religious critics of the regime. Latin American cases besides Mexico's also abound, for instance, in Venezuela, Brazil, and El Salvador, even Cuba, where the Castroite church known as "With the Cross and the Fatherland" (Con la Cruz y con la Patria) presents a suggestive parallel.[48] Most such churches fail quickly because they are official constructs and lack popular support, or can be bargained away for political gain, as with the Napoleonic Concordat of 1801 or with Stalin's efforts to make peace with Russian Orthodoxy during the Second World War. The Mexican case is simultaneously more and less impressive than many others: Pérez never enjoyed a religious monopoly, as was theoretically the case, say, with the Soviets' Living Church, Mao's Chinese Patriotic Catholic Association, or the French *église constitutionnelle* during the Terror. For the same reason, however, Pérez's Mexican Church, unusually, resisted official extirpation efforts once it outlived its political usefulness, precisely because it subsumed some historic grassroots themes: indigenous neglect, festive autonomy, agrarian yearning.

PÉREZ CALLING

Properly viewed, I hope to show, ICAM was more than anecdotally important, complicating and elucidating some larger historical questions. The Cristero War (1926–1929) is too often viewed through the eyes of central Mexican mestizo peasantries and the ecclesiastical elites that came from those same communities. The postrevolution remains synonymous with secularity. The origins of religious pluralism in Mexico are held to be exogenous, American, and Protestant. The foregrounding of indigenous Catholics' experiences offers a series of very different perspectives. While the revolution sparked cristero violence in central-western Mexico, to the south and east it inspired an indigenous Catholic revival and popularized a revolutionary concept of religious liberty, forcing confrontations between revolutionary Catholics and Roman Catholics loyal to the hierarchy. While Mexican indigenes are often seen as culturally conservative and intrinsically hostile to revolutionary anticlericalism, the popular dimension of Pérez's church shows that indigenous spirituality was oftentimes a building block of the state, not a roadblock. We see, indeed, that *callismo* itself was paradoxically Catholic, to the extent that some of its mainline reforms were guided by religious concepts. Projecting forwards, finally, the spread of a dissident Catholicism suggests that the history of religious pluralism in Mexico, often said to mushroom in the mid-twentieth century following the

Introduction

importing of U.S.-based Pentecostal religions, begins with the history of multiple Catholic denominations and the split between liberal and ultramontane Catholicisms.

Discovering ICAM is not easy methodologically, however, because of two evidentiary and conceptual problems. First, sources. No central archive exists, only scattered fragments of an institutional whole, some of which turned up accidentally over a period of years. Significant effort was needed to pick up the pieces, from the Roman Catholic curia in Mexico City, Mexican Church archives held by Antonio Celis (an ecclesiastical descendant of Pérez) in Iztapalapa, scattered issues of ICAM's 8-page, 5-cent fortnightly paper, *Restauración* (published 1925–1928, 1932–1934), agrarian reform cases, police records, Vatican archives, Episcopalian mission records, and other sources.[49] These sources are both self-justifying and self-limiting analytically. There are states about which we know little (Guerrero), and others (Puebla) where we know much more. Exploring indigenous support presents particular problems, because informants translated local disputes into the language of national church-state conflict, and because Gobernación was interested in recording priests' registrations, not contextualizing them. Occasionally, I use ethnographies as rearview mirrors. Such "ethnographic upstreaming," as Eric Van Young calls it,[50] is risky since flow implies change. I therefore try to keep the stream as short as possible, relying on (near-) contemporary ethnographers such as Guy Stresser-Péan or Roberto Williams, among others. Readers can decide how effectively this is done and how valuable the primary sources are. I think that they show a religious parastatal that was widespread and surprisingly vigorous internally. In them, we hear indigenous people talk very counterintuitively about the impact of persecution on their communities, about their religious reasons for supporting the Mexican revolution, about their expectations of priests, about their experiences of fiestas, or about the relationship of Catholicism and patriotism. Though the discrepancy between internally and externally produced sources is very great, and though Mexican Church accounts are of course mediated, internal sources are not whitewashes, as we shall see. Enough accounts by priests and laypeople survive to make this fundamentally a listening, as opposed to a reading-against-the-grain, exercise. I have tried to convey local color and pathos where possible, no matter how sectarian or pitiless the emotion. It has been said so often that there was nothing there, so the temptation to be Rankean is hard to resist.

Second is the problem of labeling. What to *call* Pérez? The term *schismatic*, which saturates the sources, is a third-party, theological designation. As such, it cannot be used without denying authenticity to ICAM, or suppressed without conferring tacit catholicity on a movement that many Mexicans believed was faithless, even diabolical. Yet why concede religious agency, say, to cristeros, but not *totonacos* who hired Pérez? The term is also situational, because the church's center of gravity can change: in Bourbon Mexico, bishops leveled charges of schism at Jesuits protesting the expulsion of the company. A century later, supporters of state churches were "schismatics."[51] I therefore describe Pérez's followers as "Mexican" Catholics (católicos mexicanos) and their antagonists as "Romans" (católicos romanos), without implying that either were deficiently Catholic or Mexican: I just foreground aspects of their identity that they also foregrounded, henceforth without scare quotes for easier reading. For what it is worth, this is in line with a shift in Catholic studies to decentering "Catholic" as a category and exploring non–Roman Catholic consciousness, a Catholic other ("other Catholics" as Julie Byrne has it).[52]

The book has six chapters. Chapter 1 rehearses the famous siege of La Soledad. Chapter 2 analyzes ICAM as a revolutionary iteration of constitutional Catholicism. Chapter 3 tracks Mexican Catholicism's revival during the Cristero Revolt. Chapters 4 and 5 explore its appeal as a spiritual adjunct of revolutionary agrarianism and local, festive religion. Chapter 6 is a prosopography of dissident Catholic priests. The conclusion buries Pérez and tracks ICAM's history post-1940. Not that this history is finished, because populist leaders still do what Calles did. In 2008 a *chavista* church, the Iglesia Católica Reformada de Venezuela (ICARVEN), was launched as a Bolivarian Catholicism. In Evo Morales's Bolivia, a body called the Iglesia Católica Apostólica Renovada del Estado Plurinacional de Bolivia (ICARBOL) appeared in 2013, preaching devotion to Christ and Pachamama. In Cuba, the recent association between the revolution and *santería*, based on the idea of spiritual decolonization, is powerful.[53] From Mexico, there are reports concerning AMLO's recruitment of religious associations as moralizing copartners in Mexico's *cuarta transformación*.[54] As long as official Catholicism exists, and politicians fear it or it is less than universal, there will be other Pérezes.

CHAPTER ONE

HABEMUS PÉREZ, 1925

ON 16 FEBRUARY 1925, Joaquín Pérez said his last Mass in Mexico City's Cathedral. Next day, he skipped work, which in his case was massing at the *altar del perdón* (altar of forgiveness), a towering retable just inside the cathedral's south door. Historically, this was the portal through which heretics passed en route to the Inquisition. At the altar, they prayed for mercy, their view of the nave obstructed by a dazzling wall of gold, as befitted blind sinners who separated themselves from the body of the church.[1] Appropriately enough, Pérez's final Mass as a Roman Catholic priest was celebrated at this traitor's gate. His next appearance, a week later in the parish of La Soledad seven blocks east, caused outrage. By then, however, Father Pérez was no more: at the altar, flanked by CROM minders, stood Patriarch Pérez, founder of a new Mexican Catholic and Apostolic Church (ICAM). There would be no turning back—and no forgiveness.

Pérez is forever associated with the seizure of La Soledad, hence with triggering Mexico's religious conflict. Days later, in fact, Roman Catholics founded the National League for the Defense of Religious Liberty (LNDLR), a civic organization that from 1926 directed an uprising against the regime. Yet La Soledad was more than a catalyst: it was a revealing *affaire* in its own right. Coming so early in Calles's presidency, it demonstrated official impatience for a new institutional order, even spiritual conformity. It likewise exposed Calles's vulnerability to press criticism, which reached an unprecedented pitch shortly after. La Soledad even framed postrevolutionary politics, renewing skirmishes between Luis Morones's CROM and supporters of caudillo Álvaro Obregón. Last, La Soledad reshaped revolutionary anticlericalism as a genre, precisely because it was a fiasco. "Liberating" churches, CROM's nationalistic mantra, produced only Keystone Cops tragedies:

baying mobs, rocks hurtling from the sky, fire engines screaming round street corners, priests scarpering, cassocks shredded. Under pressure, therefore, Calles canceled religious *cromismo*, with its Soviet-style, church-storming antics.[2] Instead, the regime changed tack, from 1926 encouraging municipal juntas to register priests independently of the Roman hierarchy. The consequences of this shift to a French-style, constitutional church were momentous. If nothing else, the change brought ICAM into contact with many indigenous pueblos, creating an unusual alliance between revolutionaries and indigenous Catholics. This will be discussed in chapter 3: it is necessary to understand, however, that Pérez's siege of La Soledad in association with CROM—which is usually seen as the whole story—was only prologue. This chapter first explores Pérez's relationship with CROM and introduces readers to the patriarch. It then analyzes events at La Soledad and their consequences.

SPIRITUAL DECOLONIZATION

When Pérez quit, he and an irascible deacon named Antonio Benigno López y Sierra had been talking secretly with CROM for weeks. Indeed, on 26 January they told CROM that they founded ICAM on 18 January, modeling it on the city-state churches of Paul's epistles and Revelation. Indiscreetly, they cited conversations with "brother Luis Morones," CROM *jefe de jefes*, who promised to propagandize on their behalf. Churches need money: on 12 February, a miracle occurred when ICAM treasurer Ángel Jiménez Juárez—supposedly a descendant of the Benemérito—found 1,000 pesos in church coffers, deposited by Pérez against "first expenses."[3] The patriarch, bankrupted months before, surely obtained the money from CROM. It is unclear how Pérez met López y Sierra, his vicar general (secretario de cámara y gobierno). Indubitably, López y Sierra was the link man with CROM: his son-in-law, Ricardo Treviño, just happened to be CROM general secretary and a federal deputy (representing Tacubaya) in the Partido Laborista Mexicano (PLM), CROM's political wing. A carpenter, ex–House of the World's Worker militant, and an "impetuous and individualistic character" according to British Labourite Joseph Retinger, the *nuevoleonés* looms larger in ICAM's foundation than Morones.[4]

That CROM plotted a religious coup weeks after Calles assumed office on 1 December 1924 is indicative of its outsized political influence and callismo's hypernationalism. CROM, a labor central founded in 1918, was a de facto pillar of state from 1920 and indisputably so from 1924 to 1928, having helped Calles to power through an electoral pact. In recompense, CROM enjoyed cabinet influence in the substantial shape of industry minister Luis Morones, once the Mexico City electricians' boss, now a bling-encrusted, gangsterish figure. *Compañeros* Celestino Gasca and Eduardo Moneda had sinecures in munitions procurement and the government printshop, but Morones was king: until CROM's political demise, part of the fallout from Obregón's 1928 assassination, he ran labor for the regime, satisfying modest demands while coercing workers' "patriotic cooperation" with Mexico's capitalist project.[5] CROM's religious putsching paralleled Calles's own state and nation building, which may be why Calles permitted it. As is well known, Calles was committed to defending Mexican sovereignty by all means. Thus, he built dams, highways, banks, schools, the tax system and currency, a civil code, a prussianized army, retroactive oil laws, and, as a parting gift, the Partido Nacional Revolucionario (PNR), the revolution's *societas perfectas*.[6] Calles also sought a near spiritual power over the citizenry, which is why he encouraged belief in an idea of the Revolution as never-ending national purpose. The regime must revolutionize everything, whether this meant teaching "revolutionary" jurisprudence in law school, canonizing "the revolutionary novel," or mexicanizing the Catholic Church.[7]

CROM support for ICAM was motivated by political rivalry with Catholic syndicates, but hegemonic religious motives should not be entirely discounted. Indeed, CROM also professed a "mixed action" philosophy including direct (political) and indirect (cultural) action. As individuals, too, some *cromistas* subscribed to an empirical, countercultural Catholicism. Treviño himself was that unusual revolutionary who admired Jesuits. His teachers at Monterrey's Sacred Heart school were jovial, nondogmatic, and tolerant of human failing, he wrote, not like parish clergy with their tales of hellfire. They taught Treviño that hell was metaphorical, a state of bad conscience (algo que llevamos dentro), while spiritual grace came from helping others. Treviño also attacked Protestantism as a cold, "political religion," and rebuked SEP undersecretary Moisés Sáenz, when he said that Mexico needed a Protestant ethic to build its middle class.[8] Other cromistas, such as Vicente Lombardo Toledano, admired the early, but not the modern, church. Morones himself, inclined to anticlerical burlesque, attributed this to traumatic altar-boy experiences in Acatlán (D.F.) that wrecked his religious sensibility.[9]

For diverse reasons, therefore, CROM decided that an aggressive expansion of revolutionary nationalism into the religious sphere would generate cultural support for the regime, mexicanize conscience, and inflict a political defeat on the Roman clergy. The idea, seemingly, was to re-create the drama of Miguel Hidalgo's 1810 grito de Dolores and declare spiritual independence of Rome. As Calles turned a blind eye, therefore, CROM placed its newspapers and "Action Group" (a secretive cadre directed by Treviño) at Pérez's service. Then, on 18 February, ICAM went public when its manifesto—"Bases Fundamentales de la Iglesia Católica Apostólica Mexicana"—was published in *El Sol*, a CROM title. *El Sol* proclaimed that the *bases*, signed by Pérez, treasurer Jiménez, and Spanish priest Manuel Monge, heralded the dawn of a democratic church. The Bible, freely interpreted, was its cornerstone; medieval practices—priestly celibacy, liturgical Latin, emoluments—were out, though Marianism was not.[10] In an interview two days later in *El Demócrata*, Pérez stoked the clergy's nationalistic feelings. Porfirio Díaz, he said, sold Mexico out to Rome by allowing the opening of an apostolic delegation. Yet every delegate was Italian: "Do *we* not have enough educated elements to direct our Christian piety?" Pérez asked. He then recalled a lifetime of struggle against Rome.

> My work began long ago . . . In the fifty years that I have spent officiating at the altar, I have learned from bitter experience that the Catholic religion, in Mexico as in all the world's Catholic nations, is no more and no less than a play run by a skillful director residing in sumptuous palaces in Rome. It shocks me that we are continually lectured by a Filippi or a Cimino, men who ought to have no authority over us.[11]

That day, Pérez sent blank loyalty oaths to Mexico City priests, promising plumb parishes to any who signed. Curia officials were disconcerted when priests started reporting visits by "the so-called Patriarch." According to one, Pérez allegedly boasted "that he counts on the support of the president, a society called the Regional Obrera, and the special help of Señor Morones."[12]

Then rumors started about La Soledad, which actually was a fitting setting for a Catholic workers' *golpe*. Once a canal dock for *chinampa* crops (Cuauhzingo), in 1633 it became an Augustinian doctrina for Nahua woodworkers, hence its first avocation, La Santa Cruz Coltzinco. In the 1750s it became Mexico City's fifth secular parish, receiving its modern name (La Santa Cruz y Soledad) in 1788 under influential cura Gregorio Pérez Cancio (1753–1789). Under his guidance, La Soledad became an urban shrine thanks to its image of Mary weeping alone on Calvary. The eighteenth-century Pérez was himself jailed in 1783 for demanding that parishioners ("purely Indians . . . the majority almost naked") be freed of the obligation to pay taxes or perform *faena*. His neoclassical church, too, had a striking motif, the first of its kind, on the facade: an eagle, beneath a crown, devouring a serpent on a *nopal*. La Soledad was thus a shrine to indigenous, patriotic Catholicism.[13] Indeed, perhaps the 1920s Pérez had patriotic reasons for choosing La Soledad. Its Virgin was patroness of Oaxaca, his home state, and gave him his middle name; perhaps he knew that historically the parish subsumed the ethnic parish of Los Mixtecos, a Dominican doctrina that was *patria chica* for Mixtecan workers in colonial Mexico City.[14] Moreover, Pérez surely knew of La Soledad's recent troubles and its surfeit of foreign clergy. A scandal occurred during the pastorate of Silvestre Hernández, who in 1922 brawled with his *vicario* after calling him a bandit and *muerto de hambre* (denoting starvation, but a strong insult in Mexico). The vicario retorted that Hernández instead of ministering read novels or dozed on a bench, while his sister fornicated with the sacristan. Parishioners demanded a transfer for their "useless" priest, but the curia kept him until 1924, when it appointed Alejandro Silva, a *zamorano* in his fifties. Though Silva was appointed ad interim, La Soledad had funds to maintain six chapels and fourteen priests, exactly half of them foreigners, mostly Spaniards though one identified as "el cura de los Árabes."[15] Like some latter-day shrine to La Santa Muerte, La Soledad was also associated with social squalor and was notorious as a sanctuary for prostitutes, street thugs, and market workers from La Merced, people as tough as the amoralist characters in José Revueltas's 1953 stage hit about the barrio.[16] Local Catholicism reflected the pervasive criminality of the barrio, then as now: in 1913 someone screwed a sign over the stoup (the stone basin used to reserve holy water) that said, "With this holy water are my sins and crimes forgiven," leading pious parishioners to object to the superstitions of "rough and ill-educated people."[17] What better place than this desperate, gachupin-ridden grotto to showcase a church revolution? On 21 February, therefore, Pérez met with Treviño and cromistas calling themselves the "Order of the

Knights of Guadalupe," a cross between Iturbide's "Imperial Order of Guadalupe" and the Knights of Columbus.[18] Piling into trucks, Pérez and his "knights" drove to La Soledad.

MEET THE NEW HIDALGO

Pérez is so identified with La Soledad that we should remember what a change in form it was for him, personally: the "real" Pérez was no militant syndicalist but a Mixtecan country cura who usually got into trouble for sticking up for indigenous parishioners. His biography is warped by black legends, but most are 1925 retrofits, such as the claim that he shot five priests in the revolution, tried to bushwhack his bishop, Eulogio Gillow, or spread Protestantism using an alias, "Padre Palma." Even without embellishment, however, *Excélsior*'s joke—that Pérez's life was like something out of *El periquillo sarniento* "but with more adventures"—rings true. He *was* a "picturesque type,"[19] but the excesses, drink aside, perhaps, were two: inciting parishioners against ecclesiastical authority; then, if bishops had recourse to the civil power, disregarding that, too. At heart, Pérez was a southern liberal patriot in a cassock, who hated the romanized church of the Porfiriato. Like Porfirio Díaz and Adalberto Tejeda, the only important figures ever to hold him in any esteem, Pérez was at home in southerly pueblos and savvy at indigenous politicking.[20]

José Joaquín Jacinto de la Soledad Pérez Budar was born in Juxtlahuaca in Oaxaca's Mixteca Baja, on 18 August 1851, to José María Pérez and María Yrene Budar. His parents had married in 1841, and were, respectively, children of Pedro Pérez and Felipa Guzmán, and José Budar and Josefa Guzmán. In addition to a sister, later his housekeeper, Pérez had at least three brothers, one older (Arcadio), one younger (Adrián), and another, Eustaquio, who died in battle. He received some private schooling, suggesting some security. He married, to María Guadalupe Viveros (1873), but was widowed after three months.[21]

Pérez's first career was military. It started with Díaz's La Noria revolt (1871), in which he served under Macario González's Mixteca command. González recalled that Pérez fought in the infantry at Tepexi, Acatlán, Chiautla, and Matamoros; then at Tlachinola under Márquez Galindo. Amnestied after Juárez's death (1872), Pérez joined Díaz's second, Tuxtepec revolt (1876), this time in the Eighth Line Batallion. All spring, Pérez fought on Puebla's southern plains or in Morelos, tasting victory and defeat; he then fought in a run of Regenerating Army victories, ending in November, at Tlachinola, Tlayacapan, Epatlán, Tehuacán, Ixcaquistla, Tepejí, and Tecoac. His brother, Eustaquio, fell at Acatzingo (June); Pérez himself showed "exceptional bravery, discipline, constancy, and selflessness," his commanders agreed. In July, Pérez turned up in Tlachinola "mounted and armed" and was made cavalry adjutant. In September, in liberal Xochiapulco (Pue.), "Citizen J. Joaquín Pérez" received a commission as auxiliary captain from fabled Puebla cacique Juan C. Méndez, in the "Tigers of Oaxaca" battalion in Díaz's Eastern Army. Like Méndez, Pérez retained Díaz's peacetime favor for a while: among his prized possessions was a signed 1877 *acuerdo* confirming his rank and pension. Until December 1877, Pérez sought new commissions on grounds of exemplary service and because he was raising Eustaquio's orphans; then he asked to be paid off because he had rheumatism, hence medical bills, yet had "received not a cent" from the War Ministry. With back pay, he planned to "retire to my part of the country, and to private life."[22]

Pérez then trained for the priesthood in Oaxaca's Institute and Seminary, but was refused ordination because of his army past. Undeterred, he pursued his vocation in Tulancingo (Hgo.), then Xalapa (Ver.), where Bishop José María Mora y Daza ordained him. Pérez celebrated his first Mass in Xalapa in 1881. His first postings as vicario were in Veracruz's highlands (Coatepec, Totula, Cosautlán) and the Tuxtlas. A lone (1925) report alleges that Pérez was suspended there, for kicking a tax collector. Several years later, he received his first parish in Juxtlahuaca, his hometown. This was an old Dominican doctrina; Pérez served from 1887 to 1889, in which time he founded the Vela Perpetua, a women's Eucharistic Adoration club. This was probably a novelty to parishioners used to venerating El Señor de los Pobres.[23] He also founded an agricultural society, the Sociedad Agrícola Progresista "Amigos del Trabajo." This was deemed political—and probably was, as Oaxacan agricultural societies were frequently created by indigenous *comuneros* to evade liberal land laws. In 1889, Oaxaca's governor accused him of sedition and his bishop, Eulogio Gillow, suspended him for the second time.[24]

Pérez was soon asking Díaz for a new commission, telling his "distinguished and dear" ex-chief that poverty required him to hock his possessions. A friend in common, a district judge, vouched for "Señor Joaquín Pérez, a son of our state of Oaxaca," reminding Díaz that Pérez had fought for him and lost a brother for the cause; "sacred obligations of *paisanaje*" thus bound Díaz to Pérez. Díaz duly promised to "bear in mind [Pérez's] desires" and celebrated "the fact that his service record allows me to grant them." By April 1891, Pérez was serving in Guerrero; henceforth he renewed his active military status (and pension) annually.[25]

In July 1892, Pérez returned to the cloth also. That month he was summoned by the Mexico City curia, probably over a jurisdictional matter because in 1893 he asked Archbishop Próspero María Alarcón to incardinate him so he might "dedicate myself to the holy ministry where your Ilustriousness determines." That was seemingly in Puebla, however, because in 1896 Pérez resurfaced there as vicario of San Juan Amecac, a few miles south of the Popocatépetl. The two subsequent years in Amecac tell us far more about who Pérez was than La Soledad. According to the bishop of Puebla, Perfecto Amézquita, Pérez arrived without letters of appointment and worked the vicaría "as an intruder" (como intruso), a word that conjured up the constitutional clergy (les intrus) of 1790s France. Pérez committed "many arbitrary acts," Amézquita claimed, yet those mentioned in communications to Rome's apostolic visitor, Nicolás Averardi (1896–1900), were mainly unlicensed masses, baptisms, and marriages. To correct such irregularities, Amézquita sent missionaries to Amecac, whom Pérez reportedly resisted with armed men.[26] Parish records paint a different story. Here Pérez emerges less as an intruder than as the leader of a secessionist movement. Indeed, Ruperto Méndez—priest of Amecac's ecclesiastical *cabecera* of Atzitzihuacán—reported in May 1897 that Pérez was involved in a "delicate affair" in Amecac and was spearheading the vicaría's bid to break free of Atzitizihuacán. That month, Pérez marched up a hill outside Amecac, "in union with the pueblo's inhabitants," and planted a large crucifix. Naming it "Cross of Amecac," Pérez proclaimed himself cura of a new parish, San Juan Amecac. When Father Méndez ordered him to recant, Pérez cocked his revolver and sent him packing. "From that day," Méndez said, Pérez performed illicit sacraments and "the people of Amecac began to be in opposition to their legitimate priest."[27] Other documents from Puebla's curia show that Pérez had previously denounced "thefts" in the vicaría that he attributed to another priest, Ysauro Sánchez.[28] Likely these were sacramental extortions because on 29 April 1897 Pérez published a broadside ("a cry for reform") which he copied to Averardi. In it, Pérez demanded that Averardi "abolish certain acts performed by the clergy of the republic," namely, the levying of parish fees according to the sacramental tariff (arancel). Poorer Catholics, Averardi was told, skipped the sacraments for economic reasons, endangering souls. Instead, Pérez proposed—as he would in 1925—that the church be funded by voluntary almsgiving. His petition, he claimed, was signed by "four thousand Catholics who hunger for the good name and prestige of Our Holy Mother Church."[29]

The authorities threw the book at him. On 30 May, troops arrested Pérez while he was leading a *novena* in Amecac. Bishop Amézquita frankly admitted to Rome that it was he who sought this intervention, as a result of which Pérez was thrown into prison in Atlixco like a common criminal. From his cell, Pérez told Averardi that he was arrested by two hundred soldiers. Later he claimed that he was tied up "like an animal" and hauled off in a coffle, a bit like the priest in Luis Buñuel's film *Nazarín*. Pérez then rotted in Atlixco jail for fourteen months while Sacred Heart of Mary religious missionized Amecac.[30] Pérez went through phases of denial, penitence, and revolt. In November 1897, he and a fellow priest, Luis G. Barrientos, petitioned Averardi and Amézquita for help, perhaps unaware that it was they who had engineered Pérez's downfall. Pérez begged them to use their influence and have him sprung from the "horrendous dive" where he had fallen sick. "On my honor as a priest and with God Our Lord as a witness," Pérez swore that all charges against him were false. His only offense against sacerdotal dignity was the severity with which he repressed some "stupid Protestants" who had established themselves in Amecac. Pérez claimed that he had broken the congregation, turned its temple into a chapel, and forced its leader to issue a public retraction. He had also toppled Amecac's mayor, Lorenzo Aguilar, another Protestant. Yet he had never turned from God's truth or his vocation. "By the special favor of God Our Lord," Pérez told Averardi, "faith, hope, and charity remain alive in my heart: I am a Priest, yet very unworthy; and notwithstanding the great sufferings that I have carried . . . never have I regretted, nor shall I regret my embrace of this perfect estate." He admitted that "my pride and *amor propio*" prevented him from seeing his own defects. If he had sinned, he fell to his knees and begged Averardi in the name of the Sacred Hearts of Jesus and Mary to forgive him.[31] Pérez also asked Amézquita for assistance, including medicine. When Pérez was released, Amézquita made him complete some spiritual exercises, which he did, then gave him some money so he might leave the diocese. Instead, Amézquita said, Pérez remained in Puebla, consorting with Freemasons and penning new broadsides against authority. Though censures achieved nothing, Amézquita again placed Pérez under suspension.[32]

Pérez certainly resumed his campaign against simony, beginning with an open letter to Averardi that the newspapers published on 25 July 1899 and in which Pérez told the apostolic visitor that he awaited a response to his 1897 petition. For good measure, on 13 August Pérez sent his sister, Dionisia, to find the apostolic visitor and communicate an "urgent matter of conscience." This was seemingly a protest against the curia in Puebla, which Pérez claimed was unjustifiably withholding his licenses and making their return conditional upon his retracting his broadsides. This he would not do, because they "contained no attack on the Catholic Church, to which I am disposed to make any sacrifice," but simply proposed the abolition of religious taxes, which, he said, even Cardinal Rampolla had described as "indelicate and sinful, since they traffic in religion."[33] Pérez told Averardi that Amézquita was being "unjust and unfair," and urged the apostolic visitor to endorse his reforms, "not for me but for the Catholics who petitioned Your Excellency."[34] Pérez thus tried to turn Averardi against his bishop. This only prompted Amézquita to complain to Averardi about his "infuriating" and "unworthy priest." Amézquita added sarcastically, "It is now said that he [Pérez] plans to found a national church. Only his own head could conceive the idea that he is capable of founding a new church."[35]

Pérez thus became notorious decades before La Soledad. In August, an anonymous priest published a letter in *El Amigo de la Verdad* lamenting Pérez's diatribes against a divine institution—emoluments—on the strength of a petition "signed by half a dozen imbeciles" and "with the gravest consequences for your scientific reputation and your priestly character." Had the Levites not tithed the other tribes? Did Jesus not say that the worker was worthy of his meat? Did Peter not berate Simon Magus for selling miracles? Emoluments were of divine institution, not simony; this being so, they could only be reformed by a papal commission, not an apostolic visitor. If the church lived on "what the faithful spontaneously wish to give," then priests would soon take to the roads with begging bowls and staffs. Pérez's idea was so outlandish that even French revolutionaries shied away from it and gave priests state salaries. Liberals had placed a noose around the church's neck, yet here was Pérez pulling it tight. Why? Liberal newspapers counterattacked. In *La Democracia* (24 August), Pérez published a third missive against Averardi, speaking for a "regular number of Catholic people" who wanted to abolish things that stained the Church's image in Mexico. This group was "stupefied" that Averardi referred the protesters to Rome rather than address the "spiritual needs" of Mexican Catholics by canceling the "impossible" sums that priests demanded. *La Democracia*'s editorialist was equally scathing: "don Nicolás" had not come to put the church in order but to have Mexicans go to Rome. If he could, he would send them even farther, "to China, for example, or to . . . the hacienda, let us say, of a certain bishop" (a reference to Eulogio Gillow's Chuatla estate). Laudably, Pérez had drawn a line in the sand.[36]

Pérez's protest soon passed into liberal lore. Carlo de Fornaro embellished it in his anti-Díaz j'accuse of 1909; revolutionary Catholic Ignacio Enríquez, *carrancista* governor of Chihuahua, also celebrated it.[37] Between times, Pérez himself reactivated his liberal persona. In 1903, we find him in Mexico City, living in Calle Pila Seca near Santo Domingo and seeking a benefice. An armchair commission in the army auxiliary saved him. Indeed, in 1904 Pérez resigned his captain's commission and was assigned to the Comandancia Militar. His exit report (1906) said he showed "good education," knowledge of canon and civil law, and administrative skills. Perhaps this was why he was then taken on as auxiliary commissar for the War Council. In 1913, aged sixty-two, Pérez left the army rather than serve Huerta, saying he had inherited some undissolved corporate property (perhaps a parish plot?) and wanted to secure it. "Presbyter don José Joaquín Pérez" then performed spiritual exercises and persuaded the Mexico curia to have him. In 1914, vicar general Pedro Benavides found "something appropriate for him," which turned out to be Iztapalapa (D.F.), site of a burgeoning Passion play that drew trainloads of capitalinos at Easter. The pageant's success generated conflicts between its indigenous sponsors and the clergy, and Pérez could handle (or else deserved) that.[38]

For once, Pérez tried to "obey the determinations of my superior," though luckily for him his superior was now vicar general Antonio de Jesús Paredes, a prorevolutionary priest.[39] Pérez also showed empathy when dealing with indigenous parishioners. In December 1914, for instance, he noted the "extreme poverty that exists in this *población*" and endorsed its petition that extra priests be contracted for fiestas but not permanently maintained ("having a priest, with whom I have an arrangement, come and help me on feast days"). In 1915, Pérez ended a local vendetta when he "reconciled"

Iztapalapa and the estranged pueblo of Acatitla. He also reduced the financial burden of the cult by "thanking"—i.e., firing, with "great sorrow"—a do-nothing vicario. This individual took the train home to Mexico City every evening, refused "many times" to account for fees earned in the vicaría of Meyehualco, and celebrated without permission in Aztahuacan (which Pérez misspelled "Hastahuacan"), "telling them that I am a carrancista and that they have no need of me." Pérez was no such thing: in July 1915, he complained that Carranza's army had stolen the parish seal and other items when it passed through. Pérez and Iztapalapa were, in sum, well matched: avoiding trouble with *mayordomos*, he reduced clerical taxes, chased off a sponger vicario, and spoke up against an abusive soldiery. He left with some social standing. Indeed, in 1918, his "friend and correligionist," judge Domingo León, asked him to endorse two candidates for deputy. Since Pérez was popular in Iztapalapa ("supo dejar bien sentado su nombre en aquella feligresía"), he was asked to back the slate.[40] Paredes now promoted Pérez, appointing him *vicario foráneo* (rural dean) of the ex-Dominican doctrina of Tepetlaoxtoc (Méx.), with jurisdiction over various parishes in Texcoco's hacienda-dominated valley. As soon as Archbishop Mora returned, however, in 1919, Pérez was demoted, to Santa María La Redonda, a historic church in Tepito, Mexico City's *barrio bravo*. His last post, as we saw, was at the cathedral's altar del perdón. When CROM found him, Pérez was seemingly in fair standing: in 1923, he marched in regalia in the cathedral's Corpus procession.[41]

The last pre-Soledad sighting comes in May 1924, when Pérez was sued in the ecclesiastical tribunal by María Larrazábal de Villafañe, wife of his cousin, Antonio Pérez Villafañe. She eventually settled for one hundred pesos—he offered twenty—because Pérez was guarantor for a tenant in arrears. Perhaps we should thank his miserly cousins, because they illegally impounded Pérez's effects, leaving an inventory. There were a few paintings: one of San Francisco Javier (a sixteenth-century missionary killed in China) and others of the Divine Shepherd and Theresa of Avila. There were also portraits of a young Pérez in country attire (de paísano) and vestments, sadly lost. Pérez's remaining property—flowerpots, an icebox, cheap prints of Hidalgo and the Virgin—was barely worth writing down. For someone whose sincerity is questioned, we might note that Pérez slept under portraits of Hidalgo and the Guadalupe. His goods were worth eighty-five pesos, and he owed a hundred: whatever he did, Pérez didn't fleece his flocks.[42]

If only, in 1925, Pérez had done what he always did: find an indigenous parish whose problems and people he understood, take their side like the old contrarian he was, then move on when an angry bishop came after him. Then he might be remembered as an agrarian cura, like Yucatán's Mauricio Zavala, or a genial provocateur, like Fray Servando.[43] Instead, audacity got the better of him under the influence of López y Sierra and CROM, whose propaganda told him that he was the new Hidalgo, "another frail old man" finishing the "Blessed Work of Liberty" by breaking Rome's chains.[44] Why Pérez imagined that he could break those bonds in Mexico City, with its dense parish networks, numerous clergy, militant Catholic organizations, and newspaper circulations and constant rumor-mills ready to expose him, is hard to fathom.

THE *ASALTO*

Capturing La Soledad was meant to prompt an uprising of Mexico City's lower clergy, but it succeeded only in stirring up parishioners and scandalizing the capital. As Father Silva later testified, at 8 p.m. on Saturday 21 February, a hundred men, some armed, burst into La Soledad, spilling on to the patio. A "tall man" (Treviño) presented Father Monge, who exhorted Silva to join ICAM. Initially, the intruders were courteous—some removed their hats—but they grew violent when Silva refused to surrender his church. Silva later claimed that he demanded to see written orders from the curia and clung to his chancel rail calling for help when he realized a coup was happening. More probably, Silva was in on Pérez's plan but got cold feet. One Spanish vicario, Laureano Valdéz, told the curia that "persons perfectly knowledgeable about [La Soledad's] administration, perhaps priests," had betrayed La Soledad's Spanish priests: the attackers knew, and said, "that señor cura [Silva] was dominated by foreigners, who restricted his freedom of action." Jesuit historian Arnulfo Hurtado, unlikely to invent divisions, accused Silva of complicity. In any event, CROM knights now threw Silva out, minus the Mass takings; Valdéz followed, minus his hat; a third priest, Elías García Calleja, was evicted at gunpoint. Later, Monge wired Calles that he and a "pious association" had freed La Soledad. "An ancient priest," aged about seventy, with a rough complexion and white hair, then entered La Soledad.[45]

Initially, the reaction was low-key. Archbishop Mora chased over Mexico City all night looking for Gilberto Valenzuela Galindo, Calles's paisano and a moderate influence as Interior Minister. A trail of calling cards demanded that Valenzuela denounce religious "barbarism" in the name of "justice and reason." If he protected Pérez, it would be "giving the executioner rights and denying them to the victim," clear proof of collusion.[46] Sunday, too, was quiet.

On Monday 23 February, however—the start of Carnival, some journalists mocked—came high drama. As La Soledad's bells began tolling at ten, the doors opened. At eleven, Monje and Pérez appeared at the sacristy door, escorted by Manuel Ruiz, the knights' *comendador*, and fellow knights, "pistols at the hip," so *Excélsior* said. At the chancel, Monje opened his mouth to say the blessing but was taken down by a group of women crying that he and Pérez were "Lutherans." One woman spat in Monje's face and punched him; another broke a heavy candle over his head; others tore at his cassock. Panicking, Monje was rescued by CROM and along with Pérez hurried through the presbytery door and into a truck. In church, the curial gazette improbably claimed, people wept on the floor, imploring the Virgin of Solitude for help; some women placed their babies on the altar, offering them to La Soledad if she would thwart "false Catholics." Outside, a crowd started ripping up cobblestones and attacking police lines. Rioting continued all evening, with numerous casualties from rocks, knife slashes, and gunshots.

That night, eyes fell on the government. In his first statement, Valenzuela swore that the regime was alien to the affray and upheld everyone's rights. It would not tolerate one group seizing another's churches: "members of the Mexican Church," he said, should not seek by force "that which the authorities are always disposed to give when requested in a peaceful manner in accordance with the law's requirements." In retrospect, Valenzuela surely wished that he had just told police to remove Pérez because his rather impartial position was contradicted that night when the first and last reciprocal communication between Pérez and Calles occurred. Pérez requested guarantees; Calles told police to provide them, wiring Pérez next day. He then told Valenzuela to obtain reports from Pérez and Mora explaining their supporters' violent behavior. This request irked Valenzuela: first Calles upheld a violent intrusion by one party; now he told Gobernación to investigate two parties. If Calles had heeded Valenzuela or reflected on the possible cost of this contradiction, he might have paused. Instead, the wire hummed.[47]

Next day, 24 February, Mass was said behind closed doors while protesters laid siege, throwing stones and drinking pulque. Pérez wired

Calles that five hundred people attended; his enemies, just as inaccurately, claimed "priests of Arab nationality" celebrated. That evening, Pérez's first pastoral was nailed to the door, pleasing some local women with its promise that next day (Ash Wednesday) Pérez would give alms to anyone who came to Mass.[48] Next morning, indeed, 25 February, Pérez crossed people's foreheads with ashes, guarded by CROM heavies. He distributed two pesos per widow and fifty cents to everyone else, two thousand in all, saying, "This is the offering that we give to the poor: we ask you to pray for the Mexican Catholic and Apostolic Church." The newspapers could not deny that many "women of the pueblo" (*El Universal*) and "humble people of the *barriada*" (*Excélsior*) attended, but they attacked Pérez with glee. *Excélsior* teased that Pérez said the Lenten oration, "Remember, man, that you are dust," in "the very language that foreigners brought from Spain." For its part, *El Amigo de la Verdad* (a Catholic daily) described how one celebrant wafted a censer "with the mannerisms proper to one whose life has been spent wielding a hoe." He was "a poor old codger, bronze in color because of the sun's ardent rays, knowing neither how to pronounce Latin nor . . . translate it." It was claimed that Pérez consecrated using Berreteaga Añejo (a cane rum), tequila, or *parras* wine, of which he allegedly quaffed several bottles a day.[49]

That day, 25 February, Mora excommunicated Pérez and placed an interdict on La Soledad. The censures, printed on handbills, posters, and in the press, were not the sulfurous rants one might expect, no doubt because Mora hoped Pérez might recant. Thus he expressed sorrow for the "painful events" at La Soledad and the souls of the "ill-advised priests" who now stared into "the abyss of schism and heresy." Pérez, a "false apostle" with "dark blots" against his name, had time to return to the fold before facing "Christ the Judge," Mora promised. Next came the theology: anyone who denied papal authority, like Pérez, was a schismatic and an excommunicate. Pérez's erroneous doctrines—like denying hellfire—made him guilty of heresy, too. The faithful must therefore shun Pérez's illicit sacraments, performed without jurisdiction. Pilgrims were banned from visiting La Soledad, because the sanctuary was defiled.[50]

The excommunication brought down more heat. Next day, 26 February, five women seized Pérez's tie at Mass and half-strangled him before CROM knights intervened. Despite the attack, a Gobernación agent counted a four-hundred-strong congregation, which was driven by "curiosity more than religiosity," but nonetheless pleased, perhaps because the intentions for the Mass were offered to the pueblo. Some even showed reverence, especially poorer women. It was worth reporting, the spy said, that "the majority of women" still left alms for the Virgin and a group of them now camped outside La Soledad, "dressed in dirty rags," hoping for more almsgiving.[51]

By now Pérez was desperate, however, because no more priests were joining him. A 26 February circular tried to win them over by again promising them new parishes, but nothing seemed to work and also the novelty was starting to wear off. Pérez looked his age, *El Gráfico* said, after interviewing him that day; with his black eye he seemed "deeply exhausted," the "eternal smile" of a week ago, gone. Rome "is hitting us very hard, I mean, very hard," Pérez admitted, though luckily for him the barrio's abattoir workers (they had a small sodality) never carried out their threat to teach him a lesson. Next day, 27 February, Pérez's sidekick, Monge, was seized on his way to Mass and spirited out of Mexico by angry Spanish compatriots. Monge left a tearful retraction with Jesuit Mariano Cuevas, who published it in the press.[52]

In fact, ICAM was already on its way to becoming an urban myth. Reported sightings of Pérez prompted ritualized spectacles of outrage in city parishes and evidenced clear sociological traits. Copycat riots were capitalino, or occurred in state capitals and factory towns, nowhere else. They started with false alarms and ended violently, often with lynchings, thus forming part of a traumatic modernity complex as Gema Kloppe-Santamaría writes.[53] The slightest thing—an Angelus struck late, denim-clad workers crossing an atrium—could result in stampedes, the drawing of knives or guns, or the breaking of human bodies. Mexico City was first. A "tremendous" riot happened at Santo Tomás de Palma (26 February) when a bellringer forgot to chime for Rosary; that day, riots happened at La Candelaria, La Santísima, and Naucalpan; three Pérezes were "seen" at Loreto (3 March), causing a fracas; a street preacher was beaten up in Peralvillo because his name was Pérez; likewise, Tepeyac workers whose denim clothes hinted at CROM affiliation. By early March, capitalino churches were barricaded; people thought that Pérez circled them in a truck.[54] Ripples spread. Paper-producing Chalco (Méx.) saw tensions in March and again in April when some hillwalkers—ironically, they included Roman clergy—were accused of casing parishes for ICAM and roughly accosted. In Puebla, a man was stoned outside El Carmen; an industrialist who resembled Pérez was half-lynched in

Analco; in Amozoc, Italian workers were assaulted because of their foreign accents. In Querétaro, factory workers were badly mauled by a crowd crying *mueras* to Pérez and a night watchman was pulled from his car and beaten. Again and again it happened: sightings, rumors, lynchings. But no Pérez—not in Orizaba, Pachuca, Huamantla, Guadalajara, San Luis Potosí, El Oro, Ciudad Hidalgo, Hermosillo, or Durango. In Oaxaca, a "schismatic" was caught in church. But actually it was a thief, El Marihuano.[55]

It is difficult not to view the tumults as a function of popular anxiety connected to industrial modernity and loss of faith. But there was also something performative about them: they were rites of religious affirmation, just very violent ones. Though Pérez looked ready "to die of starvation," *El Gráfico* reported, *fear* of him was contagious and threatened public order.[56] Then, on 4 March, Calles announced that La Soledad would be assigned either to Roman or Mexican clergy, depending on Gobernación's findings. A report reached Calles's desk next day: Gobernación's spies pointed the finger at CROM.[57] The regime's public line, however, as articulated by Valenzuela, was equivocal: Pérez had violated Silva's rights, instead of asking Gobernación to give him a church; yet the episcopate had encouraged the faithful to take the law into their hands. Thus, on 14 March, Calles closed La Soledad and turned it over to Hacienda's *bienes nacionales* section. *Excélsior* cheered ("Captain Pérez cannot believe the news"), though in fact Calles told its reporter, Manuel Becerra Acosta, that the government would give churches to people who requested them lawfully, including Catholics who wished to leave Rome.[58] On 17 March, finally, La Soledad was sealed, ostensibly to provide Diego Rivera with gallery space once Hacienda moved its contents to the Monte de Piedad for storage (all 25,599 pesos' worth, including the image of La Soledad herself). After twenty-five days, shorter than Lent, Pérez's venture was apparently over. He had not recorded any sacramental acts (marriages or baptisms) in the parish books.[59]

For a while, CROM kept up the pressure regardless. In February, two hundred people requested a Mexican priest in Tacuba, a Mexico City *municipio* with a Carmelite ex-*convento*, San Joaquín. Local *laboristas* were probably behind it: they needed CROM patronage in the 1925 municipal elections (Mexico City's last). Support also came in March from an Association of Catholic Women in Tacubaya, Treviño's congressional district; they backed Pérez because they liked the promise of free sacraments. The bishop of Saltillo, CROM's birthplace, also noted "much activity" in February: again, it boiled down to cromistas urging Catholics to elect a new bishop.[60] CROM contrived a tragedy in Aguascalientes before Holy Week, when governor José María Elizalde (1924–1925) applied the Soledad formula. First a CROM newspaper published declarations of support from knights of Guadalupe; posters announced an ICAM Mass in San Marcos, a seventeenth-century church built for Nahua and Chichimeca workers; finally, on 28 March, as barrio Catholics left San Marcos, shirtsleeve *pistoleros* led by agrarista municipal boss Jesús Flores confronted them. Insults were traded, bells tolled, and weapons drawn. As darkness fell, a battle raged, leaving twenty dead. Gobernación found that newspapers stories had agitated Catholics, whose evensong was political; no matter, the police fired at people only carrying stones. The agent could find no Guadalupan knights; until, that is, he interviewed Elizalde's officials. "These gentlemen," he concluded, "were directors of the schismatical movement." They "frankly confessed" it; some had heard Morones mention Pérez in meetings.[61]

With no more success, another callista machine—Garrido Canabal's Redshirts in Tabasco—tried to rev up ICAM that March. First came a law requiring priests to be Mexican-born, aged over forty, and married. This prompted some defections: Eduardo Coronel's, on 7 March; then José Casaponsa, cura of Macuspana, on 13 March; Víctor Bautista from Villahermosa. Garrido's attempt to elect a "red bishop" in the Merino theater failed, however, when the candidate, Manuel González Punaro, priest of the Sagrario, refused the honor. Coronel's visit to Tamulté de las Barrancas, Villahermosa's Chontal barrio, also turned violent when crowds attacked his retinue. A proposal to install a sacristan from another pueblo as church caretaker angered the principales; when a Redshirt flashed a gun, the barrio erupted. Some Chontales were beaten in reprisal, but ICAM was henceforth associated with *garridista* bullying. Sick jokes—newspapers publishing "schismatical" recipes to tempt Catholics during Lent—did not help. In any case, Casaponsa and Coronel were soon hors de combat. In 1926, a "frank, brutally frank" Casaponsa told Pérez how "he had struggled, with nothing to show for it but a good beating that they gave him in a village where they tied him to a tree all night and threatened to kill him if he continued as a cismático." Coronel was in Jalpa making *zacate* brooms; his visit to Tamulté had given him a crippled leg, because the people beat him with "great fury and cruelty."[62]

31

BACKLASH

The failure of religious cromismo not only embarrassed Calles; it was also counterproductive. First, it united Roman Catholics against him. Many were initially mesmerized, as if watching a strange meteorological phenomenon. "The storm cloud . . . is so dense and blackish that it is impossible to stop observing it," one cura wrote of La Soledad. But practical measures soon came: prayer campaigns for the "poor priests" in Satan's clutches; home exorcisms; incinerations of "satanic" ICAM propaganda.[63] A petition was launched stating that ICAM had violated priests' labor rights and common law; that seizing national property with no regard for tradition was outrageous, as "Juárez, Lerdo, Madero, Carranza . . . [and] Obregón," all understood, but not Calles.[64] The Mexico City clergy swore obedience to Mora; a relieved apostolic delegate reassured Pius XI of Catholics' loyalty (seguita unito popolo diesa chiesa).[65] Weighty pastorals damned ICAM. One from Guadalajara compared it to the dead vine in John's Gospel; its author, Archbishop Orozco, was nonchalant, smiling in his Pullman "like a Renaissance cardinal painted by Raphael" and telling reporters not to worry. But bishops of indigenous dioceses *were* worried. Papantla's bishop feared ICAM might prove serious if "red workers" joined it; Chilapa's bishop went circuit-riding to see how things stood. Still, in April the bishops presented a united front, creating a war chest and publishing a non possumus expressing "unshakable submission" to Rome.[66] CROM, by trying to split the clergy with levity, had reunited it in all seriousness.

If that was bad news for Calles, the press coverage was shocking, especially for a new, oversensitive government. Most condemned La Soledad as a common-law outrage or violation of the laicist principle. Eduardo Pallares, fired by Calles from the Jurisprudence School, took revenge in an attack in *El Universal*. To claim that the Soledad coup was valid because churches were national property was ignorant, he wrote, a fundamentalist reading of article 27, not promoting "true constitutional law" by applying law in a social medium. If law did not respect society's customs, its moral constitution, then it was just tyranny—which Juárez fought against. "For a new religion to enter the spirit and take root," another editorial read, "it is necessary for people to live through a moment of infinite anxieties, propitious for mystery." It was laughable to think that "one can open new pathways to heaven as one opens a highway . . . amid shrieking sirens and automobile fumes."

La Soledad's "sectarian character" corrupted the lay state, yet another *El Universal* report went: "It would be comical, if not so deplorable." On it went: it was cant for an official organization to support any church, let alone a "pseudoschism that mostly gives work to the hosepipes of the brave fire brigade"; Pérez's almsgiving, a stunt that applied the "laws of supply and demand" to eternal life, showed lack of faith.[67] *Excélsior* accused Calles of cowardice. The farce must stop, it cried, after another July scare: if Calles really wanted to dechristianize, he should damn well pull the churches down, not mock Catholic taste through a schism. As for Pérez, he was a pygmy, less impressive than either Lamenais (the French liberal Catholic) or Fray Servando, who had the wit not to call himself "pope of Anáhuac." If he wanted supporters, Pérez should lead "a poetic crusade, like Peter the Hermit," creating a church with "a new morality, feelings, and conception of life."[68] Popular titles went further in criticizing the president. Calles's wire to Pérez was a mistake, said *El Gráfico*. It looked as if he supported religious hooligans. When Calles promised to moralize the regime in 1924, "everyone felt callista"—not now. "The schismatics' headquarters is in Palacio Nacional," was *Omega*'s damning headline; support from "the highest government official, the *señor presidente*," had turned a criminal matter into an affair of state, a "national suicide."[69] Mexican presidents never experienced such pillorying; it is no exaggeration to see the experience as a factor in Calles's gagging law (July 1926), making press stories on morality justiciable. Apart from CROM papers, in fact, only Félix Palavicini's *El Globo* offered support. Palavicini hoped that ICAM would become the "new positivist religion" based on science and human fraternity that Auguste Comte dreamed of in later life. Like Comte, Pérez had come to plant seeds, not fell trees. ICAM's appearance was therefore healthy and should concern no one. Pérez had claimed neither to have risen from the dead nor cured the sick: until he did, Rome need not worry.[70]

It must have been doubly embarrassing to a laborista regime when Silva sued Pérez for infringing his right to work that summer. Pérez was protected by Treviño, his acting attorney, and skipped court on medical grounds, but the damage was done: newspapers lapped the story up.[71] A gratified bishop told Mora in July: "[the press] has expressed the hatred felt toward the current President of the republic, by talking against the attempted schism." Mora himself said *Excélsior*'s and *El Universal*'s reporting "deserved every praise." It mattered, too, because it fed international opinion, which was negative. The US commercial attaché reported that fears of a religious war scared investors; ambassador Sheffield feared that ICAM "may seriously involve the Mexican government" and herald a "sensational" clerophobic revival; a consular report stated that Calles had made his "first serious mistake" by leaving Pérez in La Soledad.[72]

What surely worried Calles most, however, were the rebukes of revolutionaries. They started, perhaps, with Valenzuela's back-channel opposition, which explains his replacement at Gobernación in August 1925 by Adalberto Tejeda, outgoing governor of Veracruz and a serious anticlerical. As we shall see, that was a truly significant change.[73] Most serious, though, was that Calles's support for Pérez exposed him to attacks from friends of ex-president Obregón (1920–1924), who were plotting the caudillo's return to the presidency from early in Calles's mandate. Bad blood between Obregón and CROM went back to the killing of cooperativist senator Field Jurado (1924), at least, widely considered a CROM hit. And though Obregón would not formally begin his re-electionist campaign until March 1926 (when he arrived in Mexico City promising cheap gasoline), Pérez's links to Morones made ICAM a good target for *obregonistas*. Aurelio Manrique, soon to be Obregón's campaign manager, fired the first shot by telling journalists that churches should not be founded like syndicates (una Iglesia no se funda como un sindicato).[74] Then, in March, Obregón's ex-education minister José Vasconcelos wrote a blistering piece in *El Universal* saying that ICAM was an example of thievery ("religious *carrancismo*") and "heroic ignorance." Anybody had a right to build churches, but not to "change the sign from Roman Catholic to Mexican Catholic" by force. Religious despoilment was worse than agrarismo, Vasconcelos reckoned, because it sapped society's "creative will." "If that señor, that patriarch, feels inspired," Vasconcelos cried, "let him start by planting the first stones of his church in the ground, then suffer and struggle to watch it grow." If even religion were despoilment, then "no effort would be guaranteed, and civilization would flee our land in terror."[75]

Finally, after the San Marcos massacre, Calles received a letter from the caudillo that stands as a fascinating record of Obregón's religious views and dominance over Calles. Indeed, Obregón thought that Calles should know his views, now that the "schismatical movement" was proving to be of "some political transcendence." Accompanying his letter was a long, Manichean history lesson (the farmer to the teacher), lecturing Calles that his support for ICAM endangered the revolution. In Mexico, Obregón said, there were conservatives and liberals, their function being to obliterate, not assimilate, each other. Conservatives' attachment to Rome meant that they were "incapacitated" from ending Mexico's spiritual vassalage; to emancipate the church, therefore, one would have to "improvise a pseudo-Catholic party," then storm the institution from outside. Yet the risks were huge: this might split "the liberal Party" into "pure" and Catholic wings, as liberals "grouped around schismatic priests" would soon fall under their spell. Moreover, if ICAM grew, "subtracting from the liberal camp sufficient elements to give the movement a body and create . . . a national Catholicism," the revolution would become catholicized. Liberals would then face two clerical foes, one Mexican, one Roman, "and for this change of master or yoke, it is not worth exciting the national conscience." Prominent revolutionaries would have to join the new church to give it credibility. This "Catholic and socialist duality" would be ruinous: how could revolutionaries command respect if people saw them kneeling before a schismatic priest, and faking religion? The "mask" of religion would be the revolution's "burial shroud." This was not friendly, unsolicited advice: it was a virtual cease-and-desist letter from the supremo.[76]

After this collective onslaught from the official church, the United States, the revolution, and the press, we can see why Calles desisted. CROM tried to keep Calles's interest: as early as February a "schismatic block" of students marched in favor of Pérez; then, in March, Treviño marshaled the congressional PLM—twenty deputies, three senators—to back Pérez's "Catholic-schismatic movement." Pérez preached Catholicism, not Romanism; he and Calles were new Hidalgos, the one bringing spiritual freedom, the other economic.[77] But Calles was disinvesting. In late spring, he installed Pérez in a new base, the dilapidated neoclassical convent of Corpus Christi, opposite the Juárez monument. In its glory days, Corpus Christi cloistered daughters of the indigenous nobility, including descendants of Montezuma; thus it, too, exhaled indigenous Catholic history. As soon as Pérez reopened the church, however, the Roman curia interdicted it; Corpus Christi would basically be ICAM's administrative center and seminary.[78] Elsewhere, however, Calles found himself reversing CROM-style church takeovers in the few settings where they had held. In the port of Veracruz, a committee claimed three churches for the "national religion" in March: El Cristo, La Parroquia, and La Pastora, the last a chapel for itinerant priests. They were expelled from La Pastora in May, however, when *migración* found an unlicensed priest, a Mexican national, there.[79] In the border town of Tapachula (Chis.), Father José Ramírez and a few score followers seized the San Agustín church in August, but were thrown out on Calles's orders before they could celebrate September's *fiestas patrias*.[80] Then, on 1 September, in his first *informe de gobierno*, Calles signaled the death knell of religious cromismo. All religions were respectable so long as they respected the law, the president now said.

> For this reason, when Mexican Apostolic Catholics arbitrarily seized the church of La Soledad in the capital, which was in the custody of the Roman Catholic and Apostolic clergy . . . in this way attacking freedom of worship and disposing of property belonging to the Nation without fulfilling the requirements of the law, the Executive, which has the ineluctable obligation to enforce the law and maintain respect for the institutions, could not tolerate the attack.[81]

Which was not true. It was still an embarrassing U-turn for Calles to have to make in a chamber packed with laboristas. On 3 December, Gobernación followed up by ordering local authorities to prevent religious groups from "seizing churches dedicated to the Catholic cult using violent methods."[82] Inside ICAM, the volte-face caused angst. The Knights of Guadalupe, supposedly 1,675 strong, convened ten days after Calles's speech, as we see from the only surviving minutes of a knights' meeting. Those at ICAM's round table—Supremo Gran Comendador Pérez, Hermano Gran Comendador López y Sierra, "Lieutenant Captain of the Guard" Macedonio Rodríguez, and "brothers" including ones called Maicotte and Regulez—hammered out a new strategy. They might have started by changing their cartoonish, Masonic titles; but they agreed that direct action should now mean tailing Knights of Columbus, requesting police guards for their church, and seeking transfer to a more popular parish than "aristocratic" Corpus. The problem, someone acknowledged, was that official support had cooled (el Partido Liberal se ha resfriado mucho) because people thought ICAM was dead (aparece este movimiento como muerto).[83]

CONCLUSION

Churches presented particular problems to Calles as poles of transcendental and institutional autonomy. Mexican liberalism called for church-state separation, yet Calles' nation-building urges and his authoritarian streak, fanned by CROM, told him that here were forces too powerful to leave to their own devices. An attempt was therefore made to consume them, nationalizing the church through a CROM-sponsored parastatal, ICAM. More than mere anticlerical diversion, the plan was to create a loyal priesthood, even a national church, by tapping into the grievances of lower clergy. It is unthinkable that Morones left Calles in the dark and that the president did not know what was afoot. Yet Calles, under pressure from revolutionaries, the church, Catholics, and the press, and even the United States, paid a higher price than he expected for encouraging Pérez. And in exchange for what? Pérez flopped: the patriarch's scratched, shell-shocked face soon moved journalists more to pity than contempt. La Soledad instantly showed both the impossibility and the toxicity of nationalizing the church through lightning strikes. Unsurprising, capitalino parishioners did not want their parishes violently reassigned by Brylcreemed cromistas. But what if the formula were reversed and people wanted to mexicanize their churches? What then? In mid-1925, this seemed highly implausible. But in fact, and though it was hardly acknowledged, ICAM slowly began to pollinate outside the cities and classical cromista states, such as Manuel Pérez Treviño's Coahuila, Abraham Araujo's Querétaro, or Fernando Rodarte's Zacatecas. Pérez's notoriety partly drove this process. Yet the scattershot petitioning pattern strongly suggested that ICAM's unflattering association with the popular classes and indigeneity had ironic resonance. Indeed, as time wore on it became apparent that press coverage was creating an optical illusion about ICAM, given that reports of local support were invariably buried in postscripts at the end of hostile newspaper columns, as if confirming their triviality (at least to Mexico City journalists). Yet cumulatively, they suggested that campesino Catholics were engaging with the patriarch for reasons of their own. It started with February petitions from Tenoxtitlán (Méx.) and Iguala (Gro.); then, in March, from Juchitán (Oax.), where the incumbent cura, Felipe López, led the way; next came Hule (Oax.), Ixcaquistla (Pue.), whose cura also switched, and Huichapan (Pue.), where Manuel Soriano, founder of other breakaway churches in Oaxaca and Jalapa, tried again. In April, a pro-Pérez faction opposed to crowning El Señor de las Maravillas brawled with "orthodox" villagers in Actopan (Hgo.), and another switch occurred in El Arenal (Hgo.). In May and July, changes involving bullets occurred in Huehuetla (Pue.) and Coatepec (D.F.)., where support for ICAM had agrarian overtones. In Chiapas in September, Tapachula's leading Catholic clan divided into pro- and anti-Pérez factions, with Mexican Catholics accused of "paganism." November and December saw cases in Pahuatlán (Pue.), where Father Rivera led the way, Nauzontla (Pue.), and Tenango (Hgo.), which hired dissident priest José Uribe. On *día de muertos*, two village factions clashed. True to his word, Calles moved Uribe on, for which Tulancingo's bishop called him a "true statesman."[84] Yet clearly, what was originally conceived as an official spectacular, demonstrating callismo's ability to electrify the Mexican conscience and build new institutions, was morphing into something different: a popular, grassroots experiment in religious reform. We will return to this in chapter 3. First it is important to consider exactly what the Mexican Catholic Church was.

CHAPTER TWO

"MEXICO'S NEWEST REVOLUTION"
ICAM

IN MARCH 1925, two Gobernación spies visited La Soledad. Posing as journalists, they found Pérez fraternizing with gun-toting, badge-wearing laboristas, one of whom hurriedly donned a biretta as they entered. Unimpressed by the masquerade, the agents reported that La Soledad was in reality "a political headquarters" where priests carried out "politico-religious work in agreement with Mexican Labor Party elements." In fairness, the detectives did not conceal their belief that all liberal churches were impostures: a liberal church, they wrote, "cannot be conceived, for this would constitute the very fanaticism that the Catholic Church inculcates and that liberals should combat."[1] Not everyone accused Pérez of such bad faith: Herbert Pickens Gambrell—a young Texan Baptist and Southern Methodist University history professor—was so intrigued by ICAM that he took a sabbatical to investigate. "I could discover few of the characteristics of a revolutionary rendezvous," Gambrell wrote after visiting Corpus Christi in the summer of 1925. Instead, he found promising signs of Catholic minimalism.

> We went inside. Except for the altar and the inevitable old woman selling amulets, we might have been in a Protestant chapel, so bare was it . . . Rough, concrete floors; home-made benches; a recently and cheaply built box pulpit high up on the wall; rough beams bracing a crumbling ceiling that had once been decorated with frescoes; an altar rail of pine painted red; canopies of red and blue cheesecloth over images of the Sacred Heart of Jesus and the Virgin of Guadalupe; a simple altar on which the candles were burning—certainly there was little here to attract the Mexican long used to the gaudy richness of parish churches. We

looked in vain for the confessional booth and the stations of the Cross. Later we found the reasons for their absence.

The reason, Pérez told Gambrell, was that he stood for freedom in the church: for liberty from Rome; for the defense of priests' rights against tyrannical bishops; and for the smashing of all the medieval levers that twisted the Catholic conscience.[2] Or, as one 1925 homily put it: "auricular confession, indulgences, Papal supremacy; celebrating divine worship in an unknown tongue; denying the cup to the faithful . . . ; imposing clerical celibacy; prohibiting the reading of the Bible; fomenting idolatry; selling the sacraments."[3] Pérez proposed to celebrate the sacraments for free, in Spanish, in a national church modeled on the city churches of antiquity. Exhilarated, Gambrell concluded that Corpus Christi was no cromista den: it was "headquarters of Mexico's newest, and perhaps most significant, revolution," a return to primitive Catholic purity. Gambrell realized that ICAM was "semipolitical"; thrillingly, it was semireligious. This Catholic roots movement just needed charismatic leaders and a "spiritual motif," such as *guadalupanismo*.[4]

In truth, even Roman Catholics were curious about Pérez. One educated *chilango* entered Corpus Christi in 1925, "just to see inside, never remotely with the intention of abdicating my religious principles." A year later, he confessed to hearing Pérez say Mass: did that make him a schismatic?[5] A Mexico City priest wrote to Archbishop Mora in 1926 because he worried that Pérez's sacraments, illicit under canon law, might be spiritually valid (having the desired effects). Canon law said that any priest could minister in an emergency: even if Mora suspended him, couldn't Pérez still perform the sacraments in extremis? This same debate once swirled around constitutional clergy in 1790s France and, later, among insurgent Mexican priests. A century even later, Mora's correspondent fretted that Pérez, too, had a narrow path to theological respectability. The idea caused turmoil in his soul: "many opinions emerge, deep inside me," he confessed, and in black moments, he wished something would happen to Pérez.[6] Another Mexico City priest had a rude awakening after seeing Pérez dole out maundy money in La Soledad. "Illustrious señor," he told Mora, "the schismatical movement, made with diabolical cunning and fat with devotion to the Holy Virgin, is *attracting people*." He watched them enter La Soledad, ignoring Mora's interdict. On re-emerging, coins jingling in their hands, they joked: "'You see, it was just people talking! It's the same as in all the other churches. Even the saints are the same!'" The priest forgave them. What was the point of excommunicating poor wretches from San Lázaro who only wanted to visit the Virgin of Solitude? They were ignorant, not guilty: none of them has any idea "what the unity of the church means" and most "do not know what excommunication is."[7]

In these accounts, we see different actors grappling with what we might call ICAM's ecclesiological implications; that is, its repercussions for people's understanding of catholicity and of churchness: If two bodies called themselves Catholic, what and where was the church? Was it possible to have Catholic denominations—Catholics separate from Rome? Who had the authority to confer Catholic status on people and things? Did priests need a bishop's permit to cure souls, as doctors need hospital privileges, or could they freelance? Were they defined more by obedience to hierarchy or sacramental mission? People gave divergent answers to these questions, assuming they ever thought about them. For bishops as for Gobernación detectives, admittedly, all roads led to Rome—the question was whether Rome was saintly or corrupt. For others, the boundaries of "church" and "Catholic" grew fuzzy the more they thought about them. Our guilt-ridden layman could not resist experiencing a schismatical Mass; perhaps he wanted to know if the magic still "worked." Our tormented priest feared Pérez could justify his breakaway movement using a canonical loophole. For Gambrell, ICAM was a church if it embodied a Christian origin myth. For La Soledad's devotees, meanwhile, "church" meant reassuring rituals and charity. A church that *gave* them money! "Many poor devils greatly enjoyed this novelty," Frenchman Paul Dudon reluctantly conceded after seeing it with his own eyes; but if Pérez dispensed alms, "instead of asking for them as the Catholic Church does," he would need all Mexico's oil to stay afloat.[8]

These contradictory responses should remind us that Mexico's postrevolution was a time of theological, not just political, controversy. Yet instead of the old battle lines—Catholic militants versus godless revolutionaries—we see a contest between church concepts, a culture war within Catholicism. It was an asymmetrical contest, and Pérez was bound to lose. Still, it bears repeating that the revolution did not just produce an anticlerical critique of the church: it proposed a Catholic alternative. To see this, we have to be willing to take Pérez seriously as a religious actor, not just a CROM sidekick. We also have to deconstruct "the Catholic Church" as a category and be willing to admit a plurality ("the Catholic churches"). I do not just mean in an anthropological sense—recognizing local Catholicism's infinite flavors, as in William James's metaphor of cells in a honeycomb; but, rather, in terms of organizational variety, seeing the church as an apiary of self-governing and independent, but doctrinally linked hives. Intellectually, that it is not so easy to do. No body in history has been so centered as the church; even saying "Roman Catholic" feels tautological. Our default assumption is that *non–Roman* Catholic churches—national, ethnic—cannot be "really" Catholic, no matter their protestations to the contrary.[9] To study them, as Julie Byrne observes, is thus no neutral act: it is to produce Catholics by granting catholicity to those whose bona fides many reject. If I myself am not a Catholic, why should I say who is?[10]

Nonetheless, viewing "Catholic" as a pluralistic self-ascription is necessary if we are to comprehend the ambivalence and zeal felt by liberal Catholics such as Pérez, who loathed modern Rome as passionately as they claimed to be right-thinking Catholics. For such figures, indeed, it was axiomatic that it was Rome, not they, who had abandoned the true path. Pérez himself loved to point out the moment at which, he said, Rome "strayed from the Christian path" and became tyrannical and idolatrous. It was at the First Vatican Council (1869–1870), where the doctrines of papal infallibility (inerrant teaching authority) and primacy (universal jurisdiction) were defined as Catholic dogmas. These innovations were fantastical ("the greatest absurdity"), Pérez wrote in 1925, and broke with the church's tradition of conciliar government and local autonomy. Rome, symbol of Catholic unity, had become "a truly apostate and schismatic church" due to its false claim that popes were kings and oracles.[11] Perhaps this feeling was keenly sensed by some in Mexico, where the church was palpably *made*—not born—Roman. As Elisa Cárdenas writes, the nineteenth-century assertion of Rome's authority in Latin America was a long, dialectical process that accelerated after the region won political independence. It involved devotional standardization and bureaucratic centralization, phenomena that many historians dub "romanization." It also involved historical reimaging, so that other church governance ideas were wiped and an ultramontane template—the pope as universal sovereign—was naturalized.[12]

Despite the success with which this was done, in 1920s Mexico a Catholic minority continued to contest this high papalism as a distortion of history, on both scriptural and nationalistic grounds. Jesus left "all the apostles" to shepherd the flock, not just Peter, Pérez argued in a newspaper polemic with the cura of Apan, Encarnación Anaya, in 1927. It was nonsense to read Christ's dictum, "Thou art Peter, and upon this Rock I will build my Church" as proof of "primacy in the government of the Universal Church" because "when Christ said those words, the only church to exist was in Jerusalem." As the church in Rome "did not yet exist," it was nonsensical to claim that the pope was the church's "Supreme Chief." Papal primacy usurped local rights; popes' jurisdiction extended only to Italy.[13] In a 1925 sermon, Pérez's stellar orator Benigno Gómez Ruvalcaba likened the church in Mexico to the woman beset by dragons—"the dragon called *papacy!*"—that John the Apostle saw from prison on Patmos.[14] The papal family tree, another *Restauración* story went, included antipopes, heretics, usurpers, and a woman. Were these the infallible pontiffs to whom Mexicans must submit? "Roman Catholics are not Mexican Catholics," said a 1926 tract, but "degenerate descendants" of Loyola and Torquemada, "the satanic incarnation of perversity." "Call yourself what you are: *Mexican Catholic*," a 1927 text ran: "to support the Mexican Church is to make a fatherland!"[15]

There was a crude and violently anti-Roman xenophobia at work here that was seemingly lifted from Maurice de la Châtre's muckraking epic, *Histoire des papes* (1842–1843), and other works like it. Given the pervasive nationalism of the 1920s, moreover, it is tempting to tune out the theological elements and conclude that Pérez was a romantic nationalist who happened to be a priest. As the citations show, however, Pérez mixed Christian primitivism with nationalistic touchiness. We might more accurately say, therefore, that he added revolutionary gloss to a particular Catholic style, namely, a reformist Catholicism ultimately rooted in eighteenth-century Jansenism. Pérez never claimed to be an original but, rather, "true heir" to a dissident Catholic tradition that began with insurgent priests such as Fray Servando and continued via Catholic liberals such as Doctor Mora, Juan Bautista Morales, and the *padres constitucionalistas* who supported the *juarista* Reform. As ICAM's official history had it, Pérez was the final link in an evolving "national Catholic Church in Mexico."[16] He claimed patriarchal status on the strength of this tradition. Indeed, in 1925 he told Herbert Gambrell that the rebel bishop of Porfirian Tamaulipas, Eduardo Sánchez Camacho—excommunicated for opposing the papal coronation of the Guadalupe—had once performed a "special ordination" for him, placing him in the line of apostolic succession.[17]

No matter how vaguely, this echoed the old Jansenist argument that parish priests were apostolic equals of bishops because they were descendants of the seventy disciples mentioned in Luke's Gospel, sent by Christ to heal the sick and crush serpents and scorpions, just as bishops were heirs to the Twelve. Thanks to these apostolic credentials, radical seventeenth- and eighteenth-century theologians argued, priests should not be subjected to episcopal tyranny, nor could bishops ask blind obedience of them.[18] This jansenistic emphasis on the rights of lower clergy, it bears repeating, was transposed into the canons of Mexican patriotism long before Pérez. Yucatecan liberal Lorenzo de Zavala, for instance, theorized independence as a revolt of humble curas against royalist, gachupin bishops in his 1831 *Ensayo histórico*.[19] ICAM reprised this patriotic-Catholic fusion: Pérez was a new "Redeemer," another Hidalgo, "old and venerable," sent to achieve Mexico's "second independence," its emancipation from Rome.[20]

Still, we should be careful when claiming Pérez was a "revolutionary priest" because he had little interest in theology, unlike the Jansenists, and only wanted to revolutionize the church institutionally. Here, though, we should recall that Jansenism was itself diverse. As a seventeenth- and eighteenth-century Catholic tendency, it departed from a bleak conception of fallen humanity and rejected works-based notions of salvation. Following Saint Augustine, Jansenists posited that only illumination of conscience by God's grace could save. Hence they promoted an interior, puritanical piety reflecting this inner light. As a corollary, however, Jansenists scanned sacred history in search of an elect, for purposes of imitation. They chose the early Christians, whose apostolic fervor bespoke certainty of salvation. Apostolic Christians were also said to have been egalitarian and democratic: favorite tropes here were the Council of Jerusalem, recorded in Acts, where Matthias was elected as twelfth apostle to replace Judas; or Cyprian's account of ecclesiastical elections in third-century Africa. A gloomy theological Jansenism thus focused on justification and a spiritual approach to faith; an ecclesiological kind fetishized the primitive church as a democratic, protorevolutionary forum. The first type could be weaponized against baroque religious excess, which is probably why Bourbon prelates espoused it when policing popular religion. The second kind offered scope to attack religious, hence political, hierarchy, so appealed to turbulent priests such as Fray Servando as well as those that came after him.[21]

To the extent that Pérez ever mused theologically on works and grace, he did so in eighteenth-century terms: ICAM's 1930 Constitution said that works should not be conceived in the manner "vainly propagated by the Pelagians," as heavenly down payments, but as fruits of the tree, insufficient for salvation but "agreeable to God" as evidence of living faith.[22] But really, Pérez was a latter-day Mier, a leveler of church structures, as can be seen from the numerous jansenistic *refritos* littering ICAM's manifestos. One clear affinity was Christian primitivism; the belief that Christianity's first centuries were its golden age, prompting demands that the modern church be saved by a return to ancient discipline. A related idea, since it mitigated social rank, was religious voluntarism: the suppression of religious taxes in favor of free-will giving, as a kind of New Testament throwback. Third was a belief that priesthood was defined by priests' sacramental function, not institutional obedience; hence priests could not be constrained in their ministry, even by bishops. As we will see, this idea became contentious when Mexico's bishops ordered priests to suspend public worship in 1926. A fourth idea, which will be discussed in the next chapter, was a commitment to lay patronage. Finally, in terms of its apostolic succession, ICAM claimed from 1926 to be part of a network of independent churches whose apostolicity derived from the eighteenth-century see of Utrecht, a Jansenist hotbed.

Despite their vaunted antiquity, then, many of Pérez's revamps were eighteenth-century ideas. Carey traces the history of voluntarism to Irish Catholics' eighteenth-century fight against British penal laws, thence to colonial North America.[23] Another jansenist favorite—that priests' sacramental mission trumped ecclesiastical obedience—was stated at the unofficial and jansenistic Pistoia Synod (1786), then reiterated by French revolutionary clergy and insurgent Mexican priests such as Mier and the Troncoso brothers.[24] Pérez's support for lay patronage, which emerged in his endorsement of the Calles Law, again recalled the French revolutionary church but also the practice of parish incorporation known in the eighteenth- and nineteenth-century United States as trusteeism.[25] Besides Mexican patriotism, the radical half-lives of reformist Catholicism were Pérez's main intellectual influences but not the only ones. ICAM's one theological innovation, its suppression of eternal hellfire, derived from a twentieth-century US Catholic-Theosophical body, the Liberal Catholic Church (LCC). There were hints of Spiritism and Freemasonry, too. ICAM was thus an eclectic church for revolutionary moderns that blended an eighteenth-century idea of ageless Catholicism with political nationalism and beliefs of a secular or esoteric nature. This chapter describes the contours of Pérez's Mexican Church. It first explores ICAM's primitivist Christian ethos, then its search for apostolic credentials and its voluntarist practices and form of governance. It closes with a discussion of ICAM's religious experimentation and its political response to the Church-state crisis of 1926.

BACK TO THE FUTURE? PÉREZ'S APOSTOLIC REVOLUTION

ICAM's starting point was that the church was corrupt and that to save it the restoration of primitive ecclesiastical discipline and a distilled Catholic doctrine was necessary. Christian antiquity provided the touchstone for postrevolutionary Mexico; it was assumed that ancient churches were not merely pristine but national prototypes. In doctrinal terms, ICAM claimed to be keeper of an original flame: ICAM's *bases fundamentales* (1925), Profession of Faith (1929), and General Constitution (1930) all asserted the articles of faith provided in the Apostles' and Nicene Creeds and the Bible, the latter in an appropriately eighteenth-century vernacular form (Segovian priest Felipe Scio de San Miguel's) not the Vulgate. In disciplinary terms, ICAM defined itself as a sovereign church governed by Mexican-born clergy under a patriarch. It swore obedience to national law and required that its priests be useful citizens. It further stated that priests' temporal authority was a clericalist invention: hence all coercion—taxes, auricular confession, hellfire—was abolished. To promote national sentiment and rationality, worship was celebrated in Spanish, not Latin, and laypeople were allowed to interpret scripture, though belief in the saints and Mary (code for guadalupanismo) was required.[26] Pérez believed in a purified Catholicism; the idea was to cleanse the church, laundering it through apostolic cycles en route to the future. As *Restauración*'s first cover proclaimed, ICAM was an "evolutionary religious movement" to restore "the golden age of the primitive church."[27]

Antiquity's most gilded feature was that city-state churches—such as those founded at Corinth, Ephesus, Philippi, Colossae, and

Thessalonica—offered squarely biblical precedents for self-governing national churches. This idea was repeated ad nauseam. Pérez's "Letter to the Secular and Regular Clergy of the Roman Catholic and Apostolic Church" (1925), for instance, drew parallels between ancient city churches and ICAM. Early Christendom affirmed "the real existence of national churches," Pérez wrote, whether in Paul's epistles or John's account in Revelation of the founding of the seven churches of Asia. ICAM was not schismatical; it merely revived a tradition of apostolic autonomy. This was why priests of "advanced liberal ideas" asserted Mexico's liberty from Rome. According to ICAM's 1925 program, meanwhile, "papal tyranny" must give way to a church that was "ecclesiastically self-governing . . . not humiliated by foreign priests."[28] A national "ecclesiastical body" would restore Mexican dignity and ensure compliance with the constitutional ban on foreign religious ministers.[29] A national church would also be kinder to Mexican citizens, just as the early churches had been egalitarian. Indeed, the lower clergy were promised a parish redistribution if they joined ICAM. According to Pérez's 1925 letter, "our national church" was

> inspired by the high patriotic ideal that Mexican Priests should have the right legitimately corresponding to them to occupy in the government of their church those parishes and livings which they in justice deserve; for it causes profound consternation and demoralization to see how priests of the Spanish and other nationalities occupy the best churches and parishes of the republic, while we are relegated to oblivion.[30]

Other texts promised priestly autonomy. One Profession of Faith, for instance, stated that in primitive times God had "placed first apostles, then evangelists, teachers, miracle-workers . . . bishops, priests, and deacons," but neither archbishops nor popes. Lay Catholics, for their part, were assured that a "national clergy" would be empathetic, especially toward indigenous Catholics. ICAM priests in Puebla vowed to abandon "imperial Romanism" and "take the message of eternal life to the pueblos." The "native contingent of priests" worked among the indigenous "as humbly as the fishermen of Galilee," said a 1931 pastoral from Veracruz.[31]

    Nowhere would ICAM's concern for the nation's poor be clearer

Chapter Two

than in its efforts to democratize the sacraments, again in line with primitive practice. The sacraments would be given in the fullness as Christ intended, using antique, vernacular formulas, not latinized and trafficked. ICAM's baptism rite required priests to wear purple vestments, as supposedly used in the early church, and offer recipients eternal life. Primitivist marriage, unction, and burial formulas were also published. Catechism for "the popular classes" was offered in Corpus Christi as a prelude to confirmation; the ritual supposedly imitated an old Jerusalem rite.[32] Confession and the Eucharist were given retrofits. The *sacrament* of confession ("instituted by Christ before His death") remained; but the tribunal, the confessional box, was abolished. According to Gómez Ruvalcaba, an "ex-clergyman of the Roman Church," this was done on historicist grounds, confessional boxes being instruments of psychosocial terrorism, a medieval chamber of horrors. Confessors' manuals, he wrote, taught lawyerish tricks allowing priests to absolve unrepentant murderers and adulterers. ICAM's objection that confession warped Christian conscience, we might note, was different to the revolutionary idea that confessional boxes were prurient spaces where priests ransacked women's sexual secrets, if not their bodies.[33] When it came to the Eucharist, ICAM offered communion under both kinds, in imitation of the Last Supper. "The Lord's cup must not be denied to the faithful," ran ICAM's constitution, since Christ gave His disciples bread and wine. By violating the unity of this sacrament, Rome committed apostasy. "When once you drew near to participate in the sacrament of the Holy Eucharist at your altars," *Restauración* opined, "priests gave you communion only with bread . . . but you did not drink the wine, which is His precious blood." This was "a horrendous sacrilege." Only Mexican Catholics received "the true and complete Sacrament," as Christ desired.[34]

ICAM instituted two other significant formal changes to its services, the first being use of Spanish instead of Latin—celebrating "in their own way, *a la mexicana*," as Herbert Gambrell put it.[35] As ICAM's constitution predictably explained, this was because "saying public prayers in church or administering the sacraments in a language people cannot understand . . . opposes God's word and the custom of the primitive Catholic Church."[36] Christ never spoke in Latin, Pérez upbraided the cura of Apan: was Anaya really saying that ICAM's rituals were empty because priests said "Yo te bautizo," not "Ego te baptizo"? That was Roman superstition.[37] ICAM also claimed that vernacular liturgies advanced postrevolutionary mexicanization: 1925's *bases fundamentales* did not just institute Spanish rites but used the SEP's phrase, "the national language."[38] In "pueblos where the inhabitants do not understand the national language," said another text, Mass would be celebrated in Spanish with an indigenous interpreter.[39]

Second, Pérez tried to thicken national sentiment by filling the liturgical calendar with patriotic observances. These fitted around the standard feasts (which included such "Catholic" celebrations as Corpus Christi and the Month of Mary) and usually solemnized key dates in Mexican history.[40] There were clear parallels with Protestant England, with its "Crownation Days" and providentialist commemorations of the foiling of the Spanish Armada and Gunpowder Plot.[41] ICAM created a "double rite" for San Felipe de Jesús (Mexico's first saint) and Constitution Day, which coincided on 5 February. It then celebrated the *grito* of La Soledad (18 February); the division of powers (March); Labor Day (1 May); Hidalgo's execution (30 June); Juárez's death (18 July); and Independence (15–16 September). The ritual year closed in December, with masses to mark the Guadalupe's apparition and Morelos's death. Particular emphasis was placed on cults of Hidalgo and Juárez. Pérez's seizure of La Soledad was deliberately conflated with Hidalgo's grito of Dolores: one sermon called Hidalgo the "first cismático," and described "the ancient cura of Juxtlahuaca" as his successor. This conceit was reinforced at the annual Mass for Hidalgo's death, when Pérez ostentatiously lifted the excommunication writ that royalist bishops slapped on his hero. For the fiestas patrias there were high masses, bellringing, and Te Deums attended by Knights of Guadalupe and a few revolutionary personages.[42]

Juárez's death (July 18) was another important anniversary. In 1925, Pérez led a "spiritual tribute" lauding the Benemérito for planting Catholicism's "liberty tree." It was Juárez, Pérez said, who restored the church's apostolic poverty and should be seen as "our Saint Peter, founder of the national church." This was vintage Pérez; yet ICAM's Juárez cult was equally suggestive for what it said about the interpenetration of Catholicism and esoteric spiritualities, above all Freemasonry and Spiritism. Like Madero, Pérez communed with Juárez's spirit: Juárez was "now present among us," Pérez's 1925 sermon ended, "watching us from his tomb at San Fernando and ordering us not to weaken." 1926's sermon, delivered by a confirmed Freemason, Benigno Gómez Ruvalcaba, likened Juárez to Moses, "the Great Legislator, immense caudillo of flowing beard and prodigious staff." Following "the divine and eternal law of evolution [that] raises up in every race the liberator that it needs," Gómez Ruvalcaba gushed, a "second Moses" was born in Guelatao's mountains to give Mexico freedom of conscience. Yet because Roman claws still tore "Anáhuac's virginal flesh," Juárez's spirit must descend on the *hemiciclo* opposite Corpus Christi and bring new light. "Descend from your throne," Gómez Ruvalcaba implored, "from the region of eternal light in which you are submerged . . . to give us the sacred word of the Ideal." Juárez was also entreated to use "the power of your mace" to break Romanism's chains. As we can see, this sermon featured many classical Masonic motifs, such as the mace, eagle, and staff (symbolizing power, cunning, and celestial beings' presence on earth); it also cited Masonic beliefs (God's existence as Supreme Architect of a universal "Ideal") and was written in an allegorical style that evoked a cosmic battle between realms of light and darkness.[43]

Pérez also hoped that Corpus Christi would become a national mausoleum where masses to official figures would be held. In September 1926, ICAM mourned the death of Ricardo Treviño's father; the death of seventy-year-old Ángel Jiménez Juárez, ICAM's treasurer and reputedly a son of the Benemérito, was commemorated that October; another, December, requiem was held for the soul of the father of General Roberto Cruz, chief of police (and a registered member of Corpus Christi parish); and in June 1927, ICAM prayed for Natalia Chacón, Calles's late wife.[44]

SEARCHING FOR THE OLD SOUL REBELS: PÉREZ'S APOSTOLIC SUCCESSION

For all that Pérez aped primitive Christianity and created a patriotic "Mexican" liturgy, there was no hiding that he was just a priest, not a bishop, and therefore could not really be head of a national church because he could not impart the sacrament of Holy Orders to others and in so doing perpetuate his movement. Pérez needed more than a primitive aesthetic and tricolors: he needed a credible apostolic succession. If he could not establish one, and if ICAM could not ordain priests or consecrate bishops, it would always be a defector church, unable to replenish itself. What was Pérez to do?

He could do as revolutionary-nationalist priest Gregorio Aglipay did in the Philippines, which was to redefine the episcopate as a turbocharged priesthood, a hierarchy of rank, not an order: as first priest of the Independent Filipino Church (IFI), Aglipay ordained others who consecrated him *obispo máximo* in 1902.[45] Pérez flirted with this idea, as we saw, when recalling his superordination by Sánchez Camacho: as late as mid-1926, *Restauración* said that this gave Pérez a "sacerdotal succession coming directly from the apostles," again suggesting a jansenistic parity with bishops.[46] Yet Pérez coveted bishop's status, which left him two options for creating an apostolic lineage. He could hope that a Roman bishop would consecrate him—which was very unlikely, even if Gobernación mischievously claimed in 1926 that bishop Vera y Zuria (Pue.) was flirting with the "Mexican papacy."[47] "Many Mexican prelates," Pérez claimed in 1925, pined for independence; they should take it, recalling that Vaticanism "openly conflicts with the practice signaled by the primitive church." Since none did, Pérez's third solution was to commune with another non-Roman church and have one of its bishops lay hands on him. This was what the padres constitucionalistas attempted through the Episcopalian Church; soon enough, there were disparaging, sometimes spurious reports that Pérez was tapping an array of estranged churches: Orthodox Christians, Maronites, Old Catholics, and Episcopalians.[48]

In fact, Pérez's overtures extended only as far as Episcopalianism and latterly Old Catholicism, which is to say, those European and American Catholics that broke with Rome after the Vatican Council. These were ICAM's closest correligionists, even if Gambrell lamented Pérez's refusal to align with more reformed churches (circumstances, Gambrell wrote, "would seem to call for an entente cordiale with the Protestant forces . . . but not so").[49] Initially, Episcopalians cultivated Pérez. *La Buena Lid*, the Episcopalian periodical, recalled how in the 1890s liberal curas including "distinguished padre José Joaquín Pérez" visited the Episcopalian mission in Puebla. Liturgical similarities between ICAM and high-church Anglicanism were noted.[50] Jesús L. Pérez—*La Buena Lid*'s editor—wrote in March 1925 that ICAM's launch "echoed among Mexicans of the Catholic Episcopal Church and Old Catholics throughout the world," who cheered "the apparition of a church emancipated from the Vatican." "The only gap" was "the lack of a bishop for transmitting holy orders," which the Episcopalians could provide. The Episcopalian Pérez even defended the patriarch when senator Pedro de Alva alleged in April that ICAM was unoriginal—the idea of a "national consistory" having begun with Fray Servando—and had cromista "choirmasters." ICAM was providential, *La Buena Lid* said: God often used the weak for His purposes, "so His work is not confused with that of men."⁵¹

The stumbling block to an ICAM-Episcopalian acuerdo was political. In 1925, Mexico's Episcopalian Church was itself a headless dependency of the US mainline church, missionary bishop Henry Aves having retired in 1923. He was not replaced until February 1926, when a second missionary bishop, Frank Creighton, arrived in Mexico City. The Episcopalian mission board in New York thus ran its own church in Mexico as a colony and would not appoint a Mexican-born bishop until October 1931, after Pérez died.⁵² It was unlikely, then, that the mission board would view ICAM as more than another outpost of immature, indigenous Christians, or would accept anything but a clientelistic relationship, with the promise of intercommunion and a bishop's hat as sweeteners. In this vein, in 1925 the mission board seconded one of its best Mexican priests—Gómez Ruvalcaba—to ICAM. That May, Gómez Ruvalcaba received from Bishop Richard Hulse in New York temporary license to "work with the Mexican Catholic Church, without leaving the ministry of the Episcopal Church." This was enough for Pérez to tell Gambrell that summer of his hopes for an imminent consecration at Episcopalian hands. In February 1926, vicar general López y Sierra was still promising this "extraordinary news" was nigh.⁵³

Creighton's arrival that month, however, marked a change, starting with a report in *La Buena Lid* describing ICAM as a "Mexican Orthodox"—not Catholic—Church.⁵⁴ Creighton found fault with the liberal positions of ICAM's platform; but the real problem was that Gómez Ruvalcaba had begun to militate as one of Pérez's clergy and that ICAM was competition. This seems clear from the curt letters exchanged by Gómez Ruvalcaba and Creighton that summer, in which Gómez Ruvalcaba learned that his salary had been removed from the mission budget. Creighton regretted firing him but claimed "no other course was open to me." Gómez Ruvalcaba wrote that he considered himself free of his former church and "at complete liberty to act."⁵⁵

It was at this point that Pérez looked to the Old Catholic movement, which is to say, a movement that developed within Catholic Christianity as a revolt against the dogmas of papal primacy and infallibility. In fact, the Old Catholic movement was itself fragmented, and Pérez was only ever in communion with third-wave churches founded in the twentieth-century United States by Italian, French, and Slavic migrants. Before them, however, came the Old Catholic churches of Germany, Austria, and Switzerland, which formed in protest against the Vatican Council, and the Old Catholic Church of Holland, which was Old Catholicism's mothership insofar as it preserved organic continuity with the medieval (eighth-century) see of Utrecht, independent of Rome since 1724. It is from Utrecht that Old Catholic orders, and ultimately Pérez's episcopal claims, derive, which perhaps necessitates a short digression. Briefly, the suspension and exile of jansenistic, pro-Gallican bishop Peter Codde in 1704 led to a dispute between Rome and Utrecht's chapter, each of which claimed the right to elect a successor. The chapter, citing a twelfth-century right of election and Dutch canonist Van Espen to the effect that jurisdiction over vacant sees reverted to chapters, appointed pro-vicars to govern the see, to the papacy's fury. Enter French bishop Dominique Marie Varlet (of Ascalon and Babylon *in partibus infidelium*) whom Rome rusticated to Persia in 1718. After stopping in Amsterdam, however, where his opposition to anti-jansenist bull *Unigenitus* preceded him, Varlet was persuaded to perform confirmations in Utrecht in 1719 and then, in 1724, to end its twenty-year interregnum by consecrating Cornelius Steenoven as bishop. After Steenoven died months later, the gadfly Varlet happily consecrated three more bishops.

Thus was born a branch line of apostolic succession which in the 1870s fused with the anti-infallibilist rump of European Catholicism. After congresses in Munich and Cologne, Josef Hubert Reinkens was consecrated as the first Old Catholic bishop, in 1873 in Rotterdam. The movement then spread across Europe, defining itself as a federation of communing national churches bound by ancient discipline. After Gerardus Gul's 1892 consecration in Utrecht, finally, the Old Catholic movement escaped its Germanic confines. It was Gul who consecrated the first bishop of the Polish National Catholic Church, Francis Hodur, in 1907; then, in 1908, he consecrated Arnold Harris Mathew as bishop of the so-called Catholic Church of Great Britain. Mathew, a faux aristocrat who claimed to possess Roman Catholic orders and an Irish earldom, later consecrated an Austrian priest (bishop de Landas Berghes et de Rache) in London, in June 1913; and it was Landas Berghes, fleeing internment, who took Old Catholicism to the United States. Indeed, in 1916 he consecrated an Italian priest who had quarreled with his superiors, Carmel Henry Carfora. Carfora took the title of archbishop of the North American Old Roman Catholic Church (NAORC), a fifty-thousand-strong body that ministered to Italian, Polish, Lithuanian, and Ukrainian migrants in Michigan and Pennsylvania. It was he who consecrated Pérez.[56]

Rumors that Old Catholics were making "kindly offers" to Pérez surfaced in spring 1925 in *La Buena Lid*. By August 1926, *Restauración* acknowledged that Pérez was in contact with the "Ultrajectine [Utrecht-based] Catholic Church"; in September, ICAM's synod elected three candidates for consecration; and in October, Pérez traveled to Chicago, supposedly for rest but in reality to receive consecration as "metropolitan archbishop of Mexico City" from Carfora. The ceremony was held on 17 October in Saint Mary of Grace church: as an orchestra played, Carfora, flanked by two NAORC bishops, led a two-hour ceremony in Spanish and made ICAM's first three bishops—Pérez; ex-Franciscan Macario López Valdéz; and vicar general López y Sierra. A banquet followed in Carfora's home. For Pérez, who was carrying a crook and sporting white regalia and a Bat-cape that he could only afford thanks to a Protestant benefactor, Dr. Ernesto Carrión, this camp, faintly ludicrous ceremony was a crowning moment.[57] "In the sunset of my sacerdotal life," Pérez wrote in his first pastoral as metropolitan, he had been called to restore the customs of apostolic times and purify the church. Now that ICAM had entered "the concert of all the world's true Christian churches, by obtaining, as Saint Paul puts it, *the plenitude of divine grace*," it could be said to "constitute a perfect Catholic Church in this country." Mexico thus joined the "progressive peoples" of Europe and the United States, where national churches cemented unity. Mexicans should be proud that they had won a "perfect episcopal succession" by their own means, as Rome would forever have denied them liberty.[58]

Was it "perfect"? There was something undeniably comical about the mixture of primitive protestation and pontifical theatrics: Pérez was duded up like Pius IX. In the final analysis, however, speculating as to the quality of Carfora's episcopal credentialing is to enter firmly into the world of theological right, or a metaphysical discussion about divinity, to which there is no end. Certainly, more established churches questioned Pérez's credentials. Utrecht Catholics did not recognize the Mathewite line from which he descended. Rome, of course, placed no faith in Pérez's episcopate: Mexico City's curia was told that Rome never pronounced on the "validity of such consecrations," so those ordained by Pérez could be considered *non sacerdoti* [nonpriests]. Carfora was an "ecclesiastical vagabond," an "ordinary rogue . . . willing to impose hands at a fixed price," the archbishop of Morelia learned.[59] Pérez himself was as sensitive as a wrestler to charges of fakery. On returning to Mexico, he notified Creighton of his consecration and made a shameless pitch to Mexican Episcopalian clergy, telling them to leave the "American Episcopal Church" and join Mexico's "native church" which now had three new dioceses in Mexico, Chiapas, and Puebla-Veracruz. Some Episcopalian clergy did jump ship, starting with deacon José F. Gómez. Creighton ignored Pérez's provocation, though one of his priests, Samuel Salinas, reminded Pérez that ICAM had received "disinterested help" from the Episcopalians.[60] Stung by Creighton's silence, in December Pérez attacked the American's lack of "Christian fraternity," telling him that ICAM was a "serious movement . . . worthy of respect, like all primitive Christian churches." Creighton's refusal to acknowledge this was sad; if he had doubts about ICAM's "true apostolic succession," he should put up or shut up.[61]

NO SCRIP FOR THE JOURNEY: VOLUNTARISM AND CHURCH GOVERNANCE

If ICAM embodied one apostolic virtue, it was poverty, though in practice government of the Mexican Church was as riven with factionalism, ambition, and backstabbing as was the Vatican in Pérez's mind. If he was inaccurate, Pérez was at least not hypocritical when he denounced Roman simony (sacramental rack-renting). As always, he did so on scriptural-nationalistic grounds. People should not purchase sacraments like "vulgar merchandise," *Restauración* said, but partake freely. Did Christ not command His priests "to give freely, because you received freely"? Remembering, too, how Jesus drove the moneylenders from the temple, ICAM preached that "the good priest should live off the people's alms, not sell God's sacraments."[62] "The path of Jesus Christ consists of this precept," said another missive: "'Provide neither gold nor silver nor brass in your purses, nor scrip for your journey . . . for the workman is worthy of his meat.'"[63] If priests were worth the money—the rituals solemn, the sermons stirring—contented flocks would pay up. ICAM thus suppressed the schedule of parish fees, first fruits, and tithes. Its fifth *base* was explicit: "Holy sacraments must be administered without remuneration, ending the simoniacal trade that exists in the Roman

Church." If sacraments were free, however, "for the intention or application of the holy sacrifice of the Mass only, alms given freely by the person requesting the Mass may be received."[64] That is, priests could accept a voluntary gratuity for dedicating a Mass, say to an ancestor or patron saint. This was very specific, though Pérez was not above begging for charity (for "small alms, no matter how humble"), as in a 1925 note.[65]

Religious voluntarism was introduced for reasons other than honoring New Testament maxims, not least to embarrass Roman clergy by portraying them as venal. In the countdown to the suspension of public worship in 1926, for instance, Pérez alleged that Rome was a "worse usurer than Iscariot." While "ignorant people" flocked to church for last-minute services, Roman clergy charged "the most onerous tariffs" and milked popular credulity.[66] "The Romanist priest does not just live of the altar," a 1929 ICAM broadside went,

> but, blinded by limitless greed and incorrigible simony, never thinks of lowering the aranceles—that is, the tariffs, as for any commercial establishment—or of placing them within believers' reach; on the contrary, upon his return, after the renewal of the cult [June 1929], he doubled or tripled them, without reason or conscience denying the faithful even the indispensable sacrament at the hour of death if they do not pay.[67]

This critique—that expensive offices made the poor neglect their souls—echoed Melchor Ocampo's famous 1850s diatribes. Yet the shift from regressive taxation to voluntary giving was also designed to recalibrate the relationship between priests and laity by forcing priests to rely on free-will donations.[68] While the laity was relieved of a burden, clergy would become dependent on good reviews and hence be socially responsible. A pueblo whose religion is the religion of gold," a 1925 flier ran, "is a people complicit in maintaining the greatest offense to morality as its religion . . . a pueblo that walks fatally toward its ruin." The solution was a church that banned "taxing Jesus's sublime sacrifice."[69] What that meant in practice was that Corpus Christi pre-negotiated gratuities with those, often village mayordomos, who commissioned saint's-day masses. Coyutla (in Veracruz's Totonacapan) was a case in point. Here the festive commission requested a priest for a 1929 fiesta: "in response to the petition of the inhabitants," Pérez asked when the fiesta would be held and said that typically "alms for religious services" were three to five pesos, depending on whether Mass was sung or said. Coyutla obviously accepted Pérez's going rate because the patriarch wrote back applauding its "spirit of religiosity and patriotism" and promising a priest. Future generations would not forgive him if he did not lift the "yoke of the foreignist Roman Clergy" from pueblos where God allowed his priests to work.[70]

To prove that voluntarism made economic sense, finally, ICAM reprinted the arancel used by the Roman Catholic see of Mexico. Here, an individual Mass intention cost two pesos at off-peak times, rising to seven pesos at peak times; a month of *misas rezadas* cost 80 to 100 pesos, sung Mass three times more. A Gregorian Mass—120 pesos—cost a peon three months' wages. And where did this loot go? Pérez had no doubt. "We must not allow our money to enrich Mexico's greatest enemy: *the Pope*," he wrote in 1925; "the Pope's clergy in our republic does not defend religion—it defends money."[71] As we can see, ICAM's voluntarism had a nationalistic point: to stop Rome siphoning off Mexican wealth and promote a kind of sacramental import-substitution model. ICAM was "genuinely nationalistic," said a 1931 broadside, because it "identifies with the revolutionary government that exalts the poor."[72] Thus Pérez gave a nationalist spin to a religious practice designed to make disestablished and minoritarian Catholic churches financially free from the tutelage of Protestant governments, as in eighteenth-century Ireland or the United States.[73]

For better or worse, this voluntarist ethos entirely dictated ICAM's norms and practices of church governance. On one hand, voluntarist and democratic principles were theoretically built into church structures, which stressed lay oversight of priests and constitutional compliance. ICAM's basic model of government was set out in an "accord" signed by Pérez and vicar general López y Sierra on 5 January 1926. This constitutionalized ICAM by incorporating into church affairs the legal figure of the *junta vecinal*, meaning the ten-strong citizens' junta that was empowered under constitutional article 130 to have custody of church buildings and register priests before the municipal authorities as churches' legal guardians (encargados).[74] Pérez's accord greatly amplified the operations of what he dubbed *juntas parroquiales*; these bodies, the accord stated, must consist of twelve respectable citizens (ten junta members plus an elected parish delegate known for possessing

"Christian virtues" and the priest) who would be appointed in annual parish assemblies. Juntas would have wide-ranging powers to represent the parish: the priest and parish delegate would sit in ICAM's synod, for instance, where they could vote for a new patriarch. Juntas would also care for the church fabric and, most important, control its finances. First of all, parish committees were charged with ensuring that "in their church, no tariffs or charges for any religious service or sacrament of the Catholic religion are ever introduced." Instead, priests were to receive "the alms that the faithful give piously for the maintenance of the cult and the needs of the parish ... [and the] decorous support of the clergy," as was their moral obligation. Moreover, parish juntas should administer funds: all income, "whether from *limosnas* in church, private donations, or collections," must be held by a treasurer, with 65 percent spent on parish expenses (including the cura's salary) and 25 percent remitted to Corpus Christi. Priests were thus goodwill employees of the parish, paid by laypeople. Accounts and 25 percent remittances must be sent monthly to Pérez, though significantly, if ICAM appointed a diocesan bishop to a territory then the patriarch's share would drop to a paltry 5 percent.[75]

Since priests were *supposed* to be poor, they were required (as in ICAM's sixth *base* and profession of faith) to practice a trade or profession in addition to their vocation, "following the custom of the apostles," so that they were not a material burden to their flock or tempted by simony.[76] This, indeed, was part of a general attempt to turn priests into productive citizens: for the same reason, priestly celibacy was no longer prescribed—in fact some ICAM documents described it as unnatural, Roman, and odious. Instead, priests could marry, following the order in Genesis for a man and a woman to become one flesh. Pérez himself, who never remarried, told one correspondent that following the gospels and "the ancient customs of Catholicism," priests were "at absolute liberty to live in the state most pleasing to their morality," so long as they were not libertines.[77] With their labors or their loins, therefore, and as in the church's first centuries, Mexican priests were expected to add to the sum of human plenty.

Financial considerations were certainly more important and explain many of the emphases that were placed on ecclesiastical discipline. First, priests were banned from deserting parishes in which they were registered until a replacement ("one of ours, a Mexican not a

Roman Catholic," as one cura was told) could be sent. This was to prevent Roman clergy from moving in and cleaning up.[78] Second, Corpus Christi went to considerable lengths to ensure that Pérez's monthly *derechos* were received from parish priests. Remittances, after all, represented ICAM's main income, though they were always justified as a retro practice in the sending ("as Saint Paul used to do for the Mother Church of Jerusalem").[79] Pérez's surviving archives brim with remittance correspondence, and with complaints when remittances failed to materialize. "The patriarch and I thank you," vicar general López y Sierra wrote one priest in Puebla in March 1927, "for the reports you give us . . . [and] the documents you left in this city for the Interior Ministry and the Puebla Government." Yet the priest, Emeterio Valdez, was berated for not remitting twenty pesos after visiting Zapotitlán, "for well you know the penury through which the church passes," and was told "to remember, *above all*, your duty to remit derechos" next month, so as to "normalize" church finances. In June, however, Valdéz was thanked for a giro that would substantially defray "the inflated expenses we have in Corpus Christi," especially propaganda and training. But then in July and August came further reminders "not to forget for any reason to send derechos," as ICAM had to organize its "economic business" and "be sustained by the resources of its selfless priests" alone (clearly there was now no official support). Valdéz next sent what was evidently a substantial check for February 1928 (it was Candelaria) and received a letter of "infinite" thanks from López y Sierra—"may God increase your charity and give to you by the handful"—because his earnings had "drag[ged] us out of poverty." It was thanks to such efforts that ICAM had "resolved the difficult problem of maintaining itself" and no longer relied on benefactors.[80]

Other priests received the same message or had to defend themselves against charges that their sacramental returns did not match entries in the civil registry. "It is true that I marked several *hojas* of the book of the year before last," one priest stationed in Tlaola (Pue.) admitted, but he did not celebrate a single marriage or baptism without recording it in the civil registry. "If the *partidas* for the baptisms were recorded badly, it is because, I repeat, I do not write well by hand, lacking a good script and spelling . . . but did I baptize without the civil register? No." His sacraments, he insisted, were on file, and a group of parishioners, led by José María and Manuel Torres, unfairly wanted him out.[81] Another Puebla priest reported in 1930 that his dues were unpaid because his bishop had appropriated $500, which he considered a year's worth of remittances. Tapachula's priest also fell behind on his dues in 1926 because he had to travel from Chiapas to Mexico City and pay off corrupt officials. Still, enough priests paid dues, like dean Manuel Salas Vidal in Hidalgo, that ICAM grew, certainly during the Cristero War. Afterward, conditions worsened because priests' tenures became uncertain. Zeferino Reyes, a Mexico City *ingeniero* who handled ICAM's meager funds, claimed in 1930 that he kept Pérez from starving to death. By 1931, Corpus Christi admitted that Pérez was "going through a bad economic situation" and watched "every day" for remittance letters.[82] It was, then, feast or famine.

As a structure, then, ICAM was a body that mediated between local religion and the postrevolutionary authorities, especially Gobernación, and extracted peppercorn rents from the villages. This intermediary, rent-seeking structure linking Mexico City and rural Mexico also explains many of the power struggles, and many of the abuses, from which ICAM suffered. For instance, the proviso restricting Pérez's share of local almsgiving in case of a new episcopal appointment explains the protracted battles that Pérez waged to limit the number of priests that obtained episcopal status, and to restrict priests' status whenever possible to *párroco* (parish priest) or vicario foráneo (rural dean). In theory, priests could seek episcopal status via popular election, supposedly as in the early church. In practice, Pérez thwarted them by demanding that they canonically institute new parishes or increase the number of parishes they held (from four initially to ten). Alternatively, more reports and remittances were demanded.

A good example was Emeterio Valdez, who from 1926 worked five parishes containing forty pueblos in Puebla-Veracruz as a vicario foráneo and did so, in Pérez's words, "as Saint Paul and his glorious messengers did in the first centuries of Christianity." Corpus Christi still declined a May 1928 petition by local people to elect Valdez as bishop. While López y Sierra approved the request in theory, noting the "general sympathy" that Valdéz enjoyed in highland Puebla, he determined that Valdéz operated a pastoral zone (zona de trabajos) but had not canonically founded new parishes. Thus he could not be consecrated, "worthy" though he might be. Another energetic priest, Teodoro Juárez, received this brush-off in 1928. Pérez thus used his power to consecrate to control pastoral regions, invariably appointing *foráneos* like Alfredo Arredondo López.[83] While Pérez ran things, the number of bishops did not increase beyond the four noted in 1926: Pérez (as metropolitan); Macario López (Veracruz-Puebla, eventually succeeded by Valdéz); Gómez Ruvalcaba (Hidalgo); and López y Sierra (auxiliary). In 1929, fantasy dioceses were mapped over Tabasco, Guerrero, Tlaxcala, Tamaulipas, and Texas. In reality, ICAM was halfway between an ecclesial base movement and a church Ponzi scheme; it had real congregations and parishes but no fully functioning dioceses independent of the patriarchate in Mexico City.[84]

ICAM's territorial expansion and Pérez's control nonetheless caused jealousy and battles for preeminence and income, then open challenges to Pérez's authority with the patriarch's age being a complicating factor. The main struggle was between Pérez and the able but irascible López y Sierra. In February 1928, we find Pérez expressing "unending joy" to López y Sierra, thanking him for ICAM's advances. A year later, Pérez fired his vicar general to ensure "better government of the Holy Church," which was code for ending López y Sierra's efforts to oust Valdéz as bishop of Puebla-Veracruz and install client priests, such as Pascual Luciano García. Pérez was evidently in command of his faculties, to judge from his sarcasm: López y Sierra should view his sacking as a "brilliant opportunity" to use his "laudable energies" to evangelize migrant braceros in Texas. López y Sierra duly went north, feigning obedience and dodging the bullets of Gonzalo Escobar's rebels; his successor in ICAM's vicar generalcy was Alberto Hernández de Haro.[85] Then, in August, López y Sierra took revenge, denouncing the "Iscariots" who manipulated Pérez and, in an open letter to the church, mocking "the mental imbalance of the Mexican patriarch." In some parishes, he wrote, celibacy, auricular confession, and church Latin were back.[86] Behind the scenes, Pérez and López y Sierra approached their friends, López y Sierra invoking CROM, Pérez demanding that Gobernación and Tejeda (now in Veracruz) punish López y Sierra and the "illiterate" García as rebels. Zeferino Reyes, leading a "group of revolutionary intellectuals . . . that sympathizes with the Mexican Church," told López y Sierra to stop brandishing "the ridiculous 'scarecrow' of [his] political influences," which was not too inaccurate a description of CROM's power in July 1929.[87] Wiser heads called for patriotic selflessness, as "enemies of the cause" were telling Gobernación that ICAM was crypto-Protestant. If not refuted, "with the greatest ease they will undo everything."[88] Yet the infighting continued in 1930, one side issuing letters rehabilitating López y

Sierra and the other, Pérez's, asserting its authority at a San Antonio synod (May). The synod defrocked López y Sierra and wrote a general constitution giving the patriarch ample new powers via a supreme episcopal council and a synod of clergy, church custodians, and elected lay delegates; which sounded democratic, except that the council ratified all major decisions and the patriarch not only presided over it but had the casting vote.[89]

In 1931, Pérez attempted to fix the succession in favor of Macario López, whom he wrote on 19 March urging him to become patriarch-elect for the church's good and "the Immaculate *Morenita*." Pérez was old, he said, "my head bowed by the years' weight, glimpsing eternity's peaceful shores."[90] Gobernación, still surveilling him, got the truth in June from a spy: "Patriarch Pérez is very old, so each faction in his clergy claims the supremacy as his successor . . . That is the cause of divisions in the Orthodox Mexican Catholic and Apostolic Church." After Pérez's death in October, ICAM politics grew surreal. Macario López formed a "junta of ecclesiastical administration" to elect a patriarch. Then (October 1932) López Sierra claimed election, under the title "Juan Crisóstomo I." In spring 1933, Eduardo Dávila claimed patriarchal status.[91] As we might expect, this infighting significantly undermined ICAM's effectiveness in the field.

PÉREZ AND THE UNIVERSAL MIND

Tucked away in ICAM's brief doctrinal statements were some unexpected, and unattributed, innovations. ICAM's *bases*, for instance, abolished two aspects of Catholicism that were thought to underpin clericalism: eternal damnation and the tribunal of penance. The notion of eternal hellfire was abolished on ontological grounds, as being incompatible with a loving God, and as a symbol of clerical terrorism. "Our God is a Perfect Being without anger and vengeance," ran the 1930 constitution, "therefore, He cannot condemn for all eternity a man who is His image and likeness." Instead, hell became a kind of prorated, purgatorial space where sinners would atone for an appropriate time before release. In another doctrinal shift, ICAM allowed people to read and reinterpret the scriptures and the liturgy. As Pérez told Herbert Gambrell, ICAM wanted "to get away from later additions to the Christian religion by allowing individuals to go to the Bible and reach their own conclusions.'" "The Word of God 'shall not return unto me void, but it shall . . . prosper in the thing where to I sent it,'" said another tract, quoting Isaiah. The point was to diffuse knowledge and so create a moral citizenry with a "religion of principles."[92]

These changes, which might seem humane and democratic now, were disliked widely at the time. Free exegesis smacked of Protestantism to Pérez's former Roman associates, while Herbert Gambrell called the abolition of hell a "startling slant to Universalism." It was obvious to Gambrell, too, that a biblical approach contradicted ICAM's guadalupanismo, and he quizzed Pérez and López y Sierra about this discrepancy in their meetings.[93] In fact, Pérez had not plucked these ideas out of thin air: much like the cult of Juárez discussed earlier, they derived from Pérez's long-term interest in other "revolutionary" cults, especially Spiritism (specifically Theosophy) and Freemasonry, and from his efforts to integrate these into Catholicism. Pérez did not get far down this road, but the ideological genesis of these changes is clear from reading his surviving correspondence, book catalogs, and pamphlets. Pérez was thus a liberal Catholic in theological terms as well as a Catholic liberal in political terms. He was certainly an interlocutor of other minoritarian Catholic and Spiritist movements, and to some extent, a popularizer.

For example, Pérez seemingly had some contacts with the Los Angeles–based Liberal Catholic Church (LCC) founded in 1917 by James Ingall Wedgwood, scion of the English pottery empire, and an Australian Theosophist and ex-Anglican divine, Charles Leadbeter. This curious church boomed in the 1920s United States—FDR's future running mate, Henry Agard Wallace, was an adherent—before drowning in a sex scandal.[94] Pérez found something else to excite him: a Catholic synthesis with Theosophy—that is, the evolutionary-reincarnationist Spiritist credo propagated by Helena Blavatsky in *The Secret Doctrine* (1888). In LCC hands, Theosophical belief in the evolution of consciousness toward reconciliation with a primordial Godhead was embedded in the Catholic sacraments. These rituals were not seen as remedial technologies for erasing original sin via the application of grace, LCC argued, since divinity was latent in humanity. Instead, sacraments effected an evolutionary boost, allowing humanity to know the deity whose life it shared. This being so, Catholic beliefs that accelerated humanity's metaphysical evolution should remain, while those that reflected a negative, unenlightened conception of human nature premised on estrangement from God, especially hellfire and original sin, should be discarded, along with their sacramental expressions such as aural confessional (a form of "servile cringing and abject self-abasement" that offended the notion of a "Loving Father"). As LCC's foundational documents put it (a 1926 statement of principles, a 1927 constitution), the church promoted a "Liberalist form of Old Catholicism" to improve the "spiritual welfare of humankind," with the sacraments governing a "rising process" through which believers ascended to Christlike perfection. LCC also professed a kind of universalism, a belief that all religions flowed from a common source and that, stripped of cultural specificity, they were but different ways of worshipping a universal God. Believers thus had "intellectual liberty" to interpret texts such as the Bible as they saw fit.[95]

Affinities between these Catholic-Theosophical texts and Pérez's more gnostic musings are readily apparent. Certainly we find translated LCC documents in Pérez's scattered papers, such as the 1925 LCC primer that proudly proclaimed its desire to "combine exalted mysticism and the constant witness of sacramental grace with the broadest intellectual liberty and respect for the individual conscience."[96] Given these Theosophical leanings and also ICAM's reception among southerly indigenous communities, it is surprising that ICAM was absent from the state—Yucatán—that boasted Mexico's largest network of Theosophical societies in the 1920s.[97] Still, Pérez was plugged into Spiritist circles in central Mexico, even if he could not build a popular church out of them. One Juan Félix Hernández wrote to Pérez in 1925, congratulating him on his movement and recalling their friendship in Puebla, where Hernández had used magnetism and Spiritism to heal "some priests and nuns" that Pérez had brought to him.[98] Pérez was sufficiently interested in Spiritism to receive a digest from the Hijos de la Luz called *Mensaje esotérico*: it contained communications from the Spirit of Truth on topics such as universal peace as well as book lists on topics from Theosophy to the astral plane, yoga, and vegetarianism.[99] In January 1925, too, Rufino Juanco—president of the Mexican Spiritist Federation—sent Pérez a manifesto called "The Mexican Catholic Church": it described a church to be governed by a synod and a bishop consecrated by Irving Cooper, of Saint Alban's LCC in Los Angeles. The Mexican body would claim apostolic descent via Utrecht, allow free interpretation of scripture and dogma, accept alms but charge no fees, make sacraments such as confession optional, celebrate all services in the vernacular, and suppress clerical celibacy.[100] Ethereal and secondary though such esoterica may have been, they clearly formed an undisclosed part of ICAM's manifesto.

CONCLUSION: *VIVA CRISTO, PERO NO REY*

As this chapter shows, ICAM was a church—and it *was* a church—of catholic tastes, even if Roman clergy thought it anything but "Catholic." Pérez's movement was, in many ways, an eclectic, contradictory mix of liberal churches past and present, that mixed eighteenth-century Jansenism, nineteenth-century Old Catholicism, secular-revolutionary nationalism, and forms of psuedoscientific or orientalist spirituality, among them Freemasonry, Spiritism, and Theosophy. For a nationalistic church, ICAM was surprisingly cosmopolitan, as its fleeting ties to the United States, Episcopalians, the Old Catholic movement in Utrecht and Chicago, and California's LCC attest. This should remind us that even nationalistic religions are paradoxically transnational, because they emerge from international networks. In the Catholic world especially, the centralization of spiritual and political authority at Rome led to many such borrowings of catholicity and the development of a kind of alt-Catholic underground network in which discrete movements were connected (to borrow Peggy Levitt's suggestive phrase) in "rhizomatic" fashion. ICAM was a perfect example of this running, transversal tendency, creating a church that was the opposite of the Roman oak tree.[101] ICAM also shows us that Mexico's postrevolution waged war on Rome not just from a secular vantage point, which is to say, from outside Catholicism, but from the inside, by invoking a different Catholic teleology in which the primitive had to be discerned and perpetually re-enacted to bring about the national. Pérez was in no sense a systematic theologian, yet he had his convictions and was less of a bumpkin than we assume—he was into all sorts of cosmic and religious speculation, like many revolutionaries in fact. The problem was that most Mexicans didn't care about his patriotic cult, Masonic runes, or Theosophical transcendence. Corpus Christi sometimes filled with Catholic revolutionaries, but it drew congregations of hundreds not thousands and its "register of members" had only 268 regular names (mostly women) in 1926. The pews were hardly filled week-in, week-out with cromista workers.[102]

As we shall see in chapter 3, however, the climaxing of Mexico's religious conflict with the 1926 public suspension of worship renewed interest in Pérez. Corpus Christi was "the only temple where Mass is currently celebrated," *Restauración* trumpeted in September 1926.[103] Even if vast crowds did not suddenly appear in Mexico City, it happened that some people, especially indigenous people, *did* listen to some of the things that Pérez said, especially his message of free services, lay patronage, and dispensing the sacraments no matter what. Again, it is tempting to explain Pérez's hostility to the suspension of public worship with reference to his nationalistic fervor, rather than his priestly ministry. Yet this would oversimplify what was a theological as well as a political dispute, one that revolved around the nature of the priesthood, not just constitutional article 130. In some ways, the controversy recalled the split between "citizen" and "Tridentine" priests that emerged in 1790s France when clergy confronted the civil constitution.[104] Roman clergy such as Father Anaya called the patriarch a traitor for breaking with Rome. According to Anaya, Pérez's Mass was a placebo, because in rejecting Christ's Vicar on earth, Pérez rejected Christ. Only the poor were fooled by Pérez's sacrilegious rituals, Anaya alleged; Pérez should mend his ways, because otherwise hell beckoned him.[105] That was the official church's position: priests were operatives in, and defenders of, a divinely ordained ecclesiastical hierarchy, to which they owed obedience.

In contrast, ICAM invoked a less juridical concept of priests as simple sacramental practitioners. A good starting point, perhaps, is the March 1925 sermon preached in La Soledad by Gómez Ruvalcaba and which compared the legacy of the ancients—Alexander, Caesar, and Hannibal—with those of "the humble Galilean, the divine Jesus." Jesus alone, Gómez Ruvalcaba sermonized, had conquered the human spirit through his priesthood before delegating the task to "twelve simple fishermen." Catholic priests thus had an ineluctable obligation to perpetuate Christ's ministry, regardless of any persecution and hostility that they might face.

> Never were more transcendental words spoken than those of Jesus: "And thou shalt love the LORD thy God with all thine heart, and with all thy might." "Bless and curse not"; "Bless them that curse you, do good to them that hate you, and pray for them which despitefully use you, and persecute you."[106] . . . The Church of Christ is the bearer of the Good News of the law of love, the Catholic and Apostolic Church is the faithful guardian of the holy ideal of the Nazarene and is charged never to let the light of love become extinguished in human hearts . . . Thus is our action in the breast of Jesus Christ's Church: we come with the high ideal of the Divine Nazarene; we wish to make our

> beloved fatherland great, by means of love, peace, through the fraternal leadership of Mexicans. We do not come to take away our compatriots' religious faith . . . but to give them the gift of love and the purity of immortal Christ. Free of all yoke and servitude beside that which we owe to God, we are here today at the feet of Jesus and the Most Holy Virgin to pray for our beloved fatherland, so that in her shall reign Christian peace, the true peace and invincible love of Jesus.

This sacerdotal mission was too important to be constrained, even by the church's government. Indeed, Rome and its hierarchy were now the fundamental obstacles to this mission.

> That is why, when a corporation that claims to preach Christ forgets its mission, and instead of love sows hatreds; instead of forgiving, condemns; instead of blessing, throws down EXCOMMUNICATIONS . . . ; when a "CHURCH" that says that it proclaims Christ forgets the Master's example, and instead of practicing humility becomes proud, wishing to rule the destiny of peoples . . . and instead of giving morality and education to its members, abandons them to their own wicked instincts; then that Church is not, cannot be, the Holy Church of Jesus.[107]

To Pérez, the 1926 suspension of public worship was a dereliction of duty that bishops forced unjustly on the clergy as well as the people. To Father Anaya, Pérez described it as "treason" against God: "to fail in the priesthood's sacred mission and abandon all your obligations to the Christian people." Roman clergy likewise dishonored the *patria* by rebelling against it—another "shameful" betrayal, given the "perverse intention of provoking a revolutionary conflict" to defend "the scandal of Roman supremacy." Moreover, Pérez told Anaya, he massed

> with greater fidelity than you by officiating every day, while you and all the Roman clergy have truly turned your backs on the Lord and your God, even committing the crime of depriving the Christian faithful of worship and of the Sacraments of Religion, while I . . . with my Clergy carry out my sacred duties to God's Church.[108]

With different spins, the argument that "true" priests were faithful to their sacramental ministry over and above the church power structure was repeated. At its 1927 synod, ICAM moved that Roman clergy were traitors "to the Catholic people of the republic, because they abandoned the churches, depriving the faithful of the church's sacraments . . . to promote a rebellion." How could a priest take a "homicidal rifle" into his "unctuous hands," then say, "the peace of the Lord be always with you"? asked another 1927 article.[109] Other *Restauración* pieces accused Roman clergy of ministering underground to the "moneyed castes" and excluding "the pariahs, the irredeemable who cannot pay for home masses." Only ICAM embraced the poor, sharing their suffering "like Christ on the sea of Galilee."[110] In May 1928, a priest going up-country for the first time (to the Sierra Norte) was told that "as a minister of God" he must never forget "our church's constitutional precepts, observing them even with your life" and "fulfill [Christ's] ministry to redeem the world . . . caring for the poor, the widowed, and the orphaned, attending to the sick and taking all by the hand to God's throne, for the redemption of their souls and that they may possess eternal life." What did it matter if his priests were excommunicated or had feet of clay, Pérez said, reprising the ex opere operato argument of French constitutional clergy; Christ instituted the sacraments and, as "efficacious signs of God's grace and goodwill to us," they worked so long as they were performed in His name and received with faith.[111] As we see, ICAM transposed the church-state conflict into an alternative theological key in which the issue was the apostolic-patriotic or juridical-Roman character of the priesthood. Whatever else it was, therefore, the religious conflict was a battle between a churchstate and the Roman Church.

CHAPTER THREE

THE OTHER *CRISTIADA*

Pérez's Second Coming

ON 21 JUNE 1929, interim president Emilio Portes Gil announced the arreglos that ended the Cristero Revolt. Specifically, he promised that the government would not henceforth register priests who were not canonically appointed. Textually—the phrasing matters—Portes Gil promised: "the law requiring registration of ministers does not mean that the government can register those who have not been named by the hierarchical superior of the religious creed in question or in accordance with its regulations." Given that it capped a violent religious ecstasy, this was flat, technical language. Drafted by Bostonian Jesuit Edmund Walsh, it nonetheless conveyed the seriousness with which Rome viewed Calles' tacit endorsement of Pérez's ecclesiastical freelancing. Indeed, Walsh's demand reflected a longstanding sine qua non of both Mexico's episcopate and Rome. In 1927, Vatican Secretary of State Pietro Gasparri had instructed Mexico's bishops not to resume public worship while the government retained its "iniquitous" ambition to register priests, "controlling, selecting, and rejecting God's ministers as it pleases." In 1928, one Mexican bishop wrote, Calles had contrived a "national church" by registering "unworthy" priests. It must be resisted, unless the episcopate wanted to return to the days of Frederick the Great and "sacristan governments."[1] Walsh thus demanded guarantees that revolutionaries would stop church building. Keen to distance himself from Calles and establish a modus vivendi, Portes Gil agreed, yet in doing so conceded a theological point: "canonical" meant Roman. Even if the arreglos did not mention him, furthermore, Portes Gil's statement was obviously *about* Pérez: who else was sending priests into Catholic parishes against hierarchical wishes? Yet a public, presidential statement, preapproved by Washington and Rome, would be absurd if Pérez were still the laughingstock of 1925.[2] So, what changed?

Answering this question means relativizing some powerful assumptions about postrevolutionary Mexican history. Most controversially, it means reconsidering the 1926 Calles Law (the "law" Portes Gil invoked), seeing not just draconian anticlericalism but a popular church- and nation-building instrument. Second, it means recalibrating the history of secularization in Mexico. Calles, via Pérez, wished to scare up a national church; Portes Gil, like Mussolini, hoped to induce Rome to support the state. Since destroying Pérez was key to this modus vivendi, however, it may be said that ICAM inflected the building of Mexico's secular regime and the posture of the Roman Catholic Church post-1929.[3] Appreciating this, though, requires us to reimagine the Cristero War, seeing beyond a Bajío-centric crusade to a regionalized, zero-sum contest between Catholic cultures, a war in religion premised on antithetical, yet Catholic, sentiments. Pérez himself, no less than cristero martyrs-elect, viewed the conflict providentially, as a chance to die fighting for the true religion: "I happily await the not too distant, joyous day when I will see the Father of the Lord," he wrote in May 1926,

> up in the celestial fatherland, where my Jesus lives, where the Lamb of God reigns, who has redeemed me with His precious blood alone; there, my dear brother, shall we meet face to face, praising the blessed name of my only Redeemer, He whose glory and Throne forever shine, in whose name angels and archangels, cherubim and seraphim sing in praise: Holy, Holy, Holy.[4]

Contrarian Catholicism was not exclusive to Pérez. As this chapter shows, the postrevolution saw not only resistance to Sonoran rule but also a parallel struggle in which village Catholics used anticlerical laws to take control of their churches and ecclesiastical appointments, substituting prorevolutionary clergy for Roman priests. That is, a battle over lay patronage broke out, a popular and largely indigenized controversy over ecclesiastical investitures.[5] This happened in hundreds of pueblos, denoting a different, undeniably grassroots, experience of the Cristero War: leveraging state power for popular religious and political ends. Motives, detailed in chapters 5 and 6, revolved around moiety politics, pueblo autonomy, local religion, or land. It was not only that Pérez catalyzed the Cristiada, therefore: ICAM was an essential combatant. Indeed, ICAM breathed life into an indigenous, prorevolutionary Catholicism, hence was an actor in an intra-Catholic culture war. There was something eighteenth-century about this. Following Serge Gruzinski, Mexican Catholicism functioned as a kind of "third-wave" acculturation: it reconnected indigenous religiosity and the state by matching revolutionary constitutionalism and local Catholicism.[6]

To make sense of this interaction, it is vital to contextualize the Calles Law and its constitutional basis (article 130), so that their socioreligious implications are appreciated. They are not apparent from the gnostic phrasings of the laws, let alone the sulfurous anticlericalism enveloping their execution. The Calles Law, especially, is remembered as a piece of unreconstructed clerophobia that subjugated the church by requiring priests to register with the state. Yet it was far more than that because it tagged registration to lay management of religious temporalities, that is, custody of church buildings. Priests had to register as occupants of a *church*. Nor could they register by themselves: a civilian quorum had to present them. The law's real aim, therefore, following article 130, was to create a constitutional, lay-governed church and circumvent bishops' powers of appointment. This would be done through new corporations given control of church funds and buildings, dubbed *juntas vecinales*. Being independent and civilian, juntas could hire and fire clergy, thus overriding canonical hierarchy (pope-bishop-priest). The assumption was that priests needed churches and income more than they needed bishops. If laypeople administered churches, therefore, a new piper would call the tune.

Article 130's provisions were activated by the Calles Law of 14 June 1926. Yet it is vital to understand that article 130, hence the Calles Law, drew on multiple non-Mexican sources without acknowledgment. One, as contemporary jurist Miguel Lanz Duret noted, was France's 1905 church-state separation law, which placed French churches in the hands of lay corporations called *associations cultuelles* (worship associations).[7] Yet *cultuelles* were shaped, in turn, by US Catholic experience; namely, the founding of churches by boards of trustees, following civil incorporation laws. "Lay trusteeism" proved controversial in the United States because trustees not only built churches but also asserted powers of appointment, clashing with bishops. This eighteenth-century proprietary model was paradigmatic in antebellum US Catholicism—but it, too, was a republican take on the European parish works council (fabrica ecclesiae), a figure that was common in France, Germany, and Italy, and one that was americanized by Catholics migrating from those countries.[8]

These prehistories must be recalled so that the Calles Law is not misread merely as vindictive secularization. The vindictiveness, really, was in the severity of its application. Whether the *jefe máximo* knew or cared, however, the law popularly bearing his name re-enacted in Mexico a lay-driven Catholic ecclesiology with tangled European and American roots. It was, in sum, a Mexicanized form of lay trusteeism, applied with furious anticlerical intent. Cristeros felt the law's authoritarian aspect and rebelled. Yet other Catholics, usually indigenous, saw a mechanism for exercising religious sovereignty by registering dissident clergy. Indeed, the trusteeist principle proved compatible with indigenous lay institutions, such as the mayordomía. From 1926 ICAM—the Calles Law in ecclesial form—found an unexpected constituency among highland villagers, tropical lowlanders, border people, and agrarians. Entirely absent from cities and theaters of cristero conflict, ICAM concretized this fusion of state forms and indigenous Catholicisms, a postrevolutionary churchstateness. This chapter first contextualizes this development, then traces its geography and consequences.

REVOLUTIONARY CHURCHSTATE

The requirement that priests seek registration, first drafted in article 129 but then moved to article 130, was presented to the Querétaro constituents in January 1917 by a commission of doctors and lawyers whose members were explicit that their goal was to go beyond church-state separation. This was a French and North American "legal fiction" implying churches had legal personalities. They did not: thus the state must establish dominion over, not separateness from, "religious elements." This said, churches must have a registered person (encargado) responsible for religious discipline, church buildings, and fabric. The encargado must register with the municipal authorities, who must notify the Interior Ministry in turn. Encargados were also required to register "in union with ten other inhabitants."[9] There were two active concepts, therefore, not just "registration" but also "union": state licensing was made subject to inhabitants' wishes.

What the commission did not say was that this mechanism derived from precisely those regimes of liberal church-state separation that it professed to dislike, namely, France's and the United States'. There was, then, a contradiction between article 130's liberal origins, which posited a democratic, lay-led Catholicism, a republic of the parish; and the statist, illiberal clerophobia that couched article 130 and its enforcement by Calles. As noted above, this differential, applied to Mexico's Catholic cultures, produced diverse, often tragic, results.

Conflict was foreseeable. Indeed, tensions had emerged in the first decade of the twentieth century in France, whose church-state separation bill, born of liberal disillusionment with the 1890s *ralliement*,[10] was hijacked by socialist deputies led by Francis de Presenssé, Aristide Briand, and Jean Jaurès. It was Presenssé, in fact, who imported the US idea of incorporating churches civilly as an alternative to episcopal government. The draft separation bill (debated 1903–1905) thus created cultuelles to receive churches and funds as national property. Cultuelles were presented as democratic replicas of the parish works that historically maintained French churches. This role was augmented, however, because it was proposed to give cultuelles control over ecclesiastical appointments, as custodians of places of worship. To this end, France's separation bill empowered lay corporations to let their premises to priests of their choosing, an idea that was copied wholesale in Mexico's article 130, as we saw.

There was a difference, however, because in France the separation bill's explosive provision that churches be defined as associations of faithful, not canonical entities, was hedged in the final *law*. Among Catholics, the bill awoke fears that cultuelles might install rebel or pantomime priests, what one sarcastic official called an "ecclesiastical bohemia." The bill's socialist proponents, for their part, argued that it would create an elected priesthood sensitive to people's needs. Another counterpremise—that modern republics had no business propping up church hierarchy—was defended in a brilliant speech by Jaurès in November 1906.[11] Even before this, however (April 1905), the bill was rewritten to address objections that cultuelles usurped bishops' authority. Consequently, the law of 5 December 1905 required cultuelles to "respect the rules of general organization of the religion whose practice [they] propose to ensure," a caveat (Pressensé's) so similar to Portes Gil's 1929 formula that it surely influenced it.[12] As Émile Poulat observes, this was to write bishops back into law as church managers via cultuelles' bylaws. Yet even socialists accepted this caveat because most did not want the church smashed into a thousand schismatical pieces. As Jaurès said, "la France n'est pas schismatique, elle est révolutionnaire."

Even so, the 1905 law was condemned by Pius X in two 1906 encyclicals (*Vehementer Nos* and *Gravissimo Officii*), the latter outlawing participation in cultuelles. France was also rocked by rioting that spring, especially in the "Catholic" northwest and southeast, as officials began inventorying churches for conveyance to cultuelles. In consequence, few cultuelles were founded; those that were, by Henri des Houx's League of French Catholics, were harassed.[13]

In the United States, too, radical lay trusteeism waxed with eighteenth- and nineteenth-century parish foundations in New York, Boston, Philadelphia, Baltimore, and New Orleans, then waned when the Baltimore Council (1829) made US parishioners deed their churches to bishops. Trusteeism declined further in 1875 when New York State passed a Religious Incorporations Act compelling trustees to run churches by the "disciplines, rules, and usages of the denomination to which the church members of the corporation belong." Again, this "implied trust" model seemingly shaped Pressensé's conservative amendment to France's 1905 law.[14]

In Mexico, it took a three-year religious war, not parliamentary eloquence, local legislation, and a few spring riots, for Portes Gil to say the same thing: that civil custodians of places of worship should assimilate, not efface, church hierarchies. In fairness, the Querétaro constituents barely bothered to discuss the problems of creating juntas vecinales in 1917. They simply mexicanized the cultuelles without critique.[15] The Calles Law, too, was vague as to juntas' purpose, hence its reputation as anticlerical spite: Calles gave priests thirty days to register as encargados with *vecinos*' backing, or face fines and jail. Municipalities had a month to report registrations.[16]

More than Calles, it was Interior Minister Tejeda who saw article 130's potential. Tejeda realized that revolutionaries possessed a means not just to subdue the church by making priests accept licensing laws. Actually, article 130 could be used to turn Catholicism inside-out, creating prorevolutionary parishes governed by laypeople. Thus, the day after public worship was halted in 1926—2 August, as the month-long registration period required by the Calles Law expired[17]—Tejeda ordered that juntas vecinales be formed to receive "abandoned" churches and appoint new encargados. Any priest already registered could stay, Tejeda promised.[18] Then, in January 1927, Gobernación published a law regulating article 130 that was explicit about promoting a constitutional church. Now the government stated that it did not recognize ecclesiastical hierarchy (el Gobierno no reconoce jerarquías dentro de las Iglesias) and would communicate directly with religious ministers appointed by juntas. If there were no priest, the encargado should be a respected civilian (vecino caracterizado). Finally, the law empowered lay Catholics to raise church funds.[19]

Laypeople were thus authorized to run parishes, appoint priests, and fund-raise. Ultimately, the law gave people a choice: would they go without services in support of the hierarchy's public sacramental ban, or form citizens' councils and hire surrogate clergy, thus breaking the episcopate's hold over parishes and priests and thus its political resolve? Priests feared being thrown at the state's feet; in reality, Tejeda was throwing them on the mercy of the people.

It was therefore Tejeda, both at Gobernación (1925–1928) and in his second Veracruz governorship (1928–1932), who was Pérez's enabler, not Morones. Indeed, after 1925, wires from Pérez to Calles, Garrido, or cromistas like Celestino Gasca and Ricardo Treviño went unacknowledged.[20] Tejeda, however, answered Pérez on his personal stationery, describing himself as the patriarch's devoted servant (afectísimo y atento, seguro servidor). Tejeda also received Pérez's envoys at Bucareli or in Xalapa—indeed, Pérez's authority over ICAM largely came from such bureaucratic links. "Please have recourse to Gobernación," ICAM's cura in Juchitán (Oax.) begged when a Roman cura challenged him in 1928; the same priest asked Pérez to have Tejeda administer "appropriate punishment" when an unlicensed Roman cura appeared on the scene. "The citizen governor is with us," another priest cheered after a meeting with Tejeda's *subsecretario* in Jalapa in 1930. "Please talk of this parish in Gobernación," yet another priest implored Pérez in 1931.[21] Pérez's bureaucratic control over ICAM, by virtue of Tejeda, lasted until the patriarch's death in 1931; and there is evidence that he was not above abusing it by auctioning parishes off to the highest bidder. That September, for example, one priest paid Pérez fifty pesos in silver, "deductible from a larger sum, since the señor patriarch himself insinuated to me that if I obtained that sum then he would intervene and have the [state government] assign me a parish in the state of Veracruz, with the intention that I should give derechos [parish dues, at 25 percent] and *abonos* [fees] of more or less fifty pesos." The priest, *michoacano* Pedro Infante, was shocked at being asked for so much and begged ICAM's "honorable and worthy council" to reduce his quota.[22]

That the church-state dispute was nonetheless ecclesiological as well as political and even financial—was church authority canonical or from the people?—was apparent from the acrid exchanges that followed the 1926 *cessatio a divinis*. The Roman episcopate, in September, argued that the Calles Law would "convert the church . . . into a church of the state" and must not be obeyed. Puebla's archbishop threatened to excommunicate anybody who hired "schismatical priests." And "if anyone calling himself a priest tries to celebrate Mass or minister the holy sacraments in our temples," a flier ran, people must chase the "old fool" away, honoring their ancestors' wishes to hear Roman Catholic worship.[23] Pérez's response was that if people ("legitimate builders and custodians of those buildings") wanted priests, he would send them. "Old Rome," he prophesied, was "committing suicide" by denying modern people's desire for liberty and pining for "medieval times when it could scare the faithful, like children, with the ridiculous phantom of excommunication." Priests, Pérez predicted, would flock to him once they felt the "abandonment and poverty" to which bishops condemned them.[24] Benigno López y Sierra, Pérez's vicar general, wrote that the bishops' decision to ban public worship was a betrayal of the priest's mission. He theologized that the bishops' "satanic pride" would cost them everything: they were like Ezekiel's blind king, eyes put out by God, or Belshazzar at the feast, who could not read the writing on the wall.[25]

Lay empowerment explains why the Calles Law had popular appeal. This is underappreciated: usually it is held that loyal Catholics overran church juntas and refused to register revolutionary priests, wrecking Tejeda's plans. Only one junta-backed priest—Dimás Anguiano in Alvarado (Ver.)—is said to have registered.[26] In fact, Pérez's movement extended much more widely, as seen in table 1, which lists 285 communities where ICAM priests registered from 1925 to 1938. This computes well with ICAM's totals for 1927 (235), 1928 (237), and 1929 (366), but then, church occupancies were public record.[27] Even so, 285 is very likely an underestimate, given that possession of parish seats implied possession of satellite churches, which municipios often did not register separately. Besides de facto occupations, local archives yield extra cases: Juan Alfonseca finds that ICAM was present in twenty-four communities in just two *mexiquense* districts, Texcoco and Chalco, with SEP teachers its driving force.[28] Last, it should be stressed that the count is derived from composite, including Roman Catholic, sources.

The Other *Cristiada*

TABLE 1. ICAM REGISTRATIONS, 1925–1938

State	Locality/Date†	Total
Chiapas	Tapachula,* Suchiate Mariscal, Comaltitlán, Carrillo Puerto (1925); Huixtla (1926); Berriozabal, Unión Juárez, Pueblo Nuevo (1927); San Fernando, Tuxtla,* Tuxtla-Chico, Pijijiapam (1929); Mazatán (1930); Cacahoatán (1932)	14
Chihuahua	San Isidro Guerrero (1926)	1
Distrito Federal	La Soledad,* Corpus Christi, Coatepec, Tacubaya* (1925); San Pablo Tepetlapa, San José de los Obreros (1927)	6
Durango	El Rodeo (1926)	1
Guerrero	Iguala* (1925); Tezicapan, La Unión,* Petatlán, Coahuayutla (1926); Tepecuacuilco [La Purísima, El Calvario], Manayalán, Agueguepa, Santa Teresa, Tonalapa del Sur, San Vicente Palapa, Cuescunclán, Tierra Colorada, El Rincón, Cosiña, Acayahualco, Santa Cruz, Saca Coyuca, Sabana, Venta de Palula, Palula, Sasamulco, Xalialla, Tetelilla, Tecuescontitlán, Huitlza, Tlachichilpan (1927)	27
Hidalgo	Actopan,* El Arenal, Tepejí* (1925); Tenango,* Apam,* Pachuca* (1926); Almoloya (1927)	7
Jalisco	Guadalajara (1925); San Martín de las Flores [Tlaquepaque] (1935)	2
México	San Miguel Tenoxtitlán (1925); Mexicalcingo,* Ixtlahuaca,* Jocotitlán,* Ajoloapan (1926); San Bartolo, Joloapam, Ixtacalco,* Xalostoc, Santiago Tolmán, Xometla, Amecameca,* Coyotepec,* Ixtápan, Santiago Tecalco, Atzacualoya (1927); Atenco,* El Oro,* Zapotlán, Zoyatzingo (1928); Amanalco* (1929); Tepetlixpa* (1930); San Pablo Calimaya,* Chapultepec (1932); Los Reyes de la Paz (1935); Tepexoxuca,* Joquicingo, Quictepec, Maxtleca, San Miguelito (1938); Teocalco* (1930s)	31
Nuevo León	Los Aldamas,* Los Ramones, Dr. Coss, El Bravo, China,* Las Herreras (1929)	6
Oaxaca	Juchitán de las Flores, Hule, Huajuapam (1925); Concepción Pápalo,* Loxicha,* Oaxaca [Sagrario*], San Jerónimo Ixtepec [and foranías Tepanatepec, Niltepec, Tehuantepec] (1926); Teotepec,* Tlachichilco* (1927); Pochutla* (1928); Nopala (1935)	14
Puebla	Ixcaquistla,* Huajuapam, Huichapan, Pahuatlán (1925); Nauzontla, Jopala,* Zapotitlán,* Olintla,* Huehuetla, Tapayula, Hueyapam,* Jaunahuac, Zoquiapan, Ozelonacaxtla, Zacapoaxtla,* Dimás López, Bibiano Hernández, Chipahuatlán, Nanacatlán (1926); Tetela,* Zongozotla, Santiago, Coyutla, Teteles, Ahuacatlán* [including San Francisco, San Mateo, San Marcos, San Andrés, Santa Barbara, Tepezintla], Coatepec,* Hueytlalpan,* Zitlala, Metepec, Santa Catarina, Tetelco, Tequiztlán, Casuacan, Xochitlán,* Concepción, San Martinito, Jonotla,* Ecatlán,* Tuzamapán,* Yaquihuacan, Caxhuacan* (1927); Xochitlaxco, San Miguel Tonalixco, Tepango, Chicontla, Patla, San Simón de Bravo, Yehualtepec, Ixtepec, Atlequizayán, Camocuautla, Tehuizotla, Alquizapan (1928); Santa María Actipan, Tehualtepec, Tecamachalco,* Teotozucan, Zozutla, Tlacomulco, Tlaola,* San Antonio Portezuelo, San Juan Azozac, San Simón Alcecesa (1929); Xaltepuxtla (1931); Yetla, Cutzontipa, Cuamila, Tlatlapanala, Huixtla, Tzitzicazapa, Xochinacantlán (1933)	77
Querétaro	Santa María Magdalena (1926)	1
Tabasco	Villahermosa,* Tamulté de las Barrancas, Macuspana (1925)	3

77

Chapter Three

State	Locality/Date†	Total
Tamaulipas	Matamoros* (1927), Ciudad Reynosa,* Ochoa, Camargo, San Fernando,* San Miguel, San Carlos,* Valadeces, Reinosa Díaz, Río Bravo, Congregación Garza, Cruillos Reynosa (1929)	12
Tlaxcala	San Miguel Tenancingo, San Cosme, San Francisco, Santa Catarina, San Pablo del Monte (1927); Zacatelco* (1929)	6
Veracruz	Alvarado,* El Cristo, Jalacingo,* Papantla,* Santo Domingo, Vicente Guerrero, Mecatlán, Coyutla,* Coahuitlán, Zozocolco de Hidalgo, Acayucan,* Chinameca,* Soledad Doblado,* San Cristóbal Llave, Tlalixcoyan, San Juan Evangelista, Jopala (1926); Zozocolco de Guerrero, Pajapam, Santo Domingo, Joltepec, Jaltipan, Coxquihuí,* Puerto México/Coatzacoalcos,* Santa Lucía, Paso de Ovejas,* Cotaxtla,* Tlaxicoyan* (1927); Plan de Zaragoza, Sabanas de Jalostoc, Arenal, Comalteco, Espinal,* Zapotal, Entabladero, Cerro Verde, Cerro Azul, Ixtepec, San Andrés Tuxtla* (1928); Ixhuatlán,* Catemaco, San Juan Tehualtepec, San Miguel Teotozucan, Oteapan, Cosoleacaque, Hidalgostitlán, Minatitlán,* Moloacán, Mecayapan, Santa Lucrecia, Tampico-Alto (1929); Pisa Flores [and 30 surrounding communities] (c. 1930–1935); Tihuatlán,* Amatlán,* Tuxpam,* Tamapache,* Tamiahua,* Tautima,* and Ozuluama* (1935); Chicontepec,* Tancoco (1938)	61
Zacatecas	Río Grande (1925)	1
USA (TX, CA)	San Antonio (1926); Hunter, Dallas, Waco, Natalia, Divine, Los Angeles, Consagración Martínez, Wille, Wilmington, Pasadena, Longback (1927); Alice (n/d); Gonzales, Cementville (1929)	15
Total		285 [77*]
	[†] denotes earliest documented registration/occupancy; [*] denotes parish seat, not vicaría. Sources: José Bravo Ugarte, *Diócesis y obispos de la Iglesia mexicana, 1519–1939* (Mexico City: Buena Prensa, 1941), 26–58; *El Universal*; *Excélsior*; *Diario de El Paso*; *La Opinión*; *El Dictamen*; *Restauración*; *El Heraldo Mexicano*; AICAM; AHAM; AGA; AGN; SD.	

ICAM was thus present in sixteen Mexican states, the D.F., Texas, and California. It was more regional than national, given that most churches (237, 83 percent) were in eight indigenous, central-southern states: Puebla (77, 27 percent), Veracruz (61, 21 percent), México (31, 11 percent), Chiapas (14, 5 percent), Guerrero (27, 10 percent), Oaxaca (14, 5 percent), Hidalgo (7, 3 percent), and Tlaxcala (6, 2 percent). One-third was in Puebla, another in the isthmus (Veracruz, Oaxaca, Chiapas), and a fifth in the Valley of Mexico (D.F., México, Hidalgo, Tlaxcala). Another significant concentration (33, 12 percent) was located on both sides of the northern border, in Tamaulipas, Nuevo León, Texas, and California. Foundations included scores of parish seats (77, 27 percent), again with concentrations. In Papantla and Tehuantepec dioceses, a third of parishes went to ICAM. In Veracruz and Puebla, whose parish totals were among Mexico's highest, between a quarter and a fifth.[29]

These gains were unexpected, especially over a short period. Growth was indexed to religious conflict, as all but thirty foundations (248, 87 percent) occurred from 1925 to 1930. Thus, Pérez's 1926 boast that "many churches" belonged to him was not all fiction. Despite some gaps (Morelos, Yucatán), López y Sierra's brag that ICAM stretched "from the Bravo's banks to the Suchiate's" contained some truth.[30]

Numerical support is hard to quantify. Each church had an encargado and ten-strong junta, giving an absolute minimum of 3,135 supporters. Almost everywhere, however, Pérez counted on factional support, usually a hundred or so agraristas, liberal Catholics, or indigenous families, giving 28,500 core militants. These were the people who were willing to sign petitions and fight for Pérez. Pro-ICAM petitions by villagers in Xometla (Méx.), for instance, carried fifty to one hundred signatures. In Tenoxtitlán (Méx.), 68 villagers plus the junta supported Pérez, "in conformity with the whole pueblo," so they said. The mayor of Acatzingo (Pue.), an enemy of Pérez, put ICAM's hardcore support in four villages—Actipan, San Simón de Bravo, San Simón Alcecesa, and Azozac—at five hundred. Amanalco (Méx.) was equally partisan. Here a "village intermediary" wrote in 1929 that "half the population solicited the arrival of a *padre sismático*," another half resisted, and a clique wanted "*no priest*, whether Roman or *sismático*," hence "a conflict that might spill blood" was feared. Similarly, in Yehualtepec (Pue.), four hundred villagers formed a welcoming committee for Vicente Liñán at Easter 1928. If eighteen dissenters wanted to "crush the priest," a *representante del pueblo* wrote later that a Mexican priest "comes here without difficulty, lending his services . . . without hostility."[31] Hence support for Pérez rose and fell, as rival clans competed to control a community's religious franchise, administration, and lands.

Then again, many more people came to ICAM's services on feast days. If we reckon ICAM's base as "how many served," as religious orders do,[32] allowing that 500 people attended an average fiesta, that would give 142,500 affiliates for a 174,135 total. The pattern in Apam (Hgo.), where ICAM placed its support in December 1926 at "no less than 3,000," noting that devotees of Mary swelled its ranks, was standard. Our concentric figure falls short of ICAM's inflated totals (370,000–800,000), which some accept, but is credible compared to other religious dissidences, for instance, numbers of registered Mexican Protestants (30,000) and congregants (70,000) in 1910. Really it is all we can hope for, since ICAM recorded no attendances and *Restauración*'s circulation figures (60,000–75,000) are unverifiable.³³

Corroboration comes from ICAM's petitionary growth, reflecting local responses, not central planning. ICAM resembled a network of village juntas with an itinerant clergy. As one priest, Teodoro Juárez, put it, while the pope dozed "trustingly on his laurels," thinking of palaces like Saint Francis in the dream, he was out building a new church, parish by parish, "ampoule by ampoule." The journey was "slow but definitive," *Restauración* conceded in a candid 1927 moment.³⁴

Several general factors facilitated growth. First, the 1926 sacramental strike. This created a different Catholic angst in central-southern pueblos compared, say, with highland Jalisco. In the Gulf and south, it was the metaphysical threat to festive religion, not eucharistic scarcity, that hurt. And since priests were typically wanted on sufferance—inasmuch as solemnizing saints' days kept the great cosmic wheel turning—it was preferable to hire Mexican clergy for fiestas rather than uphold a prohibition imposed by remote bishops.

Underchurching was a second factor. The states where Pérez did best, except tiny Tlaxcala, had below-average ratios of priests to population, meaning ICAM did not challenge a ubiquitous clergy. As Ricard's second-wave religious looked for gaps left by Franciscan pioneers, ICAM targeted places where Roman clergy were weak. A third, related factor was diocesan formation. The Roman sees most depleted by ICAM—Papantla (1921), Tehuantepec (1891), Veracruz (1863)—were among Mexico's newest, though others were old (México, Puebla, Oaxaca, Chiapas). This was not really a contradiction: Pérez targeted the fringes or black holes of vast ecclesiastical provinces, which Roman clergy, after centuries of neglect, were belatedly subdividing and rechurching.³⁵

A fourth factor was indigenous politics: ICAM resonated where indigenous go-betweens historically negotiated state hegemony into being. Indeed, support was strongest in "peripheral" zones—Tehuantepec, Puebla's Sierra Norte, the Huasteca—that were adept at indigenizing liberal institutions to protect local autonomies. ICAM's parish circuit, which Pérez once traversed on horseback as *porfirista* captain and cura, closely followed the geography of popular liberalism. Pérez cultivated the affinity: the Sierra Norte, he remarked, had "always been distinguished by its sons' unequaled love for the causes of liberty." He eulogized its liberal trinity—"Patriarchs Juan Nepomuceno Méndez, Juan Crisóstomo Bonilla, and Juan Francisco Lucas"—who, he said, were reincarnated in "worthy

Señor Gabriel Barrios," the 1920s cacique who gifted him churches such as Tuzamapa's and Tetela's. ICAM priest and *potosino* Alfredo Arredondo López saluted Barrios from the pulpit for "justly interpreting the spirit of the laws governing religious worship." In truth, Barrios probably opened his satrapy to cultivate Calles and slight Puebla governor Claudio Tirado (1925–1926), who called Barrios a "Romanist." Pérez, too, sensed that Tirado was "antagonistic" toward ICAM, and incited attacks on it.[36]

A fifth factor was indigenous officialdom. ICAM was often promoted by civic-religious officials: *fiscales* (lay readers), mayordomos (cultic sponsors), and principales (elected patriarchs). Indeed, juntas vecinales functioned like a callista version of the *cargo* system, the ladder of civil-religious offices.[37] We should underscore the historical specificity of indigenous officials in places where ICAM was strongest. In central-southern Mexico (Morelos, Oaxaca), fiscales were the Roman clergy's bagmen and sacramental aides: they enforced church attendance, collected religious taxes, and administered corporal punishments.[38] In Puebla-Veracruz, contrastingly, fiscales were ambivalent figures who mediated between indigenous cult (costumbre) and Catholicism, promoting indigenous saint worship in hillside shrines as well as reading liturgies in church. ICAM was thus an outlet for indigenous cultural autonomy and echoed (once again) Alan Knight's *serrano* mode of revolutionary participation.[39] Indigenous elites certainly proved more supportive than Pérez's urban liberal friends. Pleas to the latter—a colonel Limón, one doctor Régules, generals Pablo Cabañas and Ramón Fuentes, federal judge Miguel Castro—achieved few results. Castro applauded Pérez's "great work" of ending papal power, but refused to prosecute assailants of Mexican clergy.[40] Comparatively, too, indigenous support resembled the reception of lay trusteeism among marginalized US ethnies—French, Germans, Poles—who used trustee laws to fight Anglo-Irish bishops for control of churches and to install ethnic priests and rites.[41] ICAM's battles were similar: indigenous laypeople promised to adapt Catholicism to constitutional norms and defend local interests, and then they presented priests. Mexico's outraged bishops, no less reliably, echoed US bishops' tirades that trustees were a drunken, theologically ignorant, upstart rabble.[42]

Physical estrangement underwrote serrano lay patronage, too. "Day and night the rain falls, making it impossible to work," wrote one priest from Coyutla, in Veracruz's Totonoacapan, in 1928. From Zozocolco, Teodoro Juárez (a stoical ex-campesino) apologized that he could not answer Pérez's letters, because "in these mountains we have been without communication as a consequence of the torrents of water falling every day." One priest in the Sierra Norte apologized in 1929 for not sending his tithe because he had contracted malaria during the rains. Neighboring villages were separated by ravines that took days to traverse: one priest ordered to incorporate Coxquihuí and Tlaola into his circuit replied that this was "impossible" as they were separated by a four-day round trip on foot.[43] Just reaching Tlaola from Mexico City meant going by train, car, and horse with a *mozo*.[44]

There was, sixth, a culture of clerical autonomy, especially on the Tehuantepec isthmus and adjoining corridors: Oaxaca's Mixteca Baja and *costa chica*; the Veracruz leeward (Sotavento); Chiapas's Soconusco; Guerrero's costa chica. These littoral zones contained the most "apostate" priests in Mexico and ICAM was commonly spearheaded by ex–Roman Catholic clergy. Perhaps it was not so surprising that episcopal authority was tenuous here: the remoteness astonished many visitors. It took Florentino Guzmán, a SEP teacher who scouted for ICAM, eleven days to reach Tapachula from Mexico City in 1926—but the trans-isthmian landscape was unforgettable. Along the Papaloapan, the vegetation was so thick that the hollows along the banks "look live caves, even in daylight"; the isthmus's green gold—banana fronds piled high on canoes, plantations stretching for leagues—astonished him.[45] Given this distance, we might ask whether ICAM did not graft itself onto local ecclesiastical cultures, even vestigial ones. Success in Tehuantepec, for example, perhaps reflected the half-life of the Dominicans, that congregation of Jansenist and *indigenista* rebels. Some Oaxacan parishes were still Dominican-run in the 1890s, a shocked Eulogio Gillow discovered. It would take generations to overcome their baneful influence, he griped to Porfirio Díaz—yet Pérez appeared after one.[46] In a similar vein, Pérez's constituents included many *ejidatarios* in México and Hidalgo, where people most often cited extortionate sacramental fees as grounds for joining ICAM. Beside the agrarian factor, it may be that a distant memory of the Franciscans' hospitaller church lingered in indigenous Catholic culture.

WHAT HAVE THE ROMANS EVER DONE FOR US?

ICAM's local reception is felt memorably in the town cry made in Zacatelco (Tlax.) in 1929 by Pascual Luciano García, a young indigenous sacristan ordained by Pérez. For effect—and with apologies to Anglophone readers—García's homily should be read in its phonetic, rural Spanish, because it so evocatively places us among an indigenous (Nahua) audience, here in the pueblo of Zapatista Domingo Arenas.

> El día que yo yegue al pueblo de Zacatelco e sido bien resivido como de las Autoridades Civiles como demás dos mil almas, y nadien discutió en desir absolutamente nada, porque como a las Dose del Día el Presidente Municipal yamo al Pueblo para una junta que en el mismo salon de la Presidencia se iso o mas vien se le dio a conoser a toda la Jente que se encontrava como hombres y Mujeres y como de Mayores a Menores de edad, a darles a conoser la Causa que nosotros nos emos retirado del Papa. Se encontro un gran tiempo o mas vien muchos años esplotando vilmente a los Pueblos el Cura Foranio Jesús Lumbreras y cometiendo Violaciones a las Donseyas y yo como le se toda su vida porque como en el Pueblo de Zacatelco tengo algunos parientes, por eso es que yo conosco muy vien ese Pueblo y en eso en vista de las Autoridades que me dieron la preferencia en que yo les esplicara a la multitud del Pueblo, y nomás del Pueblo, sino de Pueblos lejanos como en los días Domingos es la Plaza que todos los Pueblos baja aser sus compras y a vender su comercio, por eso es que estava ese Salon como por la Caye y las demas piezas, unidas al Salon adonde se iso una esplendida conferencia yo.

García then made a revolutionary-Catholic grito.

> Entonses tome la Palabra para esplicarles a toditos el asunto por[que] abia sido a Separación de Roma con nosotros de la Iglesia Mexicana en pesando suplicarles que nosotros no eramos sismaticos y ni tampoco protestantes, sino que la Causa de nosotros era darle libertad á Nuestras Iglesias y en seguida que todo[s] nuestros sacrificios no heran balor de oro si no el balor de las nesecidades de un Pueblo o mas vien seria bajo de una limosna a lo que alcansara la[s] circunstancias de sus nesecidades, que nosotros no andavamos amenasando a los que nos pedian por caridá un Sacrificio, que nosotros yebabamos la

> misma creencia de Jesucristo asiendole caridades a los nesecitados, que nosotros no heramos como el Sesar y como los Romanos que avian de pagar todos los tributos en Oro sino a lo que Diós le socorriera a los fieles los que tuvieron a vien de faboreser al Sacerdote, y hotras cosas mas que esplique con amplitud, para darles [a] entender al mas hinorante [ignorante] y cual mas de todos los que se encontraban naiden se atrevió [a] interrumpir mi conferencia que les avia manifestado, todos como hombres y Mujeres cual mas quedaron satisfechos a mis pocas palabras que esplique todos con gusto me saludaban y me felicitaban como desian que si esa era la causa de la Separación de Roma con la Iglesia que eyos estaban sumamente conformes, como les dije que nuestras Iglesias que existen en Nuestra Nación que no heran Romanas sino que eran Mexicanas porque nosotros no heramos Romanos sino Mexicanos y bastantes cosas mas que esplique para darles [a] entender a todos y quedaron tan satisfechos con todo lo que les dije que asta alababan el gusto que haygamos establecido Nuestra Iglesia Mexicana.[47]

We can see why García's speech worked, with its peasant cadence and its emphasis on local patriotism, municipal authority, parish and market routines, attacks on clerical simony and prurience, and promises of parish autonomy and free-will religion. His listeners, indigenous women and men, listened and voted in favor only when García persuaded them he was neither schismatic nor Protestant but a Catholic promising liberty. Although García knew his interlocutors (some were kinfolk), he admitted doing battle with people loyal to the Roman cura. The experience of registering a Mexican cura seems like a popular, if factionalized, ritual, like petitioning for an ejido.

This finds corroboration in the oath ceremonies and inventories compiled when Mexican priests took over parishes. Takeovers were solemnized in a kind of constitutional liturgy in which priests signed municipal registers, swore obedience to the Reform and Calles laws, and compiled church inventories. In Tetela (Pue.), for example, Father Arredondo López was sworn in thus on Christmas Eve 1926: "Do you swear to uphold . . . the Reform Laws, the Law of 14 June past, and other laws, in your *cargo* of Catholic priest of the Orthodox Mexican Apostolic Church?" In Xochitlán (Pue.), Guillermo de la Peña swore "in accordance with constitutional article 130 . . . by virtue of the written petition placed before the patriarchate of the Yglecia Mexicana by numerous inhabitants."[48]

Civilian signatories were usually religious-political officials. In the Totonac village of Tapayula (Pue.), Macario López was registered in July 1926 "in union with the *principales vecinos* of this place." Tapayula's fiscal, Andrés Pérez, delivered the church. In the ex-Dominican doctrina of Tepetlaoxtoc (Méx.), the *principal* was Agapito Vázquez, Pérez's devoted servant (the patriarch had once been cura, hence Vázquez used an archaic valediction, *q.b.s.m.*, *que besa su mano*, "who kisses your hand"). In Coxquihuí (Ver.), ICAM's patron was "Don Salvador González," a mayordomo because he was responsible for one feast. Municipal officers sometimes led the way: in Coyotepec (Méx.), it was secretary Adrián Abad, whose "kind attentions" warmed Pérez's heart; and in Ahuacatlán (Pue.), church encargado Emilio Velázquez with "liberal elements" including Fernando Melo, a treasury official. Some militia chiefs did the honors. In Coyutla (Ver.), the *jefe de armas* and fourteen individuals led ICAM's 1927 registration; in Hueyapan (Pue.), "orthodox" Catholics and their young priest were escorted by indigenous irregulars.[49] In Santo Domingo (Ver.), finally, ICAM's promoters included municipal president N. D. Gerónimo, church encargado Miguel Gerónimo, and other Gerónimos. People sometimes grew attached to Mexican priests: Father Arredondo reported that villages around Zapotitlán (Pue.) asked constantly for him; Zongozotla (Ver.) would have Teodoro García but nobody else.[50]

That support was genuine is also apparent from parish church inventories, whose fullness suggests complicity, not preemptive "stripping of the altars."[51] Tapayula's inventory (July 1926) listed everything from an ecclesiastical bonnet and silver monstrance to wooden images, a sacrarium, chalices, and altar bell. In Zongozotla (Pue.) the fiscal handed over the sacrarium, processional cross, and 173 other pieces to the incoming priest. Father López entered Nanacatlán (Pue.) five days later with the principales' blessing. Thence he went to Tuxtla (Pue.), a Totonac pueblo whose inventory included wooden saints and fourteen pounds of wax. In Ahuacatlán (Pue.), finally, the encargado, "citizens of the commission," and tax inspector Melo compiled a 221-piece inventory listing a silver baptismal conch and amphora, an archive dating from 1700, and wooden *santos* including the patron, Saint John. Jocotitlán's inventory (Méx.) included baptismal spoons, liturgical linen, and parish tomes.[52]

Indigenous churches were thus left furnished, saints gazing into space, which again suggests complicity. After all, inventories contained utensils for births and deaths, records, and sacred images, all irreplaceable items that pueblos would never have entrusted to enemies. Contents were cataloged piecemeal, too, following no typological classification, suggesting a leisurely, not schematic, process, priests and principales conducting unhurried, item-by-item tours. Perhaps, as Joel Peña suggests, this reflected juntas' educational levels or a desire to prevent official embezzlement by mixing valuables and junk.[53] It could signal acceptance of new priests, too, with inventories often made in neighboring pueblos on consecutive days.

Tolerance of recorded changeovers is confirmed by contrasting documentation elsewhere. In Zapotitlán (Pue.) in February 1927, junta members reportedly "taking orders from Roman priests" delayed ICAM's registration, so Pérez's envoy missed the feast of San Felipe de Jesús. ICAM's registration caused "agitation and unhappiness" in Tecamachalco (Pue.) at Christmas 1928, so was canceled. Likewise in Villa Juárez (Pue.) that May, whose mayor feared rioting if "schismatic priests" took the church.[54] In some mexiquense villages, anxious mayors such as Tlaixpan's watched as "the schism, which treads through villages close by, nears our pueblo." This mayor refused to register ICAM, claiming the church was used for public prayers and should be left alone. Something similar happened in Tezoyuca and Tepexpam; at Ixtapán, "Defenders of Religion" and the churchwarden hid the church keys at Christmas 1927.[55] Evasion was one thing, yet few ICAM priests experienced sickening, *Canoa*-esque lynchings. Pérez's long-time ally, Macario López, took a beating in Zacatlán (Pue.) in 1929, where a crowd "almost sent me to the other side to live with the spirits." He escaped "certain death" by God's grace. Yet this was relatively uncommon and there were few priestly fatalities, contrasting strongly with the widespread lynchings of socialist *maestros* or Protestant missionaries in the 1930s and 1940s. Some violence was in any case generic: Roman clergy could also be stoned or flogged by angry villagers, a horrified Archbishop Vera of Puebla learned in 1924.[56]

Though always controversial, then, ICAM advanced with indigenous support, and in many highland communities a common experience of 1926–1929 was worship under new management. The pattern was established in summer 1926 as Mexican clergy reached the pueblos; it accelerated that fall as Pérez, claiming episcopal orders, began ordaining. Puebla's Sierra Norte saw the first surge. In Zacapoaxtla, Doctor José María López, "priest of the Mexican Catholic and Apostolic Church," was registered on 21 June by invitation of the principales, "there having been no cura in this community for several years." In August, Zongozotla and Tapayula were added, and by September, Ahuacatlán, though López was initially thwarted because a judge locked the church doors. By now, another Mexican priest—Father Arredondo—was in Ozelonacaxtla. In October, Pérez answered an "express petition of the most notable inhabitants" of Zapotitlán and Olintla (Pue.). By November, Arredondo was in Zapotitlán, and by December, Tetela. A third priest, Melesio Cervantes Castro, was in Olintla, prompting Archbishop Vera to denounce his bogus sacraments. That same month, Pedro Infante took over for ICAM in Hueyapan and Jaunahuac (Pue.) and Emeterio Valdéz did so in Zoquiapan because, the governor said, "a good number of inhabitants" wanted it. By 1927, Zapotitlán was a kind of rural deanery with three or four priests.[57]

From Puebla, ICAM spread into Veracruz. In July 1926, José María López claimed Nanacatlán and Tuxtla, saying an "infinity" of people wanted him. Some people must have done: Tuxtla's inventory contained painted wooden santos, saint's capes, and seven kilos of candlewax. In August 1926, Father Félix Montes de Oca broke the clerical strike upstate, in Papantla; as did Rafael Morfín in Jalacingo, a Nahua town across the state line from Tezuitlán. In September, Father Cervantes Castro registered in Totonac Mecatlán. Next month he struck against "religious foreignerism" by registering in Huehuetla, Coyutla, Jopala, Santo Domingo, Vicente Guerrero, Dimás López, Chipahuatlán, Bibiano Hernández, and Coahuitlán.[58]

The years 1927–1928 saw a second Puebla surge, spearheaded by Emeterio Valdéz, a *guanajuatense* revolutionary ordained by Pérez. In February 1927, he took over Zapotitlán, in June the Totonac villages of Jonotla and Ecatlán, and in August, Yaquihuacan. By November Valdéz was in Coyutla, as "the *creyentes* of this place desire"; in April 1928, in Jopala, "to celebrate acts of Catholic worship"; then Patla, with the backing of its "leading citizens"; and finally Chicontla, sharing duties with José de la Luz Coronado. In September 1927, Pedro Infante began celebrating in Xochitlán, then Tehuizotla. Here people wanted a cura "even if he belongs to the Mexican Catholic Church," the "even if" suggesting a quid pro quo.[59]

Another priest, Francisco Durán, began ministering in the Totonac-Tepehua township of Huehuetla in April 1928; another, Vicente Liñán, in Yehualtepec, on the valley floor near Tecamachalco. Two months later, Liñán had another llano church, at Alquizapan. ICAM now expanded into agrarianized central Puebla: in December, "citizen Guillermo de la Peña," was installed in San Simón del Bravo to celebrate a Marian feast. Next month, *poblano* Manuel Salas Vidal set up in Portezuelo and General Felipe Ángeles, though Gregoria Castillo, calling herself "the most Catholic woman in the village," threatened to ambush him with her *comadres*. That January, 175 agraristas in Actipan called for a priest "to administer the Christian religion's sacraments." Such reports filled López y Sierra with joy. "Daunting peaks of triumph" had been scaled; with such "soldiers of Christ," Catholic reactionaries would be hard put to stir up a counterrevolution.[60]

The association of ICAM with agrarianism was equally clear in eastern Mexico State, where changeovers (avowedly unanimous, really factional) peaked in 1927–1928: first was Xalostoc, which registered Camerino García Mota in July 1927; then, in August, Tolmán; followed by Coyotepec and Tecalco, where the priest was Juan Cervantes; then—reportedly—Amecameca, whose Santuario del Sacromonte was opened to ICAM at "conscious" inhabitants' behest; and last, Ixtapán, where the junta divided and there was a Mexicans-versus-Romans standoff. In 1928, there was another wave: in February, "by common accord," Tenoxtitlán sent a commission to Mexico City asking for a priest for Easter. ICAM took Atenco's church in April, prompting a melee for the keys and complaints of banishment by Roman Catholics. In May, García Mota was registered in Zoyatzingo and celebrated the patronal feast. In July, Emeterio Valdéz registered in Coyotepec; and a tenacious Mexican Catholic group in Tepetlixpa, near Morelos, registered Pedro Infante in August.[61]

In Hidalgo, the issue was whether agraristas could bring in Mexican priests to support the ejido program or whether people should resist them on grounds that their ancestors were Roman Catholic. In Tenango, Pérez claimed three churches and three thousand followers, mostly agraristas. Opponents of these "restless and turbulent spirits" said, "We do not oppose them putting their Ideals into practice; what we oppose . . . is that the [ICAM] Minister occupies our Temple, since this was built by our elders so that the Roman Catholic and Apostolic cult be celebrated in it."[62] This conservative argument did not always work: Jocotitlán's church (Méx.) was under construction when it fell into Pérez's hands, so there were no ancestral wishes to offend.[63] Elsewhere on the pulque plains, in Apan (Hgo.), "numerous" agraristas wanted a 12 December Mass in 1926; two priests registered in Pachuca's Asunción church two months later; and in Ajoloapan (Méx.) thirty miles away, forty people brought in a Mexican cura. Farther south, in December 1926, Pascual Luciano García went to the Nahua village of Tenancingo (Tlax.), an ICAM stronghold decades later. As usual, priests here were imported or selected from the ranks of lay religious officials. Few Roman incumbents flipped, though some liberals did: Jocotitlán's cura, Tiburcio Cortés, was one; *jalisciense* Ricardo González, in El Oro, another; likewise, the curas in agrarianized Mexicalcingo and Ixtlahuaca (all Méx.).[64]

DECENTERING THE CHURCH

In southern regions, ICAM resembled a jigsaw puzzle with missing pieces but clear likenesses. In Guerrero, it enjoyed a coastal presence but less of an inland one. Two days into the 1926 clerical strike, two Roman curas, Porfirio Castañeda and José María Fonseca, registered in *costa grande* municipalities (between Acapulco and Michoacán) including La Unión, Petatlán, and Coahuayutla. Here, unusually, ICAM ministered to *mulato* peasants who ranched and sharecropped cotton. Sadly, we have no details. Southward, in the *mineral* of Tezicapan, Juan Gutiérrez swore to "obey and uphold" the Calles Law. And still farther south, in the costa chica's hinterland (Acapulco to Oaxaca), three Mexican curas set up in Tepecoacuilco—an Augustinian ex-doctrina populated by Nahua weavers and muleteers—after the junta asked Pérez to celebrate its fiestas in February 1927. They were there at Easter when Victoriano Bárcenas's cristeros dragged Father Arredondo from a nearby church in Manayalán and shot him. Pérez raged that cristeros were "Romanist Iscariots," but ICAM was checked, remaining confined to Tepecoacuilco in the 1930s.[65] Arredondo, the Mexican clergy's Father Pro, received exequys in Corpus Christi in April, though there was no coffin because the tropical climate had made it necessary to inter him quickly—"a burial in some corner of the village," a priest wrote. Thus, López y Sierra prayed over Arredondo's bloodied relics and claimed that the "sacrificial lamb's name" would be written in gold in church annals. In private, Mexican clergy were afraid. "If the situation becomes difficult due to revolutionary disorder," López y Sierra told Emeterio Valdéz in 1927, "pack your bags and come to the city." "You do not know the intense grief that weighs in our souls," he mourned. Still, the Saint Bartholomew's massacre never materialized, and this was one of only four priestly fatalities between 1925 and 1940, the result of encountering cristeros. The same was true, perhaps, of seventy-two-year-old Felipe de Jesús Ochoa, murdered in 1928 in his Guadalajara church. Two other priests died in Puebla (one in June 1927; Vicente Liñán in 1932).[66]

In Oaxaca, ICAM was present in four of the state's seven subregions (the Mixteca Baja, Cañada, costa chica, and isthmus), plus Oaxaca City, but not in the Central Valleys and sierras. Oaxaca was virtually the only capital to have juring clergy, prominently, Mauro de Jesús Merlin, who swore on the Calles Law and received the Sagrario in August 1926. In the Mixteca Baja, a hundred miles north, Pérez had more support, but this was his patria chica. Indeed, Pérez used networks of kinship like those eloquently described by Ben Smith. In Juxtlahuaca in October 1926, Pérez empowered a nephew, thirty-one-year-old Pedro Pérez Villafañe, and a cousin, Manuel Pérez Villafañe, to find priests. In Tlapancingo, another nephew, General Agapito Pérez, scared up priests, distributed copies of *Restauración*, and reported to Calles's *estado mayor*. Correspondence between the senior Pérezes continued all winter, uncle Joaquín hoping that Agapito would make ICAM known to all, "not only our relatives, friends, and acquaintances in this region." Pérez's Oaxacan in-laws also included an aspiring *profesor normalista*, Francisco Ulloa Ayala, and "squadron captain Adrián Pérez," leader of Tisetla's Volunteers.[67] In Calihualá, finally, near Guerrero, yet another nephew, Benito Méndez, reported "how many priests there are . . . and whether they are willing to receive our parishes." Some were. In January 1927, Pérez's nephew recruited Silvestre Miguel Ondilón Sánchez, whom Pérez appointed cura of Tlachichilco after discerning that he was a "true soldier of Christ."[68]

There was more support in the *cuicateco* township of Concepción Pápalo, in the Cañada, adjoining the Mixteca, which registered José Velasco (October 1926). Likewise, there were registrations in Oaxaca's coffee-growing costa chica, between Juquila and Pochutla. Here were Maximiano Amador, cura of the Zapotec parish of Pochutla, who reopened his church for the feast of San José in 1928, causing the patriarchate "great surprise"; and Andrés Urbina, cura of Loxicha, another Zapotec pueblo, who registered in November 1926. Details are few. Happily, the case of Teotepec, a Chatino parish near Juquila, provides better insights into Oaxaca's juring clergy, represented by Aureo Castellanos López, who withdrew from his church in August 1926 and went up-country. A year later, however, on 27 July 1927, he reappeared in Teotepec, swore fealty to the Calles Law, and said Mass. He celebrated all winter, missing neither the Guadalupan feast nor the Epiphany, which he celebrated in Nopala. Here diocesan investigator Ausencio Canseco intercepted him.[69] The exchange was revealing: Castellanos told Canseco that he ministered on state authority because it was one thing to be doctrinaire about canonical discipline in Oaxaca, another in parishes like his. Rather than negotiate "delicately" with Calles, the episcopate foolishly called a strike and "threw excommunications" around like thunderbolts, with the result that worship was decaying. If Castellanos did not formally recognize Pérez as superior, he voiced identical liberal views concerning the primacy of priests' mission over hierarchical politics and submission to the state. Oaxaca's vicar general wrote disbelievingly, ordering Castellanos to end his "depraved attack" on authority. Yet Castellanos massed as he pleased, calling his detractors dupes of Satan; if he were cismático, he accepted excommunication. Locals wondered about the lawfulness of his sacraments years after the Cristiada.[70]

There were juring priests in Tehuantepec, too, led by Miguel ("Miguelito") Guillermo Fernández, párroco of Ixtepec in "liberal" Juchitán, who swore on the Calles Law in 1926. Despite warnings from Niltepec's cura that ICAM was Protestant, Miguelito massed in Ixtepec and Juchitán, and was found presiding over feasts in "distant villages." In Tehuantepec, ICAM had local backing, and its priests roamed where they wanted. Even with the arreglos, registrations were not annulled: Roman clergy were outraged that they must celebrate in "tiny chapels, called *posas* or *velas*," used for popular feasts such as the May Cross or Emerald Light, while Miguelito had five churches. This was because he was close to Tehuantepec's mayor, "who always favors the *intrusos*" ("intruders," again recollecting 1790s French constitutional priests). *Juchiteco* liberals, meanwhile, calling themselves "true Catholic, Apostolic Mexicans," denounced the annual edicts published against ICAM by Tehuantepec's Roman bishop. Miguelito, insisting that ministry was "the most sacred thing in his life," remained until 1930, then quit on health grounds, prompting the apostolic delegate to ask whether he had recanted (he hadn't).[71]

It was the same story on the isthmus's Gulf terminus. In September 1926, a diocesan priest registered in two old Nahua delta ports, Jaltipan and Chinameca, and US consuls knew of another juror in San Juan Evangelista. Two months later, in November, Miguelito began massing in Acayucan, returning for December's Marian cycle to perform "masses, baptisms, marriages, etc.," according to a Roman cura who watched him. This priest was livid when his curia did not agree that Miguelito "profaned" Acayucan's church. Indeed, the curia preferred that Miguelito visit so the building could stay open for lay worship when he was away, and told their priestly informant to avoid confrontation. Seemingly he did not, given that ninety-seven agraristas turned on him, claiming that he "shared out all the santos . . . to his *viejas*, his lovers," before fleeing for Cuba. Either way, by spring 1927, pro-ICAM groups in Pajapam and Puerto México (today Coatzacoalcos) sought Miguelito's services. Then, in August, Pascual García was registered in Jaltipan. Stipends in indigenous ports and Puerto México, a young oil town, proved rich enough that Pérez sent two disastrous priests, Adolfo Briones and Antonio Munive, to Acayucan in 1928. Their moneygrubbing plunged ICAM's isthmus church into anarchy.[72]

ICAM developed farther up the Veracruz coast. In San Andrés Tuxtla, a Mexican priest took over in 1929, with sixty supporters claiming that their ex-cura had removed "some small images, here known as 'pilgrims,'" from church. One wonders if joining ICAM was an attempt to get them back. In February 1929, Tampico-Alto, upstate in the Huasteca, brought in a Pérez priest.[73] By this time, the region's most infamous juror, Dimás Anguiano, a sixty-four-year-old liberal and *colimense*, had been working Veracruz's leeward plains for years. Indeed, as cura of the port of Alvarado, he wired Calles the moment his eponymous law came into effect, offering his registration as a "work of nationalism in support of the Mexican Catholic religion." For this his bishop excommunicated him, "with anguish in my soul," and prayed for his repentance. By mid-August, Anguiano was in the El Cristo shrine on the old sea wall, ministering to *jarochos*. By spring 1927, his leeward circuit included Soledad de Doblado, Paso de Ovejas, Cotaxtla, Tlaxicoyan, and San Cristóbal de la Llave. Wherever he went, he proclaimed that it was "the bishops themselves" who made priests leave. Anguiano was harassed by some municipalities loyal to governor Heriberto Jara, Tejeda's rival and interim replacement, and in Soledad he was arrested. Even Tejeda refused some requests for licenses—to celebrate household baptisms in Cardel, for instance, which had no church—yet Anguiano was still going strong in 1929, having ministered to thousands.[74]

ICAM's other southern bastion was the Soconusco, historically the starting point of the trade route (cattle, indigo) linking the isthmus and Puebla/Mexico City but by the 1920s a coffee-growing and ranching borderland. Here, in 1925, a fight broke out at the old cow town and labor hub of Tapachula (Chis.) between two factions for control of the neoclassical *parroquia* of San Agustín. The struggle, lasting years, pitted Catholic revolutionaries against a Catholic plantocracy (and Roman clergy) that managed migrant Guatemalan and Mexican labor. Fifty-three members of a "Mexican Catholic and Apostolic Congregation," fronted by Elías de la Cruz, a mayordomo, then rose up, arguing that Mexican cult would create "nationalist feeling" in Tapachula. ICAM scored a victory in October 1926, when its cura—*queretano* José Ramírez—was registered in San Agustín, an act he called "a second national independence." Alas for him, the municipal elite wrecked the occasion by delivering the church without silver or vestments, making it difficult to celebrate. Thus began a violent dispute over a church that symbolized not just religious divisions but the auspices under which a mixed labor force would be run. Indeed, ICAM soon spread inland to foothill municipios such as Unión Juárez, Tuxtla Chico, and Cacahoatán, as well as coastal plains communities like Mazatán. Tapachula aside, these were younger pueblos than Chiapas's highland communities which had expanded into forested spaces between coastal coffee *fincas*. Village lands were imperfectly privatized, too, hence villagers had few incentives to toil for *finqueros* who instead recruited seasonal Guatemalan laborers. By the 1920s, village factions were developing as the accepted criterion of community membership—residency or *vecindad*—was subjected to the stressors of migration and revolutionary nationalism, with attendant exclusions in agrarian, educational, and religious affairs.[75]

Far up north, Tamaulipas's coastal borderland was another *foco*. Here the religious crisis revived a historic interconnection between civil and ecclesiastical power after ex-Roman cura José Laurencio Reinoso launched ICAM in Matamoros in 1927. His petition for Ciudad Victoria's churches was opposed by Roman Catholics on grounds that only "ignorant people" could want his sacraments, but, by 1929, when Bishop López y Sierra carried out a pastoral visit, ICAM's circuit had expanded to municipios including Reynosa, Ochoa, Camargo, San Fernando, Río Bravo, and Reinosa Díaz, plus smaller communities such as Congregación Garza and Cruillos. People came, in caravans of cars or on horse, to confirm their children; there was still faith in Israel, *El Heraldo Mexicano* reported. In the sierra around Reynosa, another ex-*romano*, Melesio Guerrero, conducted indigenous missions and sent Pérez tithes. The pueblos had "a true desire to hear the counsels and teachings of the Holy Gospel," he wrote. Given Portes Gil's aversion to CROM, it surely helped that ICAM's clergy were well known politically. Father Guerrero was a friend of Portes Gil's *maestro* and of his father-in-law, who ran the Nuevo Laredo customs house. Guerrero also officiated at Portes Gil's wedding. After the arreglos, nonetheless, Portes Gil turned his back on ICAM, forcing Guerrero to concentrate his efforts in San Antonio (Tex.). Pérez also made him priest of Los Aldamas (N.L.), where *buenos vecinos* called him saying that the Roman cura visited only once a year to raid the collection box. Guerrero claimed his ministry was validated by a village plebiscite, but he was still awaiting registration in March 1930. He thus resorted to subterfuge, opening a "school" where he taught catechism. Nobody disturbed him, though the Monterrey curia warned that a well-known priest was schismatizing in Los Aldamas, Doctor Coss, El Bravo, China, Las Herreras, and Los Ramones. God allowed this apostasy, it said, so as to decant impure priests from His clergy.[76]

THE *ARREGLOS*

This *radiografía* of ICAM explains why the Roman episcopate wanted Portes Gil to disown Pérez: the patriarch had hundreds, not a handful, of churches. Portes Gil, for his part, was keen to break with Calles's religious policy and encourage moderate figures in the episcopate who might steer the church back toward mutually supportive relations with the regime. The sycophantic bishop of Chihuahua called Portes Gil "a new Constantine."[77] Yet if the Roman Church, post-arreglos, rediscovered its vocation as a national church, where did that leave Pérez? As it turned out, there were clear parallels between Rome's decision to sacrifice the cristeros and Portes Gil's decision to scuttle ICAM, whether out of hatred for Morones or institutional realpolitik. Certainly, the campaign was concerted. Even before the arreglos came a decree (18 June) ordering La Soledad's return to Roman clergy.[78] Vexatious demands that Pérez produce his clergy's theology degrees and restore Corpus Christi followed. Refusal of a permit to adorn the church with murals of Quiroga and Motolonia (the artist was to have been a young Covarrubias) was another sign of waning favor.[79] Then came circulars to implement the arreglos and force Mexican priests out. One mandated the return of church annexes. Then, on 15 August, came circular 33, asserting the federal prerogative in the regulation of external religious discipline and stating that any churches unoccupied when the arreglos were signed should be returned "specifically to priests of the Roman Catholic Church." Churches occupied before then—by definition, the incumbents were ICAM's—could be reassigned to Roman clergy if their occupation were "unjustified."[80] Pérez was thus on notice, on terms that were subjective.

The deliberate nature of Portes Gil's decision to accommodate Roman clergy could be seen in the fact that a well-publicized test case occurred in Tamaulipas, his home state. Here it was reported a week after the arreglos that "Mexican-Roman" priest Antonio García y García had reappeared and demanded the return of the parroquia in Matamoros, prompting ICAM to appeal directly to the president. Had Gobernación's circulars not promised that ICAM's legal occupations would be respected? Matamoros's municipal president promised likewise in a telegram of 5 July—yet Portes Gil countermanded the order and returned the parish to Roman hands, prompting criticism from liberal opinion, *El Heraldo Mexicano* said. It was unconscionable, Father Guerrero told Pérez, that Mexican priests should be ousted, having obeyed the law all along. That it was his paisano and compadre who did the ousting must have been hard to take.[81]

Portes Gil also promised alacrity. Gobernación predicted that a new Registro General de Sacerdotes y Pastores would be completed in spring 1930, assuming that Roman curas now registered as encargados. Pascual Díaz, the appreciative archbishop of Mexico, now authorized Roman Catholic clergy to register because the Portes Gil regime had provided guarantees and was debarring impostors "who trick the faithful, passing themselves off as Catholic priests." Díaz even had Mexican tricolors flown ostentatiously from church towers. Catholic papers cheerfully read ICAM's last rites: "the schismatic church . . . ceased to exist today," crowed one after the arreglos.[82]

While Díaz and Portes Gil buried the hatchet, Pérez protested the arreglos to attorney general Enrique Medina, who assured him (July 1929) that ICAM's rights would be raised with Portes Gil. Pérez's efforts to procure an interview with the president were nonetheless rebuffed.[83] Pérez could therefore do little but denounce the "diplomatic arrangements" as an injustice to patriotic priests who submitted to the law all along, instead of a "foreign master."[84] In private, a demoralized Pérez scrutinized Providence. "Long and sleepless nights have we spent, deep and serious meditations have we performed, to pinpoint the Spirit of Christ in the world's current turnings," he wrote. But he could find no answer as to why Portes Gil bargained with the "King of the Vatican."[85] Some correligionists, for instance Luisa Reboulen, Pérez's faithful correspondent in southern Veracruz, found silver linings: Rome now accepted the principle of ecclesiastical registration, she wrote, which proved that ICAM had never been an apostasy; "Mexicans' fiery character" had caused a tragic religious misunderstanding, which she hoped was now over.[86]

High politics soon filtered down to the municipios, however. A devotee of Pérez's in Progreso (Ver.) described new clashes between "schismatics" and "simoniacs"; the Roman cura now expelled "schismatical people" from Mass, claiming the Virgin herself had appeared and commanded it.[87] In Puebla, conservative governor Leonides Andreu Almazán (1929–1933)—a friend of the clergy—took aim at the Barrios *cacicazgo* and ICAM.[88] In reality, then, the arreglos ushered in a competitive game of musical chairs as Mexican and Roman priests fought over churches. The main difference was that the federation had changed sides. Even so, and as we shall see in the conclusion, the clashes often lasted well into the 1930s, if not beyond, again showing that Mexican Catholicism had entered popular culture. Serrano chieftains, for instance, resisted Almazán's efforts to purge ICAM, as in Tlaola, whose *ayuntamiento* renewed Francisco Durán's registration in August 1929, and Patla, whose mayor remained friendly (quedó en amigo de que yo fuera a sacar la fiesta). Thus, Durán ended, "though the romanos make war on us, we still have supporters." In 1931 and 1933, Tlaola's principales still backed ICAM (la Autoridad Municipal de Tlaola ha trabajado mucho por nuestra causa). Zongozotla's and Xaltepuxtla's did, too: here representatives alleged that Roman curas treated them as "vassals" and charged twenty pesos for Mass, four times ICAM's price.[89]

In the Puebla valleys, Mexican Catholicism permeated land disputes and *almazanistas* and agrarianized Mexican Catholics fought pitched battles. In Yehualtepec, "fanatics" and women backed by "señor governor Almazán" tried to "bring in a Roman Catholic cura by force, against the pueblo's will," leading to "bloody conflicts," wrote a representante del pueblo. Almazán had no right to "impose a cura whom we qualify as a mocker of Christ's religion," an instrument of landlords, and "a raper of maidens," others wrote. In some places—Tecamachalco, Teotozucan, Zozutla, and Tlacomulco—Almazán prevailed, a Catholic source reported, yet ousting ICAM required force and Pérez had "many more pueblos."[90]

Outside Puebla, the war of attrition continued. In Hidalgo, ICAM occupied Almoloya and other churches in 1930, while in Tenancingo (Tlax.) two curas remained in 1933. In México, finally, ICAM kept its northern and eastern bases (Xometla, Coyotepec, and Xalostoc),[91] and expanded where religion dovetailed with secessionist village struggles, as in the municipio of Tenango, south of Toluca. Here in 1932, Aniceto Trujillo was registered in several churches around Calimaya, just north of the cabecera, after local authorities recognized ICAM as "a distinct sect from the Roman." What they really meant was distinct from Tenango; people in Tepexoxuca, south of Tenango, felt the same aversion to the cabecera, and in 1938 they contracted another ICAM cura, Felipe de Jesús Vázquez Aguirre. Vázquez soon had hundreds of militants in Joquicingo, Quictepec, Maxtleca, Zictepec, and San Miguelito. In essence, ICAM offered villagers freedom from a "fanatical" headtown, the dignity of local cult, and a path to municipal status. Apologists declared that Mexican priests also "spread the true Catholic religion among the proletariat," which again hints at agrarismo. The hated cabecera was a danger zone. Indeed, a near-lynching occurred in 1938 when Mexican Catholics and an eccentric priest—"Pope" Eduardo Dávila—entered Tenango. The Roman cura sounded the bells and Tenango Catholics beat Dávila, stole his archive, and dumped him on the edge of town.[92]

South of Mexico City, around Popocatépetl, another cluster of ICAM villages emerged by 1937, as shown by an order to Roman clergy in Amecameca to halt the schismatics' labors. One Roman cura reported that Father Fernández de Haro was "sustaining and propagating the schism," using "prudent" conduct to "trick many faithful in surrounding parishes." Local authorities protected him, and he threatened Romanists with jail if they invaded his terrain. There was some religious substance: Teocalco, eight miles south of Amecameca, had not been tithed since ICAM took over in 1930; in Tepetlixca, a Jesuit source notes that Fernández paved the church's earth floor and consecrated a new bell from 1934 to 1938, so local cooperation was evidently key. Fernández promoted Marianism, too, placing alms at the Guadalupe's feet in Tepeyac and distributing prayer cards. Thus, these were satellites for whom Mexicanization brought material and religious gains. When the government tried to replace Fernández, locals jeered the Roman cura. A hail of stones forced him out.[93]

In Veracruz, ICAM signified independence of Mexico City and integration in Adalberto Tejeda's statewide movement. By August 1929, Tejeda was reportedly in "open conflict with President Portes Gil's government" over the arreglos and his League of Agrarian Communities (LCAEV) was protecting ICAM in the municipios. In Los Tuxtlas—a lacustrine region with a famous Cristo Negro and Virgin—the mayor and agraristas defended ICAM gun in hand, moving ICAM's priest, Adolfo Briones, to applaud their "heroic" conduct. If Briones worried that he would have to find priests for Tejeda and give kickbacks to mayors, he had a clientele. People came from both Tuxtlas (San Andrés and Santiago) and their sister village, Catemaco, he said. Perhaps the droves existed, for Briones worked the shrine at Catemaco, where Nahuas venerated a lake sprite under a Marian avatar. Briones claimed that the ex-Roman cura had embezzled 10,000 pesos from sanctuary coffers but was himself unscrupulous. Surprisingly, Briones never claimed Otatitlán's Cristo Negro shrine; perhaps clergy were unwelcome, for around this time (1931) local officials decapitated the image and took a match to it.[94]

In Acayucan, sixty-five miles south, the muncipio installed a Pérez priest, though some pious *acayuqueñas* complained to Portes Gil that the authorities showed "partiality toward enemies of our religion," "sullying" the arreglos. Indeed, the municipio gave "unlimited help to those we consider 'schismatics,'" suggesting "agreement with the state's superior authorities" to support ICAM. They recalled Portes Gil's promise to respect only priests "approved by superior ecclesiastical authority." In fact, it was Ortiz Rubio's national property directorate that responded, closing Acayucan's church on grounds that falling masonry "endangered the faithful." This was a pyrrhic victory for the *damas*, since "schismatics" roamed the villages and the parish was not sealed until 1933, with Tejeda gone.[95]

Though Tuxpan's mayor would not touch it, we find support for ICAM in northern Veracruz, too: "Because of a change in the authorities, everything has changed for the cause I follow," Teodoro Juárez wrote in Zozocolco, on the Sierra Norte escarpment, in 1930. He and José Varela still had churches in Mecatlán and Coyutla. In 1931, ICAM had six priests on the Veracruz-Puebla line and the numbers were increasing. In December 1935, Amatlán's Roman Catholic vicar forane identified ten ICAM priests in northern Veracruz, one a "bishop" with headquarters in "Quisquigüe" (Coxquihuí); and, he wrote to the US consul, "there are five [more] in the parishes under my charge," namely, Tihuatlán, Tuxpam, Tamapache, Tamiahua, Tautima, Ozuluama, and Amatlán.[96] In central Veracruz, too, Dimás Anguiano carried on. Brandishing old telegrams from Calles and talking up improvements to El Cristo—whitewashed walls, an atrium shaded by coconut trees—Anguiano claimed it was "public knowledge" that he suppressed parish fees, "leaving the faithful at liberty to give such donations as they wish." That Roman curas boycotted him showed their contempt for "the pueblo's economic liberty in the church." Letters, from the apostolic delegate and Freemasons who wanted the church for a school, failed to dislodge him. The Roman bishop, Rafael Guízar y Valencia, believed the port's alcalde protected him. ICAM's occupancy of El Cristo ended in 1939.[97]

If things got trickier post-Tejeda, ICAM had entered Veracruz's Catholic vernacular, as Teodoro Juárez learned after a 1938 sojourn on the oilfields. In "lands isolated from all discourse"—Chicontepec—he "waged the fight" for churches and found so much spiritual hunger that he needed help. For a time he was aided by Father Heraclio Ortiz, a relative, it was said, of Guadalajara's archbishop Ortiz (1901–1912), though unfortunately Ortiz had little stomach for the fight. When Juárez moved on to the Zacamixtla and Tancoco oilfields for Holy Week, however, roughnecks and indigenes would not let him leave. "Thanks to God, I am officiating after some days in which, more or less, I did not," Juárez reported.[98]

Farther south, ICAM's rollback was more political. In Tehuantepec, Miguelito complained that Roman curas encroached on Juchitán the second the arreglos were made public. Another Mexican priest worked the isthmus in 1932, but generally, ICAM dwindled as clergy resubmitted.[99] A protracted battle was waged in Tapachula, where Father Ramírez promised to see things through, like the apostles. Enemies were everywhere. He battled officials for licenses, an experience he likened to "banging my head on the ground," yet despised priests who crawled back to Rome. In feverish dreams he saw Roman clergy lining up on the Guatemalan side of the Suchiate, waiting to cross. Hostile pamphleteers worked him over psychologically, calling him a prodigal son; petitions for San Agustín's reassignment littered the streets. Ramírez, sensing an "implacable fall," was losing churches by September: Berriozabal, San Fernando, Tuxtla, Pijijiapam, Huixtla, and Tuxtla Chico, to the flock's "great sadness," he said. Still, he could not be removed from Tapachula. Another ex-romano, Urbano Gómez, was in Motozintla.[100]

In the end, ICAM foundered because of internal divisions following Pérez's demise (October 1931) but more because the influence in Chiapas of a regional force, *garridismo*, proved toxic. First Father Ramírez confronted a rival ICAM priest, Salvador Castellanos. When Ramírez was seriously challenged in Tapachula in February 1932, however, it was due to centralization in the local PNR, which was now run by Lorenzo Bravo, municipal boss and string-puller for syndicates of haulers, feminists, market-traders, bootblacks, and sinophobes.[101] Bravo's coalition demanded that San Agustín be converted into a school; Bravo attacked Ramírez, urging that "the veil of ignorance that *el clero*, whether of the Orthodox or Roman schools, has cast over the eyes of the people" be ripped away. Soconuscans should not be exposed to a foreign—in his words "Guatemalan"—religion. This was of a piece with Bravo's xenophobic efforts to chase Guatemalans off ejidos.[102]

Garrido-style defanaticization was repudiated by incoming state governor, Raymundo Enríquez, a callista (1932). Enríquez duly reinstated Ramírez (March) and reprimanded PNR bosses for making "common cause" with Rome by punishing a patriot priest. But then Garrido weighed in, urging San Agustín's secularization in the name of "revolutionary civilization." In what was surely a first, Roman Catholics and Garrido agreed: Ramírez must go. Rioters stormed San Agustín on 19 March, accusing Ramírez of stealing church property. All Ramírez had done, he claimed, was to scythe corn in the church garden. Nonetheless, *caciquil* and municipal hostility prevailed, and he was out. In June, Ortiz Rubio withdrew San Agustín from use.[103] Ramírez had worse humiliations to come. First, as priest of Cacahoatán, the mayor taxed him four pesos per Angelus. In May, he naïvely asked Garrido for help: his "only ambition" was to minister legally, "for I am a Mexican, not a Roman, priest." Garrido's reply—that all religions deformed the mind—was cold. Worse,

Chiapas's next governor, Victórico Grajales (1932–1936) made Ramírez perform garridismo's signature rite, the *quemasantos* (saint-burning) in 1934. That December, Ramírez built a pyre in the Parque Revolución, "spontaneously" renounced his faith, and threw his cassock and bonnet on the flames. It seemed like the end, yet days into Cárdenas's presidency, letters from Chiapas's Mexican Catholics started arriving.[104]

CONCLUSION

The Calles Law is conventionally seen as tyrannical because its effort to civilianize church government took no account of what Lanz Duret called *el hecho católico*—the fact of Mexico's catholicity, hierarchy included.[105] The law was constitutional fundamentalism. Yet ICAM's history invites us to reconsider Mexico as "Catholic fact" and posit Catholicism as an unstable value. Not everyone naturalized the Roman clergy's presence or supported the 1926 suspension of worship. In the Bajío, steeped in ultramontane piety, the Calles Law caused a seizure. Yet many indigenous Catholics supported ICAM's juring priests as a way to advance religious interests. Indeed, ICAM was not just a church of powerful, cynical men but of Nahuas, Totonacos, Tepehuas, Cuicatecos, Zapotecos, Mames, agraristas, and campesinos. To the extent that ICAM was popular and fused ethnic, religious, and state forms, it was religious state formation. It grew once Tejeda reactivated the constitutional bond between churches and investitures, turning juntas into sovereign corporations on French and US lines. Indigenous Catholics wielded this power more willingly than we think, probably because church juntas assimilated easily to village corporations such as mayordomías. More than a pyramid, ICAM was a revolutionary confederation of lay-led congregations, equivalent in scale to two or three Roman dioceses. Many indigenous Catholics thus practiced religion through the state. Very deliberately, but incompletely, Portes Gil broke the link when pacting with Rome.

There was more to ICAM than bureaucratic manipulation and indigenous gullibility. As long as Roman clergy could not church the highlands, isthmus, and coasts, margins were left for other Catholicisms. It remains to show how ICAM fitted around indigenous lives. Yet indigeneity is the reason, one suspects, why ICAM is forgotten: even Calles would not exploit it for propaganda, which he would have had Pérez fulfilled his task of building a "modern" national church in Mexico

City.¹⁰⁶ Perhaps the entanglement of Catholicism, revolutionary constitutionalism, and indigeneity should not surprise, historically. The church Pérez attacked was only standing because it had, centuries before, driven out mendicant priests on crown authority and seized their churches in "possession ceremonies" remarkably like those of 1926. More than a CROM putsch, ICAM resembled Bourbon secularization, right down to the participation of indigenous notaries and witnesses in violent church handovers, ecclesiastical appeals to the *audiencia* (not Gobernación), and the furor that one generation of priests did not deserve to inherit what another had built.¹⁰⁷

Figure 1. Eyes straight ahead, ex-cavalryman and Catholic priest José Joaquín Pérez Budar prepares to launch his Mexican revolutionary church, Tacubaya, February 1925. Fototeca Nacional #24817. Photo courtesy of the Instituto Nacional de Antropología e Historia, Mexico.

Figure 2. Adalberto Tejeda, Calles's interior minister (1925–1928) and governor of Veracruz (1920–1924, 1928–1932), was Pérez's most loyal official patron. Fototeca Nacional #28940. Photo courtesy of the Instituto Nacional de Antropología e Historia, Mexico.

Figure 3. Ricardo Treviño, Labor Party deputy and Pérez's CROM minder at the siege of La Soledad. Fototeca Nacional #29585. Photo courtesy of the Instituto Nacional de Antropología e Historia, Mexico.

Figure 4. The power behind the throne: Luis Morones shadows Calles. Fototeca Nacional #44341. Photo courtesy of the Instituto Nacional de Antropología e Historia, Mexico.

Figure 5. Echoes of the eighteenth century: neoclassical *callista* allegory. Fototeca Nacional #44344. Photo courtesy of the Instituto Nacional de Antropología e Historia, Mexico.

Figure 6. Schoolgirls perform flag ceremony at Calles's inauguration. Two months later, the regime would extend revolutionary nationalism into the church sphere. Fototeca Nacional #44382. Photo courtesy of the Instituto Nacional de Antropología e Historia, Mexico.

Figure 7. A *callista* welcoming committee waits for caudillo Álvaro Obregón on the station platform in Mexico City, 30 March, 1926. Note the cold, determined stares. In truth, it was Obregón who had come to intimidate Calles and his supporters, including Pérez. Front row, L-R: governor Carlos Riva Palacio of Mexico State; Calles; agriculture secretary and ex-torero Luis L. León; labor minister Luis Morones; San Luis Potosí federal deputy Gonzalo N. Santos; Banco de México director Alberto Mascareñas; general Eulogio Ortiz. Fototeca Nacional #45028. Photo courtesy of the Instituto Nacional de Antropología e Historia, Mexico.

Figure 8. *Bomberos* turn their hoses on Roman Catholic rioters besieging the parish of La Soledad, February 1925. Within days, copycat riots would break out in cities all over Mexico. Fototeca Nacional #45597. Photo courtesy of the Instituto Nacional de Antropología e Historia, Mexico.

Figure 9. Patriarch Pérez crosses women and children with ashes in the parish of La Soledad, Ash Wednesday, 1925. Critics alleged that Pérez drummed up recruits in La Castañeda mental hospital. In truth, Pérez's followers were nearly all indigenous Catholics, and almost none of them lived in Mexico City. Fototeca Nacional #174538. Photo courtesy of the Instituto Nacional de Antropología e Historia, Mexico.

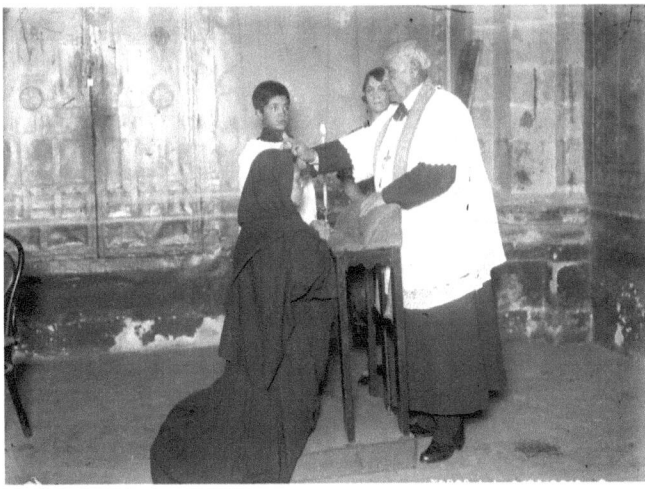

Figure 10. Patriarch Pérez crosses woman devotee at La Soledad while two acolytes look on, Ash Wednesday 1925. Fototeca Nacional #174553. Photo courtesy of the Instituto Nacional de Antropología e Historia, Mexico.

Figure 11. 1903 broadsheet showing Our Lady of Solitude, as venerated at La Soledad. DP867950. Photo courtesy of the Metropolitan Museum of Art, the Elisha Whittelsey Collection, the Elisha Whittelsey Fund, 1946.

Figure 12. Facade of La Soledad, c. 1925. Originally a parish for indigenous Oaxacans working in Mexico City, from the eighteenth century La Soledad became a monument to patriotic Bourbon Catholicism and latterly a decaying urban parish patronized by market people, prostitutes, and street criminals. Fototeca Nacional #175384. Photo courtesy of the Instituto Nacional de Antropología e Historia, Mexico.

Figure 13. Main altar, parish of Santa Cruz y Soledad, c. 1900. Photo courtesy of Archivo Histórico del Arzobispado de México, Mexico City.

Figure 14. Spanish priest Father Manuel Monge, Patriarch Pérez, and ICAM treasurer, Ángel Jiménez Juárez, February 1925. Photo courtesy of Centro de Estudios de Historia de México Fundación Carlos Slim.

Figure 15. Father Antonio Benigno López y Sierra, Pérez's vicar general. Photo courtesy of Father Antonio Celis García.

Figure 16. Indigenous priest Father José Cano. Photo courtesy of Archivo Histórico del Arzobispado de México, Mexico City.

Figure 17. "Bell of the parish church of La Soledad, the first to ring out after the *arreglos*" [Campana del templo de la Soledad, primera en sonar después de los arreglos]. Photo courtesy of CESU-AHUNAM.

CHAPTER FOUR

"OUR BELOVED PEASANTS"

ICAM on the Ejido

IN OCTOBER 1926, Calles's agriculture secretary Luis León stood up in Ixtayopan (D.F.) and addressed agraristas enjoying an alfresco banquet. León prophesied that ejidos would elevate indigenous people so that they soared like the arrow fired at the sun by the Nahuas' "heavenly archer," Motecuhzoma Ilhuicamina (Archer of the Skies). In more Christian terms, León next promised that ejidos would liberate indigenous peons by upholding their natural right to enjoy the fruits of their labor. Nor had Calles forgotten the "peasant middle class": if these peasants opposed the revolution, the government would "pardon their sins" and "redeem them" with irrigation trenches and credit.[1] León's baroque rhetoric mixed developmentalist tropes with traces of Nahua cosmogony and Catholic theology (natural law, sin, and redemption). If Ixtayopan's ejidatarios politely applauded, León's speech revealed something vital, if counterintuitive, about callismo. Namely, that it owed some philosophical debts to Catholicism—no matter how deeply buried under anticlericalism. Sometimes the influence was just rhetorical, as with the *Agrarian Catechism* (legal compendium) issued by León's department. In other ways, it ran deep, deeper than the fascist corporatism with which Calles is commonly associated.[2] As noted in chapter 3, the Calles Law aimed to re-create a French- or US-style constitutional church. Calles' agrarian policy—so often viewed in technocratic terms—also borrowed from Christianity, though here the debt was to Germanic, Christian-inspired cooperativism. For all its priest-baiting, callismo was steeped in empirical religion and Christianity was the love that dared not speak its name.[3]

This was partly thanks to youthful Catholic intellectuals and bureaucrats, such as Manuel Gómez Morín (creator of Calles's rural credit schemes and latterly PAN) and Vicente Lombardo Toledano (CROM culture secretary, later CTM boss). These cultural caudillos argued that the ejido's success ultimately depended on an ethical transformation rooted in Christian principles, not mere redistribution. Ejidos required fraternal cooperation. Yet here was a problem: how to moralize a reform that the archbishop of Mexico denounced in 1925 as theft? This dissonance helps to explain why dissident religious actors—ICAM, Protestants, Mormons, and Mennonites—were encouraged to infiltrate, even theologize, ejidos in the 1920s and 1930s.[4] For their part, ICAM priests worked to erase the stigma of agrarismo, allowing Catholic campesinos to mobilize with fewer inhibitions, thereby facilitating regime construction. The affinity between Calles-era agrarianism and ICAM was strong: the three states with most Pérez supporters—México, Veracruz, Puebla—were also top three in terms of ejidal *dotaciones* (grants) under Calles.[5] Within states, there were particular concentrations of ICAM-affiliated agraristas. A good example was the *altaplanicie pulquera* or Mexico basin (cuenca): that is, the arid, maguey-lined, pulque-producing plateau covering northeast México State (Cuautitlán, Zumpango, and Otumba districts), the Mezquital and Apan plains of Hidalgo, and much of Puebla and Tlaxcala. This region's pulque estates, whose fermenting, milky bounty was siphoned to Mexico City by rail, were the acme of Porfirian agro-industry, hence, under Calles, targeted in a flagship (but barely studied) land reform. For upwardly mobile plains agraristas, Mexican Catholicism was an identitarian weapon in ejidal politics. A more conservative example comes from Veracruz: here ICAM appealed to indigenous comuneros in the northern Huasteca and southern Isthmus who sought a cultural gateway into Adalberto Tejeda's Liga de Comunidades Agrarias del Estado de Veracruz (LCAEV), thus a way to overpower municipal elites supported by Roman clergy.

Agraristas' need to feel justified was rooted in their Judas status as a despised minority. For that reason, the synthesis of Mexican Catholicism and agrarismo was complicated, vengeful—far darker than revolutionary elites' sunny parables. Indeed, as agrarismo acquired religious overtones, sectarianism toxified village politics. Pérez, quoting chapter and verse (the disciples' pentecostal fellowship), boasted in 1928 that ICAM taught agraristas Christian brotherhood: on ejidos in Puebla and Veracruz, Christianity was practiced with "proper purity and sanctity."[6] The reality was more Cain and Abel, because campesinos learned that religious affiliations could be used as political mobilizers, to excuse rank partisanship, or as a criterion for restricting access to land. Religious commitments could

113

Chapter Four

be visceral, yet to condemn agraristas as bigots is to ignore how hard a road agrarismo was, how often the boot was on the other foot, and how factional village life was. Some Roman clergy staked their authority on damning agrarismo, turning land disputes into theological affairs. Despite often bloody consequences, therefore, agraristas were also conscious dissenters by default. The "campesinos, ejidatarios, [and] natives" of Tehuizotla (Pue.) who switched to ICAM in 1928 explained their defection thus: "Even if the señor cura belongs to the Mexican Catholic and Apostolic Church, we know that his offices in no way differ from those that priests dependent on the Roman papacy used to perform. But being the same, they enjoy the protection of the constituted authorities because they comply with the law of religious worship."[7] These agraristas distinguished between sacramental and institutional Catholicism in a way that allowed revolutionary participation with a clear conscience. Why not make such judgments? Their enemies did.

This chapter explores the entwining of Mexican Catholicism and agrarismo, which was central to ICAM's consolidation and also delivered popular Catholic support for the regime. It does so in two settings, the Mexico basin and Veracruz. For context, however, the chapter first explores the religious implications of callista land policy.

A CITY ON THE HILL? THE EJIDO AS CHRISTIAN CONCEPT

The idea that agrarismo was Christian was not invented under Calles—indeed it was part of Zapatismo. The essential claims derived not only from Sermon-on-the-Mount socialism but also from natural law: just as nature gave peasants ownership of their bodies, it was argued, so it conferred a natural right to enjoy the fruits of labor. Most prominently, perhaps, *tapatío* lawyer and Catholic Zapatista Miguel Mendoza López Schwerdtfeger argued in *¡Tierra Libre!* (1915) that the "*true* right of property" was to one's body and, by extension, the work it performed. Landownership corrupted natural law, allowing parasitical owners to charge rent on others' work. Private property should be abolished, with peasants cultivating nationalized fields and enjoying "the integral product of their labor." Mendoza claimed his "new juridical concept" of work-property was inspired by Catholic theology, namely, Paul's dictum, "He who does not work, should not eat." Mendoza was no marginal figure: he authored the Convention's Agrarian Law and was Obregón's National Agrarian Commission (CNA) secretary.[8]

A kindred, if eclectic, spirit was poblano liberal Catholic, Vicente Lombardo Toledano, who in the 1920s ran CROM's cultural wing, the Grupo Solidario del Movimiento Obrero (GSMO). Through schools and propaganda, Lombardo spread a Christian apology for agrarismo. The revolution was Christian, he said in 1923, a crusade "in the name of the gospels."[9]

That year, he wrote a pamphlet, *El reparto de tierras no se opone a las enseñanzas de Nuestro Señor Jesucristo y de la Santa Madre Iglesia*, whose cover featured a Diego Rivera sketch of a peasant plowing while his wife and baby sat on the ground with a Mauser rifle for protection. The Sacred Heart hovered above this Holy Family, emitting light rays. Besides disarming militant Catholic symbols, the slogan ("Distributing Land to the Poor is Not Contrary to the Teachings of Jesus Christ Our Lord and the Holy Mother Church") was designed to silence curas who preached that agrarismo was theft. A footer ("The Mexican people fought and suffered for ten years hoping to find the Word of Our Lord Jesus Christ") implied that the ejido was gospel truth in action. Inside, Lombardo juxtaposed theological proofs. Leo XIII's workers' encyclical, *Rerum Novarum*, followed Aquinas in stating that property must be "communicated" among the poor. Lombardo then rehearsed the Sermon on the Mount, which—he believed—was the most important event in history. Specifically, Lombardo reproduced verses describing the hungry as righteous ("Ye are the light of the world") and implying that the ejido was Matthew's city on the hill.[10] Next, Lombardo claimed that article 27 revived a primitive Christian weal that the "bourgeois system" had broken. Proof lay in article 27's insistence on property's social function, which echoed the teachings of Saint Ambrose, Milan's fourth-century bishop. Once personal needs were satisfied, Ambrose said, property robbed the commonwealth and should be shared. The ejido was an Ambrosian covenant guaranteeing sustenance for all. Finally, Lombardo rehearsed the natural-law defense of agrarismo. To liberals, private property was sacrosanct, yet this violated workers' ownership of labor. Should property rights be invested in the harvest or the field? Lombardo said the former, to stop the rich from gorging on rents while workers "turned their hands, which God gave them to break free from bondage, into shovels for digging their own graves."[11]

Catholic ideas thus pervaded 1920s agrarismo. The strongest influence, however, was the cooperativist system developed by Friedrich Wilhelm Raiffeisen, mayor of Weyerbusch (1818–1888). Though a Protestant,

Raiffeisen's model of Christian mutualism was adopted widely by Catholics. According to Raiffeisen, parish cooperatives should replace village institutions such as commons that insured peasants against market forces until capitalism stripped them away. Without defenses, peasants were at the market's mercy, underselling crops to speculators or borrowing at usurious rates in bad years. In *Credit Cooperatives* (1866), Raiffeisen proposed that peasants emancipate themselves by forming cooperatives. Banks would advance cheap loans to individuals if their fellow cooperativists pledged their crops as security, each becoming responsible for the others. Eventually, cooperativists could capitalize their own banks. Shared liability was key, Raiffeisen said, because it encouraged moral responsibility and Christian fraternity; this was why parishes were the ideal base for cooperatives. Capitalism's biggest evil was spiritual, its violation of love thy neighbor. Raiffeisenism would allow peasants to grow and rechristianize capitalism.[12]

Given callismo's vaunted secularism, it is remarkable how strong the Christian influence on agrarismo was—albeit with ejidos replacing parishes. This can be seen in the genre that defines callismo: the technical manual. A 1925 pamphlet rehearsed Raiffeisenism's history and reported how Calles, having discovered the system on his European tour, was bringing it to Mexico. Cooperatives advanced peasants' "moral and material good," allowing them to grow "from debility to strength, poverty to independence." The religious aspect was stressed: cooperatives would be Mexico's "soul"; with "faith and constancy," they would "redeem the great Mexican family." A dozen SEP manuals taught how German peasants drove speculators away by creating cooperatives, staking their crops to secure loans, then buying machines or seeds. Mexico must do the same, SEP literature suggested. "Do we mean to go on despoiling our neighbor?" a 1925 tract asked, invoking love-thy-neighbor: usury was attacked in another biblical formulation as "the root of all evil in Mexico." Mexico must find "twelve apostles of cooperation," said another text, as Germany had Hermann Schultz-Delitsch (founder of Catholic workers' banks) and France had Charles Gide (Christian economist and uncle of novelist André Gide).[13]

Mexico had Chihuahuan technocrat Gómez Morín, creator at Calles' behest of the Agricultural Credit Law and National Bank of Agricultural Credit (BNCA), in February and March 1926, respectively. The credit law allowed farmers and ejidatarios to form a Local

Agricultural Credit Society (SLCA)—essentially a revolutionary cooperative—and obtain BNCA loans secured against the value (up to 75 percent) of the SLCA's harvest. This leveraging was based on the idea that work was an asset. Yet the law's *spiritual* purpose was explicit: SLCAs, it said, must promote peasants' "economic and spiritual improvement." Gómez Morín was near-messianic. He told one correspondent that his was the first scheme since slavery to harness the labor of indigenous Mexicans, yet he would lead them *out* of bondage: with God's help, SLCAs would change Mexico as much as human intervention could.[14]

These ideas were inscribed in Calles' flagship Law of Ejidal Patrimony. Published in 1925 and written by another Chihuahuan—León—the law is incorrectly remembered as a homestead decree "privatizing" the ejido. In fact, it was designed to moralize ejidos and boost production by ensuring that *labor* was not expropriated by corrupt bosses. To prevent ejidal commissars from reassigning plots with standing crops, León required that ejido lands be divisible only once, when the ejidal grant was executed. Occupancies, recorded in the Registro Agrario, would be based on *labor*, not property, rights: untilled *parcelas* were forfeit. Clearly Raiffeisenist in spirit, León's law rehearsed the old natural-law argument against accumulation: ejidatarios "owned" parcels as owners of the *work* in them.[15]

The regime thus believed in Catholic-style cooperativism, centralized through the ejido, SLCA, and BNCA. The idea was to encourage peasants and ejidatarios to pool resources and then, unmolested by speculators, to exercise a natural right, "disposing of the means that nature has placed within reach to work for a future for themselves and their families." Through Christian cooperation, peasants would become "modern agriculturalists," what Calles called the "middle peasant."[16]

From mid-1925, ICAM began glossing agrarismo. Seemingly it was the arrival of peasant delegations at Corpus Christi that summer which turned Pérez's attention to the pueblos. After one visit from Coatepec (D.F.), Pérez published a flier consoling his "brother peasants," who had quarreled with Roman clergy over fees and been denied Mass. Agraristas had "a right to practice their religion" and if it were not respected, they should switch churches and call themselves Mexican Catholics.[17] Subsequent propaganda was attuned to León's missives. An August pastoral, "To Our Beloved Peasants," denounced Roman curas' practice of excommunicating agraristas and promised that God was on

117

agraristas' side, because He condemned "all privileges and abuses with which the strongest despoil His weakest creatures." Pérez then promised that ICAM would work "for the good of all who cultivate the fields in order to achieve a better economic position, enjoying the integral product of their labor and making use of that right which God Our Lord gave to all creation, to live from and enjoy the blessed earth."[18] In summer 1926, as the religious conflict heated up, *Restauración* started carrying Lombardo's tract.[19] Finally, a September pastoral, "Agrarianism in Mexico," reported that ICAM clergy were touring ejidos and salving agraristas' consciences. Eminent philosophers—"Bentham, Montesquieu, Hobbes"—held that property was a limited right, just as theologians agreed that "God's plan" was for property to serve all. Ejidos created "a superior social state," Pérez noted (another of León's phrases) in which all "freely exercise their rights and enjoy the product of their honest labor."[20] León returned the favor. "We have met *curas agraristas*," he speechified in August, "who truly practice Christ's doctrines among their flocks." These sons of Motolinia and Morelos shared the peasantry's sufferings—but were never found in bishops' palaces.[21]

For their part, Roman Catholics were incensed at attempts to inoculate agrarismo with Christianity. Miguel Palomar y Vizcarra—the lawyer who pioneered Raiffeisenism in Mexico—was aghast at Calles's belated "discovery" of Christian principles. "The virus of sectarianism has taken the name of agrarismo," a bishop wrote, and crept through rural Mexico "like poison."[22] But how did campesinos respond?

ICAM ON THE PLAINS

Considering how revolutionaries demonized pulque, the destruction of Mexico's pulque estates is nowadays forgotten. Supposedly to invigorate the national diet and economy, however, but also from political rancor toward the "pulque aristocracy," revolutionaries resolved to tax and ejidalize pulque out of existence. That meant attacking the three hundred or so plantations that shipped eight hundred thousand pints of fermented cactus milk to Mexico City a day. Obregón, instinctively protective of haciendas, wanted to repurpose the plantations and make nonalcoholic maguey derivatives such as paper or, fantastically, gasoline. Calles, more prosaically, wanted to replace the estates with barley-growing ejidos servicing a "modern" agro-industry: brewing. While spiraling duties shuttered the *pulquerías*, therefore, plains estates—wilting maguey crowns, mile upon serried mile—would be broken into moated parcels for intensive farming. Ejidos, not haciendas, crystalline beer, not stagnant "Indian" pulque, were the future. Of course, it was never going to happen like that. Only magueys could create sap from windswept crust; without irrigation, ejido barley would turn to parchment. Nonetheless, ejidalization of the *zona pulquera* was pushed through, first in Tlaxcala (1919–1923), then Hidalgo (1921–1927) and México (1926–1930). Over thirty dotaciones were finalized by 1929, halving pulque production relative to 1920 and stimulating barley cultivation. Calles was thus the main architect of a sector-wide reform long antedating Cárdenas's collectivizations.[23]

Pueblos northeast of Mexico City were thus politically significant as protagonists in callismo's garden fantasy. Perhaps inevitably, this implicated them in Calles's religious project. Possibly with official prompting: CROM leafleted plains estates in 1925, *hacendados* reported; cromista José Ortiz Petricioli, Morones's biographer, ran the mexiquense Local Agrarian Commission (CLA) from 1926 to 1930, an important post.[24] Still, the agrarian process also reflected local conflicts relating to class, ethnicity, and religion that were as unyielding as *altiplano* soil. As a survey of ejido files from the ex-districts of Apan (Hgo.), Cuautitlán, Zumpango, and Otumba (Méx.) shows, an association between ICAM and agrarismo developed. Usually this happened where semi-independent peasants were trying to prize open an entrenched pulque-producing system in the teeth of hacienda and clerical opposition. Intervillage rivalries played a part, more so the ambitions of sharecroppers, pastoralists, and *rancheros* who identified with callista institutions and portrayed themselves as politically meritorious. Widespread mobilization could be seen in that two-thirds of Mexico's ejido-based SLCAs were located in this region. Such cooperatives—Xometla's "Cosecheros de Trigo" (Otumba), Coyotepec's "Benito Juárez" (Cuautitlán), Almoloya's "Sociedad de Pequeños Agricultores" (Apan)—obtained ejidos and BNCA loans.[25] Rather than effect some Weberian transformation to capitalism in the cuenca, however, ejidos became mired in factional, often sectarian, politics. As ejidatarios put body and soul on the line, they turned to ICAM as a religious prop. If religion was instrumentalized, this was a *struggle*, not a rosary afternoon. To win land and municipal power, agraristas needed state backing, guns, and godly fighting-talk, not pious sentiment. Across the plains, then, agrarian disputes broke out, with different groups fighting under rival Catholic colors.

The pattern was set in maguey-growing Coatepec (D.F.), near Tepeyac, in July 1925. Pérez appeared here on San Miguel's day and celebrated a Mass that led to a pitched battle in the square and the stabbing of the official who authorized the ceremony. Mexico City reporters described another senseless outrage, yet this time Pérez exercised his right of reply, insisting that Coatepec's better citizens (principales vecinos) hired him because of the Roman clergy's rack-renting. A Gobernación spy who spoke with parish mayordomos confirmed that, effectively, a Basilica of Guadalupe priest demanded fifty-five pesos to say Mass, so mayordomos hired Pérez for half. The feast then unfolded "with the greatest order," until attendees and "contrary elements" clashed outside. The spy realized that the real purpose of the Mass was to consecrate Coatepec's agrarian faction. Indeed, Pérez's key supporters were the Tinoco clan, leaders of a pugnacious agrarista movement. *Barrio alto* (uptown) agrarian bosses—merchants like thirty-one-year-old Juan Tinoco—were at that moment pushing for additional ejido lands for Coatepec. The quarrel between Basilica clergy and Coatepec's mayordomos gave them a chance to perpetrate a church coup. The Tinocos told Gobernación's spy "of all the abuses committed by priests from La Villa, which is why they resorted to schismatics." They also cried "that everything in the church belongs to them, and they would not let any Romanist priest occupy the church again." True to their word, the Tinocos guarded Pérez and posted armed sentries on the roads to prevent Roman curas returning. Agrarista gunmen then circled the town, riding on the running boards of a car like Bonnie and Clyde. Their foes claimed that the clan coveted fiesta takings, yet the main purpose of defecting to ICAM was to legitimize the ejido by association with the santo.[26]

These realignments were common. In Xalostoc farther north—the village sat on grassy plains below nopal-strewn hills—an ejidal petition was lodged in 1920 because inhabitants wanted land from El Risco estate to grow barley. Yet the petition languished until 1925, when Primo Sánchez took over the agrarian committee. The Cristero War saw two developments. First, Xalostoc switched to Mexican Catholicism in June 1927, when ICAM priests celebrated the patron, San Pedro. Second, Xalostoc's ejidal petition was approved, first provisionally, with 238 families taking possession of 238 hectares in March 1927, then definitively in December 1928. Once again, this was a multistranded convergence with callismo: agraristas embraced not just barley-growing and ejidos but ICAM. Once more, the leaders were upwardly mobile ranchero types who used official means to consolidate their control over land. The agrarian census is the best document: it shows that nearly all would-be ejidatarios owned donkeys and cows, sometimes herds of them, plus oxen, horses, goats, sheep—even stud bulls. Agrarista chiefs, Sánchez included, had more.[27]

Farther north again, there was violence in Ixtacalco (Méx.). The case was tense, thanks to the enmity of dog-in-the-manger estate owners and agraristas whose prospects depended on estate lands. But local hacendados would not rent them out, the CNA noted in 1926; landowners also thwarted Ixtacalco's ejidal petition by subdividing their estates. Agraristas, led by Macario Pallares, protested that the fractions were a latifundium not agro-industrial units exempt from expropriation. To no avail: Calles, deceived by "anti-agrarista" lawyers, denied Ixtacalco's petition in August.[28] The Cristero War gave agraristas opportunity to close ranks with the regime by supporting its religious policy. In August 1927, agraristas asked "Metropolitan Archbishop Pérez" to send a priest to celebrate the "sacred Catholic religion," that is, a Catholicism purged of "foreign" elements. Henceforth there was a twin struggle to control Ixtacalco's church and win ejidos. "We of the Mexican Church," Pallares said, "more rightfully because we are Mexicans," should have the church. Roman Catholics led by Romualdo Contreras, a cacique who ran the pulque trade, violently disagreed. "A certain hatred exists between them and us," Pallares told the government, because "we are busily establishing the Mexican Catholic Religion in our pueblo." He himself wanted to end "the obscurantism in which Roman religion has kept us" and eventually donned a cassock.[29] Pallares's band captured Ixtacalco's church in December 1927; Easter services (April 1928) coincided with the launch of another ejidal petition. Yet this prompted a revenge attack in which assailants defaced church walls, smashed the altar, and beat up the fiscal. Undeterred, agraristas continued to assert their revolutionary-Catholic identity. Their "sacred right" to land was being violated, they wrote in 1929: Contreras and their ex-cura "invade even the liberty of our consciences, imposing on us the Roman Catholic creed, which we detest with all our heart as the instrument of landowners and their allies to keep us in obscurantism, poverty, and slavery." This was why, "making use of our liberty of conscience," they joined ICAM, "incorporating our *templo* into that church at the start of the Roman clergy's rebellion against the institutions of our fatherland." If the land petition still lagged in 1931, Ixtacalco's agraristas had a church.[30] The point, either way, is that religious change helped to turn agrarista guilt into self-righteousness.

The case of Tepejí, on Hidalgo's Mezquital, was especially suggestive of the material and religious pressures agraristas felt. Alleging an 1893 despoilment, Tepejí received a three-thousand-hectare ejido in 1924. In protest, the Caltengo estate's British owner fired coal furnaces on ejidal land, protested through his legation, and claimed agraristas grazed illegally and starved his cattle of water. US-owned estates leveled similar claims. Here the contest acquired strong religious connotations. Agraristas remembered how Caltengo employees abducted their leader, Guadalupe Juárez "El Judas," in 1923, "cruelly whipped him," threw him in jail, and razed ejidatarios' huts. Early in 1925, someone let estate cattle overrun the ejido, ruining the corn: by summer, agraristas were starving. Were that not bad enough, their cura, Simón Gómez, evoked biblical famines. As one hacendado told the archbishop of Mexico: "in the pulpit [Gómez] strives to make the faithful aware that in His Commandments God orders us not to steal, and that agrarismo is simply theft authorized by the government." Agraristas hated him, believing "that the Father was not there to discharge his sacerdotal mission but to help the landlords." The landowner feared agraristas might bushwhack Gómez ("I know those people"). With some license, this reads like a bleak, composite parable with famines, floggings, fat and lean cows, and a Judas. It is unsurprising that agraristas, watching estate cattle chew their corn, should have embraced ICAM in 1925, though disappointingly the land file has no details. In 1927, Tepejí adopted the ejidal-patrimony regime and donated lands for the construction of Calles's Requena dam.[31]

Eastward—on Apan's and Almoloya's cold, dry plains—more agraristas sought spiritual insurance. Here were Mexico's biggest pulque estates, the ones filmed by Sergei Eisenstein, hence Apan's 1921 petition alleging that vecinos possessed "not one furrow of land" to farm. Yet Obregón would not help because a French huckster, Elie Delafond, was promising to make sugar and gasoline from maguey. The regime also feared that agraristas would milk the maguey dry, "then abandon their lands, as has happened in other cases." Moreover, Apan retained a townsite for shacks and corn patches. Let that be enough, the CNA said, because the *indígenas* were peons, not farmers. Apan's agrarista bosses, the CNA reported, were "ambitious and troublesome men" who wanted to "seize the *magueyeras* and become pulque merchants." Calles offered more encouragement. When Apan's pulque estates refused to renew agraristas' sharecropping contracts, agraristas formed a SCLA (the Sociedad de Pequeños Agricultores) and received BNCA loans in 1926. Calles denied Apan's ejido petition that March because petitioners could use BNCA money to buy land, which they did. Results impressed the government: "municipal estates" now grew barley under BNCA auspices, León boasted; speculators—who once bought peasants' harvests cheaply for Army forage—had been chased out. Now the BNCA commercialized peasant grains and soon agraristas would have threshers. León hoped that the co-op would soon self-capitalize.[32]

Religious innovation accompanied agrarian change. In their 1921 petition, agraristas likened themselves to Israelites enslaved by pulque barons and friars "who, in the confessional, threaten all who solicit lands with hell." It was therefore a godsend when "revolutionaries fleeing persecution in other states" reached Apan in March 1925. The revolution they preached, one agrarista wrote, was "a matter of salvation."[33] By 1926, Mexican clergy were active in Hidalgo. One priest reported that a "compact crowd" came to Mass in Apan that December; "our church has not come to modify the sacred dogmas of the immaculate religion of He who was crucified on Golgotha's hills," he sermonized.[34] Apan's agrarians exhibited theological sophistication. When *El Diario de Apam* endorsed their excommunication in 1927, agraristas responded, recalling how "Jesus, barefoot and hungry, preached fraternity [and] love thy neighbor." Rome had turned His "beautiful program" into "criminal idleness" and Communion into "fool's gold solemnity." What right had curas to "annihilate peons' consciences" on landlords' behalf? The letter's ending, a virtual ICAM-agrarista creed, is worth quoting at length.

> We are Catholics, because we believe in God; but we cannot be Romanist, because we are Mexicans before we are Romans, pure Mexicans, of the clearest Indian blood, and this is why we [reject] a Catholic adulator like the Pope in Rome, who does not know our situation or understand our needs or our poverty, unless told by a pack of foreign clerics—*gachupines*,

gabachos, Italians—who come to Mexico only to traffic in our ignorance and pain. We are *católico-mexicanos*. There is no fundamental difference between the Mexican Catholic Church and the Roman Catholic Church; if priests of the latter attack the former with naked fury, this is because they fear that all Mexicans, in supreme fulfillment of their duty, will abandon the so-called Pope once and for all, to join those who are beginning this reformation in our country, which does not prejudice belief in God but, on the contrary, benefits the Mexican family ... Let all Mexicans stand beside the Mexican Church, for the collective good of our nation, and beside the constituted government, to defend the integrity of our *raza* and our institutions ... Far beyond, in the other life, we will make our account to God, not through the offices of a foreigner, but a person who knows and comprehends our necessities and agonies, a Mexican! Brother agraristas, open your eyes. If you doubt our vision of Heaven, come to Almoloya, where we are excommunicated by the Romanists because priests of the Mexican Church have resumed the cult in our church; and you will see that our granaries are full, our cooperative has funds, and our families are happy while we work our fields, scythes in hand, souls at peace, hearts content.[35]

Agraristas in Ajoloapan (on the Hidalgo-México border), also battled clergy, landowners, and municipal authorities. Here it was realized that the suspension of public worship allowed religious dependencies (vicarías) to become independent of parish seats by registering a Mexican priest—thus they could escape Roman curas' supervision and freely solicit land. Soon enough, Ajoloapan's agrarista leader, thirty-nine-year-old Antonio Hernández, claimed the church for ICAM. Authorities in the parish and municipal cabecera, Hueypoxtla, tried to block the move, which went ahead after Hernández wired Gobernación for a permit. Alfonso María Arías duly celebrated the patronal feast in December. Pious women barred the church doors and there was fighting, yet the conflict was really a turf war between Ajoloapan and Hueypoxtla: Arías stated that Hueypoxtla's municipal president himself "told the señoras to resist, so as not to give room to schismatical priests." Another bone of contention was agraristas' attempt to introduce religious conformity so as to restrict access to ejido land. As distraught Roman Catholics wrote, Ajoloapan's Mexican Catholic agraristas "deprive us of our ejidos if we do not second their ideas." Father Arías also shunned them at the altar "because he says we are not his supporters." Once again, religious affiliation governed access to land. Henceforth, "the schismatical party" of agraristas and their opponents did battle each summer to decide who might carry the Virgin through the streets for the Assumption. The symbols were threadbare—a Cristo with missing limbs, a Virgin in tatty robes; yet the material consequences of their possession were very significant.[36]

Mexican Catholic hegemonies were not unusual: Coyotepec (Méx.), near Cuautitlán, provides another example. Coyotepec had one land dispute with Xalpa, an ex-Jesuit hacienda whose lands it solicited in 1917. Villagers, many of them ex–estate sharecroppers, received an ejido in 1923. Yet this dispute was considered trivial compared with Coyotepec's sixteenth-century feud with next-door Teoloyucan: the pueblos fought "bloody battles" every spring, "epoch of the green grass." Last, there were internecine disputes between Coyotepec's agrarista and anti-agrarista factions. Under Calles, agraristas kickstarted another ejidal petition for Teoloyucan land, formed the "Benito Juárez" SLCA (receiving a twelve-thousand-peso BNCA loan), and purged "antis" from village institutions. With intermittent success, anti-agraristas tried to stop them. In a ten-year saga of peasant violence, Mexican Catholicism became the agrarista religion. An Easter 1926 incident inscribed this identity in blood. That day, anti-agraristas led soldiers into Coyotepec, promising to "put an end to half-naked, sandal-wearing agrarian bandits." Some agraristas were roped behind horses and dragged through cactus patches: the torture was repeated "without compassion," victims' relatives wrote, though their families wept, "as when the Mother of *Jesucristi* cried for Him." Though agrarista leader Tiburcio Rodríguez was jailed for the "crime" of procuring the pueblo's "daily bread," his comrades swore that anti-agraristas ("bloodthirsty vipers") would pay.[37]

Perhaps Coyotepec's priest drafted this agrarista Passion because that August he broke with Rome and joined ICAM. Religious change was thus managed by an incumbent priest, which solidified it: according to the mayor, the "vast majority" of vecinos became "adepts of the Mexican Catholic cult." Political changes were dramatic, too. In 1927, agraristas led by Hilario Castillo wrested back control of the ejido. They then launched the new petition, supposedly based on Coyotepec's primordial titles, for lands "stolen" by Teoloyucan. Agraristas claimed to see Coyotepec's old boundary stones standing in Teoloyucan fields. The CLA urged caution. Yet the decision to solicit land "possessed as ejidos by Teoloyucan" was endorsed in a rowdy May 1929 plebiscite.[38]

As in Ajoloapan, efforts were made to impose religious conformity and silence anti-agraristas, who were encouraged by the arreglos. Some antis urged Gobernación to remove ICAM's priest, Juan Cervantes, saying he was a policeman in a cassock. Others said it was intolerable that Coyotepec's Roman Catholics must hear Mass secretly in Teoloyucan.[39] Protests prompted a clampdown. That November, seven hundred agraristas denounced Roman curas as "lackeys" of landlordism. They would have "no friars who leave us in ignorance" but "friar[s] of the Mexican Religion." Mexican Catholics also enforced church attendance. Those caught hearing Mass in Teoloyucan were tied up, fined, or jailed. Agraristas would "sustain the schism at any cost," prisoners wrote, invading the "sacred ambit of conscience . . . to make us believe, that the schism is the true religion." Sectarian land-grabbing was rampant: "The *reparto de ejidos* is a powerful weapon for winning adepts for the schism. The lands given to us Roman Catholics before are now taken from us, and those of us with plots have an impossible choice: 'either you're a schismatic with land, or a Roman Catholic without.'"[40]

The case was discussed in upper circles. Mexico's apostolic delegate, Leopoldo Ruiz y Flores, demanded that the governor end this "abnormal" situation, in which people were despoiled "because they do not want to become schismatics." The archbishop of Mexico demanded Coyotepec's church, saying "schismatics" had abandoned it. According to Coyotepec's mayor, two ICAM priests, Francisco Fernández and José Lorenzo Sánchez, ministered in the 1930s. The government declined to evict them, though it reprimanded Fernández for loaning out a religious icon in 1931. In 1934, there was a renewal of hostilities with "priests of Vaticanism": Sánchez was roughed up by anti-agraristas crying "¡Viva Cristo Rey!"; Fernández's car was sprayed with bullets. Coyotepec's Mexican Catholics were defiant. That March, three hundred reported that "to date, we have been able to conserve the church of our pueblo in the power of the Mexican Orthodox Church." "In this way," Hilario Castillo wrote, "we will defanaticize our villages, breaking Roman friars' iniquitous monopoly." Thus the file ends, but not, one suspects, the vendettas over grass, territory, and dogma.[41]

Xometla (Méx.)—in Acolman, near the Teotihuacán pyramids—saw even worse sectarianism.[42] Here, beside the Mexico-Puebla railway, good communications and land allowed campesinos to think of sending milk and grain to Mexico City, "each vecino . . . building his house on a perfectly cultivated plot." These rancheros could also ship pulque. "Good quality maguey" abounded, the CLA wrote: "the zona pulquera that reaches to Apan's plains begins here, the industry providing inhabitants with another livelihood." Yet the desire for bigger herds and magueyeras brought Xometla into conflict with Spanish-owned estates—San Antonio Acolman, Nextlalpan, Santa Catarina—and local political/ecclesiastical elites. As before, it was better-off peasants—the wealthiest families on Xometla's agrarian census—that ran the ejido and Mexican Catholic movement, the Juárez clan especially (brothers Ismael, Juan, Marcos, Nicolás, and Catalino). Their hatred of Spanish foremen and Acolman's mayor was intense, and it worsened as their land petition received provisional (1921) then definitive resolution (1924). Agraristas complained of Spanish overseers' abuses: in 1923, one used his lariat to beat children tending ejidal cattle; in 1924, Santa Catarina's "gachupin administrator" fired on ejidatarios and had two unfortunates flogged for haymaking.[43]

Once more, the struggle was between village and estate producers: hacendados claimed their properties were small "agro-industrial units" whose alfalfa fields and modern milking installations exempted them from expropriation. The CNA found that in reality Spanish estates hogged Xometla's "magnificent pastures." Rather than farm them, they sharecropped them, concealing a monopoly by fractioning their estates and hiding behind the Spanish legation. The Obregón government backed agraristas on paper, expanding the provisional land grant in 1924. Yet Obregón did nothing when one estate, Santa Catarina, planted magueys to defer agraristas' occupation. Federal troops even watched as hacienda gunmen carted off fenceposts marking out Xometla's ejido.[44]

Frustrated villagers thus welcomed callismo. With CNA supervision, agraristas took possession of their ejido in February 1925. The *procurador de pueblos* found that the *reparto* was working, though violence still occurred: someone tried torching ejidal crops and an estate employee nearly brained Juan Juárez with a shovel, but ejidatarios now hit back, organizing patrols and posting lookouts in the church tower. In November, agraristas traded blows with soldiers who came looking for a fight. Four agraristas were carried off and clubbed with rifle butts in Acolman's jail, but increasingly it was eye for an eye. The decision to join ICAM in August 1927 reflects this context. That month, forty-four agraristas led by the Juárezes marched into Acolman and compelled the municipal clerk to register "*presbítero* Camerino García Mota, of the venerable Mexican Catholic Church clergy," as Xometla's cura. For the next two years, only Mexican cult was celebrated in the pueblo.[45]

The 1929 arreglos brought more violence. Agraristas at once denounced Roman priests for celebrating illegal acts of cult in Xometla; they wanted them out, arguing that "we represent the majority of the vecinos . . . and are firmly resolved to continue belonging to the Mexican Catholic Church." The Juárezes, writing as "members of the 'Cosecheros de Trigo'" SCLA, even asked the BNCA to uphold their religious claim, stating that

> there has been lacking neither religious worship ministered by members of the Mexican Orthodox and Catholic Church nor genuine approval of the whole *vecindario* . . . because all such acts are in Spanish, a language we more or less understand; and because in this cult all simony is prohibited, which is to say, there is a ban on the tariffs established by notorious Romanism, whose clergy is formed by birds of prey of evil portent, and which long exploited our pueblo.

They remembered the cristero years as a time of ejidos, credit, and free religion.[46]

The showdown came in August 1929 when Acolman's hated municipal president, Joaquín Lozano ("a rich young man . . . despotic and tyrannical") came to Xometla with police chief Luis Amaya and others to install a Roman, cura, Luis Méndez. According to Nicolás Juárez, a "fracas" between the pueblos ensued when Lozano forced the church doors and "Mexican Church partisans" confronted him, citing majority wishes and Portes Gil's decision to protect registered clergy. The Juárezes alleged that Lozano lashed out with a whip and pulled a gun. Lozano stated that someone rang the bells and he was assailed by forty people, men and women, "led by brothers Marcos, Catalino, Nicolás, and Juan Juárez . . . armed with carbines, pistols, sticks, iron bars, and stones." The mob seized Lozano and trounced him, breaking his nose with a rock while apparently insulting Portes Gil "for allowing the resumption of Roman worship." Police chief Amaya, riding to the rescue, turned back when a bullet winged his horse. Militiaman Alberto Romero was shot from the saddle. He and Lozano were then dragged to the station, to be sent captive to Mexico City. In a veritable *3:10 to Yuma* sequence, the Juárezes who put them on the train held guns to their heads and threatened to shoot if the cacique's henchmen fired.[47]

This battle—an outburst of agrarian, political, ethnic, and religious tension—was suggestive of the emotional and religious wellsprings of popular callismo. And of the high stakes: after the shootout, indeed, Lozano called in the army and six Juárez men were jailed along with three women and Xometla's *comisario del pueblo*. There were reports that Lozano sexually abused the wives and sisters of agraristas. Thus, fears that Acolman's Hispanic elite had lost control of its *sujeto* were calmed by displays of sexual, military, agrarian, and religious dominance.[48] Unusually, however, Portes Gil upheld ICAM's occupancy of Xometla. In August came an *amparo* barring the Roman priest from ministering; at this, jubilant agraristas drove around Acolman in a truck, whooping it up and insulting the mayor. From the Texcoco and Belém jails, the Juárezes demanded their freedom, alleging that they were victims of a "fanatical" ayuntamiento. "Reactionaries" were exacting "revenges, calumnies, and intrigues against Ejidatarios . . . because we belong to the Mexican Catholic Church." Such measures included removing the church bells, requiring written retractions, and preventing the registration of Mexican priests. María Galindo, a self-described "señorita who has fought for liberty," prayed to the Sacred Heart and asked Pérez to visit the incarcerated Juárez brothers. The Juárezes asked the patriarch to stand their bail. That November, finally, Portes Gil released the brothers while putting Xometla's feuding Catholics on the spot by ordering that the church be removed from public use. This brought rare unity. At Easter 1930 both factions met, with Roman Catholics agreeing to share the church with "persons who from ignorance or conviction embrace the Mexican religion." A truce was agreed, though officials were "almost certain" bloodshed would follow.[49]

In the end, Mexican Catholics regained control after a 1931 appeal by the patriarch and a government investigation which found that Romanists were a disengaged majority and Mexican Catholics a substantial, militant minority. The Juárezes' leadership of Xometla's

"Pro-Education Committee" saw them regain control of the church annexes for a school. In 1934, the brothers resumed their petitions for Mexican priests, reflecting "the aspirations of this community." A federal agent who convened a plebiscite found that "only a numerous group of so-called schismatics" attended. One wonders what methods were employed to get this result. Still, in March 1936, Eduardo Dávila—"Head of the National Orthodox Mexican Catholic and Apostolic Church"—told Cárdenas: "On this day I have taken custody of the church . . . all in the pueblo being liberal and adepts of the Mexican Church."[50]

ICAM IN VERACRUZ

If ICAM gave a religious edge to land reform near Mexico City, in Veracruz, it was associated with Adalberto Tejeda's state-level agrarian radicalism (1920–1924, 1928–1932) and, paradoxically, conservative-indigenous politics. Thus its appeal to Tepehua, Totonaco, and Nahua peasants in Veracruz's northern Huasteca and southern isthmus, and its absence from the class-based, coffee-estate agrarismo of central Veracruz. The association was strongest, too, during later *tejedismo*, when Tejeda, resigned from Gobernación, contested the conciliatory religious policies of presidents Portes Gil and Ortiz Rubio. ICAM thus reflected Veracruz's ethnic-agrarian specificity; it was not just an autocratic attempt to perpetuate callismo on the Gulf (the standard view).[51] Indeed, Tejeda wanted a peasant movement free of federal control, thus devised a strategy that relied on state-level bureaucracy, municipal elites, and organized campesinos. To break Mexico City's stranglehold over ejidal grants, Tejeda relied on state laws authorizing municipalities to lease their public lands. By recategorizing lands as "public" and drafting forced tenancy laws (1926, 1930, 1931), Tejeda gave 495,000 hectares of land to 70,000 campesinos. Peasants were the heart of his "ejidal state," but had to defend it electorally and with guns. Thus Tejeda organized his Liga de Comunidades Agrarias del Estado de Veracruz (LCAEV) in 1923. A key strategy was for LCAEV to contest municipal elections: victories ensured that municipios' powers as land surveyors and appeal courts were at peasants' service. From 1929, Mexican Church coups consecrated municipal captures and underscored revolutionary dominance on the religious plane.

The LCAEV-ICAM link seems counterintuitive, nonetheless, given LCAEV's erstwhile affiliation to the Liga Nacional Campesina

(LNC), a leftist body dominated by firebrands like Tampico oil worker Úrsulo Galván. Thus we must note that in June 1929, Mexico's communists cut ties with Veracruz agraristas following Tejeda's decision to defend Portes Gil's "bourgeois" regime against Gonzalo Escobar's spring mutiny. In any case, LCAEV was a mosaic. In central Veracruz, with its plantocracy and dense population, class-based politics predominated. Elsewhere, LCAEV mobilized indigenous groups characterized by geographical isolation, weak economic integration, and ethnic ties. As recent historians note, Tejeda succeeded because LCAEV was able to work through bureaucratic and classist, or traditional-ethnic (including religious) structures, integrating incompatible peasantries.[52]

In indigenous zones, people wanted communal agrarismo. Rather than receive polygons of land, then assign ejidatarios fixed plots therein, it was hoped that ejidos would restore communal access to land. Communalist practice was usual until the nineteenth-century liberal reparto, when peasants had roaming rights over large common tracts. Such mobility was imperative in Veracruz's piedmont and southern lowlands, where slash-and-burn cultivation quickly exhausted the soil, where tropical vegetation quickly reclaimed farm clearings, and peasant crops (corn, coffee) thrived at different altitudes, requiring peasants to migrate between noncontiguous plots. Communal practices were syncretized in the liberal privatizations of 1880s Veracruz, in which many pueblos opted for a figure called the *condueñazgo*; that is, a regime in which commons were divided into lots that were then subdivided among groups of indigenous shareholders (condueños). As joint-stock companies, pueblos assimilated liberal law while keeping communal access within lots. Condueñazgos also perpetuated patriarchal authority, with lot chiefs dominating political-religious posts in perpetuity.[53]

Indigenous agrarismo in Veracruz actualized these principles. For instance, LNC accepted that ejidos could encompass diverse property regimes, either on a communalist or parcelary basis. Many southerly agraristas were, in fact, *comunalistas*. That is, they lodged ejidal petitions for a restitution (restitución) as opposed to the standard gift (dotación), while interpreting this to mean restitution of communal practice as well as territory. Comunalistas thus waged war on two fronts: first with municipal, mestizo elites opposed to agrarismo; second, with agraristas who accepted federal-style, individuated ejidos. Veracruz peasants thus bifurcated into comunalistas who worked through LCAEV, town councils, and Tejeda's bureaucracy; and a rival, younger, "agrarista" strand that sought patronage from Mexico City's Agrarian Department and did not care about communal practices. In this context, ICAM became a cultural signifier of communalist ascendancy. In some places, as in 1930s Soteapan, comunalista hegemony was shown in revivals of Carnival, the old maize festival; elsewhere, in the *volador* dance—a kind of aeronautical Totonac maypoling. In other places, ICAM provided festive cover for a communal order. Thus in the Nahua village of Pajapan, for instance, which registered an ICAM priest in 1927 as it cranked up an ejidal petition under the lot system. Thus in southerly, LCAEV-run municipios—Acayucan, the Tuxtlas, Chinameca—and in northern Veracruz, in the Tepehuas' adoptive homeland.[54]

The association of ICAM with LCAEV politics became clear in violent clashes occurring in summer 1929 over both the arreglos (Roman clergy resumed public worship in Veracruz on 1 August) and the rancorous municipal elections held in September. Coming weeks apart, these statewide tremors inevitably merged. So ugly did the election become that Tejeda used emergency powers to depose forty-one hostile municipal regimes and directly appoint civil juntas (juntas de administración civil). This was autocratic, yet municipalities were key to his agrarian reform. Given Tejeda's support for ICAM, moreover, and Portes Gil's desire to normalize relations with Rome, the arreglos complicated an already tense renovation of local powers. Indeed, there were fears that Portes Gil might hobble Tejeda's LCAEV by pushing candidates backed by the newly founded PNR and its local bagman, landlord's friend, Arturo Campillo Seyde. Priests' registrations were symbolically important: appointing a priest underscored LCAEV hegemony, hence the likelihood of a quick land reform.[55]

A good southern example was tobacco-growing San Andrés Tuxtla. In the 1920s-1930s, San Andrés was run by the "Partido Rojo Sanandrescano," founded by revolutionary veterans loyal to cacique Manuel Azamar and later afiliated to Tejeda's LCAEV. In 1922, party militants petitioned for restitución of commons dissolved in 1884. Though this petition failed—San Andrés, once part of Cortés's marquisate, had no primordial titles—a dotación bid yielded seventeen ejidos by 1932, all marked out on municipal lands, thirteen of them favoring Nahuatl-speaking communities. Thanks were due to cacique Azamar, who moonlit as CLA boss and San Andrés's mayor (1922–1924,

1930–1932). As such, he both approved and enacted ejidal petitions on municipal lands, even if he sometimes angered agraristas by favoring old comrades-at-arms or commercial growers. Despite his abuses, tejedismo clearly inclined to Nahua wishes. ICAM, for its part, came to symbolize Tejeda's independence of Portes Gil and this agrarista ascendancy. This was shown after the arreglos, in July 1929, when two priests, one Mexican (Adolfo Briones) and one Roman (Manuel Carreiro), attempted to register. According to Carreiro, mayor Juan Jacobo Torres, with police and agraristas, violently installed "schismatic priests" on 2 August, the day public worship resumed. Torres invoked Tejeda's "direct instructions" to prefer curas who complied with the Calles Law; Rome's rebellion "dirtied the heavens," he said. Violence then erupted as Roman Catholics roamed the streets, threatening to lynch Torres. Briones, surprised mid-Mass, was saved by "armed agraristas" when a mob stormed his church. LCAEV thus had a partisan association with ICAM. After the incident, Briones "obtained a permit to arm partisans of the Mexican Catholic Church," surely agraristas. The civil administration chief stated that Briones's supporters were, in fact, "a numerous group of perfectly armed and munitioned campesinos." There was more violence in August when Briones went visiting, leaving his churches unattended. In days, federal agents were "invit[ing] schismatic priests to leave the churches." Then, just as quickly, "schismatics" were again found officiating to agraristas.[56]

Mexican Catholic cult thus finessed LCAEV's triple lock (religious, agrarian, and political) on municipal power. In Catemaco, a sister pueblo in Los Tuxtlas, there was a similar attempt to consolidate political, religious, and agrarian power. The lands here, declared national property in 1833, were rolled into a large estate administered by Lucas Alamán until Catemaco, having no colonial titles, began buying land back in 1837. An 1856 purchase of lands used by its *cofradía*, named after the Virgen del Carmen, completed the recomposition. Yet liberals undid these efforts in 1860, transferring ownership of all the pueblo's lands to the municipio of Catemaco. Indígenas, henceforth at the mercy of the municipal elite, were left landless but for a few paddocks after the liberal reparto of 1888–1890. Hence Catemaco's ejidal petition of 1921, which saw its agrarian committee and Sindicato de Obreros y Campesinos wage a long battle with the municipal government and federal agrarian commissions. The municipio settled colonists in Catemaco to pad out the agrarian census with supporters; Mexico City "lost" Catemaco's ejidal petition. But then, in 1928, the Sindicato relaunched its petition, allied with new mayor Rafael Pérez Vidal, and invited ICAM in, as we saw in chapter 3. The way was clear for a strong expression of support by Tejeda. Indeed, with Tejeda's support the CLA gave Catemaco a provisional dotación of 2,530 hectares in December 1929. Conservative elements retook the municipio in the 1930s, but at least Nahua agraristas had their land.[57]

What may look like religious thuggery, therefore, or contrarian anticlericalism to show that Tejeda followed his own drum, was tied to sensitive ethnic equilibria and historic agrarian processes. We find the same combination of religion, *comunalismo*, and tejedismo in the swamp-filled, lowland municipios of the Coatzacoalcos delta, such as Acayucan and Chinameca. These mixed (Nahua and Popoluca) pueblos originally migrated upstream from Veracruz's coastal plains in the colonial period to avoid Spanish cattle and plagues. Inland they adapted, running feral (cimarrón) cattle and torching hillside slopes to grow corn. Over time, they became riverports in the trans-isthmian trade, sending cattle by barge to Veracruz, thence to the slaughterhouses of Puebla and Mexico City. As agrarian communities, their lack of definition defined them. *Fundos legales* were never formalized and estate cattle trespassed freely: the last hoofprint of a Spanish cow showed where the range ended. Thus, port pueblos with Náhuatl-speaking peasantries doubling as muleteers and bargees skirmished with coastal ranges. Agrarian violence between estates and "squatters" was perennial but diffuse.[58]

Acayucan's antagonist, the Cuatotolapan estate, was still standing when liberal laws (1869, 1878, 1889) mandated the dissolution of indigenous commons. In 1869, Acayucan proposed to divide its lands on the basis of its colonial endowment, which it claimed included parts of Cuatotolapan and public land. A dispute as to whether Cuatotolapan's 1614 *merced* mentioned Acayucan dragged on until commissioners, including Acayucan's cura, found in Cuatotolapan's favor (1896). By then, the Development Ministry had already reclassified all Acayucan's land as municipal territory, allowing the municipio to effect a "general" reparto; that is, one open to Acayucan's *gente de razón*, not just ex-comuneros (1888). The ex-community came close to recovering its disputed territory in 1897 when Cuatotolapan's new owner surprisingly agreed to recognize Acayucan's boundaries. Again, however, the municipio trashed Acayucan's hopes, claiming ex-comuneros had imprisoned officials in church until they endorsed the deal. The 1888 reparto stood. In 1906, despairing *acayuqueños* joined a doomed Mexican Liberal Party (PLM) revolt.[59]

This panorama explains indigenous acayuqueños' suspicion of mestizo-dominated municipios/parishes, and their interest in agrarismo. In 1917, the CLA endorsed Acayucan's demand for a restitución, Governor Cándido Aguilar sidestepping the problem of missing titles and vague boundaries by simply ordering that *ocho sitios de ganado mayor*—thirty thousand acres—be restored, as if the fact of Acayucan's colonial patrimony were self-evident. The CNA rejected this restitution as nonsensical. Acayucan's agraristas subsequently fell in with Luis Morones's (not the Flores Magóns') Mexican Labor Party (PLM). Under these auspices, Acayucan resubmitted its claim in 1922. Local laboristas enlisted Tejeda's support, arguing that the *"naturales* of this city" lacked land for corn. The battle for Acayucan's lands had been waged "generation after generation," a laborista wrote; Tejeda could settle it. Tejeda did so, sending engineer Álvaro Fernández canoeing upriver in search of the mythical townsite in 1923. Alhough Álvarez asked old-timers on the riverbanks where Acayucan's 1614 boundary stones were, he couldn't find any. With changing river courses, reforestation, and inaccurate toponyms making a mockery of his map, Fernández realized what Tejeda had really asked him to do, which was to pinpoint a revolutionary Eldorado "scientifically," so Tejeda could expropriate it, in 1924. In 1925, CLA engineers traced the ejido.[60]

Ejidalization set off a violent contest for municipal control. In 1923–1924, agraristas complained of persecution by Acayucan's "disastrous Green Party." Some agraristas landed in the Ulúa's dungeons. Savage repression followed in 1928: that April, Acayucan's "Hilario C. Salas" syndicate reported that police and a local judge murdered two agraristas and jailed others, including leaders Manuel Villano and Hipólito Landeros. Agraristas' houses were searched for guns, though only old hunting muskets were found. This repression prompted a more determined participation in tejedismo. In March, ICAM was registered in Acayucan's church; and by December, agraristas were asking Tejeda for guns.[61] By August 1929, as angry *damas católicas* informed President Portes Gil, the local authorities were violating the spirit of the arreglos and giving "unlimited help" to "schismatics," meaning "unattached priests who are therefore contrary to the Catholic Church." Two ICAM priests, Adolfo Briones and Ricardo González, visited Acayucan, making the women "think that some agreement exists with the State's Superior Authorities to support such irregularities." The women asked Portes Gil to decertify "schismatics," appoint a new civil authority, and register a priest "approved by the superior ecclesiastical authorities." The bishop of Tehuantepec likewise harangued Tejeda in September.[62]

That was election month, though, and the LCAEV/ICAM alliance was preparing to hold the municipio. "With Mexican curas, we are content," Acayucan's agraristas told Gobernación in October, "because they do not rob or trick us, or meddle in politics like other priests who . . . support the candidacy of [José] Vasconcelos, who will be the one to finish off communalists, agraristas, and all kinds of *sindicatos*." Agraristas claimed that their old Roman cura was a philanderer who forfeited his church by fleeing during the Cristiada. The cura in question, Arturo Huguet, repaid the insult in kind but corroborated ICAM's relationship with agrarismo. As Huguet wrote in November, Briones "today set himself up as chief of the agraristas, who are the only ones who help him and his woman." In Huguet's estimation, this "ruinous" alliance was disturbing the peace and causing commerce to stagnate. Briones himself was "an extreme alcoholic . . . in everything immoral," though in fairness sex and drink were on everyone's minds as Huguet wrote. Indeed, he did so at the end of Acayucan's patronal feast, Saint Martin of Tours (11 November), with its "danza de arrieros y morenos": this was an innuendo-laden frolic in which masked "muleteers" danced through the streets brandishing sticks and pursuing "Morenos"—indigenous men wearing their *novias*' frocks.[63] What aggrieved Father Huguet, perhaps, was the concentration of political and festive power under ICAM and Tejeda's LCAEV. Briones was still going in 1930, though the federal government began to exert pressure through Hacienda, which demanded that Briones vacate the church or fix its crumbling tower. In 1931, Hacienda closed the church, though Briones continued to work his village circuit until 1933. In 1934, Lázaro Cárdenas confirmed Tejeda's 1924 ejido grant.[64]

Chinameca's files also show that festive commerce was central to agrarista support for ICAM. Here "more than two hundred campesinos" (virtually the whole ejidal census) embraced ICAM in 1926. Yet in 1928, Roman Catholics led by Avelino Jaurigui regained the municipio, closing the church and sacking its junta. Agraristas charged that

Romanists were sectarian ("they do not accept curas who have recognized the law . . . and aim to stop them from officiating"). They themselves wanted to bring back pilgrimages and trade. Petitioning Pérez in June (nativity of their patron, Saint John the Baptist), they stated that "suppression of the cult and our religious feasts has brought, in consequence, the neglect of our industries and commerce"; holy days were "the means through which our *negocios* were favored with returns." This was why they "demand cult again today" and priests "to invigilate our Saintly Religion." Jaurigui, meanwhile, had a Roman cura minister secretly while the church stayed closed. Agraristas demanded the reinstatement of Evaristo Torres's church junta, which "several times brought in the cura who obeys the law, as the vast majority wants." If Gobernación did not intervene, the agrarians would topple Jaurigui's faction, "so they cannot obstruct the workings of the cult and make us look like fanatics." "For us it is all the same whether Roman or Mexican curas come," they added: "What we want is that there be divine worship" and a fiesta "[where] we can baptize our children, since it would be very sad for us if the pueblo's feeling were obstructed by two or four people." Jaurigui was withholding the baptismal registers and funds for restoring the sacristy. Villagers had promised free labor to complete the work.[65]

Agraristas, once again, wanted communal feasts, not clandestine religion. In Chinameca, as elsewhere, they obtained them after LCAEV candidates won the September 1929 elections. The "agrarista element," wrote one Bibiana Ortiz, then installed a church junta composed of "people of the same *gremio*," which in October brought in Mexican priest Antonio Muníve (he "cannot even read and write," Ortiz claimed). Yet Mexican priests were untouchable because agraristas placed armed men in church. They also used the alms deposited by villagers to pay Muníve, who lived illegally in the *casa cural*. Despite his flaws, ICAM was to agraristas' liking and endured well into the 1930s. In August 1935, Chinameca still had Mexican curas: Teódulo Alarcón, and, still, Muníve, whose superior said rather generously that he was well known and "esteemed by all *católicos de corazón*."[66]

There was more support for ICAM in northern Veracruz, in the hinterlands around Poza Rica and Tuxpam. Religious partisanship was premised, again, on communal ejido access; it differed, though, in that the converts were indigenous migrants exiting Puebla's borderlands for

Huastecan municipios such as Ixhuatlán de Madero. Dozens of Mexican Catholic agrarian communities were founded here from the 1930s, mostly by the ethnolinguistic group known as the Tepehuas ("Lords of the hills," from Nahuatl, *tépetl*). Indeed, ICAM was the church many Tepehuas chose after their odyssey to Veracruz. As a group, Tepehuas were first described (in the sixteenth-century *Relación de Huexotla*) as natives of modern-day Hidalgo. Three centuries later, however, they left the *hidalguense* township of Huehuetla and trekked south, stopping ca. 1900 in *another* Huehuetla, this one in Puebla and ethnically Totonac. Perhaps it was the name. Nonetheless, coexistence was tense: Totonacs considered themselves Tepehuas' ethnolinguistic forebears, and for this reason it seems that some *huehuetecos* viewed Tepehuas as poor relations.[67]

Tepehuas had been in Huehuetla for a generation when they re-entered the record: in 1926, *Restauración* reported another blow against "religious foreignerism" when Father Melecio Cervantes Castro reached Huehuetla. Castro was hired to solemnize Huehuetla's *fiestas titulares* and those of nine other villages.[68] Soon after, however, in the late 1920s, hundreds of Tepehua families left Huehuetla; possibly there were religious fallings-out, or perhaps Huehuetla was experiencing agrarian compression. What is clear, though, is that they began resettling in Ixhuatlán, a hundred miles north—their third municipio in so many decades. Probably they came here because Tepehuas already lived in Ixhuatlán's sujeto, Tziltzacuapan, where the newcomers settled. Then, in 1935 (or 1932 or 1938, the sources vary), Tepehuas started bivouacking on Tziltzacuapan's hillsides and founded a separate *poblado*, Pisa Flores. Over time, *pisaflorenses* raised conical shacks with mezzanine altars holding Catholic saints and costumbre figurines. As their animals grazed, they dug.

Holding this ground was not easy, however, as a review of Pisa Flores's ejido file (courtesy of anthropologist Williams García) shows. Pisa Flores would eventually stand on lands granted to Tziltzacuapan in 1719 that were later subdivided as lot number 5 of the Ixhuatlán condueñazgo in the 1880s. In theory, the subdivision sufficed to give hundreds of condueño families ample shares; except a fifth of shares went to gente de razón from the Acatlán estate, who asserted pueblo residency. Two British-owned estates also encroached, likewise a US company that bought them out in 1920. The problem, then, was that gente de razón dominated the condueñazgo, monopolizing the best land and killing for it. By 1926, mestizos possessed 172 shares, ex-comuneros 56. Incoming Tepehuas thus had to navigate aggrieved ex-comuneros and commercial and mestizo growers. Still, the Tepehuas were fortunate that in 1928 the gente de razón overreached themselves, petitioning for all remaining 1888 lots as an ejido. They also made the mistake of inviting the Tepehuas to sign the petition, to pad out the census with names and so justify the larger expropriation. This time the Tepehuas got the knife in first. Not only did Tejeda reject the gente de razón's 1929 bid: he supported a rival ejidal bid launched by the Tepehuas in their own right.[69]

In revenge, Tziltzacuapan's mayor shot the Tepehuas' leader dead. Henceforth, there was a vendetta between rival agraristas: Tziltzacuapan's *comité del centro* (or "Piedra Grande" faction) and Tepehuas' *barrio bajo* group. Blood was shed. In the 1930s, as stated, the Tepehuas left Tziltzacuapan for Pisa Flores. This was not an immediate solution, because for years Pisa Flores had no political status and hence could not request ejidos. The conflict abated when Ixtlán's agrarian commissioner censused Pisa Flores in 1937; in 1940, an engineer surveyed; and in 1943, the Agrarian Department received Pisa Flores's *solicitud* for an ejido. Fearing expropriation, Tziltzacuapan's mestizos now conceded that the old 1888 subdivision should be redone more equitably, which Tepehuas accepted. Thus, lot number 5 was resurveyed and divided between Tziltzacuapan's mestizos and pisaflorenses. Pisa Flores never received an ejido, therefore, but a condueñazgo of 952 hectares in 1943.[70]

Once more, we see Veracruz indígenas pressing for communalist solutions to their agrarian problems. In Pisa Flores's case, moreover, ICAM was built into the community from inception and became the majoritarian, even exclusive, religion. The Roman cura of Tuxpan told his bishop in 1936 that nearby pueblos were a vale of tears; between them, Francisco Durán ("governor of the schismatic church") and Satan placed thorns in his path, making him suffer "most bitter moments." Pisa Flores itself entered a long relationship with ICAM priest Hieronymus von Monte de Honor, who entered Pérez's circle in 1929. As Pisa Flores's cura, Monte de Honor endured jailings and beatings at the hands of Ixhuatlán's Roman Catholics, and spurned tempting offers to make him recant. His pastorate nonetheless lasted for decades. By 1959, he was assisted by another priest, Jesús Gutiérrez, whose enemies accused him of performing *brujo* rites in church. Monte de Honor's life story was as mad as Sir Edward James's surrealist garden in nearby Xilitla.[71] But he was no fair-weather friend of the Tepehua. When Williams García performed his classic fieldwork in the mid-1950s, he found him building a church and tending parish affairs in Pisa Flores's Tepehua hamlets.[72]

CONCLUSION

Exhaustive sweeps of ejido files might reveal all cases in which peasant revolutionaries supported ICAM. Nonetheless, in flagship cases (México, Veracruz) dissident Catholicism became part of agraristas' repertoire and a morale building element for the regime. ICAM removed some Catholic angst from the land petitioning process and gave agraristas a sectarian identity that could be politically liberating. The blooded, defiant agraristas we have met here are worlds away from the guilt-ridden cannon fodder deployed against cristeros in the Bajío. Sometimes participation involved pragmatic compliance with Calles's religious policy, but many elements—standing firm against beatings, arson, and bullets; giving back punishment—were hard to fake and needed force of will. That ICAM appealed to diverse peasantries (the would-be farmers of the pulque zone, conservative Gulf comuneros) also mitigates against a flat, instrumental reading. In these areas, battles over land became marked by new religious differences; perhaps because the battles themselves had convoluted ethnic, political, and agrarian backstories, meanings that religion could subsume. Regime rhetoric imagined peasants working in Christian solidarity. The actual experience was a cross between the sectarianism of the Ulster Plantation and the Maya-on-Maya violence of Guatemala's October Revolution. ICAM justified cruel religious *limpiezas* and naked partisanship. The experience nonetheless provides a striking example of how a religious parastatal could legitimate and facilitate regime building. Agraristas lived on the edge and accepted tough odds: what harm could it do to feel that God was on *their* side?

CHAPTER FIVE

"ACÁ TODO ES VIDA"

ICAM as Local Religion

IN MARCH 1928, the US consul in Puerto México (Ver.) reported on the local religious situation. "Clergymen of the 'Mexican Catholic Apostolic Church,'" he wrote, were traversing the isthmus, "conduct[ing] services, such as 'baptisms,' 'confirmations,' and 'masses,' with great success." He believed that indigenous backwardness explained this apostasy.

> The majority of the population being in the same intellectual stage of development as that in which their ancestors were at the time of the Conquest, they are not concerned with questions of dogma or whether the services be conducted by Roman Catholic or "Mexican Catholic" clergymen . . . This district is an intellectual backwash of the Mexican Republic and no religious or national questions take root in the minds of the inhabitants.

Seven years later, a different US consul interviewed the Roman Catholic dean of Papantla in northern Veracruz. The dean protested that fifteen "schismatic church" priests were celebrating fiestas, deceiving Totonac elites ("such of the Indians as can read") with false papal bulls. In the dean's view, too, "the incredulity of the ignorant natives" explained why "so-called schismatic priests" found success. The consul himself wondered if there might be other reasons. Papantla was a "rich Indian section," he noted, with lively fiestas "staged by the Indian population under the patronage of the wealthier Indian class." Fiestas such as Corpus Christi were dramatic, "the participants enduring not only corporal torture but also making material offerings of value in both gold and precious stones."[1] Thus, he intuited, ICAM's popularity was meaningful: priests helped Totonac elites to purify themselves through gory penitences and gifting to the saints.

Chapter Five

With some exceptions, then, educated officials and Roman clergy rubbished indigenous Mexicans who did not practice Catholicism in "modern," superaffiliated terms and hence did not shun Pérez as "real" Catholics should. These reports, coming years and hundreds of miles apart, nonetheless corroborate an important trend: the rallying of indigenous Catholics to Pérez, hence the forging of a mediated alliance between local Catholicisms and the regime. Pérez's priests were stunned at the animation of many pueblos on the central plateau, Gulf, or isthmus. "Our cause enjoys the best of times and beautiful hopes in this region," wrote Guillermo de la Peña from Puebla's Sierra Norte in 1928, "and I am pleasantly surprised by the sympathy we count on. Only Corpus Christi is dead; here everything is life."[2] "I arrived without incident," wrote José Luis Lazarini from Actipan (Pue.) in 1929,

> save walking three-and-a-half leagues on foot, since the señores to whom letters were sent, in order that they should send people to meet us, did not receive them because the post officer is an enemy of ours . . . I never thought [actipenses] would prepare such a reception for me as the one they gave, for I do not deserve it: peals of bells, confetti, the throwing of flowers wherever I walked, in sum an overflowing of happiness, and all as I say unmerited, for on the inside I felt pity toward these people, so full of respect and different to those in Coyotepec . . . For now, I do not complain of all the attention that they give me, because I feel like a count from the days of the viceroys, with squires, domestics, waiters, and servants who anticipate and fight to fulfill my every wish . . . So, for now, I am on my *Ínsula*.

Pérez perhaps missed the baroque allusion, to the island (ínsula) of Baratavia that crowns Sancho governor in the *Quixote*.[3] Neither Lazarini nor de la Peña had much incentive to exaggerate, however, because Pérez taxed priests' income at 25 percent: the more multitudinous the chronicles, the more dues owing.

Historiographically, however, this fervent picture seems unlikely because we imagine that Mexico's postrevolution, with its saint-burnings, was toxic to indigenous Catholicism.[4] Even historians who note provincial support for ICAM are skeptical: the usual, reductionist line is that this was performative anticlericalism, state bosses falling into line behind Calles.⁵ Yet this is spectacularly to avoid indigenous actors themselves. In contrast, this chapter argues that support for Pérez was essentially religious—so long as we carefully define what was "Catholic" about it. Instances of ultramontane piety in ICAM can certainly be counted on one hand: a Month of Mary, marred by failed crops, in Coyotepec (Méx.); the (Italian) Forty Hours devotion, tried in Tlaola (Pue.); a Sacred Heart club in Tapachula (Chis.).⁶ Conversely, ICAM appealed to indigenous sensibilities where it fitted around local, patriarchal, and agrarian forms of Catholicism.

Religious partisanship was complicated, except in *Restauración*'s nationalistic stories. Two motives predominated, one spiritual, one political though associated with religion. First, in the context of the Cristero War (1926–1929), ICAM promised an indigenous Catholic renaissance: the resumption of fiestas and agrarian rites (costumbre), hence prestige for elites who sponsored local religion. Second, by creating Catholic denominations, ICAM created religious differences that mapped onto other conflicts. Besides land disputes, the most common were jurisdictional conflicts between satellite pueblos and headtowns or internal tussles between indigenous and Hispanic groups. We read these vendettas imperfectly, through partisan sources that euphemize local battles in the language of church-state conflict. Rarely was it so simple as deciding to register a Mexican or a Roman priest. Catholic cult was enfolded into the agricultural and planetary cycles, pilgrimage commerce, and local autonomy. It intersected with indigenous spring rites (la gran costumbre), though archival sources rarely allude to this. Village politics were factionalized and impenetrable. Some indigenous groups installed Mexican priests as a snub to mestizos linked to Roman clergy, or to lure Gobernación into supporting them. Mayordomos (festive patrons) pressed ICAM to slash stipends or endorse feasts of which Roman clergy disapproved. There were secessionist struggles pitting indigenous vicarías against mestizo-dominated (de razón) parishes. At stake, then, was control of local religion and all it represented: supernatural favor, territory, political power, and civil-ecclesiastical autonomy. Struggles took years to play out. Interpersonal violence and a niggardly, Montagues-versus-Capulets clannishness pervaded everything.

Roman claims that pueblos welcomed Pérez unknowingly were thus self-serving; there was nothing naïve about it. Witness the game-like encounter recorded by Miguel Darío Miranda, Roman prelate of Tulancingo (later archbishop of Mexico), in Chicontepec (Ver.) in 1939.

Chapter Five

Miranda rode in as apostolic visitor[7] to reinstate a Josephite priest who had been ousted by a *padre cismático*. Yet he found a divided parish, men leaning Rome-ward, women to ICAM. Alleging that Satan had stolen the clapper, Miranda's supporters sounded assembly by striking the church bell with a stone. Miranda then cried that the cismático was really just a butcher and he a bishop. Such majesty might have worked in Miranda's native León. Not here. "The women had devised a plan," he diarized. First, they chased his horse away to stop him leaving; then, disingenuously, they pressed him to say Mass and confirm. "At once I saw the ambush," he wrote,

> for if I performed the confirmations and people gave me money, that would give the schismatic his opportunity to attack me, saying, "You see, he only comes here to take your money" . . . On the other hand, if I refused any stipends, then this would set a precedent, which I could not do, since it was not convenient to establish "customs" that could not be maintained afterward. With serenity I took charge of the situation, and said to them: "Very well, I shall leave on foot, and when you have brought my horse down, send him after me . . ." They still had one card to play, which was to tell me that I should wait for a military escort, because the road was dangerous. "I don't need an escort, I am not afraid, I have only come to do my duty. Farewell and God bless you . . . ," and with determined strides I marched back down the dusty road.[8]

Miranda was intelligent enough to learn from such defeats.[9] Yet what stands out is how Chicontepec's women won a premeditated clash over their religious "rights" by negotiating between Catholic options. Their wish list included worship without fees, a veto over church investitures, and, granted some license, respect for Nahua churchpeople (the butcher-priest).

Indigenous Catholics were always thinking about politics. "The religious problem is not mentioned here," a SEP bureaucrat told Pérez in 1926. But "here" was Chiapas's impious capital, Tuxtla, so he checked himself: "As I have yet to depart for the pueblos, I can tell you nothing of peasants' frame of mind concerning establishment of the Mexican Church in this zone." As it turned out, a line of lowland pueblos reaching

Guatemala joined ICAM. In México state, the problem was that indigenous people would not *stop* reading the newspapers, one priest lamented in 1929. "It would be pointless to list the difficulties that must be overcome in the pueblos," he said, "the more so if these be indigenous, like the one where I find myself." That was Tepetlixpa, Sor Juana's hometown, where political soothsaying was a sport: "I say this because as soon as people saw that the newspapers mentioned an *arreglo religioso*, it was as if they were told 'the old Father's coming back,' and the situation turned black [medio color de ormiga]." Fearing ICAM's decline post-Calles, people stayed away and the priest could not pay his dues. As Pérez's loving son, he felt ashamed.[10] Clergy misconstrued such shifts as "Indian" caprice, but they reflected knowledge of a changing religious and political scene, if not indigeneity as situational fact. If pueblos were not ahistorical essences but adaptive sites in fields of changing relations dominated by state and church, then such recomposition *was* indigeneity.[11] Thus, indigenous people could transition from Roman to Mexican auspices, as once they transitioned from mendicant to secular clergy. There was little sense of contradiction, because a "real priest" was someone who ministered *right*: leading the fiestas, in sync with the seasons, rains, and corn; reverencing wooden saints, preferably with flights of baroque oratory; marrying and baptizing; not rack-renting; stepping carefully around the principales. Priests who could do these things walked a flower-strewn path, never mind canonical provenance. It was not that indigenous people couldn't "tell the difference" between clergies, as Roman clergy alleged, but that they held them all to identical, endogamous standards.

Pérez's main achievement was servicing villages' festive needs and creating a Catholic network called ICAM that he represented before Gobernación. He was no polyglot indigenista savant like Father Ángel María Garibay, still less a proto-liberationist with a theology of inculturation, like some 1970s *obispo rojo*.[12] Yet he was well known in the pueblos and neither afraid nor contemptuous of indigenous Catholicism, which he genially accepted as religious Mexicanness. For all that capitalinos mocked, in the sierra even his wizened looks and grandiose title were assets. Pérez was antediluvian yet he had plausibility as an indigenous patriarch—an ecclesiastical version, perhaps, of "patriarch of the Sierra" Juan Francisco Lucas, or his old C.O., Juan Méndez. It was as pueblo-Gobernación go-between, not Orthodox graybeard, that Pérez lived up to his title as church father. As journalist Alfonso López

Guerra (a son of Tlatlauqui, Pue.) told traveling merchants in Lagunillas in 1928, Pérez knew the sierra "perfectly," having toured it since 1877. He enjoyed "good relations with the *señores tlatoanes* [from Nahuatl, *tlatoani*, "lord"] as people of authority here are known." These patriarchs held Pérez in "true affection and unctuous respect"; his prestige won "many adepts."[13]

From 1926, ICAM rhetoric reflected these *pueblerino* roots. *Restauración* published sackcloth-and-ashes stories recalling mendicant histories like Mendieta's *Historia eclesiástica indiana*, with its tales of priests eating *nopales* among the heathen. While effete Roman clergy ("eunuch priests") abandoned the people, Mexican priests took "the dusty road for a bed, a rock for a pillow, and the sky's canopy for a roof."[14] Another pastoral promised to "redeem" indigenous Mexicans: ICAM would fill the revolution's religious "void" with "the doctrines of the Man-God, Jesus Christ"; the spirit of Las Casas, "no stranger to the unredeemed Indian's tears," was reborn.[15] This rhetoric—with its unredeemed Indians and hero-priests—resembled SEP *indigenismo*, but people responded. We see this in two sections. The first explores how a church synonymous with CROM was able to synthesize with village Catholicism. The second shows how ICAM became a religious vehicle for pueblo politics.

SAN PÉREZ

As chapter 3 shows, numerous pueblos evaded the 1926 suspension of public worship. Yet it is important to understand that such decisions were themselves rooted in Catholicism, given that the ban on public worship necessarily entailed a prohibition of the religious feasts on which village well-being depended. Fiestas mattered in central-southern pueblos because Catholicism was a corporate affair, the overriding concern being propitiatory, saint-based cult, not individual pursuit of sacramental grace. As anthropologist Manuel Gamio noted in his 1922 study of Teotihuacán, to be Catholic was to participate in a group enterprise. "A Catholic," he wrote, "is someone who goes to Mass, confesses, and joins in with all the fusillades and rockets, as well as the dances and primitive representations with which a determined saint is celebrated." A "non-Catholic," no matter how devout, did not do these things: such a person, Gamio noted, "ceases to belong to the group and is not considered worthy of the name Catholic." Gamio's depiction of indigenous primitives ("rudimentary Catholics") offends; yet the observation concerning group identity is valid.[16] It explains, for example, how the abstentionism of Roman clergy might be interpreted as "not Catholic" and lead people to consider other options. Gamio, of course, never anticipated this: in his view, *teotihuacanos* were incapable of such choices. When teotihuacanos were asked if they were Catholic or Roman Catholic, he found, "they do not know what to say and end up saying that probably they are just Catholics."[17] As we shall see, indigenous Catholics did know what to say. Given choices, they chose deliberately.

A relevant contextual factor was that the Roman Catholic presence in many areas where ICAM did best was comparatively recent. The Roman sees of Tulancingo (1863), Tehuantepec (1891), Papantla (1922), and Huejutla (1922), for instance, were recently created and run by Rome-educated, Bajío-born bishops, whose pious rigor did not necessarily go down well. Under Mora y del Río, the archdiocese of Mexico adopted a hardline, repressive policy to local Catholicism: after hearing reports of scandalous fiestas—straw bulls dancing into church, bizarre rituals involving dead squirrels, saints carried off at night, *limpias* with altar linens, drinking—Mora banned processions (1908) and Passion plays (1921). Rafael Guízar y Valencia, a fellow michoacano and bishop of Veracruz, was less strict, but there was no mistaking his puritanical 1920 command: "sacramentalization of the pueblo." Perhaps he might have done things differently had he known that Totonac Catholics had a deep history of rebelling (1836, 1885, 1886) against fiesta prohibitions and religious taxes.[18]

The 1926 suspension of worship created new flashpoints. People in Xometla (Méx.) protested the imminent "scarcity of priests" to Mora in July 1926. "Do not forget us," they begged—or they might "forget God's worship." Lead signatory Trinidad Juárez was one of the agraristas encountered in chapter 4 and the driving force behind ICAM in his pueblo. In Santa María Magdalena (Qro.), people wrote to Pérez expressing anger that "Romanist clergy" left them in "an atmosphere of uncertainty" by suspending public worship. And in Tenoxtitlán (Méx.), "many faithful" asked Pérez to lead a 1928 feast and clear the backlog of baptisms and marriages. Anger at the cessatio a divinis was palpable: "we are being made fools of for want of a priest to impart these sacraments." If village clans (González, Cárdenas) led the way, there was obvious popular support: an escort brought the priest from Mexico

City, a crowd was at the station, and post-fiesta a hundred people wrote thanking the "gracious señor patriarch." Roman curas' condescension to indigenous Catholics cost them. The cura of Acayucan (Ver.) stopped a boycott against ICAM because women led it. Citing Paul's injunction against "women governing in the church," and claiming that acayuqueños were "extremely indolent," he preferred to risk an "Indian" schism than foment gynocracy—and got his wish. In Jonotla (Pue.) in 1925, a scandalized archbishop Vera thought himself "on a mission to Africa" after finding totonacos worshipping a stone Virgin by a waterfall. In 1927, the parish divided, with mestizos upholding the strike and totonacos calling in Pérez to preside at their Marian shrine.[19]

Many pueblos disregarded the religious conflict until *their* saint's day, then implored Pérez for priests. The calendrical distribution of village petitions reveals seasonal clusters. A spring cycle—from February to May/June—tracked the planting of summer corn and the winter corn harvest; after a hiatus came the main harvest surge in late summer/autumn. That was the peak: as a breakdown of patron saints' days in ICAM-affiliated pueblos confirms, the biggest celebrations fell in the second half of the year (interestingly, this contrasted with cristero mobilizations, which peaked earlier in liturgical time, the main "booms"—1927, 1929—occurring between Lent and Easter). Surveying 267 pro-ICAM communities, the most common titular saints were the Archangel Michael (29 September, 17 cases), Saint Francis (4 October, 15 cases), and Saint James (25 July, 14). Fourth was the Virgin of the Assumption (15 August, 11), ahead of the Guadalupe (5), though collectively Marian avocations were twice as popular (34) as Christological ones (17), such as the Lords of Chalma or Esquipulas. The top four were regionally significant, colonial saints. Santiago and Francisco—like Domingo (8 August, 4) and Agustín (28 August, 4)—were associated with religious conquest. La Asunción and San Miguel recalled the secular church's seventeenth-century consolidation, in Mexico and Puebla, respectively. La Asunción was the see of Mexico's patroness (1656); San Miguel, a Satan-crushing "viceroy," appeared near Puebla in 1631.[20] If meanings changed, one thing is obvious: people were hitching ICAM to the old ritual year, not taking orders from CROM.

A few examples from Pérez's almanac must suffice. Pajapam's mayor (Ver.) wanted a priest in March 1927 to solemnize the patron, John of God (a sixteenth-century hospitaller-soldier saint). Four priests were wanted for Tenancingo's (Tlax.) fiestas in March 1928, with stipulation for a saintly homage and Mass for San José, while Santo Domingo (Ver.) needed a priest to lead pilgrims to Monte de Chila in April 1929. Next month, a priest was wanted in Tampico-Alto (Ver.) to revive the *feria* of El Señor de las Misericordias, a sixteenth-century Christ Crucified. Commerce was in "lamentable decadence," people wrote, and "countless children" unbaptized "for want of a priest of the Catholic cult." A Mass would draw pilgrims, thus trade. That month, "sons of the pueblo" of Ixhuatlán (Ver.) walked to Puerto México to find a priest. Towns such as Xalostoc (Méx.), with its fiesta of Saints Peter and Paul (29 June), closed the first cycle: their 1927 fiesta had five priests, sports, and fireworks.[21]

In autumn, the harvest cycle began. In 1927, Coxquihuí (Ver.) wanted "to celebrate the fiestas that take place in this village from 6 September," meaning a fortnight-long cycle climaxing on Saint Matthew's day (21 September). The feast of the Archangel Michael a week later—marking the rainy season's end—saw invitations from Tenancingo, Xometla, Tenoxtitlán, and elsewhere. In October, the Totonocapan and isthmus feasts began. In 1926, Melesio Cervantes celebrated titular fiestas in ten Totonac villages: Santo Domingo, Huehuetla, Vicente Guerrero, Bibiano Hernández, Dimás López, Chipahuatlán, Mecatlán, Coyutla, Coahuitlán, and Jopala. In Juchitán (Oax.), Father Miguelito received invitations from across "the *istmeño* region." In Santo Domingo (Ver.), to give a December example, the church encargado told ICAM's envoy, "Kindly come in person and celebrate the two masses we desire, one of which must be tomorrow." The petition was urgent ("tomorrow" was Christmas day) and reads like an instruction.[22]

For most indigenous Catholics, it was the solemnity of the fiesta, not the priestly office, that dignified the priest. Priests were king for a day. Tacit expectations were written into the primers they sometimes carried, such as Emeterio Valdéz's Spanish-Totonac lexicon. It explained how to ask for water, fodder, and a bellringer. Most useful, one suspects, were the translations "when do your fiestas start?" (Tun quiltamacó natzucuy min Pascuas) and "I want to baptize my child" (Lacasquina natacmunuy qui excata).[23] Priests were expected to mass, spend some days baptizing and marrying, then go. Life between fiestas was thankless, especially in arid postings like Almoloya (Hgo.). Here vecinos begged Benigno Gómez for a visit in February 1930. It was assuredly fiesta time, because in previous years he had stayed a fortnight, celebrating at a fiesta with bellringing, fireworks, and colored paper flags "suspended wall to wall from the houses." Parishioners even carried him in procession to the parroquia, where he officiated beneath a retable of the Apocalypse. In other months, however, indifference was total. "Had I known that I was going to fall into this hole, I would not have come," José Varela wrote of the same village one May. Mass takings were a few cents: "In this village, they want priests only for banquets, not the day after." Another priest wrote that he would practice medicine to survive. "This town is sad, so sad," said yet another priest, Fray Agustín Mójica, in August: "Nobody comes here, nobody stops. What a life!" Mójica was just in from Actipan (Pue.), which came alive for fiestas, as we saw. But it, too, was bleak between-times. "It is impossible to sustain myself here," Mójica wrote; people gave food and a few coins, but there was no ministry ("absolutely nothing") and his presence felt "undignified and shameful." "A *fiestecita* every two or three months run by the mayordomo... how am I to support myself like this?" Eventually he worked out that he was meant to rotate to greener pastures, not stick around like an incumbent country priest: at the end of the month he was leaving, he told Pérez in January 1930, because priests in Huitzilan (Pue.) needed help.[24] José de Jesús Gómez experienced poverty in Tlaola (Pue.) in spring 1931. Even though the "greater part" of local villages "support the Mexican Church," Gómez wrote, "the meager *entradas* in this parish are absolutely short of what is needed to sustain me," creating a "powerful motive" for leaving. That August, however, came the fiesta of the Assumption. Now Gómez found that it was "entirely possible to continue as cura of this village, because I have now received... the charity of the kindly people in the pueblo."[25]

Local Catholicism did not suffice to support resident priests, therefore, except in large towns. Some ICAM priests started naively: newly ordained Francisco Fernández asked Pérez if he should publish marriage banns. Nobody was going to read them.[26] In general, indigenous Catholics demanded high Mass and nonreiterative sacraments (baptism, marriage) on feast days, reiterative ones (daily Mass, confession) rarely. In Puerto México in 1928, communion breads were stamped and only a priest was needed to consecrate them—but then it was Corpus Thursday. Father Arámbula asked Pérez to send communion wafers to Actipan in 1929, "thirty of the large kind, two hundred of the small." Again it was Corpus, suggesting that unusual numbers of people communed on this feast. José Lazarini also asked for communion breads for Actipan's autumnal fiesta. It was not just the Eucharist that people evaded. Several curas said their churches lacked holy oils (sending some was a "matter of conscience," said one), so people obviously died unshriven.[27]

The "popular" sacraments—a relative term—were rites of passage performed during lulls in fiestas. Surviving tallies, accompanying remittances, keep score. José de la Luz Coronado, working the villages round Ixtepec (Pue.), received 213 pesos for 119 acts in June 1928, mostly baptisms (61). He stayed three days in any town, so likely these were festive spin-offs. Vicente Liñán in Xochitlán (Pue.) celebrated ten baptisms and eight masses, including ones for the Guadalupe and the dead, in March 1929. He earned seventy-six pesos, remitting nineteen to Pérez. Next month alms were seventy-five pesos (19 for Pérez); and, in a fallow July, thirty-three pesos, with nothing (no hubo limosna) in the second fortnight. In Almoloya, baptisms yielded six pesos in February 1930, while José Gómez celebrated twenty baptisms in Tlaola in May 1930 "and no more," plus a few marriages, one in articulo mortis. Pencil-written baptismal and marriage tickets from Zapotitlán, Huehuetla (both Pue.), or Acayucan (Ver.), tell identical stories. José Ramírez, who remitted twenty-five pesos monthly from Chiapas, did better. Teodoro Juárez in Zozocolco (Ver.) in September 1928 performed sixty-three acts for eighty-three pesos, remitting a quarter to Pérez. In March and April 1930, he received about forty pesos, insufficient even for a sacristan; after deducting money for wine, his per diem, and Pérez, nothing was left.[28] Confirmation rates were higher because confirmation required a bishop and hence was associated with major fiestas, as when Macario López visited Tapachula (1926), López y Sierra toured Hidalgo and Guerrero (1928), or Mójica went to Puebla (1929). López reported 201 confirmations in one place, López y Sierra 753; Mójica found "many people to confirm." Pérez took four hundred confirmation tickets to one Federal District pueblo.[29]

Income from saints'-day masses and sacraments, rarely quantified, subsidized everything. Francisco Durán refused to leave the Sierra Norte to renew his Gobernación permit in August 1929, "because fiestas hereabouts are beginning": Lletla wanted him in August, Patla for the Nativity of Mary (8 September), then Tlaola, with thirteen client villages. "For that reason," Durán wrote, I do not want to leave."[30] There were, though, limits to what pueblos would pay, and Pérez's voluntarist idea made hagglers of priests. Emeterio Valdéz in June 1929 said a Mass in Coyotepec (Méx.) for three pesos, on promise of a larger gift (limosna) for Corpus. A Tlaola mayordomo paid José Gómez thirteen pesos for a 1931 Mass; some mayors and mayordomos—Félix Hernández in Chumatlán, Emilio Torres in Ahuacatlán—threw in railway passes, mounts, and hens for plucking.[31] Pedro Infante, meanwhile, recalled Macario López's pastoral visit to Coyotepec in 1931, and the "humble services" he performed for his bishop, "helping him to lay hands on hens, taking him out for *paseos*, and going with him to make sure that the mayordomos paid him the eight pesos that were agreed by the encargados of the pueblo's fiesta." This was fair, yet the stipend made a "bad impression" on López, who complained. Infante augmented the sum personally, protesting that "I have six years' service in the Mexican Church, and the church has not had to lament any great faults of mine," save capitulating to Coyotepec's mayordomos.[32] The only way to accumulate was by touring. Luis Games Flores—a scoundrel—hogged the May 1929 fiestas in southern Veracruz, according to Pérez's confidant Luisa Reboulen. "Seeing there were many fiestas in the villages," she wrote, Games "dispatched them all, officiating in Oteapan, Coxoleacaque, Hidalgostitlán, and Minatitlán." Thus he "gathered money in abundance," for these annual feasts drew "immense agglomerations of people." Games "remain[ed] only in those places," never his parish.[33] Ricardo González grew tired of hearing about Adolfo Briones's moneygrubbing in Acayucan (Ver.): "He doesn't give a damn about the growth of souls, so long as the money comes in."[34]

Generally, ICAM priests were beholden to lay officials. The usual interlocutors were mayordomos, fiesta sponsors whose service entitled them to ascend the village's civil hierarchy (hence, mayordomos often doubled as principales, alcaldes, and secretarios). Officials also included fiscales, sacristans who tended church saints and figurines used in costumbre, and *cantores* (choristers). It is important to historicize these roles, and to note that the politically integrated mayordomía system was a recent, nineteenth-century construct that emerged once the props sustaining colonial cult—endowed confraternities, Indian bluebloods—died off. Essentially, mayordomías subvented religion by rewarding lay sponsors with power, converting cultural into political capital. The system was patriarchal, not socially leveling.[35] By the 1920s, however, it was buckling as romanization depleted the local religious calendar, pushed new associative forms, and exalted priests' authority. New economic routines also favored mestizo over indigenous elites. The 1920s religious conflict was important, perhaps, because it paused this process: Roman curas withdrew, leaving churches in lay hands. The Calles Law allowed mayordomías to direct the cult autonomously of mestizo mayors and Roman párrocos. In some pueblos, therefore, juntas resembled state-backed mayordomías, a new politico-religious hybrid, not the hated inspectorates of the Bajío. There were hints of local religious revivalism.

Interestingly, local Catholicism allowed for such assertiveness theologically. Manuel Gamio found this *alabado* (praise) to the Archangel Michael on Xometla's altar in 1922:

> Blessed are you Saint Michael
> Of the heavens and beautiful earth
> For God has desired to name you
> Miraculous prince.
>
> You are Mary's guardian
> My God has charged you
> With the care of my soul
> And to be my advocate
> In the agonies to come.
>
> With delight we ask you
> To spare us from Lucifer
> From hell and its power
> Spare us loving father
> God save you, Oh Michael!

We can see why Gamio copied it. In a few lines, it sketches the pueblo's relationship to its patron. The supernatural pairing (Michael, church defender, versus Satan) is conventional, but has local, telluric qualities (prince of the earth). Moreover, Gamio's informants told him that the archangel sat in judgment over clergy, punishing those who performed perfunctory cult or showed ill-will (mala gana). Gamio heard of priests who were unhorsed after speeding through Mass and who begged San Miguel for mercy on their knees.[36] In this context, it is easier to understand why some pueblos, including Xometla, switched out their clergy during the cessatio a divinis for what they probably interpreted as a dishonoring of their *santo*.

That pueblos had notions of "good" and "bad" priests is apparent from many mayordomos' letters to Pérez. Some established brief tenures: Zoquiapan's junta (Pue.), wanting a priest for "several days," issued a one-week permit. Others demanded punctuality. Being late, as Coyotepec's Easter celebrant was one year, or imposing on one's hosts early, as a priest did in Santo Domingo (Ver.), brought reprimands. There were riders about splendor: "The fiestas approaching," Pedro Infante told a comrade in Tepetlixpa (Méx.), "we must find another priest . . . because the mayordomos want three priests, not two." The third man must be "competent," lest "some accident" befall him (which sounded ominous). Aniceto Trujillo, hired by Coxquihuí (Ver.) in 1932, had to mass day or night. Some villages required indigenous language speakers. Tuzamapán (Pue.) hired Laurencio Reynoso in 1927, but, discovering he did not speak Totonac, rejected him after reading in an old tome that *ministros de culto* must speak the pueblo's language. Only the authority of Jonotla's jefe de armas dissuaded them.[37]

Considering how often indigenous Catholicism was mocked as near idolatrous, it is surprising how often mayordomos insisted on pulpit eloquence: good sermons were sometimes required in registration documents, as in Coyotepec. Pulpit drama was especially desirable. José Lazarini's anxious style flatlined in Xochitlán (Pue.), so mayordomos fired him. Indeed, two "old servants" of Pérez, early supporters of ICAM, warned of a "critical situation" in 1929: Lazarini's lack of pulpit presence, which made him look weak. Lazarini was a "most competent" priest but "so young and lacking in preaching experience . . . projection, and the power of words" that people did not respect him. Fatally, Lazarini complained from the pulpit that almsgiving and church attendance were low, after which a delegation rebuked him. He was told that *xochitlenses* were harvesting ("están todos en los meros travajos") but that when the crop was in his sponsors, "with society's agreement," would give more. The church would fill for the Assumption, Xochitlán's patronal feast. On fiesta's eve, however, Lazarini got stage fright, so mayordomos sacked him. "We are being made fools of," its churchpeople upbraided Pérez, "preventing a romano from coming when you are not attending to us or keeping discipline among your Priests."[38] Lazarini recognized his lack of charisma ("in this I am clumsy and lack eloquence, and know not what to do," he wrote). He was haunted by his predecessor, Vicente Liñán, whose rapturous farewell sermon he witnessed. Even as Liñán climbed the pulpit staircase, xochitlenses wept and asked for blessings "from this padre that they love so." It reminded Lazarini of a famous circus clown he had seen as a boy, Ricardo Bell, who had people laughing before his routine began. "Liñán is the one who can carry these people," the "only one." This was not just impostor syndrome: the most pro-Roman source imaginable, *La Razón*, conceded Liñán's virtuosity, reporting how he seduced one congregation with "honey-dripping words" and sobbed with emotion during his sacrilegious Mass. The dramatic effect, *La Razón* said, was electrifying; it transfixed women especially, through "true Catholics" resisted.[39] Liturgical performance mattered everywhere. Tlaola's grateful authorities told José Varela in 1930 that "no priest who ever officiated in their church had celebrated a Mass as solemn as the one they had felt." *Felt* (palpado), not heard: yet, Varela railed, Roman clergy had the "cynicism" to call his masses invalid. Pedro Infante embellished his sermons "with images and rhetorical figures"; while Pascual Luciano García had an effective, rustic style, as the 1928 sermon he gave at Mazatán's (Chis.) Marian feria showed ("Desde que yo eyegado la jente acanbiado de pareseres o les e caído de simpatía al Pueblo que casi todos por cualquier asunto se dirijen a mí . . . abisto los sermones que yo selebro, y los sermones que él se las da, les aparesido bien lo que yo hago, barias personas desean que mejor yo me quedara").[40]

Mayordomos were quick to show authority to get what they wanted. Father Varela, a smash hit in Tlaola, was unacceptable on Puebla's plains. San Simón de Bravo (Pue.) would not have him: the pueblo did not wish it, the junta wrote, and thanked God for José de Jesús Gómez. If it must be another cura, let it be Isauro Flores; people liked him, and he would keep Roman clergy out. Varela caused another mutiny in Yehualtepec when replacing Manuel Salas Vidal. ICAM's rural dean, sent to adjudicate, reported that Yehualtepec "would sooner change back to Romanism than accept F. Varela. Here they will only have *Manuelito*, and if another padre comes, they will ignore him." This determination irked Varela ("Have you not seen how they treat me? These pueblos!"). Yet the dean knew the truth: "When people in the pueblos accept and esteem a priest, he lacks nothing and complains of nothing."[41] If not . . .

Priests' indiscretions, above all sloppy cult, financial improbity, or hints of disdain, were the main reasons why principales fired them. In 1931, José Gómez was banished from Tlaola (Pue.) after taking payment from mayordomo Félix Garcés and sending a substitute priest who then double-charged, causing "intrigue." Over the course of eight months, Gómez had "more or less gotten to know the señores of the village," and believed that "the mayordomo of the fiesta was in my power." But he was not, and sacked Gómez. Teodoro Juárez similarly underestimated Huitzalan's (Pue.) principales. He could handle his "Indian" opponents, he thought, because few would challenge him (como son indios, unos cuantos son mis contrarios). Likewise, Fray Mójica, who made so poor an impression in Puebla that several towns shunned him. Once provoked, Varela wrote, indigenous people rarely forgave (no siendo de razón, no entienden de satisfacciones). Mójica got another shellacking from Almoloya women (Hgo.) after an acolyte gave a blessing with the *santísimo*, which they knew only priests could do. In Tepetlixpa (Méx.), Pedro Infante's position became untenable after some church funds vanished. The last straw was his decision to cancel dawn Mass and, pettily, his mother's talking down of the parish.[42]

When indigenous elites liked a priest, he was immovable. San Simón de Bravo's vicario, Jorge Celis Casillas, was prevented from attending ICAM's 1930 synod because locals suspected Corpus Christi might redeploy him: "they grew truly enraged" (verdaderamente bravos) and "will not let me go to Mexico City, for fear I will not return." Guillermo de la Peña refused to leave his Puebla parish in 1929 when Pérez tried to second him: his six hundred faithful would have nobody else. Also in Puebla, actipenses took to Pascual García: "no priest, Roman or Mexican" had done so much for them, they said in 1931, or "suffered so much for the pueblo." If Lazarini's timid persona alienated Xochitlán, it unexpectedly endeared him to Coyotepec's fierce agraristas, who liked their studious, pious priest. Lazarini's "correct attentions . . . fulfill the law of God," they said; they were resolved "like heroic Cuauhtémoc" to keep him, which in their case was saying something. Xalostoc eulogized José Melgosa; Emeterio Valdéz was described by Santo Domingo's (Ver.) jefe de armas as his *compadrito* and was asked to pray for the pueblo during a flu outbreak.[43] It is counterintuitive to think of ICAM in affective terms. Yet given the historic neglect from which many indigenous Catholics suffered, it was not surprising that attentive priests stirred up strong feelings in them. Indigenous elites forgave priests a lot if they showed respect and dramatic flair. Actipan's junta endorsed Antonio Munive, whose homosexuality dogged him elsewhere, because people took to him. When one of Pérez's envoys arrived to depose him, a crowd of men and women, led by the sacristan's brother, stood shoulder to shoulder, stones ready. When Francisco Durán's homosexuality became known in Tlaola in 1930, locals demanded a return to Rome. Yet the cura who told Pérez of the scandal involving "Sr. Durán's personality" said that if he wanted to save Tlaola he must approach "well-known and respected" Francisco Torres and take his advice (de voca de él). Torres, as municipal secretary, indeed had influence and used it to uphold Durán's tenure (according to his daughter, Torres also had healing gifts, suggesting shamanic power). In Ahuacatlán, tax official Melo was the key *principal*; he and some laypeople appointed Durán as their *cura párroco* in early 1928, seemingly unconcerned by rumors of homosexuality; yet this time Pérez vetoed a local decision, saying that it was impossible for Durán to be párroco, given his "limited experience and youthfulness." This was perhaps a reference to Durán's private life, though Pérez said he opposed the appointment because Ahuacatlán's principales had not consulted him.[44]

Festive chronicles must be carefully read, as *Restauración* embellished them, yet accounts of deflated fiestas also came in. In Ixtapan (Méx.) in 1928, the church emptied because people went to a lay (and Roman) Mass in Atenco. Jaltipan's priest admitted one year that local "fanatics" tried to stop the fiesta, which went ahead after an order from Veracruz governor Abel Rodríguez, who intervened at Calles' behest. "It is known by you," Lazarini told Pérez, "that I personally do not like the pueblos, still less dealing among *indios*."[45] These reports lend credence to enthusiastic ones. Xometla's junta (Méx.) printed a flier announcing 1927's feast of San Miguel and leafleted neighboring villages, as if promoting a county fair: fliers promised a five-day fiesta, Mass with a bishop, fireworks, a banquet, and "customary dances." For the latter, "companies of Saint Jameses [Santiagueros]" battled moorish captains and Pontius Pilates, caparisons swaying, swords clashing. Possibly these quadrilles represented Santiago's triumph over the Moors or the four *Truenos* (thunders) that anthropologists say held up the corners of the Nahua cosmos; or perhaps they were simple good-versus-evil contests, as Guy Stresser-Péan (who saw many such battles) believes. This was not a lone festive account. For one 1928 feast in the Puebla lowlands, the band of San Pablo de las Tunas struck up as the priest's car pulled in, a Marian flag was unfurled, and he walked under floral arches on streets thick with confetti. In Zapotitlán (Pue.), Alfredo Arredondo López thought that 1926's Guadalupan fiesta "surpass[ed] those of previous years." In the Nahua town of Jaltipan (Ver.) in 1928, finally, Pérez's envoy was humbled at Candlemas. "Without exaggeration," he wrote, five thousand people and two bands awaited: "From the train station to the *curato*, I was driven in a car that was literally covered with flowers... carnations, gardenias, tuberoses, and other blooms." The year before, another priest estimated that five thousand people came to the station; he walked into church under a floral arc de triomphe.[46]

PARISHES WITHIN PARISHES

Fervor was partly political, and ICAM was often lured into secessionist politics, that is, subjected to towns' efforts to declare independence of parish seats. That was especially so where conflicts reinforced what archbishop Vera y Zuria of Puebla called the "the ancient and terrible division between *Indios y castellanos*,"[47] mestizo and indigenous rivalry. Certainly, the desire among indigenous wards to become "polities unto themselves" was old: as Benjamin Johnson writes, it characterized the quarter-sections (tlaxilacalli) of pre-Hispanic *altepeme*; colonial sujetos likewise wanted to escape headtowns (cabeceras) that exacted tribute or faena. Thus, subcommunities would present themselves as de facto centers ("institutional givens") whose autonomy the authorities need only recognize. The eighteenth century was a golden age for this secessionism (the Bourbons encouraged it to deplete indigenous cacicazgos),[48] but the 1920s and 1930s saw a revival, perhaps because political status (categoría política) determined eligibility for ejidos. Pérez himself (chapter 1) knew the power of secessionist aspirations. The religious crisis was important, too, because it decentered religious authority by closing churches. Sujetos thus had a chance to register priests of their own, becoming de facto parish seats, holding fiestas, and making a preemptive case for political autonomy, as Puebla towns did when paying municipal school taxes.[49]

None of this was lost on ICAM's base, which comprised numerous subject communities. Fewer than half the communities registering Mexican priests (127, 48 percent) were municipal cabeceras; only a third were parish cabeceras (70, 30 percent).[50] On the contrary, ICAM petitions often articulated resentment at cabeceras. Xometla's enmity toward Acolman's "fanatical" mayor reflected its historic status as a *visita* of Acolman's Augustinian priory. Tenoxtitlán's Mexican Catholics enjoyed registering a priest in the hated cabecera, Jocotitlán, thereby usurping its role as parish seat. Alquizapan (Pue.) registered a priest in 1928 but requested guarantees for fear that its "fanatical" headtown, Juan N. Méndez, would inflict reprisals ("cruelties").[51] Some pueblos—such as Actipan and Yehualtepec (Pue.)—were still waging eighteenth-century battles to escape bullying cabeceras (Acatzingo, in Actipan's case) or, hypocritically, to dominate their sujetos, as Yehualtepec did after absconding from Tlacotepec. The conflict between Actipan and, Acatzingo, three miles distant, is a dramatic example. Led by auxiliary mayor Guillermo Domínguez, Actipan backed ICAM and registered a priest during the Cristero War; as the church-state conflict was resolved, however, actipenses faced reprisals from Acatzingo's returning Roman cura, who "mesmerized" the municipal president into canceling ICAM's registration in January 1929. When Mexican Catholics reinstated a priest—Salvador Arámbula—in June, there was violence. Subsequently, 448 *acatzinguenses* denounced "grave outrages against our persons and interests by schismatic elements" and demanded that the "schismatic group" be barred from the parroquia, "which by tradition is ours." They alleged that schismatics stormed the building one night, fighting through "a furious crowd." "All the evils" in Acatzingo were caused by Arámbula, who "injects deviant ideas into the ignorant masses' spirits." Yet 175 actipenses refuted this, damning "Romanist tyrants" and affirming their continued loyalty to the Mexican Church.[52] Arámbula himself became anxious on discovering that his supporters, many of them agraristas, were locked in a vicious battle with "Romans" from Acatzingo. "You cannot imagine how bad things are getting here," he told José Lazarini in August: his "Romanist brothers" had tried to poison him, now he was terrified of what actipenses might do to avenge him. The atmosphere was heavy with dread: "We're in it now, and there's nothing for it but to come out on the far side of this hell," he continued, "for you know very well the commitments that one acquires with these merciless, schismatical agraristas." When in the pulpit, Arámbula wailed, "I always preach peace and that there be no more talk of 'Romanists,' but God knows how I shall ever get out of this."[53]

Actipenses took revenge on 15 September—a holiday—when a Roman Catholic family tried to bury a dead child. Mourners alleged that cismáticos defiled the open grave, filling it with rocks; as the cortege neared the templo, it was attacked by "the schismatic priest and a multitude of persons professing that creed." Machetes flashed, rocks pounded, blood was spilled. Terrified pallbearers kept going to Acatzingo. Mexican Catholics claimed self-defense: they were an "immense majority" in Actipan, yet Acatzingo harassed them by sending Roman clergy on to their turf. It was unjust that they "be deprived of the right . . . to conserve a church of our own." Moreover, 251 people wrote, "the Roman clergy hates us in an unchristian manner, holding us contrary to their church." In December, there was another confrontation when Arámbula, returned to his Roman obedience, marched into Actipan with Acatzingo's mayor, "people alien to the community," "pious women," and soldiers. Actipenses fought back, and for years hence only Mexican priests were allowed; a blow came in 1931 when President Ortiz Rubio closed Actipan's church, citing complaints that Mexican Catholics showed "a wildness bordering on savagery" (predictably, there was rioting when Acatzingo's mayor sealed the church). Next year, however, Mexican Catholics forced the doors, the custodians lamenting that "the majority group has decided that, for better or worse, the church will open." ICAM was in charge in 1934.[54]

Reports of actipenses' enthusiastic fiestas make sense when tagged to this violent struggle for self-determination: it was a way to portray Actipan as a parish-in-waiting. Just as eagerly, Acatzingo denounced actipenses as "savages" who should be punished. These fault lines were common. In Tehuizotla (Pue.), twenty-five miles south, a few hundred agraristas wanted to register a Mexican priest in February 1928 and asked that their cabecera, Molcaxac, allow him to work "with complete liberty." Yet the ayuntamiento ("in accordance, we believe, with the Roman priest of that place") thwarted them. Tehuizotla's agraristas thus asked the state governor to punish Molcaxac's "fanatical" priest and officials, ensuring that the municipio "in no way obstructs the practices pertaining to our Mexican Catholic religion." Receiving no answer, Tehuizotla's "campesinos, ejidatarios, [and] natives" turned to Gobernación, complaining that Molcaxac's ayuntamiento demanded endless proofs of the priest's bona fides when Gobernación already had him on file. The state governor, too, showed a "spirit of conservatism" and hoped that "ministers dependent on Rome will recover their former glory." As everyone ignored them, Tehuizotla's petitioners took matters into their own hands as the 1929 patronal feast approached. Now, "Romanists" reported, ejidatarios "instigated by the schismatic priest" persecuted them. "Our creed being different to that which the majority professes," the victims wrote, agraristas "oblige us to attend the ceremonies and festivities of the *cura sismático* who ministers in our pueblo." One "Romanist" had been struck in the face with a machete, losing seven teeth; another had been cudgeled and robbed, and three more shot.[55]

Another well-documented case of Catholic separatism was Tenancingo (Tlax.), a Nahua village nestling in La Malinche's skirts. Its campaign for municipal status (achieved 1930) was in full flow during the religious crisis, and separation from its parish, San Pablo del Monte, was desired. Indeed, three fiscales who petitioned ICAM for a priest in March 1928 signed as the "Junta Directiva de San Miguel Tenanzingo que gestiona la erección de una parroquia." And, according to oral history, Tenancingo's estrangement from the diocese of Puebla started earlier, during the revolution (1918–1919), when its *tiaxcas* (principales) asked the cura of San Pablo, Father Montiel, to celebrate a Mass with three priests. Montiel agreed, but, not finding two other priests, hired a deacon and sacristan, Pascual Heredia García, who for unknown reasons gave the sermon. Despite Heredia's lay status, the sermon was a hit, and villagers asked him to remain for Easter, which he did, performing sacraments after Montiel fell ill. Heredia was so successful that the inhabitants protected him when Montiel ordered him out. Emissaries from the archdiocese were stoned. Oral histories suggest that Heredia later grew tyrannical, hiking prices, consorting with women, and excommunicating rivals. It was probably this that drove tiaxcas to depose him and register ICAM priest Pascual Luciano García in 1927. García led Easter and Pentecost services, for which people rang bells, threw flowers, and played music. He also consecrated a chapel to the Blessed Sacrament and a "rogation bell, for when storms are unleashed over the mountains," hinting at an agrarian religion. His influence helped Tenancingo to win municipal status and he ministered until his death, in 1948. In the 1950s, ICAM was majoritarian.[56]

Sometimes cabeceras opted for Mexican Catholicism, as we see in complaints from Yehualtepec's *fiscal mayor* that a priest (Manuel Salas) had gone awol in August 1930. A priest, the fiscal told Pérez, must curry local favor, especially now that ICAM was attacked on all sides post-arreglos. Yet "Father Manuel, instead of making us one pueblo does the contrary"; his neglect of Mexican Catholics exposed them to political attack. He should remember that he, "without his parishioners, is worth nothing." Next month, Yehualtepec's officials made the stakes plainer: while Yehualtepec once lorded it over its sujetos by virtue of its parish status, its satelites now had a Roman vicario and three of them—Zozutla, Tetzoyucan, Tlacomulco—were "requesting political separation so as to reconstitute themselves as a *municipio libre*." Yehualtepec's fiscal and principales wanted to crush this movement, and demanded Pérez's support: "This being one of your principal churches . . . Your Grace should care for it, lending us the full weight of governmental authority so that this Authority may defend revolutionary principles and the faithful's beliefs." They needed action, not words, "because we are suffering in ways that perhaps Your Grace cannot imagine."[57]

A battle of wills between Afro-indigenous peasants and cacique Alberto Páez broke out on central Veracruz's leeward (Sotavento). Here ICAM was drawn into a conflict between the Cuyucuenda cattle estate—the name deriving from the *kimbundu* (Angolan) for "plantation"—and hamlets that were seeking to re-establish a colonial pilgrimage rout over estate land. This was a novel variation on our theme: client hacienda villages seeking right of way (possibly grazing rights) on estate land, not parish status. Thus, hamlets such as Mata Cabestro and Los Robles petitioned Dimás Anguiano to come the twenty miles from Veracruz to celebrate the feast of the Virgin of the Aparecida in 1927. Anguiano was to celebrate in a white colonial chapel located on Cuyucuenda land, right beside the *casco*. Herein dwelled the Aparecida, known as "La Virgen de la O," because of the O-shaped *embouchure* that colonial *mulato* confreres made when singing her praises. Anguiano was on his way when told that Páez, the hacendado, "claiming to be owner of said chapel," would stop him. Devotees accused Páez and one José Lara of purloining alms at the shrine, and of doing so for decades. The Roman curia knew this to be true, devotees said, and interdicted the chapel, though Páez bribed officials and reopened for business, keeping the Virgin's utensils and jewels for himself. As Páez intimidated the petitioning villages, they had not known how to exercise their rights. But then they heard of ICAM and approached Anguiano, who urged Gobernación to reopen the chapel and punish Páez. Anguiano himself had a permit to minister in all three municipios embraced by Cuyucuenda (Soledad de Doblado, San Cristóbal Llave, Tlalixcoyan) plus a letter of invitation from local notable Pío Lara, averring that Mata Cabestro and Los Robles wanted him ("he gestionado vastante su ida a Cuyucuenda . . . ya mucha gente sabe que Ud. vendría y que con eso se les compondría la fiesta"). Yet Páez refused to yield, even when his wife asked him. The attorney general launched an investigation in January 1928, surely reflecting Tejeda's concern for ICAM and, perhaps, anxiety about central Veracruz landlord gangs such as La Mano Negra. Unfortunately, the resolution is missing from the file, though one hopes Páez got his comeuppance and villagers heard their Mass.[58] Perhaps they did, because by autumn Anguiano's beat included not only El Cristo in Veracruz, with its ancient driftwood Christ, but also hinterland towns north and south, from Chichicaxtle to San Cristóbal Llave. Here Anguiano massed on All Saints,' evidently drawing a crowd since the church junta and police conspired to detain him and extract a hefty *mordida*. Though the authorities resented Anguiano's "investiture," they had little choice but to let him work because he had permits.[59]

In addition to center-periphery conflicts, there were intracommunitarian, barrio-level conflicts in which class and ethnic interest, not jurisdiction, were in dispute. These mainly occurred in headtowns, which is unsurprising since mestizo elites were concentrated there. Often we have the impression that indigenous and de razón cliques were waiting to get their hooks into Mexican priests the minute they dismounted. Father Durán made a "general confession" in 1928, admitting that he had slandered the patriarch before Ahuacatlán's (Pue.) municipal president, by saying that Pérez liked a drink. He now retracted these statements, however, saying wealthy *beatas* had coached him ("I was advised to break with the sismáticos and stay as a Romano by the Cuevas sisters and doña Barbara, who said that the romanos were coming back and the sismáticos were finished"). Ahuacatlán's principales ("Don Fernando Melo, Umberto Sosa, Cacho Sosa, and Don Lolo") convinced him to stay as cura, though he was only a deacon.[60]

In Ixcaquixtla (Pue.), a valley pueblo with a Churrigueresque church, ethnic divisions were explicit. Here an indigenous *principal*, Pedro Cancino, launched ICAM in November 1928 when he petitioned the ayuntamiento to register a priest according to "our wishes." The Marian cycle was approaching, so a priest arrived and was taken to the town hall "by a group of inhabitants of this community, documenting that he is appointed cura of the parish church." Yet the mayor refused to register him, demanding endless *oficios* and "losing" the church keys. Cancino claimed that "almost all the inhabitants" supported him—certainly, a hundred people filled the ayuntamiento—while "five or ten, including the authorities," did not. The ringleaders were municipal secretary Francisco Orea, his sister's pious women friends, and Spanish cura Bonifacio Balbuena. Unfortunately, they had pistoleros. When ICAM's priest took to the pulpit, indeed, armed men burst in shouting "¡Viva Cristo Rey!" and soldiers were called. Undeterred, Cancino continued to hire priests in 1929, because Mexican Catholics were "not merely a faction . . . but genuinely the pueblo." He himself was "special commissioner for this Villa's inhabitants, excluding so-called 'people of reason' [los llamados "de razón"]," which said it all. In June, for the patronal feast (John the Baptist), Cancino found a priest to satisfy people's desire "to feast on the day of our Patron Saint, with the religious rites according to our customs." Again, the fiesta committee self-identified as indigenous and denounced the "people pompously called '*de razón*'" for bringing "anarchy" to Ixcaquixtla. Local agraristas, led by Nicolás Simón, also weighed in, warning Portes Gil that "my pueblo . . . petitioned via the proper channels" for a "Mexican Church priest," but was obstructed by an "an upstart" municipio. If it continued, agraristas might use violence to recover "the rights of my pueblo."[61] Thus, Ixcaquixtla's Cristiada was really a sectarian feud between mestizo and indigenous Catholics.

Some townships divided into mestizo and indigenous parishes, such as Jonotla in Puebla's coffee-growing Sierra Norte. Here intra-Catholic differences reinforced a split between mestizo planters and Totonac peasants who participated in a dual (Marian and costumbre-based) religion. Religious politics assumed a revivalist character after Emeterio Valdéz registered first in the parish of San Juan Bautista ("the main church") in 1926, and then, finding no takers, in "the so-called 'Santuario del Peñón [Shrine of the Rock]'" in March 1927. This, he discovered, was a rough-hewn edifice which Totonacs built part-way up a huge rock dominating Jonotla. A waterfall cascaded to the canyon floor far below. The shrine was dedicated to the Guadalupe in her local avocation, "La Virgen del Peñón": indeed, it housed a stone Virgin, eight inches tall, who miraculously revealed herself in a rockfall witnessed by a young boy, Fidel Alejandro, in October 1922. Valdéz's March registration coincided with the spring agricultural cycle and, as anthropologist Gregory Reck shows, the Marian cult itself was linked to fertility, specifically, to Mary's symbolic coupling with a pluvial male deity: the rock—*Tlaloctepetl* in Nahuatl, *Tlaloc Sipij* in Totonac—was venerated as the home of Tlaloc, Jonotla's mythical founder and Nahua rain god.[62] In social terms, Reck adds, intra-Catholic divisions overlaid the stresses of economic modernization: while mestizo growers observed parish rituals, the shrine expressed defiance against mestizos associated with the coffee economy and official Catholicism. If so, Marianism was a symbolic reassertion of the indigenous economy, what Reck calls Jonotla's "Virgin-maize complex," and ICAM administered it. By July 1927, Valdéz had "still not taken custody" of the parroquia, the mayor reported, though he had "passed through this community on various occasions" to minister. He did so, however, exclusively in the Totonac shrine; that April he stated that indigenous devotees provided "the only support for religious cult in this place." Alms were generous: Valdéz's accounts totaled 360 pesos just for 15 March, with Mass collects adding 93 pesos by month's end. On the day of writing—27 April—Valdéz raked in 183 pesos, meaning 636 pesos in one month. From this, he used 300 pesos to pay two employees—likely sacristans—leaving 350 pesos. ICAM's conformity to Totonac habits was echoed in sacramental observance, where takings were paltry. As Valdéz noted, "to date [April], no baptisms or marriages have been celebrated." This, he alleged, was due to "fanaticism," but really, *jonotecos* had no need of him once Marian rituals had realigned the cosmos.[63]

Reflecting generally on ICAM's Totonac and Nahua appeal, we might note that anthropologists identify revolutionary anticlericalism as a powerful degenerative factor in indigenous costumbre, as this was tagged to Catholic ritual. Thus, argues Stresser-Péan—whose lifetime of fieldwork in Puebla began ca. 1938—ethnographic-archaeological evidence shows that from the mid-1920s many villages buried their ceremonial wooden drums and suppressed local fertility cults as the prestige of Nahua-Totonac seers, no less than Roman clergy, collapsed.[64] The Cristiada, together with economic out-migration and roadbuilding, were the death knell for costumbre, spring rites in which pueblos renewed ties with life-giving male and female mountain deities and their saint-gods before attending Mass. Formerly, Stresser-Péan shows, costumbre involved visits to shrines at villages' cardinal points, where people sacrificed fowl or pigs to the Thunders, divine pillars of a rectangular, nahuatlized cosmos identifiable as Saints John the Baptist, Alexander, Gabriel, and Gregory. Seers celebrated mountain deities by playing horizontal, "female," wooden drums (teponaztli), and vertical, "male," drums (huehuetl) that were kept in churches or shrines. At night they placed corn dollies and paper, bark, or straw figurines on shrine altars, feting them in dancing and drinking sessions led by *curanderos* and fiscales. A priest's Mass was the fiesta's climax, because corn would not grow without cult to the Sun-Christ nor Mary, his mother.⁶⁵ Jonotla's account tantalizingly suggests such a dual celebration, sponsored by indigenous officialdom. It is not hard to imagine, therefore, that ICAM provided a safety valve for indigenous elites and associated religious practices including costumbre as these came under pressure from mestizaje, capitalism, and romanization. Contemporary portraits of ICAM-run churches hint at this. In 1930s Huehuetla (Pue.), British diplomat-folklorist Rodney Gallop saw wooden drums, "maize dolls" drenched in fowl's blood, and figures in ecclesiastical garb, one wearing a biretta—a pity he did not ask who they were! Indigenista-muralist Miguel Covarrubias, visiting Cosoleacaque's (Ver.) big whitewashed church in 1942, saw "rows of gaily painted niches and vitrines along the walls . . . containing awkward wooden statues of saints, garishly painted, with staring glass eyes, all alike in size as if to establish their equality." The altar was "decked with embroidered napkins, candles, bouquets of flowers, braziers for copal incense, clay pigs, and ears of corn"; "primitive drums and a wooden palanquin" stood nearby. Clergy were "conspicuously absent" as "town elders take charge of the ceremonies."⁶⁶

There were no buried drums in Pisa Flores (Ver.), either, when Mexican Catholicism was taken there by Tepehua migrants from Puebla in the 1930s. Instead, anthropological data (mainly from the 1950s) suggest that the twinning of Catholicism and costumbre was central to ICAM's success. Here a corner of the townsite was reserved as a shrine for the small paper or bark saints (muñecos or halasítnit) that Tepehuas worshipped, though ICAM also permitted costumbre in its church (tahkín), a stone building that doubled as a native oratory (lakachinchin). As in Totonac religion, saints were linked in sets of masculine and female pairs (*camas*), the most important being the Sun-Christ (witcháan) and the feminine moon and Marianized water goddess; then the Cross, tahkín, earth, corn, and star. Mexican Catholicism thus allowed Tepehuas to regulate public religion, hiring clergy to celebrate feasts such as San Miguel and select sacraments (Mass, baptism, confirmation); but otherwise ICAM left church-based cult in indigenous actors' hands, and sometimes the Mexican priest himself was an indigenous religious specialist. Jesús Gutiérrez, who succeeded Father Monte de Honor as priest and died in 1959, was accused of practicing witchcraft as well as Catholic rites. By allowing devotees to be Catholic while observing Tepehua rituals, ICAM shored up the indigenous elite. For the fiestas patrias, curanderos led rituals commemorating the pueblo's mythical founders.⁶⁷

In Jaltipan (Ver.), a sixteenth-century delta port founded by coastal Nahuas fleeing plague and cattle, Mexican Catholicism joined a political struggle between indigenous and conservative elites, the latter backed by Heriberto Jara's state government (1924–1927). Jara opposed Tejeda's handling of religious policy and manacled ICAM: Veracruz's 1926 religious law, anticipating the arreglos, stated that only "hierarchical superiors" (Rome) could make parish appointments. In January 1927, however, ICAM arrived. That August, came Pascual Luciano García, the thirty-three-year-old indigenous sacristan we met in Tlaxcala. His religious credentials are doubtful (one document has him as an ex-seminarian from Puebla) but not his indigeneity. Macario López, who recruited him, condescendingly called him "that little Indian [aquel Indito] from Nativitas." In Jaltipan, García suffered persecution but eventually prevailed by catering to Nahua tastes. His first task was to celebrate the fiesta of Saint Rose of Lima, which drew four thousand people from across the isthmus, followed by Señor San Miguel in September. Supporters included *mayordomo de las fiestas* Eutiquio Anzúres and the church notary.[68]

After a promising start, Jaltipan's authorities accused García of profiteering. This was not an elected ayuntamiento, however, but a Jara-appointed junta de administración civil. García's supporters claimed he was punished for challenging a cacicazgo led by Jara's *comisionado gobernador*: Jara's hirelings "assaulted" the church, removed the bells, and jailed people "for the simple fact of being Mexican Apostolic Catholics." Then, in 1928, García was ordered from Jaltipan on pain of arrest. Blaming this on "the municipal political authorities," García begged Pérez to contact Tejeda, who probably intervened since the warrant was not enforced until mid-1928, after Tejeda left Gobernación (May). In June, however, García was arrested after police stopped a Nahua woman for carrying an image to church for a blessing. García was charged with organizing illegal processions. "I have suffered a real via crucis," he told Pérez: "I fear for my life." In September he was arrested again, for rebellion, according to his brother, Melquíades. That was a virtual death sentence, and indeed, García was ferried between Salina Cruz (Oax.) and Puebla to keep him incommunicado. Then, in November, García was released; two weeks after Tejeda began his second governorship (1 December), García was appointed "first priest."[69]

Evidently he was a pawn in Tejeda's and Jara's rivalry. Another complication was that Pérez betrayed García because he suspected him, along with vicar general López y Sierra, of plotting.[70] Thus, in January 1929 Pérez sent a replacement priest, *tlaxcalteco* Antonio Munive, to Jaltipan. Munive canceled Candlemas, a major feast, locking the church and saying that García would never say Mass again. Munive "was such a swine," García wrote, "that he would not ask for my help through gritted teeth . . . though he was overloaded with baptisms." The parish president denounced Munive's "harsh character" and refusal to lead a novena for La Candelaria. Such abuses never happened under "our beloved Father *Pascualito*," parishioners wrote; they demanded his reinstatement.[71] Instead, García established himself twenty-five miles away in Puerto México, where he was sheltered by Luisa Reboulen, an influential widow and devotee. Obstinately, Pérez kept harassing him: it was said that Munive's supporters were "ready to kill don Pascualito," because he acted like "boss" of the isthmus. García was livid that Pérez assailed him, leaving the pueblos without cult and violating his "canonical rights": this was why Rome mocked them, García said, yet it was he who had revived the faith of the indigenous ("ise despertar los indígenas a reconocer que avia Dios y patria").[72] Local people seemed to agree. In September, García returned to Jaltipan with the backing of indigenous officials and new *tejedista* authorities run by local fixer Juan Carranza. In September, 160 Mexican Catholics told Gobernación that they did not want clergy "who supported the cristeros" and that "we love our Mexican Father, defender of our pueblos." Over four hundred people signed a November petition backing García, by which time he ministered in twenty-two pueblos, up the coast to Pajapam and upriver to Minatitlán and Acayucan.[73] Now that García had "mesmerized" local Nahuas, in Munive's words, he turned on him. Jaltipan's municipal secretary ("great friends with Father Pascual") denied Munive permission to minister; people shunned or spied on him, save Manuel Aragón and his wife ("*presidenta* of the Holiest Virgin of Guadalupe" sodality), who sheltered him. Munive was "dying of hunger because of don Pascual's bad faith," unable to earn a cent. Meanwhile, Pascualito officiated as he pleased, in new towns like Cosoleacaque. While other priests took steps "without a lantern," García trod confidently.[74]

Reading this saga, ICAM seems like a politico-religious movement connecting local and state cadres. Yet traction depended on genuine affinity with local Catholicism. Even Munive's supporters conceded that Jaltipan's mayordomos esteemed García, because he "contented the pueblo with ceremonies and sermons." García himself claimed to have ended "all the abuses that Roman Fathers committed in the pueblos," including sacramental fees. He himself "administered everything for a limosna, which is how I was able to win over all the villages." Additionally, García said, Nahuas were "the only ones to show any interest in the conservation of their traditional church," thus he enlisted them in his building campaign, "to which the whole pueblo contributed." Problems, he averred, began with a refusal to give Jara's civil junta its cut, after which he faced a "war without quarter." Sixty women corroborated this account: "the señor cura has known how to put [the junta] in its place, ensuring that what the pueblo contributes voluntarily with its small donations . . . is respected." Two hundred men praised the "indefatigable and good Father" for rebuilding a church that was "abandoned into God's hands." García's reverence for the Nahuas' images, meanwhile, was notorious: he was "personally repainting all the church images, and he has changed all the old tatters that once clothed the icons," the men wrote. Not just altar saints, but old, cracked effigies found "relegated to the most complete oblivion." It would be fascinating to know which saints these were, and who had junked them and why. Luisa Reboulen saw him do the same in Puerto México: "the images are his beloved children—he repairs them, dresses them, cleans them, and tends them with maternal affection."[75] Curating indigenous Catholicism paid dividends. Reboulen told Pérez in May 1929: "Concerning Canon Pascualito . . . I tell you that he enjoys great affection in this City," for he overcame a lack of education by giving himself "body and soul" to the church. "The faithful are his brothers; he treats and serves them with solicitous affection . . . Can more be desired of a priest?" If Pérez did not protect him, the romanos would return: she told parishioners that God would not allow the church to fall into Roman hands again, "after such bloodshed." And she "dearly begged" for García's return, "since there is a great deal of work with the feasts in the villages."[76]

In Chiapas, finally, a pitched battle for churches on Soconusco's coffee coast and the Mexico-Guatemala border broke out. As seen in chapter 3, local revolutionaries saw ICAM as a useful device, until garridismo's regional advance saw cura José Ramírez forcibly recant his beliefs (1934). This should not make us conclude that ICAM had no religious base. Here, again, ICAM was rooted in local Catholicism, especially in divisions between *ladino* clergy and indigenous churchpeople. This was a borderland, too, where shifting boundaries had long created space for Catholic curios (who could forget Rugeley's harlequin priest, roaming the Petén in multicolored breeches and high heels?).[77] The career of Tapachula's Roman cura, however, Eudaldo Martínez, was straight out of *Balún Canán*. We know because a confidant of archbishop Mora wrote a secret report in September 1925, explaining why the parish had fallen to ICAM. Though "schismatics" were a minority, Mora's informant reported that ICAM was attracting aggrieved laymen who deplored Martínez's conduct. They included two locally prominent figures, Germán Rizo and Manuel Chacón Cárdenas, plus indigenous sacristan Elías de la Cruz, who the informant described disdainfully as a "church mouse" and "someone not to be feared." The "true motive" for Pérez's schism was thus personal. No wonder. The informant explained how Martínez, arriving in 1917, lodged rent-free in Dolores Chacón's house. When his benefactress died, relatives were stunned to find, tucked inside the will, "an IOU in the señor cura's favor, signed by her, for 18,000 pesos." This "scandalized one of the heirs [Chacón], and this person is now director of the cismáticos." Martínez's sexual abuses caused further outrage. On arrival, he shacked up with "a concubine named Ignacia Bustamante, with whom he had a son"; he left "another señorita," a Comitán indígena, in an "interesting condition"; and raped a girl in the Hijas de María named Dolores Argueta ("abusó de ella"). When her family protested, Martínez sent her to a village in Guatemala, where he still visited her. The cura also neglected church affairs to tend his own, having an estate and shares in a banana plantation. His laziness in church alienated De la Cruz, "a humble Indian who always used to be at the cura's side" but was now "one of the schismatical directors." Mora's informant believed that the revolt would end if a "moral Father" went to Tapachula.[78]

Soon Father Ramírez was presiding at San Agustín. "I say Mass and compulsory prayers every day without interruption," he wrote in November 1926. For his part, De la Cruz, restyled as Knights of Guadalupe commander, began sponsoring feasts for ICAM, beginning with the 1925 fiestas patrias, the Guadalupan feast, and the 1926 feast of Saint Cecilia. Except for the music (*marimbas*, not brass) and patriotic flag-waving, the fiestas were like those elsewhere.[79] De la Cruz also liaised with local pueblos, because, unusually, village Knights of Guadalupe branches existed in Chiapas. When San Agustín filled, too, it was because Mam and Zoque villagers came to Tapachula. "In this city," a Roman Catholic woman wrote in 1931, "vecinos who believe in the so-called Mexican Schismatic Church do not exist." She did not mean that San Agustín was empty—just that educated ladinos steered clear. Two of them, in fact ("two señoritas"), snuck inside in March 1927 and removed the prized image of Saint Augustine, a whitewashed saint holding a miniature church in outstretched left hand, like a baker admiring a neoclassical cake. Nonetheless, this pious dama continued, ICAM drew "Indians or ignorant people, who in their simpleness or inculture, believe that the practices taking place are the same as those that they are used to seeing from childhood, with no change in canonical validity." The ethnic description, if not the value judgment, was right: as ICAM deacon Alfonso Arias confirmed at Easter 1927, it was "Tapachula's humble inhabitants" and "tributary populations" who sat in the pews.[80]

So Ramírez toured the pueblos. He first founded a chapel in Suchiate Mariscal, whose "inhabitants . . . gathered fervently to lift their prayers to God." His sermons exalted indigenous "humility" and he used the Suchiate as his font; in 1927, he baptized a "young man of good position"—Palomec, son of Hermenegildo Chol—in its waters. These are mere details, true, but they give the impression again that ICAM attracted indigenous elites. Later Ramírez was escorted to Huixtla, where *Restauración* admitted that "antagonistic elements" shouted insults. But people in Berriozabal requested services in July, as did the Mam pueblo of Motozintla. By 1929, petitions came from the border: a handwritten one with sixty-six signatures, half bearing women's names, from Tuxtla Chico; another, signed by forty-three people from Unión de Juárez; one from three hundred people, evenly split by gender, in San Fernando, though this was upstate. Mazatán's Roman Catholics, finally, denounced Ramírez in 1930 for blessing a church bell, performing "many baptisms," and leading candlelit processions and collecting alms in the plaza.[81]

The combination of Mexican Catholicism and indigeneity in border municipios, where increasing numbers of inhabitants were Guatemalan, was distinctive. One wonders, as Nolan-Ferrel does in her study of agrarismo, whether revolutionary Catholicism appealed because it consecrated a kind of religious citizenship, either for borderland Mexican pueblos experiencing inward migration or migrants themselves. It is striking that Ramírez turned the Suchiate—a.k.a. the Mexico-Guatemala border—into a Mexican Jordan. Surely there was poetic license in his accounts; yet clashes between romanos and *mexicanos* in Tapachula were recoded as battles between Catholic *mexicanidad* and "Roman" Guatemalenness. In March 1932, Ramírez was chased from San Agustín by a crowd comprising the wives of ladino elites and "foreign" women who then occupied the church. "Due to one lot of sectarian fanatics or the other," a cynical eyewitness added, Tapachula was "a marketplace where people insult, argue, or gossip about one another." Yet when soldiers ended the occupation (5 April), women detainees were turned over to Migration, not Gobernación or Hacienda, which respectively had legal power over matters of worship and churches.[82] Despite hints of transnational conflict, ICAM's basic utility as an indigenous Catholic medium was clearer, as a 1935 petition by "Apostolic Mexican Catholics" shows. Gobernación had by now closed San Agustín to prevent fighting. Yet Vidal Becerra, president, spoke for "several thousand *congregados*" when demanding its reopening "for the practice of our cults, which consist of prayers, the lighting of candles, and the placing of wild and other flowers [on the altars] . . . We choose, as a rule, the nonintervention of any priest, since we desire to work solely in conformity with our own good judgment, without committing censurable acts . . . On the contrary, we desire to serve our Catholic pueblo in order that the good religious practices that our fathers and grandfathers left us do not disappear; and because, on exiting this world, we hope to take with us the satisfaction of having complied with the wishes of our elders."[83]

CONCLUSION

Mexico had a popular revolutionary church, but in practice it was *far* from the classical French prototype. It offered a pragmatic, saint-oriented religion, not a cult of reason: priests had to reintegrate the supernatural and village orders at climactic points of the ritual year. Adore the saint, preach with gravitas, defer to principales, agree a price—and little else mattered. When priests were away, people did as they wanted—which was how they wanted it. ICAM tapped into, and accepted, indigenous Catholicism, undercutting its hegemonic rival. It was Catholicism plus costumbre, not syncretism. In a country where indigenous pueblos were exploited as a resource, or deemed incomplete, this was something novel, even if ICAM fell short of its own reformist rhetoric. ICAM promised Catholic liberty to indigenous people, so got dragged into local politics. There was some evidence of high-level manipulation. Yet, if the regime had possessed enough power to orchestrate a national church centrally, it wouldn't have done it how Pérez did it, traversing Mexico's poorest states, its sierras and tropics, yielding to quarrelsome principales, splurging on saints and rockets, stitching together a serape of ethnic stripes, like a Mexican coat of many colors. Outside Mexico City, ICAM was less the sick joke portrayed in Catholic historiography than it was a popular indigenous church in Pérez's image.

CHAPTER SIX

BRONZE PRIESTS

Mexican Revolutionary Clergy

PATRIARCH PÉREZ HOPED to create an ecclesiastical "bronze race" of patriot priests, but French ambassador Ernest Lagarde described a motley crew: six adventurers, "from the worst elements of the clergy," their leaders notorious for "unedifying conduct."[1] For Bishop Méndez of Tehuantepec, likewise, Pérez's priests were "the Church's trash." Editorialists alleged that Pérez's priests were policemen wearing cassocks sewn in CROM factories; they were so ignorant, one said, that people could expose them by speaking Latin. Allegedly, ICAM priests in Veracruz stole pyxes, chalices, altar cloths, and vestments; Tapachula's priest allegedly played revolutionary airs—"La Adelita," "La Cucaracha"—on the organ in drunken masses; a Mexico City priest supposedly "wrestled" with church *encargada* Dalila Flores on a pulque-soaked sacristy floor, while another prepped for Mass by rutting with a buxom indigenous woman he called his "sister."[2] Hypocrisy, lucre, grog, sex: it was ironic how fast Pérez's Roman Catholic enemies found the old anticlerical repertoire when facing clerical opponents themselves. Why hadn't they shamed such vicious priests before? If even half the allegations were true, conversely, why should we care about these Friar Tucks?

One reason is that Pérez's clergy was more of a "chip off the old block" than Roman prelates cared to admit. This is what Lagarde said about Mexico's *Roman* clergy: "coarse, ignorant, greedy, and dissolute ... In matters connected with morals as well as those concerning dogma, the clergy has in no way directed its efforts to edifying the masses."[3] This said, the careers of Mexican priests, many of them ex-romanos, give unusual insights into the flawed lives of priests in postrevolutionary Mexico, an ecclesiastical "hidden transcript."[4] Their peccadilloes are legible, because ICAM interacted constantly with officialdom and had no curia to bowdlerize its archives; Pérez's surviving personnel files can be sensationally indiscreet. A century on, though, the record humanizes its subjects; unusually, we hear priests owning up to theological doubt, sexual urges, and marital and political angst. Some were rogues, others tormented: many had more colorful stories than the martyred boy-priests we so often hear about. Second, Mexican clergy were more numerous than we think: there were minimally 130 of them, equivalent in personnel terms, perhaps, to two Mexican dioceses. This was not a huge total; nor, in context, was it trivial. Nationally, ICAM siphoned off 5 percent of the Roman clergy's 1926 total of 3,600, though it was actually less because Pérez ordained an unknown number of priests.[5] Yet a brute comparison takes no account of the fact that ICAM was a regional movement with no presence, say, in the Bajío, northwest, or Yucatán. If we compare its strength to numbers of Roman clergy residing *only* in dioceses where it competed, following Gobernación's 1929 ecclesiastical census, the like-for-like picture is more even. North to south, 215 Roman curas reported from the sees of Papantla, Huejutla, Tulancingo, Puebla, Huajuapan, Chilapa, Veracruz, Oaxaca, Tehuantepec, and Chiapas. Thus, in Mexico's underchurched center-east and south, Pérez's clergy totaled two-thirds of Rome's (60 percent) within a few years.[6] ICAM paled against France's or Russia's revolutionary clergies, but in strength was comparable to other minority clergies in Mexico: it equaled the number of indigenous priests trained by the Bourbons in the whole eighteenth century (117), for example, or the Protestant pastorate of 1910.[7]

A related, third reason is that ICAM revealed some interesting, sometimes historic, fault lines among the clergy. One trait was a jansenistic commitment to defending the lower clergy. Indeed, Pérez called on poor, untenured priests to fight for their rights against haughty upper clergy. Even Lagarde sympathized: Mexico's lower clergy lived in "degrading," "menial" conditions, he wrote. Pérez promised to end such "wretchedness."[8] Pérez also revived the practice (more than the theory) of indigenous priesthood by ordaining Nahua and Totonac churchpeople ad hoc: fiscales (sacristans), cantores (choristers), curanderos (healers). The clearest analogy is not the Franciscan convent at Tlatelolco, but Samuel Ruiz's campaign in 1970s Chiapas to ordain indigenous lay specialists (tuhuneles) to the diaconate, even if married.[9] More from expediency rather than a liberationist urge to inculturate, Pérez ordained indigenous men versed in local Catholicism.

People who received Pérez's holy orders did not usually consider them fake. Hence this chapter treats ICAM's clergy as a group, one that included liberal clergy punished for their dissenting theological views; unbeneficed clergy who could not afford to suspend public worship; deacons or seminarians whose career paths were blocked; Catholic freethinkers; priests who saw in the revolution a chance for sexual liberty (to marry or conduct same-sex affairs); indigenous churchpeople who formalized their authority by donning cassocks; Episcopalian priests seeking to escape missionary control; and ex-revolutionaries. Some were talented, others indeed scandalous. Overall, Pérez's misfits—his Caneks, Fray Servandos, and whiskey priests—were united by rejection of Rome and a searching for liberty in the Church. They were diverse, "priests of the revolution," not revolutionary priests.[10]

WHO WERE THEY?

Mexican priests were called so many things that it is useful to say what they were not. First, they were not impostors pretending to be Roman clergy. Then as now, this was common; but since differentiation from Rome was the point, Mexican clergy never hid their affiliation. Second, they were not coerced. Shotgun "schisms" in which *federales* gave captured priests a choice—apostatize or face the firing squad—did occur: some generals played this game, mainly as a counterinsurgency tactic in cristero parishes.[11] It was psychological cruelty. When Eulogio Ortiz ordered Father Morones (Aguas.) to say Mass on pain of death, Morones

> spent all that night and next day submerged in a terrible anguish and dominated by a frightful nervousness . . . I imagined him [Ortiz] propagating the false news that I had become distanced, in my manner of thinking, from the Mexican Prelates . . . that the big Mexico City papers, getting the story from some rag here or in Zacatecas . . . would splash the front page with this headline in capitals: "FATHER MORONES, FINDING THE LAWS REGULATING WORSHIP TO BE JUST, HAS RESOLVED TO SUBMIT TO THEM"; next I imagined the terrible discouragement that this news would cause among those with whom I had worked; I now saw them—and this wounded me to the soul—raising their fingers and pointing me out me as a SCHISMATIC, a *cowardly soldier*, who at the height of battle turned my back on my own and went over to the enemy camp with *arms and equipment*.

Chapter Six

Morones said the "schismatical" Mass on his knees, confessing beforehand to the sacristan, "so he should not take me for a comrade of Patriarch Pérez." He dreaded Judgment Day, when God would reveal if he sinned or not.[12] Such coercion was manifestly untenable. Third, then, and returning to our caveats, Mexican clergy were not Protestants, though Gobernación received many contrary complaints. Some Episcopalians enlisted, but rumors that Pérez was awash with missionary green were false; most Episcopalians who joined were Mexicans frustrated by US mission board refusals to consecrate native bishops. More reformed churches, even the Salvation Army, stated candidly that they were unconnected to Pérez.[13]

TABLE 2. MEXICAN CLERGY, 1925–1940

Name	Orders	Date	State
Aguilera Robles, Francisco	RC	1925	D.F., TX
Agustín Cortés, J. J.	MC	1928	—
Alarcón, Braulio	MC	1930s	Méx.
Alarcón, Teódulo B.	RC	1928	Ver., Pue.
Amador, Maximiano	RC	1928	Oax.
Anguiano, Dimas	RC	1926	Ver.
Arámbula, Salvador	RC	1928	Pue., Ver.
Arévalo, Lucio	MC	1925	—
Arías, Alfonso María	MC	1927	Méx., Chis.
Arías, Juan M.	MC	1927	D.F.
Arredondo López, Alfredo	MC	1926	Pue., Gro.
Bautista, Víctor	RC	1925	Tab.
Briones, Adolfo F.	MC	1928	Ver.
Bustamante, M. M.	MC	1926	Chih.
Campos, Francisco	MC	1933	Ver., Pue.
Cano, José S.	RC	1935	Méx.
Cano Ballesteros, Rubén Darío	MC	1928	Ver.
Carreño, José F.	MC	1925	D.F.
Carrión, José Antonio	P	1927	Méx.
Casaponsa, José	RC	1925	Tab.
Castañeda, Porfirio M.	RC	1926	Gro.
Castellanos L., Aureo	RC	1927	Oax.
Castellanos, Salvador A.	MC	1928	Chis., Tlax.
Celis, José Othón	MC	1928	D.F.

Name	Orders	Date	State
Celis Casillas, Jorge	MC	1929	Qro., Gto., Pue.
Cervantes, Juan F.	MC	1926	D.F., Méx.
Cervantes Castro, Melesio	MC	1926	Pue., Ver.
Cervantes de Castro, Miguel	MC	1927	—
Céspedes, Samuel	P	1927	D.F.
Chávez Trigueros, Raymundo	MC	1927	D.F., Méx.
Coronado, Ángel	MC	1928	Pue.
Coronado, José de la Luz	MC	1930s	Ver.
Coronel, Eduardo A.	RC	1925	Tab.
Cortés Villaseñor, José N.	MC	1928	Pue.
Dávila Garza y Pardo, Eduardo	MC	1928	D.F., Pue.
De la Garza Treviño, Santiago	RC	1933	Ver.
De la Peña, Guillermo R.	MC	1928	Pue.
De Anda y Soto, Severano	MC	1926	Jal.
De Lara, Antonio (Fr.)	MC	1926	D.F.
Domínguez, Donato	MC	1930s	Méx.
Durán de la Vega, Francisco	RC	1926	Pue.
Espinoza, Miguel	RC	1927	D.F.
Fernández, Francisco	MC	1930	Méx.
Fernández, Miguel Guillermo	RC	1926	Oax.
Fernández de Haro, Alberto	MC	1926	D.F.
Flores, Manuel	MC	1932	Pue.
Flores, Isauro M.	MC	1931	Pue.
Fonseca, José María	RC	1927	Gro.
Gabiño, Gabino J.	MC	1930	D.F.
Games Flores, Luis A.	MC	1928	Ver.
García, Pascual Luciano	RC	1926	Tlax., Pue., Ver.
García, Teodoro	MC	1929	Pue.
García Mota, Camerino	MC	1927	Méx.
Gómez, José de Jesús	MC	1930	Pue.
Gómez, José Filogonio	P	1931	Pue.
Gómez, J. Urbano	RC	1931	Chis.
Gómez Ruvalcaba, Eleuterio B.	P	1925	D.F.
González, Ricardo Vázquez	RC	1928	Méx., Ver.
González, Roberto T.	MC	1926	Cal.
Guerrero, Melesio	RC	1928	Tamps., N.L.
Gutiérrez, Juan B.	RC	1926	Gro.
Gutiérrez, Rafael	MC	1925	D.F.
Hank, Jorge Mariano	MC	1929	D.F.

Chapter Six

Name	Orders	Date	State
Heredia, Pascual	MC	1927	Tlax.
Hernández, Eduardo	MC	1931	Pue.
Hernández, José María	MC	1928	Pue.
Infante y Tapia, Pedro	RC	1927	D.F., Méx.
Iñíguez, José B.	MC	1927	—
Jiménez Juárez, Ángel	MC	1925	D.F.
Juárez, Teodoro	MC	1927	Pue., Ver.
Juárez, J.	MC	1928	Ver.
Lazarini, Jorge	MC	1929	Méx.
Lazarini, José Luis	RC	1928	Ver., Pue.
Liñán, José Vicente	MC	1928	Pue.
López, A.	MC	1925	—
López, José María	MC	1926	Pue., Ver.
López, Felipe	RC	1925	Oax.
López Valdés, J. Macario	RC	1926	Pue., Cal., TX
López y Sierra, Antonio Benigno	RC	1925	D.F., TX
Maldonado, Alfonso	MC	1928	—
Maldonado, Antonio	MC	1930	Ver.
Maldonado, Tiburcio	RC	1928	Méx.
Melgosa, José	MC	1927	D.F.
Merlín, Mauro de Jesús	RC	1926	Oax.
Mójica, José Agustín (Fr.)	RC	1925	Méx., Pue.
Monje, Manuel Luis	RC	1925	D.F.
Montes de Oca, Félix	RC	1926	Ver.
Montoya, Elías	MC	1928	TX
Morfín, Rafael	RC	1926	Ver.
Muníve, José Antonio Toribio	MC	1927	Ver., Pue.
Ochoa, Felipe de Jesús	RC	1925	Jal.
Ondilón Sánchez, Silvestre Miguel	MC	1927	Gro.
Orihuela, Fausto	P	1927	D.F.
Ortíz Rodríguez, Heraclio	RC	1934	Ver., Mich.
Pallares, Macario	MC	1928	Méx.
Pérez, Adolfo	MC	1925	D.F.
Pérez, Ángel R.	MC	1932	D.F.
Pérez Budar, José Joaquín	RC	1925	D.F.
Pérez R., Miguel	MC	1928	—
Placencia, B. G.	MC	1928	—
Rábago, Antonio (Fr.)	RC	1932	N.L., TX
Ramírez, José	RC	1925	Chis.

Name	Orders	Date	State
Ramírez, Rubén D.	MC	1928	Pue.
Rangel, Salvador	MC	1925	D.F.
Rebollar, Leovigildo	RC	1926	Méx.
Reyes, José E.	MC	1932	Ver.
Reynoso, José Laurencio	RC	1926	Pue., Ver., Tamps.
Rivera (no first name)	RC	1925	Pue.
Rodríguez, Antonio T. M.	MC	1927	Méx.
Rodríguez-Fairfield, Emilio	MC	1938	Cal.
Rodríguez y Durán, Alberto Luis	MC	1926	Cal.
Rojas Vargas, Elías	MC	1937	Pue.
Ruiz, J. Joaquín	MC	1927	D.F.
Salas Vidal, Manuel	RC	1929	Pue.
Sánchez, José Lorenzo	RC	1932	D.F., Méx.
Sánchez Rangel, Roberto	MC	1925	D.F.
Santibáñez Prieto, Adolfo	MC	1928	D.F.
Soriano, Manuel	MC	1925	Pue.
Trujillo, Aniceto María	RC	1932	Ver.
Urbina, Andrés	RC	1926	Oax.
Uribe, José	RC	1925	Hgo., Pue.
Valdez, José Emeterio	MC	1926	Pue., Ver., D.F.
Varela Pallares, José	MC	1928	Ver., Pue.
Vázquez Aguirre, Felipe de Jesús	MC	1938	Méx.
Velasco, José	RC	1926	Oax.
Vieyra, Salvador	MC	1928	D.F.
Von Monte de Honor, Armín	MC	1929	Ver.
Total			128

Table 2 records the names of 128 Mexican clergy, more than historians or hostile propagandists admit.[14] The hardest thing to ascertain is the provenance of holy orders. Ex-Roman curas leave paper trails, but priests with presumptively Mexican orders might still be ex–Roman Catholic deacons or seminarians, not ab initio priests. ICAM claimed that many of its priests were ex-Roman curas, and of those whose orders are known (75, 57 percent), the majority *were* Roman Catholic (44), then Mexican Catholic (25) and Episcopalian (5). Ex-Roman clergy were probably just in the minority overall, however, because many of the remaining fifty-three priests were ordained by ICAM.[15]

Then again, there were an unspecified number of romanos who

shared Pérez's angst but wavered about going public. Take Mauricio Jacobo y Calvo—archpriest of the Basilica of Guadalupe, no less—who tried to depose his abbot and seize Mexico's shrine on 31 July 1926. He did this by barging into the Basilica while municipal officials inventoried the contents and swearing obedience to the Calles Law. Only the officials' prevarication—they said they would register him later—prevented a sensational coup. Thwarted, Jacobo y Calvo was ordered to quell rumors of a schism by the curia, bringing him to his senses. His loyalty to Rome was unbreakable, he now said; he tried to seize the Basilica to prevent the shroud from falling into evil hands. Yet, he could not explain why he went to Bucareli beforehand, twice, to meet with interior minister Tejeda. He also struggled to explain why he asserted his canonical right as the *cabildo*'s "second eminence" when claiming the shrine. Thus, when the abbot ordered him out, crying, "I am the abbot!" Jacobo y Calvo screamed back, "And I am the archpriest!"[16]

De facto Mexican clergy created a larger, shoaling movement. Other priests on our list *personally* opposed the suspension of public worship as a dereliction of duty; thus they communed with Pérez, without necessarily submitting to him. Father Rivera in Pahuatlán (Pue.) said that he had "not changed his religion but simply washed his face" of Roman dirt. Oaxaca has more examples. Thus Father Velasco in Oaxaca's Cañada, who obeyed "the laws ruling the fatherland's destiny" from 1926; or Mauro de Jesús Merlin in Oaxaca City, who told the governor "that he does not agree with the clerical strike to which Oaxacan clergy are forced to submit" and urged priests to break it.[17] Liberal church subcultures existed, then, and Pérez tapped them by evoking the Jansenistic maxim that priests' spiritual powers could not be limited by anyone. "Not one day have I stopped saying Mass," he wrote; it was "sheer arrogance" to hold that "outside the Roman Church, one may not practice the Christian priesthood."[18] The more east or south of Mexico City, the more this resonated. Bishop Guízar in Veracruz had to distinguish between "rebel" and cismático priests to save face. He judged Dimás Anguiano a "schismatic" for backing Pérez in print; yet Rafael Morfín, who refused to end public worship in Jalacingo, was a "perverse" rebel. Then again, Morfín was Guízar's paisano and seminary buddy: when another priest pointed this out, Morfín branded him a "whisperer." Rebels in Veracruz became cismáticos if they blabbed to the press; otherwise Guízar pretended they were contrarians—which wasn't very theological. Guízar finally suspended Morfín for rebelliousness, not schismatizing.

Even this showed an arrogance "worthy of the Gods of Olympus," Pérez cried, given that Morfín's ministry met with Jalacingo's approval.[19] Such outcasts often gravitated to Pérez: in 1931, after years of disobedience, Urbano Gómez (Motozintla, Chis.), swore loyalty to ICAM, "to which I belong de facto" having always obeyed the Calles Law, "even at the cost of disagreeing with the Bishop of this state."[20] Episcopalian clergy, again, were special cases. Reportedly, numbers of them joined ICAM in 1925, including Antonio Carrión (a *veracruzano* registered in Xolox, Méx.), Fausto Orihuela (who supported Antonio Paredes's carrancista church in the 1910s), Samuel Céspedes, and J. L. Pérez, "a priest of the Mexican Catholic and Episcopal Church founded under President Juárez."[21] Here, perhaps, ecclesial affinity was misconstrued as ICAM militancy because of High Anglicanism's historic affinity with liberal Catholicism in Mexico. Yet other Episcopalians (José F. Gómez, Benigno Gómez Ruvalcaba) were key to ICAM. The line separating ICAM from high-church Episcopalians and ecclesiastical nonconformity was thus fuzzy. All told, there were degrees of ecclesiastical "bronzeness" in Mexico, just as shades of ecclesiastical "brownness" existed in Nazi Germany.[22]

BISHOPS

Pérez was the figurehead, but much of ICAM's work was done by three men who became its first bishops: Antonio Benigno López y Sierra, Macario López Valdéz, and Benigno Gómez Ruvalcaba. All were career clergy, after a fashion: ex-Roman Catholic deacons, seminarians with minor orders, or priests, they came to ICAM via the Episcopalian Church or, in Macario López's case, the Franciscans. Roman Catholic propagandists painted them as debauchees, but the main documented crime before 1925 was leaving the clergy to marry. They were all aged forty to sixty-five and sons of Jalisco or Aguascalientes. Geography is a key detail: all thus trained in Guadalajara's seminary, whose liberal reputation ca. 1860–1900 was notorious. At different times, indeed, Eduardo Sánchez Camacho (Tamaulipas's rebel bishop) and Agustín Rivera (the archetypal liberal cura) were on the professoriate. As late as 1899, Bishop Eulogio Gillow complained that Guadalajara's un-Roman spirit left "a bitter aftertaste of liberalism" in his mouth. This bitterness had not dissipated fully even under Archbishop José de Jesús Ortiz y Rodríguez (1901–1912); one of his nephews joined Pérez.[23]

Pérez appealed to a lost generation of liberal clergy. One such—

tapatío Antonio Benigno López y Sierra (1861–1937), ICAM's vicar general—also had important if discreet regime connections. One was to CROM: his daughter, Sara López Escobar, married PLM deputy Ricardo Treviño in 1922. López y Sierra was thus father-in-law to ICAM's CROM handler. More interestingly, he had *compadrazgo* with Calles. His older brother and virtual namesake was pedagogue Benigno López Sierra (1855–1907), who in the 1880s moved to Sonora at governor Ramón Corral's invitation. There, in Hermosillo's Primera Municipal school, López Sierra taught a teenaged Calles, later giving him his first teaching post. For Calles, this was a formative influence. Sailing for Europe in 1923 with Treviño aboard as secretary, Calles was elated to discover that *Sarita* Treviño was his mentor's niece.[24]

López y Sierra's ecclesiastical credentials were mixed. The Mexico City curia discovered that he attended Guadalajara's seminary and was ordained deacon. When registering as priest of Tepetlapa in 1927, López y Sierra claimed to have been a priest since 1888, which probably denotes the year of his deaconate. Later, he joined the Episcopalians, probably ca. 1910 because he later revealed that Rome suspended him *in sacris* in 1911 and that his last ministry before 1925 was in the Church of Jesus. This was probably a reference to the Iglesia de Jesús (the ex-juarista, latterly Episcopalian church). Indeed, in 1919 López y Sierra was lauded by *La Buena Lid* as a deacon and "brilliant" contributor to its pages. The Roman curia alleged that López y Sierra was immoral and was once caught in flagrante in church with a woman. The reality was mundane: he married, twice, first Esther Escobar; then, Soledad Carmona Gutiérrez-Bocanegra. He had eight children.[25]

As López y Sierra largely ran ICAM's affairs, he was key. Indeed, ICAM suffered from his 1929 estrangement from Pérez. The row left Pérez "sick with bile" and determined to prevent López y Sierra from succeeding him. For his part, López y Sierra dubbed Pérez an "obstructive mummy" and warned that ICAM would be finished without his connections to Ricardo Treviño and governors such as Carlos Riva Palacio. Pérez, he said harshly, was "a decorative figure," but "the development and greatness that the Holy Mexican Catholic and Apostolic Church came to have, in its beautiful and triumphal days, was due to the impulse of my efforts." López y Sierra relocated to San Antonio, his sermons drawing crowds of braceros. In 1932, he returned to Mexico, bizarrely calling himself John Chrysostom I.[26]

Doctor Macario López Valdéz, who took ICAM into the Puebla

Sierra, was an old indigenista priest. Born around 1884 in Aguascalientes, he entered the Franciscan order, working in Querétaro (1905) and then Sinaloa's historically Cahíta pueblos of Ocoroni and Mocorito (1906). The Franciscans found him to be obedient (cause for neither "complaint nor disgust"), with a "genuine vocation for the religious state." Until he left to marry: in 1910 he went to Los Angeles and took up chiropractic medicine, returning to Mexico in 1925 to join Pérez. Seemingly the Franciscans tried to stop him by promising to restore his licenses, but it was too late. He went to Puebla and remained in ICAM's ranks until 1931, though Hurtado suggests he later returned to Rome as Tlalnepantla's *vicario cooperador*. Ideological vim suggests not: "God shine a ray of divine light on this pueblo," he wrote Pérez in 1929, "so that it awakens from its ignorant slumbers and arises from the shadows of idolatry." Mexicans adored "man-made images," especially the "golden calf of the Vatican," for which they gave their lives, mocking the blood shed by Christ."[27] López was a Catholic primitivist. "It would be convenient," he told Pérez, "to do away with priests' black cassocks and require another color, like the one used by Saint Peter, midway between red and brown," in imitation of the apostles. Priests should "share our alms with the faithful, as if we were their brothers."[28]

Eleuterio Benigno Gómez Ruvalcaba was another jalisciense (b. 1887) but a different kind of liberal Catholic. He studied in Guadalajara's seminary, receiving the tonsure and minor orders in 1906. Later he idealized the experience. On entering the seminary, he recalled exchanging his "ill-matching threads of yore" for a black suit, struggling with Immanuel Kant, and feting visiting bishops. When given the tonsure, he felt humbled from "the razor's first cut"; on receiving minor orders, he dreamed of "emulating Paul of Tarsus" and going on a mission, with "hopes of reforming the world." He dreamed of the "intimate psychological moment" when he would leave the seminary for "the world and its swamps." Yet when he did leave, three years later, the curia alleged "serious offenses against morality," though all that is on record is Gómez's marriage to fellow tapatía Rebeca G. de Gómez.[29]

In 1914, the Episcopalian Board of Missions hired Gómez and ex-seminary friends branded him an apostate. His appointment letter described him as an ex-professor of Guadalajara's Normal School who had been received into the diaconate and "proved his worth by his missionary activity." From 1919, Gómez wrote many articles for *La Buena Lid* affirming his rank; it was the Episcopalians who, in 1921, ordained him to the priesthood. From 1921 to 1925, he did "native Mexican work" in Mexico City, Nopala (Hgo.), and mexiquense villages where he staged pastoral plays and taught people to make cedar nativity crowns. He was, apparently, a barnstorming preacher. Certainly he was prized by missionary bishop Henry Aves, who paid for him to receive a life-saving operation in in 1920. This prompted a reprimand by mission directors in New York, who scolded Aves for giving the impression that "native clergy" were entitled to medical care.[30]

Mission board attitudes partly explain why such liberal clergymen wagered on a nationalist entity like ICAM. In spring 1925 Gómez requested secondment to ICAM, ostensibly to perform a fact-finding mission. This was granted, likewise his resignation on 1 May; Episcopalian bishops had no desire to absorb another Catholic spin-off, as with the juarista Church of Jesus in 1904.[31] Gómez was one of very few Mexican priests to work in the callista bureaucracy: also an alumnus of Guadalajara's Normal School, Gómez taught in a Mexico City *escuela oficial* while preaching for ICAM, SEP confirmed. Anticlericals attacked this moonlighting, but SEP accepted Gómez's assurances that one vocation nurtured the other. SEP reports described "a cultured teacher" and "unequivocally liberal" Freemason. Indeed, Gómez believed in an empirical Catholicism open to scientific, esoteric, and political ideas. As he wrote in 1923, he wanted to sow "the seeds of the most pure Catholicism," yet a faith "purified, ennobled, by a perfect knowledge." Gómez believed science could perfect religion, just as religion tempered science. One 1920 sermon proposed that "true" education revolved around two "poles," "Science and Virtue," one learned in school, one in church. Both were of God ("rays emitted by the divine sun, lights emanating from an immense, eternal, and loving focus called God"). Yet moderns erred like medievals in cultivating only one. Fanaticism—religion without wit—was evil. Yet to have science without virtue was to be "puffed up with vanity," repeating Satan's words, "'I will not serve.'" Only an integral education could create "citizens of earth and heaven."[32]

Like Ivan Ilich, Gómez believed in Catholic psychology. At a 1919 Episcopalian convention, indeed, he outlined what he called a theory of "Christian psychology." Religious inclinations, he wrote, were a gift from God that made Christians "superior beings." Closely observing Catholicism's elect—the saints—he discerned three faculties ("psychic forces") that he likened to the sun's elements: sentiment (fire), intellect (light), and will (heat). Sentiment tempered "bastard" passions with love and intelligence discerned divine revelation, but following a religion was an act of will. If psychology could bend the will to conscience, then the superheroism of the first Christians could be recaptured. In dreams, Gómez saw Peter and Andrew on "hideous crosses," Saint Lawrence sizzling on a griddle. They had not flinched, nor must modern priests.[33] Priests must be modern saints, Gómez told the 1920 Convention, not through sterile mortification but as "teachers of the pueblos ... consoling those who suffer." They must wrap Christ's doctrines in science and criticism, learning secular as well as sacred disciplines and working in a "vast sphere of action" to eradicate material as well as spiritual hunger. The task was hard, so priests must run and swim, building "muscles of iron."[34]

Gómez also believed in an ecumenical Christianity. He upheld, for instance, the Catholic practice of unction as "a very ancient ... truly apostolic ecclesiastical custom." The liturgical formula antedated the Nicene Council, thus, only a "fanaticized" Protestant could object to it. Yet he hoped, too, that the Anglican Book of Common Prayer might be added to the Catholic liturgy, creating a "primitive unity of prayer" among Christians. All traditions were worthy and perfectible. Episcopalians' aversion to the phrase "Thanks be to God" was silly: Augustine and Paul used it. Catholic celibacy was wrong: marriage was "blessed and just," Paul said, and only a church that admired "pasty celibates and hysterical virgins" would need rods and cilices to silence the "universal law" of human love. Religious tolerance was admirable: "God is the center, and religions the radii, of a circle: all lead to God." Gómez was a questing priest, a believer in muscular liberal Christianity and science, but no fiend.[35]

José Emeterio Valdéz was an old revolutionary. Born in 1879 in Tarimoro (Gto.), he joined the Constitutionalists in Michoacán and had a checkered career. Accused of desertion in the face of the enemy (Villa) in 1915, Valdéz somehow obtained a colonelcy in the third regiment of the northeast in 1916. That year, he became mayor of San Miguel de Allende, provoking claims that he was an unelected grafter who enriched himself. Valdéz was arrested that November, on Obregón's orders, but escaped from the National Palace guardroom. Later court-martialed, he was saved by Dr. José Siurob, Guanajuato's military governor (1916–1917), who confirmed that Valdés held a mayoral office but could not be accused of usurping it as all mayors were military appointees in 1916. Siurob then described how he made Valdéz state comptroller because he was beyond reproach. Indeed, in 1920 he described Valdéz as "an old

Liberal Party fighter who has distinguished himself by his rigor toward clericalism." Valdés for his part insisted that Obregón victimized him. The caudillo, he alleged, stripped him of his command in front of his men, then served military justice on him. Valdéz was cleared of desertion, and, in 1918, of a charge that he failed to discipline a lieutenant who threw a young schoolteacher named María Rodríguez over his saddle and raped her.[36]

Though rescued by Siurob, Valdéz's army career was finished. In 1926, while living in Tacuba, he entered ICAM. Perhaps Pérez recognized a fellow soldier-priest, because he soon ordained him. Regardless of his antecedents, Valdéz was an effective mobilizer, and by 1927 was ICAM's *consentido*: ICAM owed its Puebla and Veracruz success to him, López y Sierra wrote. Pérez unfailingly prayed for him ("so that God will assist and protect you") and he was urged to return to Mexico City if cristero violence required it. Unfortunately, the photographs and reports that Valdéz sent to Pérez are lost.[37] We know, however, that Pérez briefly considered appointing Valdéz as patriarch-elect in 1929, and perhaps with this in mind sent him a crucifix that he deemed "a true relic" because it was the one he wore for his 1926 consecration. Though Valdéz married in 1932, he never left ICAM. In the 1950s, he opened a new branch in Iztapalapa in the Federal District, which still exists.[38]

Other revolutionaries who joined ICAM were adventurers. The most colorful was Hieronymus Maria von Monte de Honor, whose life story was as fabulous (and probably concocted) as his name. He turned up in Mexico City in 1929 claiming to be a Viennese aristocrat wishing to minister to Austrian Old Catholics. Perhaps to evade the ban on foreign *ministros de culto*, Monte de Honor claimed to be a naturalized Mexican employed in the War Ministry's Technical Commission. He had qualified for this, he claimed, because he had seen action with the Austrian Imperial Chasseurs on the western front—which he punningly insisted on calling "the field of honor" (el campo de honor). After the war he moved to Chicago, where the Old Catholics ordained him; thence to Mexico, where he read medicine before joining up. Incredibly, Gobernación detectives confirmed his essential story, reporting that thirty-one-year-old Monte de Honor was a son of count Arminius Von Kunewal-Reinharts-Brum and baroness Maria Malvine von Monte de Honor; he had served in the First World War and, most recently, flown bombing and aerial reconnaissance missions in the campaign against Gonzalo Escobar's mutineers (1929). His ecclesiastical training began in the Vienna seminary before concluding in Chicago. Quite why hardboiled detectives should credit this fantastical story is hard to fathom. Perhaps they were impressed by the coats of arms on his wall or the framed dispatch bearing War Minister Joaquín Amaro's signature. The most surprising thing about Monte de Honor, however, is that latterly he devoted himself single-mindedly to promoting ICAM among Tepehua peasants in Veracruz, from the 1930s to the 1970s. Persecuted at first, he won the Tepehuas' support by living like a peasant and allowing costumbre in church. Jesuit sources, unlikely to flatter, say he doubled as a *maestro rural* and married a woman who left him on finding him in his glad rags. He died in 1984. A last letter stated that hospital nuns betrayed him to two Roman bishops, whose invitation to recant he refused.[39] While this harmless Ruritanian vanished into the Huasteca, a darker, narcissistic figure emerged in Mexico City: Eduardo Dávila Garza y Pardo (1896–1985). His first role in ICAM (1928) was as cantor in Corpus Christi. Before this, a career with the Constitutionalists, who he joined in 1913. Dávila leapfrogged from corporal to sergeant in days; he made captain in two years, major a year hence (1917), then colonel (1920). By then, he had participated in sixty *hechos de armas*, in México, Puebla, Morelos, and Guerrero. Dávila erred in 1920, however, sitting out the Agua Prieta revolt. When it succeeded, he lost his commission. As a priest, he was highly opportunistic: Monte de Honor ordained him in 1931, though Dávila claimed that a rogue Roman bishop did so. In 1932, he proclaimed himself ICAM's leader; then, in San Simón de Bravo (Pue.) in 1933, he had himself elected "Pope Eduardus I." His "pontificate" was a series of mad schemes. In one propaganda photo, his face was pasted over a picture of Pius IX. Then came a flirtation with fascist Goldshirts (1935), foundation of a Masonic club (the "Great Anáhuac Lodge"), macabre plans to parade Pérez's remains in Mexico City, and a patriotic stunt to recruit priests into the Mexican fighter squadron flying sorties in the Pacific war (1942). More credibly, indigenous Catholics accused him of running a cacicazgo in Tlaola and racketeering in religious images. Dávila's long, bizarro life ended mysteriously in Mexico City, two days after the 1985 earthquake. Somebody had cut his throat.[40]

CLERGY

ICAM's pastorate was populated by liberal clergy, nationalists, ecclesiastical proletarians, grafters, and those seeking presumptive liberty. Only a small minority of priests rebelled; those that did often viewed themselves as victims of a church that was stacked against them. Pérez's clergy thus exposed class divisions in the church and, more interestingly, stubborn "non-Roman" views among clergy. This can be shown variously. It is again surprising how many ICAM priests hailed from "liberal" regions: south Jalisco, the Puebla highlands, Oaxaca, the Huasteca. From southern Jalisco came "very liberal" priest Ricardo Vázquez González (born Tapalpa, 1858); tapatíos José Uribe and Fray Agustín Mójica; José Reynoso, another alum of the Guadalajara seminary; Guillermo de la Peña (Teuchitlán, 1903); Heraclio Ortiz Rodríguez (ICAM bishop from 1933); José de Jesús Gómez (Ocotlán, 1907); and Salvador Arámbula (San Gabriel, undated). Dimás Anguiano was colimense, but when he was born (ca. 1853), Colima belonged ecclesiastically to Guadalajara.[41] A younger batch came from central-southern Mexico. For instance: Francisco Durán (Tenancingo, Méx., 1902); Juan Cervantes (Teloloapam, Gro., 1902); Antonio Muníve (Huejotzingo, Tlax., 1897); Miguelito Fernández (Jalapa, Ver., ca. 1883); Pascual Luciano García (Nativitas, Pue., 1897); Adolfo Briones (Atlixco, Pue., 1898); Alfredo Arredondo López (SLP, 1883).[42]

It seems that Pérez drew from skipped generations of liberal priests from Jalisco and central-southern states. Hardly any came from cristero strongholds such as the Bajío, though such places were veritable priest factories. The exceptions were "priest and printer" José Melgosa (Purépero, Mich.); Francisco Aguilera Robles (Celaya, Gto.); and Pedro Infante y Tapia (Ario de Rosales, Mich.), ordained by Archbishop Ruiz y Flores in 1922.[43] It was a question of ecclesiastical culture, therefore, as well as rank. Aguilera Robles, for instance, received holy orders in 1909, probably in Mexico City, since a 1913 *hoja de servicios* shows him serving as auxiliary priest in indigenous hidalguense and mexiquense parishes. In 1918, he was made *vicario fijo* of San Mateo Chapultepec, but left because it was *incongrua* (nonstipendiary). In the 1920s, he was incardinated in Yucatán, making such an impression on Archbishop Guillermo Tritschler that he was talked of as a future bishop. Aguilera translated pastoral manuals into Mayan, which he learned, served as undersecretary, and ministered to foreign priests in Mérida. The main obstacle to his elevation, said Tritschler, was "natural modesty." Then, however, the young priest penned a critique of (ex-archbishop) Crescencio Carrillo y Ancona's tract, *Don Joaquín García Icazbalceta y la historia guadalupana*. Carrillo fancied himself the scourge of the Guadalaupe's historicist critics, so by deflating him Aguilera Robles became suspect.[44] By 1924 he was back in Chapultepec. In June, he was suspended in sacris, a decision that caused him "the gravest hurt" and wrecked his honor and income. "I have given no grounds for suspension," he pleaded. It later transpired that he was suspected of "Jacobin" views. His denials to Archbishop Mora are suggestive.

> I know the enemy systems hostile to us and our religion, from the Pelagians and Donatists who were condemned with the Aryans in the time of the illustrious bishops Saint Ambrose and Saint Augustine. These systems developed afterward under different forms: Protestants, Lutherans, Masons, ... To these were allied the systems of [German Idealist philosophers] Fichte, Schelling, Kant . . . all gathered subsequently in the Jacobin system, whose bases are calumny, defamation, dishonor for all, and respect for nobody . . . Nowadays, these systems appear under the veils of socialism, the Bolsheviks, Soviets, Communists, agraristas, et al., whose bases are to respect neither civil or ecclesiastical authority; nor a Supreme Being, creator of all that which exists; to destroy all capital, and to proclaim equality. There are many people who fully and knowingly sustain these errors; others sustain them without knowledge or for temporal convenience . . . I do not wish to cooperate with, nor lead even indirectly, support for errors destructive of our Catholic principles.

In another letter to the curia, however, Aguilera Robles came out fighting.

> I do not support the Jacobin system, destructive of Catholicism, and believe that I should not involve myself in it. But if I am not allowed to continue serving [the archdiocese], I shall conform and use the free will that I possess to seek my subsistence as I wish in or outside Mexico City; but without you telling me, as the Illustrious Señor said, that I must leave Mexico City because you do not want bad priests like me here. If I have no civil or ecclesiastical crimes against me, I have no obligation to heed such comments, unless these are proved juridically.

Aguilera Robles did not consider himself a "bad" priest—just one who was conscious of his canonical rights. His reputation went before him. On 3 March 1925, Pérez approached him, as "a priest filled with the highest Christian virtues . . . a cultured and liberal man," and asked him to become "a principal part of this patriarchate." Aguilera Robles eventually jumped, and was active in the 1930s, though some Mexican clergy suspected him of spying. We last find him in 1944, corresponding with US Old Catholic bishop Carmel Carfora.[45]

All Mexican priests articulated an idea of the church as a national entity; for most, this was a stubborn ideological commitment, hence the betrayal they felt when Portes Gil signed the arreglos was comparable to the loss of faith in Rome that cristeros felt. "Because of our just and noble cause," José Melgosa wrote in 1929, "I am obliged to continue working in secret with those who steer the tiller of the Mexican Church." He lamented "the intrigues and bad faith that have been attached to *my entirely liberal attitude*"; it was "unjust" that after two years ministering under the law he was expelled from his churches. José Ramírez, cura of Tapachula (Chis.), was proud that he "was one of the first priests to abandon the despotic temporal power of the Vatican" and recognize, "like a good Mexican," the Calles Law. He was distraught when Chiapas's government turned on him in 1934 ("government, which should be the first to protect me as a Mexican priest . . . is the first to attack me").[46] Similarly, Miguel Guillermo Fernández ministered in Ixtepec (Oax.) through the Cristiada because he was "a Mexican before a Roman," and in 1927 accepted appointment as Juchitán's foráneo from "His Illustriousness, the Metropolitan Archbishop who collaborates and coexists with our supreme government." The state had every right to fix external religious discipline: "as a professional priest," he obeyed the law, which gave him the right to demand state protection. "As a true Mexican," he told Portes Gil in July 1929, he should not be despoiled to benefit Romanists who "bloody our soil and insult our government and its laws."[47]

Dimás Anguiano, vicario of Alvarado (Ver.), was another old liberal who rebelled against his bishop, Nicolás Corona. Anguiano was unwilling to lose his meager income when the cult was suspended. Indeed, the very next day he wired Gobernación offering to perform a "work of nationalism in favor of the Mexican Catholic cult." As the first priest to break ranks, he received a telegram from Calles, the canonical suspension coming days later. By September, he was in Veracruz and roaming the Sotavento, remaining there until 1931. After the arreglos local Freemasons attacked him as a holdout; he tried to convert them.[48]

There were liberal priests, then, who intellectually or viscerally disliked the church's self-image as a supranational sovereign society and cleaved instead to the Gallican idea of a national church. Unsurprising, some of these priests came out of the liberal professions. Guillermo de la Peña was a doctor turned priest who "worked for the pueblo's good not only through the holy ministry but also through my work in medicine." His viewed himself as the enlightened priest par excellence, though one comrade thought him boyish and an intriguer.[49] José Lazarini, a lawyer with a *despacho* on Donceles, had received minor orders in the Mexico City seminary before Pérez approached him in spring 1928. Initially Lazarini refused priestly orders because of an appointment as secretary of the first circuit court. Pérez ordained him that June, however, sending him to Xochistlán (Pue.). The arreglos shook Lazarini, and he bid for a position in the Roman clergy, telling the apostolic delegate that he had sabotaged ICAM, "turning" poblanos back to their "old beliefs." By now, he wrote "my labor is solely to finish off the schism." Shunned, Lazarini stayed in ICAM: by the 1930s he was in Calimaya (Méx.).[50] Other priests who joined Pérez did so professing disillusionment with Roman Catholic immorality. One ex-romano, Salvador Arámbula, trained in the Veracruz seminary and received holy orders in Cuernavaca. Hurtado claims that as a seminarian he truanted and drank, yet Arámbula's sermons spun a different version: "Ask me about their conduct," he dared, referring to the Roman clergy, "I came from them!"[51] A few priests resembled the ascetic, primitive prototype. One of these was Aniceto María Trujillo (b. Calimaya, Méx., 1868) who struggled to graduate from Mexico's Seminario Conciliar (his Latin was poor) yet was welcomed by the Franciscans in Cholula. Receiving holy orders in the 1890s, he went on missions in México, Guerrero, and Puebla with a massive crucifix about his neck. His asceticism impressed Rafael Ibarra, bishop of Chilapa, whom Jesuit sources say considered Trujillo a saint. Trujillo also worked as a chaplain in Cuernavaca and in Jaltipan (Ver.) in the 1910s, where anticlericals accused him of moneygrubbing. This was out of character, given his locusts-and-honey past. He joined ICAM in 1932, when it was penniless, ministered for years in Tepetlixpa (Méx.), and retired poor to Mexico City.[52]

Economic resentments, especially toward Spanish priests, motivated others, as the Spanish legation realized when it counted four hundred peninsular clergy in Mexico and jibed in-house about native priests' "ignorance, indiscipline, and lack of religious spirit." Teodoro Alarcón, for instance, left Puebla's Seminario Conciliar for ICAM in 1928 because he resented the Spanish clergy who monopolized Puebla's best parishes. Pérez ordained him in 1931, and then began a long career among indigenous Catholics in Puebla and Veracruz: in 1944, Hurtado tracked him through Yetla, Cutzontipa, Huixtla, Cuamila, Xochinacanatlán, Tlatlapanala, Xaltepuxtla, and Tzitzicazapa. In the 1950s, he was in the Huasteca.[53] Ricardo Vázquez González, a seventy-year-old jalisciense "of the most liberal kind," had more complex economic motives. González (he used his maternal surname) broke the sacramental strike in October 1928 in response to a petition for a Mass in the *mineral* of El Oro (Méx.). In fact, he had been working since August as a "priest of the Mexican Catholic and Apostolic Church" in Yehualtepec (Pue.). And by August (1929) pious women in Acayucan (Ver.) complained that "cismático priest Señor Ricardo V. González," had taken over. His base, meanwhile, was the Jesús María church in Mexico City. Noting this, the curia investigated, finding that he was "aggrieved at the manner in which an ecclesiastical superior dealt with him," leaving him unable to provide for himself. González, too, wrote letters to the government insinuating "how Spanish priests enjoy advantages over Mexicans" and denouncing his superiors' "bad conduct." González's confessor, absolving him in January 1930, mistakenly thought that he had not yet defected, "though he was tempted . . . not from conviction but true necessity."[54]

González's letters reported a litany of abuse in Roman ranks, starting with a superior, Vicente Díaz, who invited him to mass in the chapel of San Jerónimo, then refused to pay him on the pretext "that I take thirty minutes, while his misa rezada takes an hour and a quarter." González, with "thirty-eight years reading Latin," would not have his delivery questioned; the difference, he uncharitably said, was due to the chaplain's stutter. González also launched fierce attacks on the high clergy, on vicar general Pedro Benavides (a "brutish animal") and auxiliary bishop Maximino Ruiz (a "criminal" who reserved rich parishes for Spanish cronies). González demanded fair pay for the lower clergy ("Saint Matthew says, restitute or condemn"). He aired another complaint with interior minister Tejeda in a September 1926 interview. González explained how the archdiocese of Guadalajara transferred ownership of a house in which he had shares to a *prestanombre* who opened a Catholic girl's school there. González, who "worked like a peon" to buy his share, was not compensated. Tejeda's agents verified that the house was used as a school; Calles himself exempted it from closure because the students were indigenous. González, then, was either wronged by the Guadalajara curia or angling for bounty. Shamefully, he promised to denounce Spanish priests (yo daré datos) if Tejeda assisted him.[55]

Yet there was no denying the misery in which Mexico's ecclesiastical underclass lived, and the exploitation they sometimes suffered. José Uribe was a tapatío who took holy orders in Monterrey (1894) and burned through auxiliary curacies in Nuevo León, Mexico City, and Hidalgo. His crowning achievement was an eighteen-year stint in Peralvillo, a poor Mexico City barrio made notorious by Porfirian Jack the Ripper "El Chalequero." Uribe's own career resembled that of Saint Dismas, the good thief, with its mixture of impropriety and penitence. In 1918, members of La Magdalena's (D.F.) Sacred Heart Association accused him of purloining cultic items. Then, in 1924, allegations surfaced that he conned a widow into leaving him property and a journalist started a campaign against him. If Uribe sinned, however, he atoned. He was chaplain to the Mexico City poorhouse (Asilo de Mendigos); then came the years at Peralvillo, where parishioners praised his "goodness" in 1924; then a redemption shot as chaplain of La Institución (a prison), which in Uribe's own words showed him "the gutter of the city." He himself requested the post as so many Peralvillo people were incarcerated; he tended them, spreading the cult of Our Lady Refuge of Sinners, an Italian footpad's devotion, "of which," curial records note, "he is an ardent devotee."[56]

By 1925, Uribe was rusticated to Hidalgo. He could cope with that, but when he confessed to violating canon 2388 (banning priestly marriage) he was suspended, tipping him into revolt. In summer 1925, a starving Uribe joined "the virtuous patriarch" in protest against the Roman hierarchy's "despotic and anti-Christian attitude." In open letters, he praised Pérez's efforts to "free the multitude of priests oppressed by high Roman Clergy, simply because they are not those favored by fortune." He also attacked clerical inequality: dioceses lacked priests, but Mexico City had three hundred *miseros*, priests retained as private celebrants of the wealthy. With no cure of souls, they spent afternoons watching plays or Gaona's corridas while "thousands of *fieles*" had no Mass. Uribe demanded a rational distribution of clergy; let all priests baptize, preach, and heal the sick, as Christ said.[57]

193

That, of course, was the old Jansenist trope about the seventy disciples, but Uribe's revolt was guilt-ridden and lasted only a year. It still made the Roman curia appreciate him. Indeed, in June 1926 it absolved Uribe of the censures incurred "on joining the Mexican Church of Corpus Christi" and offered him a parish in Puebla. His recantation, "by God's mercy," was effected by a Jesuit who made him promise to end his marriage. Describing himself as a wretch who apostatized "at a bad moment," Uribe now tendered his resignation at ICAM. Post-Cristiada, he remained in Peralvillo, assisting his priest nephew, Luis Sepúlveda, and promoting Our Lady of Refuge. Rehabilitated, he died in 1937.[58]

José Cano, who ministered in Tenancingo (Tlax.) and Los Reyes (Méx.) as late as 1935 was another economic refugee. Leovigildo Rebollar, weighed down by "censures incurred in the Schismatic Church of Corpus Christi" in 1926, had been *vicario auxiliar* of various parishes since 1920 including Cuautitlán and Metepec. Iztapalapa, too, though he requested a transfer in 1918 on learning that parishioners had lynched a predecessor. He would work anywhere but begged for a post where he would "not depend on the señores curas, who I respect but with whom I do not lack difficulties."[59] The pattern recurred outside central Mexico. In 1932 in Camarón (N.L.), Monterrey's curia suspended another alleged cismático—Antonio Rábago—though people protested that this Franciscan was a saint who visited the sick and ministered for free. "Is that schismatical?" they jeered. Yet the párroco who employed Rábago portrayed a religious who worked "as an envoy of the civil government" and usurped authority. Forced out, Rábago said an emotional final Mass, saying he could not understand how such bad blood could exist between priests.[60]

It is hard not to feel for these conflicted, hungry souls, and for most of those who suffered as sexual beings. Manuel Luis Monge, from Lugo (Galicia), was Pérez's first recruit; though enemies alleged that he was a gun-toting *rojillo*, in reality he was a poor priest who took comfort in the flesh and saw ICAM as a chance to give the hierarchy its comeuppance. Reaching Mexico in 1903, Monge was assigned to "difficult villages" such as Atlacomulco, where a neighboring priest reported in 1910 that he was succumbing to "old weaknesses": relationships with women. Monge rashly admitted a violent animosity to this snitch, and in punishment was moved to an auxiliary post in Sultepec (near Guerrero), under an "unjust" cura who, in Monge's words, "crushed" his vicarios. The priest beat Monge's domestic, paid him one month in three, and worked him all day in the confessional, thus reserving the paid sacraments for himself. He likewise kept all Mass intentions save those of the dawn Mass, which Monge celebrated. The cura also sent Monge to far-flung pueblos, then pocketed the fees. And his constant complaints to the curia jeopardized Monge's licenses. A charge of bination (eucharistic double-headers) made Monge livid. He had never done that and was tired of "working as a slave ... at the whims of an ambitious and cruel señor cura."[61]

The curia moved him to Otumba, then suspended him in 1912 because the "señora who helps him" was providing kindnesses of the flesh. Month after month, Monge begged for the return of his licenses, accepting his faults ("I am guilty, I know"). But his clothes were now rags, he sobbed in August, and he was hungry; by November, he begged only for a reference written "with charity" that might let him escape the flea-bitten Morelia guesthouse where he was living. He implored the Mexico City curia not to "close the door which, perhaps for my salvation, the God of mercy is opening for me."[62]

Unsurprising, Monge bore a grudge against authority. For all that, this bespectacled, startled-looking Galician made an unconvincing rebel. The press mocked his humdrum government job (he was a penpusher with Ferrocarriles Nacionales) but also sexualized his young wife, Magdalena Mercado, with whom he had four children. Protesters hounded him and, five days after La Soledad, abducted him. Monge's wife reported hearing a fracas outside their Coyoacán home, after which he disappeared. His whereabouts became a newspaper sensation. A published retraction failed to satisfy curiosity, and soon it transpired that Monge was kidnapped by angry members of the Spanish colony assisted by Jesuit Mariano Cuevas, as priest to the Real Congregación Española. By June, Monge was in Galicia; the bishop of Lugo asked if he might rehabilitate his former priest.[63]

Another pathos-filled case was Franciscan, José Agustín Mójica, who acted as Corpus Christi's párroco in 1925 and impressed some Episcopalians with his sermons. He should not be confused with a famous contemporary: fellow jalisciense, Franciscan, and namesake José Mójica, whose operatic tenor entranced Caruso and led to starring movie roles alongside Tito Guízar.[64] Our Mójica was a forty-one-year-old religious whose motive for joining Pérez was the patriarch's abolition of obligatory celibacy. Certainly, in 1917 he had "slipped up with a young woman," as a result of which her relations and carrancista revolutionaries (though this was probably an exculpatory touch) forced him into civil marriage. The couple consorted secretly until 1925, when Mójica fled his convent, joined ICAM, and cohabited. In July 1926, church authorities offered to lift his censures if he abjured the "schismatical sect of the Mexican Church." He did, and all might have been well had the curia not assigned him two *ligueras* (LNDLR members) as chaperones. The women guarded him zealously to prevent relapses, but took it upon themselves to punish him by rationing his intentions for Mass. By 1927, Mójica was going weeks without celebrating and facing a "serious economic problem": how to stop his household from sinking, taking his mother, a soap-making sister, and her five children down with it. Mójica himself used worn-out shoes and second-hand underwear.[65] The discovery that Mójica was again consorting with "a señorita" in 1928 led to more censures. God was "tired of tolerating my faults," he admitted, yet he was "completely ill-prepared to sustain myself outside my profession." Suspension left "four doors wide open to me: the street, prison, the hospital, or the grave." He chose a fifth, ICAM: from 1929, Mójica ministered in Puebla and Hidalgo. In 1931, however, he was readmitted to the Roman fold after a "time of trial." He felt like "an unfortunate pariah," he said, *sin Madre*. He regretted his "important place" in Pérez's "terrible schism," but couldn't really say otherwise. That year, Mójica, absolved of apostasy and marriage, was incardinated in Monterrey.[66]

These were common scenarios. Pedro Infante revealed his wife in 1929 after she fell sick with influenza and he needed help. An uncomplicated sinner, Antonio Maldonado in Puerto México (Ver.), reportedly enjoyed trysts with the sacristan's wife and then sat contentedly in the square, reading the newspapers and having his boots blacked.[67]

Some of the most fascinating, because unusual, accounts, concerned homosexuality. Francisco Durán, who curial records place as Roman vicario fijo of Acazuchitlán (Méx.) or a member of the Congregación de la Misión (a Vicentian congregation devoted to the poor), joined ICAM ca. 1926. The Roman curia believed that he was ready to abjure his error that July, yet then we find him working for ICAM in Puebla's Sierra Norte. He admitted to some theological doubts, telling his ICAM superiors in 1928 that he was "Schismatical in body but spiritually Roman," and asking for their understanding, "bearing in mind that I am young and inexperienced." He was forgiven, for in 1929 we find him in Coyutla and Tlaola, reporting "useful works."[68] That year, however, Durán repeated his transgression, writing to a Roman cura that he never broke with Rome in his heart, "only in appearance," and "never denied one dogma." He still celebrated in Latin, "not *castellano*," "as I was raised in the Catholic not Protestant faith." In another, ingratiating letter (capped with the slogan "*¡Viva Cristo Rey!* Death to the Mexican patriarch!"), Durán begged the cura to "arrange what I most desire, with all my soul, in these moments—to unite with the Roman Church."[69] Probably Durán hoped to be saved from revelations of his homosexuality. In spring 1930, indeed, Pérez heard of "difficulties" in Puebla and sent José Varela to investigate. Varela found people in Tlaola looking ashamed, so asked why. Some señoritas asked Varela to forgive the language they were about to use, then said that their priest embarrassed Tlaola "because he is a PUTO—which is quite how they spelled it out to me [De que es un PUTO, haci con todas las letras me lo expresaron]." The women then said that "they would prefer [Durán] to have a concubine, and would provide him one, because after all he is a man." Varela wanted Durán banished as "a duty before God and all humanity."[70] Another priest, Teodoro Juárez, found out more. For Tlaola Catholics, Durán's *defectillo* was to be "a man who does not like women," but teenage boys. Surprisingly to us, Tlaola women were less angered by Durán's pederasty than sexual competition for young males ("open competition, without quarter"). Juárez found that Durán shared the curato with a "family" of men but shared his bed with one *jovencito* ("duermen los dos juntitos, no sé conque objeto"). Again surprisingly, Francisco Torres—Tlaola's powerful *secretario*—advised absolution: if Durán sent his "family" away and lived discreetly or chastely, he could stay. Torres never meddled in people's private lives; when on duty, Durán was diligent, and "everybody, except for some fanatics who call themselves *romanistas*, esteems him."[71] At year's end, Durán was still ministering in Tlaola and Huauchinango, though Chicahuaxtla snubbed him. In the 1930s, he was in Coxquihuí with "Reverend Father Santiago de la Garza Treviño," an old liberal priest and Oratorian from Tamaulipas. From 1934, Durán was in Las Tuxtlas (Ver.).[72]

The case is interesting for what it said about indigenous views on homosexuality, which was tolerable if secret or platonic, and its supposed impact on women's reproductive choices: priests, meanwhile, were *expected* to want heterosexual companionship. Similar stories dogged Tlaxcalan José Antonio Toribio Muníve. He was honored to serve a church, he told Tejeda, that was led by a Mexican and obeyed the law. As priest of Jaltipan (Ver.), Muníve was thought conscientious by Pérez; Muníve once sent Pérez a missal as well as derechos. Muníve also chided Mauricio Eríes, church junta leader, for neglecting baptismal records. This was important, he said, because some indigenous asked ICAM to rebaptize their children, thinking it meant extra grace; without baptismal registers, priests would need to be "clairvoyant" to stop this superstitious practice. Yet when Muníve was sent to Yehualtepec (Pue.) in 1930, a "black cloud" descended; in the words of investigating priest Manuel Salas, people "accuse him of sodomy." Muníve denied having "the shameful defect," though Salas found him in hiding because Yehualtepec was agitated. Muníve asked Salas to remember how Christ bathed Mary Magdalene's feet and the parable about casting the first stone.[73] This case ended in a canonical trial, which Salas suggested to placate Yehualtepec's mayor; Salas threatened to report Muníve's "nefandous crime" to Gobernación if he dared to abscond, reminding him how it punished "deviants" (indirectos) who hid their sodomy behind the cloth. A private ecclesiastical hearing (in foro interno) was preferable, he warned Muníve, thanks to the merciful canon law adage, *de internis neque Ecclesia iudicat* (not even the church may judge inner dispositions). But if the civil power claimed him, "your destination will be the Islas Marías," Mexico's Devil's Island, where "deviants" (homosexuals, fanatics, addicts) were worked to death in salt lagoons. If Muníve confessed, Salas would be merciful because "I value you as a friend and priest. I mean to say, let us wash our dirty laundry at home."[74] The punishment, demotion and suspension, forced Muníve to cancel a lucrative Mass in Panzacola (Tlax.), a railway town. If his suspension were not lifted, he wrote in May 1930, he would have to "seek my daily bread with the sweat of my brow," reverting to campesino life. He hoped that Christ and Mary would forgive his "failings" as heaven was filled with saints with "the same defects" (arriba hen el cielo ay santos de primer orden, que tubieron los mismos defectos pero rogaron con umildad y subieron libres de sus faltas). In a second letter, he asked for compassion because only God could judge humble, uneducated priests. If suspended, he would "hang up my cassock." A terrifying Gobernación summons, to his relief, produced a new permit to minister, not jail; and in August he went home to Portezuelo to minister, promising no relapses, "otherwise, the Islas Marías await me."[75]

This case is intriguing because it showed that ICAM recognized areas where state supervision was unwelcome. Muníve's indigenous roots also bring us to our final category: the aspiring priests, often campesinos or indigenous religious specialists, that Pérez ordained. They were the best and worst, and ICAM priests with conventional backgrounds complained about them.[76] Some were downright scandalous. Adolfo Briones had the right theological grudges (the confessional was a "den of prostitution and crime"; Pérez had freed Mexicans of "slavery to the Roman Pontiff"), yet people in Acayucan (Ver.) remembered a drunken Lothario who stole church jewels; people in San Andrés Tuxtla (Ver.) promised to kill him if they saw him again. Luis Gamez Flores was another pilferer: Jaltipan's encargado reported that he stole church funds and a surplice. And in 1937, penniless Elías Rojas Vargas confessed that "Pope" Dávila "induced me to go with him to a pueblo in his care, so that I might assume the position of priest." Rojas found the sacrilege easy, until asked to reserve the santísimo, which his conscience would not let him do, so he quit.[77]

They were not all so unscrupulous. Indeed, many such priests received ab initio training, even if this lasted only one or two years, much less than for a Roman Catholic seminarian. A seminary of sorts existed by 1926 at Corpus Christi ("where a group of young men studies theology and philosophy . . . in accordance with the libertarian principles of the century"), yet it must have been a shoestring operation, given Pérez's 1929 admission that his "greatest difficulty" was funding it.[78] Nonetheless, people volunteered to teach, usually liberal types such as Rodrigo Amadeo Sequeiros, a Spanish salesman who was shocked by Mexicans' deference to Rome; a cura called Arturo Gómez who offered to teach Latin and physics; or Ángel Herrera, who wanted to teach "in the name of libertarian emancipation."[79] In reality, most novices were identified by other priests, and trained in situ, which is why campesinos figured prominently among second generation Mexican priests. Ricardo González, our old liberal cura from Jalisco, was always "preparing men for Your Excellency [Pérez] to ordain," since there was "a need for padres." On one occasion he traveled to Acayucan (Ver.) to recruit a priest but found that he was "strange and without aptitude."[80] "About the young man you say you have instructed for ordination here as priest"—López y Sierra told a subordinate in 1927—"we will gladly ordain him if, after examination, he shows that he is effectively trained in his duties."[81] From Zozocolco (Ver.), Teodoro Juárez sent several young men to Corpus Christi because they showed "religious spirit" and education.[82] In Puerto México (Ver.), Luisa Reboulen referred "a Catholic señor" who asked "if it is true that the Holy Mexican patriarchate helps Mexican Catholics who wish to study to receive holy orders." This individual had three years of *prepa* but was orphaned and forced to quit. He had served as an acolyte, spent time with clergy, and could "officiate the Mass and some other offices."[83]

In reality, Corpus Christi was a finishing school not a seminary, and priests usually learned through a form of SEP-style action pedagogy. Nonetheless, there were periodic exams in Corpus Christi or in the field. Emeterio Valdéz was grilled about how "to exercise the sacred ministry with all piety and decorum" in late 1926; in 1933, Francisco Campos had the same performance-based exam.[84] Training was therefore formalistic, not theologically exhaustive, which made it a pantomime in Roman Catholic eyes. Examinations could nonetheless be brutal. One deacon, Rubén D. Ramírez, was so criticized by López y Sierra in 1928 that he quit, to do "another kind of work, in which he would not have to sacrifice his very dignity." Emeterio Valdéz rebuked López y Sierra for occasioning this "moral and material loss" (perhaps this was the origin of their festering dispute). Valdéz is worth citing at length because his letter conveys ICAM's precisionist approach.

> After the celebration of the Mass by señor presbyter don Teodoro Juárez, assisted by the young man in question [Ramírez], both complained to me about the injustice of your observations, since each was in the right concerning the execution of their acts. For, consulting the rubric immediately upon our return home, it was confirmed that you were in error, though it is conceded that you were in the right in some small part concerning the preparation of the chalice. This should be done by placing the chalice with the right hand in such a place as can be reached comfortably from the epistle and the *corporales*,[85] and not at the distance of two paces as you told both me and them. We also agreed that you were entirely in the right to say that, to read the epistle, the celebrant should be in a standing position; and that, concerning the offices of the deacon, you were only in the right when you stated that [the deacon] should have knelt on the left hand side of the celebrant at the moment of the confession. Concerning the ringing of the bell three times at the moment of the offertory, I confess that I am

guilty because this is how I have taught that it should be done—the reason being that this is what I learned in all the parishes and churches of the [Puebla] Sierra, because that is the custom in that region. On the assumption that they will go there to officiate, it can be deduced that I have believed it my duty to prepare them in accordance with the customs of those pueblos.[86]

ICAM's defense to charges of theological shallowness was thus that it opened the religious estate to underdogs and respected local custom more than the rulebook. Some Mexican priests showed genuine humility about their lack of education: as José Filogonio Gómez, a campesino trained by the Episcopalians and ordained by Pérez, wrote in 1931,

The Lord is not unaware that in me He has the clumsiest of priests in terms of lacking college instruction and the solid principles—philosophy and other priests' things—that are needed to place oneself without hesitation at the head of a church, like a competent priest; which, in truth, God knows I am not, but my purpose has always been to be one, and I have not lost my vocation since my gentle childhood, as I showed the señor patriarch when he deigned to interview me for the first time . . . I live in gratitude to him for the many considerations that he knows how to show each of his ministers.

Gómez, who had heart, remained a Mexican priest into the 1940s, then found success with the Episcopalians: a plaque in San José de Gracia (Mexico City) commemorates his time as dean.[87] Some priests of this kind felt like impostors. "I was ordained as presbyter, in accordance with the ritual," Jorge Othón Celis wrote in October 1929, having joined ICAM in 1928. His rapid ordination scandalized his sister, Ernestina Celis, a Josephine religious, and even he had doubts because later that year Rome absolved him of heresy. Still, by 1932 Celis was back in ICAM.[88] Francisco Fernández was another doubting Thomas. When sent out in in September 1929, he wrote often to Pérez about marital cases and asked him for a book of Easter sermons and Loyola's spiritual exercises, but used scare quotes when recalling "my 'sacerdotal' ordination." Vicente Liñán was another lowly recruit: a Roman cura found out that he was once a "miserable porter" in a Monterrey theater—but he had theatrical style and his performances, theologically sound or not, could move people to pious tears.[89]

Pérez also ordained indigenous cantores and sacristans, not just poor aspirants. These churchpeople already had intimate knowledge of local religion, and ordaining them was a way for ICAM to win friends locally. Other priests sometimes resented them. When José F. Gómez asked for assistant clergy in 1931, for instance, Isauro M. Flores and "Señor J. María [Hernández]" appeared. This surprised Gómez, because he knew the men to be village cantores. "I did not know that these señores had been prepared as Priests," he wrote, "knowing that one of them worked as a complete campesino." Yet, he continued, "when we least expected it, I learned that [vicar general] Santibáñez was to consecrate them and that, from one hour to the next, they became señores curas; and I found it strange that this was so." The ex-cantores became his enemies ("They started to attack me, because I said that I did not have faith in them and had never seen any Priests like that"). Flores's rusticity, at least, pours forth in his few letters. In one he asked for oil of catechumens, for driving out evil during baptism (necesito saber de los Óleos Catecumenos . . . o como podré aser para la vendición del Hagua Bautismal). In Puerto México, too, Luisa Reboulen was disgusted when the church was entrusted to two "two Indians," one of whom she thought was immoral and the other "stupid." They turned out to be the sacristan and cantor. Reboulen especially disliked that they opened the church for nocturnal cult.[90] Elsewhere in Veracruz, in Santa Lucrecia (today Jesús Carranza), Antonio Munive baptized with the help of one María Mayo. She was *ermita* (hermitage) president, likely a midwife or healer. In Olintla (Pue.), too, Teodoro Juárez knew, the cantor went to Puebla City and came back with holy orders months later. Juárez feared that the countryside "would be flooded with these priests."[91] Pascual Luciano García was the archetype—an indigenous sacristan and seemingly an ex-Franciscan novice—and as we saw in chapter 5, he was the most successful: as one ICAM congregation wrote, García "conquer[ed] the pueblos, making sure to leave them in peace as a result of the good teaching that he gave to the indigenous."[92]

CONCLUSION

There was, then, a clergy of the revolution, though generally it was a coalition of downtrodden ecclesiastical types. Evaluating any religious corps presents an old methodological problem in that ecclesiastical sources, when accessible, thicken around transgressions, normalizing the deviant. That is especially true for ICAM, given its political associations: Pérez's enemies in the Roman clergy thus aired exposés of priest defectors; latterly ICAM divided into rival factions that "fessed up" one another's' secrets. There is obvious truth to Roman Catholic claims that Mexican priests had feet of clay, but that was a truism and was designed to make ideological variance itself seem dirty. Most Mexican priests said Mass fairly diligently. ICAM had its ignoramuses and money-grubbers, with one documented pederast (Durán) and one madman (Dávila). The usual vices, however, were concubinage (or marriage), and, above all, ideology, specifically, variants of ecclesiastical nationalism, which could be rooted in anything from old-school liberal Catholicism to the Pauline letters and hispanophobia. Many Mexican priests expressed simple patriotism and a concern for their livelihood, coupled with a vague post-Jansenist theology stressing priests' right to celebrate. They believed in a different kind of church, given that the most common element was rejection of a super-romanized, super-hierarchical edifice with an associated class structure. A range of minorities objected to that: liberal Catholics; Anglo-Catholics; seminarians who abandoned religious careers; proletarian priests; others who protested celibacy vows; those who thought that church government was a national matter. Some had primitive Christian fantasies, others spent years among indigenous people. Last, there were people to whom Pérez made holy orders accessible: campesinos with vocations, indigenous churchpeople. Pérez was inferno-bound, many thought; but perhaps his biggest crime was to lead a band that was brown and poor, an underclass, not an underworld.

CONCLUSION

PÉREZ IS DEAD, VIVA PÉREZ

HISTORY REMEMBERS PÉREZ as a Catholic traitor, but this book has tried to show that he was more than that. Not just a CROM patsy, Pérez was a rebel who mediated the exclusion felt by indigenous Catholics and some lower clergy. He played a significant role in Mexican indigenous history as orchestrator of a revolutionary alt-Catholicism, and in some ways was a kind of empirical liberation theologian. ICAM began as CROM agitprop but became a pueblo-centric medium through which the regime channeled indigenous religious support during the Cristero War, and beyond. The existence of a revolutionary Catholicism seems counterintuitive, because historians have been quick to conflate Catholicism with *cristerismo*. Yet Pérez opens our eyes to a radically different pueblerino experience of the 1920s and 1930s. In this sense his movement was not just a critique of Mexico's Catholic establishment but serves as a reminder of how slow the historiography has been to place indigenous and mestizo Catholicisms on equal footing. Zooming out from the war-torn Bajío, the *conflicto religioso* was anything but a Catholic epic. Rather, religion was weaponized in sectarian struggles for village supremacy between "Romans" and "Mexicans," just as support for the Calles Law was used to negotiate recognition of indigenous religion or ejidos. There were multiple religious conflicts: the real "schism," perhaps, was between indigenous heartland Catholicisms and the "Rosary Belt" pieties of the center-west.

Besides changing our perspectives on the Cristero War, ICAM's history complicates some historical master narratives. One is the secularism of the postrevolutionary regime, which was clearly mitigated by religious preferences when it did not evidence some reformed Catholic and usually Gallican-type ideas. Some callistas were anticlerical as outraged *Catholics*. They hated Rome, yet some laws and reforms, including agrarian policy and the Calles Law, had religious fingerprints all over them; callismo thus exhibited a paradoxical, reform-minded catholicity, not just brash secularism. Evidently, too, the regime derived some religious legitimation from ICAM and favored it, at least until 1929 when it tried to cancel the revolution's main religious experiment. This attempt to reconstitute Mexico's religious field bureaucratically is redolent of Jason Dormady's "informal religious corporatism,"[1] state-managed religious pluralism relying less on a free market than the multiplication of patronage ties between the state and churches. In this sense, ICAM contributed to Mexico's lopsided religious modernization and made indigenous Catholics more aware of their religious rights. Its history is really the history of indigenous people's efforts to leverage federal power to reclaim control over their religious lives, festivities, and economies, sometimes by exercising denominational choice within Catholicism. That bandwidth, in and of itself, should make us question the idea that religious modernization was exogenous, tagged to Protestantism and the rise, ca. 1950, of a religious marketplace.

As a Catholic parastatal, ICAM was of particular concern to Rome. We saw this in the 1929 arreglos. By the same token, Pérez was probably a factor in the Roman hierarchy's development of an indigenous apostolate in the 1950s, not least in sees such as Miguel Darío Miranda's Tulancingo, whose priests competed directly with ICAM. One of Miranda's barnstorming priests, Nahuatl-speaking Santiago Aguado, led a pastoral team through ICAM hotspots such as Tlaola (Pue.).[2] Whatever else Pérez did, then, he revealed a Catholicism with a bronze face that the official Church had long taken for granted.

ICAM's history complicates another trope: "romanization." Evidently there was resistance to this in indigenous parishes, for all that Mexico had long felt Rome's gravitational pull in terms of discipline and orthodoxy by the 1920s. ICAM's popularity reminds us that something of "Bourbon" Catholicism (neo-primitive, statist) remained at the grassroots, not least in sees such as Puebla or Mexico that were historically run by superenlightened prelates. Perhaps we assume too easily that reformed Catholicisms were emotionally "cold," hence uninspiring, to indigenous people. That is to infantilize indigenous Catholics as people only capable of emoting, or to focus on the theological aspects of reform, not more ecclesiological ones. As it turned out, indigenous people were willing to embrace a constitutional church if it served their wishes for greater parish autonomy, village fiestas, and lower religious taxation. Pérez was no great reformer, of course, but he was more than just an ecclesiastical delinquent: he knew highland pueblos and parishes as well as anyone and in the 1920s he continued to act in accordance with a personal Catholic reform project of long standing that favored religious voluntarism and indigenous self-determination. To those that supported him, he offered a kind of religious sovereignty, expressed in lay control of religious appointments, fees, and fiestas. Indeed, reducing Pérez to the status of a lone church arsonist has long obscured the pressures that really brought his movement into being and briefly gave indigenous Catholics a competitive advantage: historic competition between ecclesiastical and political elites over the administration of indigenous communities, and efforts to assimilate or abstract the Church into or out of the nation-state.

PÉREZ HA MUERTO . . .

To the end, Pérez was news, if only because people wondered whether he would recant. Over the years, stories circulated that he suffered from an illness requiring bromide pills (used to treat convulsions) or alcoholism. News that Pérez was rushed to Mexico City's Red Cross Hospital on 5 October 1931 suffering from uremia—blood toxicity caused by kidney failure—saw reporters and clergy descend on his bedside. Bernardo Portas, a forty-nine-year-old Orizaban Jesuit, reportedly obtained Pérez's recantation next day and absolved him, having sought permission from Archbishop Díaz y Barreto via telephone. Newspapers exulted: Pérez repented before dying, *La Prensa*'s afternoon headline on 9 October proclaimed: his retraction would "cause a sensation among all the inhabitants of the republic."[3] The archdiocese of Mexico published Pérez's "spontaneous retraction" and ordered the faithful to commend his soul to God. After a lifetime of revolt, Pérez reportedly bowed out saying this:

> I abjure all the errors into which I have fallen, be they against the Holy Faith or the legitimate authorities of the one, true, Holy Roman Catholic and Apostolic Church. I repent of all my sins and ask forgiveness of God, my prelates, and all whom I have scandalized with my errors and conduct. I swear that I wish to die in the breast of the Holy Roman Catholic and Apostolic Church, trusting in the goodness of Jesus Christ Our Lord, and

of my loving mother the Holiest Virgin of Guadalupe; I believe all that the Holy Church teaches us and exhort all the faithful not to stray from her because she is the sole arch to salvation.[4]

We can and should be skeptical, because Pérez was committed to ICAM and unrepentant by nature. He had seen off confessors before: in 1928, he teased one priest who got past his housekeeper by promising to sign a retraction next day, only to try to "dazzle" his confessor into joining ICAM ("Conclusion: I could not administer any sacrament, nor extract any written retraction").[5] Not once, until isolated by clerical rivals in his death throes, did Pérez desire to recant: as late as June 1931, he was out visiting in México and Puebla, "receiving displays of affection and respect from my pueblos."[6] *El Universal* noted that when Pérez was admitted to hospital he was unable to recall his age and too weak to stand. His actual last words—spoken to a gunshot man who asked how he was feeling—were: "Very bad, my son, this is now ending." Only after the recantation was publicized was Pérez's body released: in a final indignity, Pérez was measured up with *ixtle* string and put in a cheap coffin. A nocturnal vigil was held in Corpus Christi, where Pérez's coffin was draped with a tricolor. His funeral rite was Mexican Catholic. He went into a pauper's grave in the Dolores cemetery.[7]

Pérez was thus sequestered in death, his apparent retraction signifying the inevitable victory of orthodoxy over schismatical pride. Coming two months shy of 1931's Guadalupan quadricentenary, Pérez's death was convenient to the episcopate. For President Ortiz Rubio, it drew a line under callismo and consolidated the arreglos (seven months later, indeed, Ortiz Rubio withdrew Corpus Christi from public worship).[8] Yet Pérez's retraction was contrived and in truth could have been signed by anybody. First there was doubt about the absolution: ICAM claimed to have shriven Pérez before hospitalization.[9] Then there were formal defects. Though notarized, the retraction does not bear Pérez's signature, just his fingerprint (inked by someone else), a crudely drawn cross, and a squiggle. With the exception of Portas, all the witnesses who swore that Pérez dictated and signed were medical students.[10] Given the church's desire to cancel Pérez, in sum, it looks like metaphysical ambulance-chasing.

One retractation led to others. Adolfo Santibáñez Prieto, ICAM's administrator, repented in 1936 that he had "officiated as a priest in the schismatic church" yet now "comprehended the error in which I found myself." He received absolution, observing that Rome treated remorseful sinners gently: he was the missing drachma in the lost coin parable. Pedro Infante returned to his Roman obedience in 1937; Manuel Salas Vidal, from Tecomaltán (Pue.), also did so proclaiming his sorrow for "the errors, which I detest and abominate, of the Orthodox Mexican Catholic Church."[11] Still, these inquisition-style confessions mattered little because Mexican Catholicism had entered indigenous Catholic culture: more than it was reducible to personalities, or callismo, it was a dissident tendency married to the unmet social, spiritual, and political needs of indigenous Catholics. If those needs were unmet, Mexican priests might reappear.

. . . ¡VIVA PÉREZ!

As they did, for instance, during the anticlerical *sexenio* of Adolfo Ruiz Cortines, when Alberto Fernández de Haro founded a seminary in Tlalpan. Here he ordained Leonel Montes of Tenancingo and others: Faustino Martínez, Pedro Sánchez, Zacarías Zacarías, Juan Cervantes, Daniel Salas. Some trainee priests from Roman seminaries were also recruited. Hidalguense Rubén Fidel Mayorga trained in El Salvador, then Xalapa and Montezuma (New Mexico), but was ordained by an Old Catholic bishop in Brazil and admitted to ICAM; by the 1950s he was leading processions in Hidalgo villages such as Tizayuca and Reyes Xolos.[12]

Again, these developments must be seen in relation to the efforts of indigenous elites now allied with PRI to retain power in their pueblos by controlling public religion. In 1951, Tenancingo Mexican Catholics complained that they had been in possession of their church for decades, with the same minister serving for eighteen years. Yet now a "minoritarian group of vecinos" who worked in the La María textile factory were being instructed by the owner, "a foreigner and Spaniard named Eloy Pellon," to transfer the parroquia to a Roman priest. Violence was imminent, petitioners warned, "since the majority of the pueblo wishes to remain in the Mexican Church." Petitioners wanted Gobernación to uphold their rights and warned of disorder. Troops were sent in 1952, then Gobernación made a Solomonic decision: the parish would be given to Roman Catholics (the last resident Mexican priest left in 1955) yet Mexican Catholics would control the municipio, dominating town-hall appointments, roadbuilding, and faena commissions in Tenancingo's four barrios. Since Roman Catholics refused to perform faenas directed by Mexicans, they became excluded from state largesse. Mexican Catholic support remained strong in Cruztitla barrio, and Tenancingo remained 25 percent Mexican Catholic ca. 1990. A religious, PRI-affiliated minority thus constituted a dominant political group.[13]

Elsewhere in Tlaxcala, in Nopalucan, the old admixture of local religion, federal patronage, and autonomy drove a defection to ICAM in 1954. Trouble began when locals reported a miracle ("the appearance of the little feet of the Niño Jesús at the foot of a tree") only to find that the Puebla curia dismissed the apparition. In May 1955, angry Catholics registered ICAM priest Teódulo Alarcón, who endorsed the miracle, and converted en masse. The archdiocese of Puebla quickly raised Nopalucan from vicariate to parish and sent a cura, Simón Vázquez, and a team to reappraise the miracle. Too late: locals rejected the "Roman padres"—a government spy said—"because they were Mexican Catholics and had nothing to do with the Roman Church." The Roman cura then alleged to state authorities and the archdiocese of Puebla that Mexican Catholics fired pistols at his jeep. The complaint enabled state troops to arrest Alarcón in March 1956 and escort him over the state line. This felt like an injustice, because Gobernación's agent stated that Nopalucan was "completely unified around the Mexican Catholic Church." Alarcón was carrying out a "work of proselytism, like any religious minister," and his tenure should be upheld against the Roman cura and state government. On it went. In 1960 Mexican Catholics protested that federal writs were being ignored by state officials and "fanatics" who disliked ICAM's free sacraments.[14]

Something similar happened in Huetxoyuca (Pue.) in 1957, with a complication: simony. Here people voted to join ICAM "due to the neglect in which the church and inhabitants of this pueblo were kept by the Roman Catholic parish authorities in the cabecera of this municipality." The Roman cura, who disliked ascending to this hilltop village, charged exorbitant fees. Thus, in January people wrote to Ruiz Cortines informing him of their switch to Mexican Catholicism; the letter was signed by the ejidal commissar, church fiscal, and many inhabitants. In February, Gobernación endorsed the registration of two ICAM priests, Agustín García de la Cruz and Ángel Bueno Bonilla. Again, however, the state government backed the Roman archdiocese and sent troops to close the church. As Gobernación's agent put it, people were united behind ICAM and outraged by the state authorities. In the agent's opinion, this "dangerous" situation should not be allowed to continue, because it could result in clashes between villagers and state police. Gobernación learned of similar defections elsewhere, as in Coatepec (Pue.) in 1951, where people quit the Roman church after the cura criticized their church decorations, or Texoloc (Tlax.), where people joined ICAM because they felt neglected by their Roman pastor.[15] In Tutoltepec (Hgo.) people requested a "national church" priest in 1944, though the authorities were fearful of dividing the village.[16] In Agua Blanca de Iturbide (Hgo.)—the Iturbide was a sixteenth-century evangelist—people demanded a Mexican priest that year because they rarely saw a Roman priest and wanted parish status. To obtain them, they repaired their church and built a priest's house and school. Even Agua Blanca's Catholic Action bosses admitted that the disappearance of funds entrusted to the old Roman cura had encouraged "a certain distance" to grow between the Roman diocese "and those who call themselves the principales of the pueblo." The Roman diocese's response ("they should consider that pueblos with parish status have more right to be attended than does Agua Blanca, which is still not a parish") spoke volumes about why such tensions arose.[17] There were still agrarian cases, though the incidence diminished as Roman clergy stopped anathematizing the ejido. Yet ejidatarios in Tebanco (Ver.) requested ICAM masses into the 1940s, likewise Jalostoc's (Méx.) agrarian-religious elite.[18]

ICAM had a late resurgence in Chiapas. In Mazatán, near Tapachula, principales who founded a Patronato Pro-Construcción del Templo Católico between 1949 and 1965 were outraged to find that "great quantities" of money had been siphoned off by the Roman cura to pay for cinematic and sporting events. Thus patronato leaders "appointed on their own authority the (schismatical) bishop of Chiapas, Fray Agustín García de la Cruz," Gobernación noted. Its spy suspected that there were other issues, but the judicial file with its "countless" injunctions was impenetrable. The federal and state authorities could not decide what to do with Mazatán's church, but they feared "cruel happenings" if they closed it before 8 December, the patronal feast. Any official who dared to do so should remember that it was twenty-five miles back to Tapachula along a lonely track.[19]

An air of frustration enveloped a famous case: San Juan Chamula (Chis.), where ICAM was adopted by PRI-affiliated principales who resented the rising strength of San Cristóbal's liberationist clergy—the see was governed by "red bishop" Samuel Ruiz—just as they feared Protestant conversions. Mexican Catholic affiliations followed the arrival of liberationist priest Leopoldo Hernández in 1966. Hernández wished to denounce local structural inequalities, in line with Ruiz's "Misión Chamula." This was unwelcome to some, especially as Hernández began to require greater sacramental preparation and to decentralize ritual practices by training indigenous *catequistas*. He also refused to honor Chamulans' indigenous deities. In 1969, local elites expelled Hernández, breaking with the diocese of San Cristóbal; the municipal presidency then asked ICAM for a priest. In 1979, ICAM spread to Petalcingo, again because of disputes over liberationist ideas, yet here it was the Roman priest who switched sides. From Petalcingo, ICAM entered the municipios of Yajalón, Tumbalá, and Sabanilla, as well as ejidos such as El Puerto and Flores Magón. In essence, ICAM was a rearguard defense of indigenous costumbre and the elites ensconced in the *carguero* system and PRI. By the 2000s, Chamula gravitated back to Rome—in 2001, Ruiz's successor, Bishop Felipe Arizmendi, visited. Henceforth, Roman and Mexican priests swung between acceptance and ostracism, depending on their relationships with the principales.[20]

For the first time in decades, too, in 1960 ICAM acquired international notoriety when it offered support to the leadership of the Cuban revolutionary church, Con la Cruz y con la Patria. This action followed the suspension in sacris of Father Germán Lence, the Cuban Pérez, who along with militant fidelistas disrupted bishop Enrique Pérez Serantes's reading aloud of a furious anti-Castro pastoral, *Roma o Moscú*, in Santiago cathedral that November. Pérez Serantes, an erstwhile supporter of Castro's, suspended Lence in December. At this point, Lence wrote a letter that was read on Cuban television denouncing Pérez Serantes's attack on ecclesiastical freedom. In private, Lence reportedly said that he would use Pérez Serantes's edict to wipe his own arse. More public support was offered by Castro himself, who applauded this "distinguished priest," and by Lence's admirers in Mexico. That same month, indeed, letters of support for Lence from the Mexican Catholic and Apostolic Church (signed by vicar general José F. Xavier Cortés) appeared in *El Mundo* and other newspapers, intensifying the controversy.[21] From the 1960s, ICAM had urban success. In Tuxtla Gutiérrez (Chis.), ICAM boomed after Zoque Catholics clashed with Roman clergy over cult to San Pascual Bailón, a sixteenth-century Franciscan promoted as a eucharistic saint in Guatemala and canonized in 1690. During a 1650 typhus outbreak, the saint became associated with death and venerated as "King Saint Pascual," a colonial Santa Muerte. A Chiapanecan cult existed by 1872, and the famous image—a life-sized wooden skeleton in a wheeled coffin—was attracting pilgrims by 1902. Roman clergy waged campaigns against the image, moving it church to church and banishing it in the 1930s, ostensibly to prevent a revolutionary quemasantos (saint-burning). Subsequently, the icon—dubbed San Pascualito Bailón—was worshipped in a chapel near Tuxtla's market and became an important object of cult, its May fair pulling in Zoques, curanderos, Spiritists, and brujos. Then, in 1954, the Roman Catholic bishop maligned the cult and refused to consecrate the chapel if "that box"—his words—were not thrown out. *Pascualitos* and Roman Catholics clashed violently that December for control of the chapel. Then, on a visit to Tuxtla in 1959, President Adolfo López Mateos's secretario told devotees that they must register a minister if they wanted official guarantees. At this point (1960) pascualitos turned to ICAM bishop Agustín de la Cruz, who henceforth presided over a hybrid cult consisting of indigenous Catholicism, *curanderismo*, and PRI-style civil religion. By the late 1960s, the fair was attended by Chiapas's state governor, and featured Zoque incantations, the state marimba, limpias with candles and herbs, Catholic liturgies, and prayers for Chiapanecan liberals. As a climax, Saint Pascual's coffin was opened, and his image paraded through a street carnival enlivened by brass bands and free *pozol* (fermented gruel).[22]

ICAM finally made inroads in Mexico City, fifty years after La Soledad. In the 1970s Eduardo Dávila reappeared with another priest, José Enrique Cortés Olmos, and claimed the church of San Antonio Abad, off the Calzada de Tlalpan. In 1979, the Roman archdiocese tried to dislodge them, yet because the church belonged to a state bank, NAFINSA (Nacional Financiera), interior minister (and liberal historian) Jesús Reyes Heroles confirmed ICAM's occupation.[23] It is hard to separate his gesture from hostility among PRI hierarchs to 1979's papal visit and its challenge to PRI laicism. Conversely, the most successful Mexican church in the capital—José Camargo Melo's Our Lady of Guadalupe by the Parque Balbuena, near Benito Juárez Airport—was presented as a *priísta* Basilica, with tricolor-painted towers and a holiest of holies to rival Juan Diego's cloak: a bleeding Host. Camargo, a former Mercedarian (religious of the Blessed Virgin Mary of Mercy), broke with his order in 1978, having served as chaplain of the church known colloquially as "La Guadalupita" since 1973. He then joined ICAM and received episcopal orders. Since 1978, Camargo's branch of ICAM has centered on a bleeding Host, to which devotees attribute miraculous cures of terminal illness and addiction. In a 1978 letter to Archbishop of Mexico Ernesto Corripio Ahumada, Camargo celebrated the miracle which, he said, placed a "a true cross" on his shoulders and made him an object of persecution. His burden was unlike the "cardboard crosses" of everyday Christians, for he beheld a daily theophany. Thus he would not cling to the "false virtue" of slavishly obeying Church hierarchy. Thus he scoffed at a curial "notification" warning the faithful to avoid him and Pope John Paul II's instruction to mend his ways.[24]

As Carlos Salinas prepared to reform constitutional religious articles and sweep away the legacy of 1917, a sensational trial occurred. In April 1991, Camargo was thrown into the Reclusorio Oriente on charges of despoiling La Guadalupita's Roman clergy. It is not hard to see this as a demonstration by the Salinas regime to the Roman Catholic clergy of its bona fides and of its rejection of old school PRI anticlericalism. Speaking to reporters through bars, Camargo alleged that his occupancy was as valid as his Gobernación permit and that his arrest was the result of a deal struck between the Roman curia and Salinas. Mexican Catholics descended on the prison waving tricolors or barricaded themselves in La Guadalupita. *Granaderos* had to keep order during the trial, in which the Roman Catholic advocate conceded that "many people" in *colonia* Balbuena supported Camargo, but that the principle of "popular election" had no legal force. It was alleged that Camargo had been arrested for threatening to murder a Roman cura sent to remove him in 1989, not because of realpolitik. Camargo was released, and soon had churches in tough neighborhoods including Iztapalapa, Tláhuac, Iztacalco, and Ecatepec. He also runs a migrant church in Ileah, Florida.[25]

Camargo Melo's barrio bravo Mexican Catholicism, with its baroque miracle, popular nationalism, and embrace of Mexico's *olvidados* (addicts, migrants), brings us full circle. The pattern of 1926–1929 thus repeats, with permutations, because Mexico is still Catholic and governments periodically find the device of a state church politically useful. There is, always, a Catholicism of the damned that the official Church never fully assimilates and that is periodically receptive to new promises. This is why, of the best-known revolutionary schisms (France's église constitutionnelle, the Soviets' Living Church) only Pérez's still has a tangible base and an evolving place in its country's religious vernacular, thanks to its popular roots. As Corripio Ahumada recognized in 1985, the archdiocese of Mexico still faced "grave problems" caused by Pérez's "Mexican schism." There are today municipios such as Pisa Flores (Ver.), where Mexican Catholicism is the sole religion, because it coexists with corn ceremonies celebrated by Tepehua seers in the shrine-church (lacachínchin). It is not hard to imagine future "Mexican churches" premised on new social categories or taboos (priests' or devotees' sexual orientations or gender, devotees' migrant status), as opposed to staid, twentieth-century nationalism. Let us give the last word, then, to Rubén Mayorga, who drove ICAM in the 1950s. "Nobody is perfect in this world," he wrote to his old, Roman, archbishop in 1960: yet when people judged him he hoped they would have in mind "the image of Christ which exist[ed] in the mind of His Holiness John XXIII" when he called the Second Vatican Council, and show "pity and mercifulness to the fallen."[26]

NOTES

INTRODUCTION

1. A.k.a. Orthodox Mexican Catholic and Apostolic Church (IOCAM). I use the original title.
2. AHAM/MDR, c. 148/exp. 85, Paul Dudon, "Le Chaos Mexicain," cited in Ricardo Cox Méndez, "Cosas de México. El Gobierno de Calles y el Cisma Religioso," 1925; *Omega*, 9 Apr. 1925, "¿Quién Es el Patriarca Pérez?"; AMPV, c. 98/exp. 710/f. 5867, *El Faro*, 25 Jul. 1926, and c. 103/exp. 735/f. 7665, *La Opinión*, 18 Dec. 1928, "El Patriarca Pérez Se Ha Vuelto Loco," "Poliantea"; *Excélsior*, 7 May 1925, "La Victoria del Capitán Pérez."
3. AHAM/DB, c. 60/exp. 46, "Al Auto-Obispo López y Sierra y a su Porristica Feligresía"; Conflicto Religioso, c. M-R, *Segunda Pastoral del Ilmo. y Rvmo. Sr. Dr. D. Jenaro Méndez del Río, 4° Obispo de Tehuantepec* (Habana: Imprenta la Milagrosa, 1928). *Gaceta Oficial del Arzobispado de México* 23, no. 4 (15 Apr. 1925), "El Pretendido Cisma: Juicio contra los Asaltantes."
4. *El Demócrata*, 18 Aug. 1925, "Católicos que Piden Devuélvase el Templo y Virgen de la Soledad." AMPV, c. 106/exp. 745/f. 8508, *La Opinión*, 22 Aug. ("No Aparece la Virgen de la Soledad"), 25 Aug. 1929 ("Estaba en el Nacional Monte de Piedad: La Empeñaron los Cismáticos del Patriarca"). *Omega*, 9 Apr. 1925, "¿Quién Es el Patriarca Pérez?" AHAM/MDR, c. 148/exp. 92, Hearst reporter John Page, Mexico City, n/d. Pérez's recantation is Jesuit legend: Hurtado, *Cisma mexicano*; Gutiérrez García, "Apuntamientos"; Moctezuma, *Conflicto religioso de 1926*, 1:308–13; Parsons, *Mexican Martyrdom*, 18–19, 22–23, 177–78.
5. Butler, *Popular Piety*, 117.
6. Jorongo: poncho. AHAM/DB, c. 47/exp. 39, *Desde Mi Sótano*, 10 Apr. 1927.
7. Sicilia, *Concepción Cabrera de Armida*, 444; Weis, *For Christ and Country*, 124, 148.
8. *Excélsior*, 7 May 1925, "La Victoria del Capitán Pérez." Medina Ruiz, *Calles*, 96, 98. Riva Palacio, *Martín Garratuza*. Romero, *Vida inútil de Pito Pérez*. Some fiction writers still consider the idea of a Mexican pope to be high farce. See Reyes de la Maza, *Juan Xóchitl I*.
9. Medina Ruiz, *Calles*, 96.
10. *El Amigo de la Verdad* (9 Mar. 1925, "En el Templo de La Soledad el Patriarca Cismático Está Consegrando con Berreteaga") first claimed Pérez consecrated using "Indian" specie. The myth was popularized by "Pito" Pérez, who celebrates a Mass "worthily using the cassock of my brother, Joaquín," and jests that if priests drank *aguardiente* in the Mass, they would be "sweeter with their congregations" (Romero, *Vida inútil de Pito Pérez*, 21, 121–22). However, claims that indigenous Catholics consumed transubstantiated maize/agave derived from colonial homiletic practices, such as the Franciscans calling communion bread *tlaxcale* (Nahuatl, tortilla). In the eighteenth century, secularizing bishops attacked such calques as sacrilegious. *Cartas pastorales y edictos del Illmo. Señor D. Francisco Antonio Lorenzana y Buitron, Arzobispo de México* (Mexico City: Imp. del S up. Gobierno del Br. D. Joseph Antonio de Hogal, 1770), 98 and 98n2.

11. *Todo ha de ser mexicano / Y de origen nacional / ¡Nuestro diablo es el "Nahuál" / No el Luzbel, diablo romano! . . . ¡Es nuestra herencia, y por eso / De sangre no nos hartamos / Por culto la derrotamos/ Y hacerlo bien es el progreso!*). My translations. Simmons, *Mexican Corrido*, 395–97.
12. Moctezuma symbolizing Calles. Vasconcelos, *El Desastre*, 303–5.
13. AHAM/DB, c. 60/exp. 46, *La Razón*, all 1928, "Los Léperos del Cisma" (25 Nov.), "El Cisma en su Base Mujeriega" (9 Dec.), "El Cisma Callista y sus Cretinos Observadores" (7 Sep.), "Los Chuchos Hambrones del Cisma" (21 Oct.), "A los Títeres de Calles, Pérez, y López" (30 Sep. 1928), "Los Payasos del Cisma Calles" (4 Nov.); "Los Decentes y Pulcros (???) (¡¡¡) del Cisma Callista" (11 Nov.).
14. Antonio de Nebrija, 1444–1522. *Excélsior*, "Los Sacerdotes Cismáticos Celebraron Dos Misas Durante la Mañana y Dieron la Ceniza a los Feligreses" (26 Feb. 1925).
15. McCullagh, *Red Mexico*, 29–30, 165–67.
16. Given a starting point of 1524—when the first Franciscans disembarked in colonial Mexico—church and state will not have been separated for longer than they were conjoined until the year 2195. Of course, anything could happen by then.
17. AHAM/MDR, c. 71/exp. 6, Leopoldo Ruiz to Mora, Morelia, 26 Feb. 1925
18. Meyer, *Cristiada*, 2:143–66.
19. The 1917 canon law code defined schismatics as those who refused to submit to the Roman Pontiff or commune with his church. They were technically distinguished from heretics (deniers of dogma) and apostates (deserters from the faith). *Schismatici* incurred excommunication and, if priests, suspension. Miguélez Domínguez et al., *Código de derecho canónico*, 289–90, 294, 297–98, 305–6, 361–62, 464–65, 499–500, 547–48, 835–36, 844, 859.
20. Cannelli, *Nación católica*, 185–86.
21. The latter are explored elsewhere. Butler, "Christ Stopped." Miller, "Iglesia Más Mexicana."
22. Díaz Arciniega, *Querella por la cultura "revolucionaria,"* 44. Pérez Montfort, "Iglesia Cismática de 1925"; and "Iglesia Cismática Mexicana"Patriarca Joaquín Pérez."
23. Lisbona Guillén, *Persecución religiosa*, 275–317; Ríos Figueroa, *Siglo XX*, 116–24. Ramírez Rancaño, *Patriarca Pérez*.
24. I have piloted some arguments elsewhere: "*Misa a la mexicana*"; "*Sotanas Rojinegras*"; "God's *Campesinos*?"
25. Bastian, *Disidentes*, 320. Crewe, *Mexican Mission*, 3, counts 277 doctrinas.
26. As registered with Gobernación: Iglesia Católica Apostólica Mexicana; Iglesia Cristiana Católica Apostólica Ortodoxa Mexicana; Iglesia Ortodoxa Católica Apostólica Mexicana Comunidad Antigua Católica de México; Iglesia Católica Apostólica Ortodoxa Mexicana Independiente de San Pascual Bailón. Zalpa, *Enciclopedia de las religiones*, 59–74.
27. Ricard, *Conquista espiritual*, 420–21n16: "Esta situación explica posiblemente el intento, por otra parte insignificante, de producir un cisma bajo el gobierno de Calles . . . [E]se intento fue precedido de otros en 1859, en 1866, y durante la época de Carranza; de igual manera, notable es el hecho de que el 'Patriarca' de la Iglesia Mexicana, creada durante la época de Calles, José Joaquín Pérez, era un indígena mixteco."
28. As Estrella Ruiz-Gálvez Priego tells us (in "Conquista espiritual de México,"

Ricard in part projected French anxieties concerning Catholic modernism onto Mexican history and lamented that ecclesiastical authority was built on a narrow foundation, notwithstanding the success story of the "religious conquest."
29. Coatzacoalcos see (scrapped 1534) ran from Alvarado (Ver.) to Tabasco and Tehuantepec to Soconusco. Jiménez Abollado, "Cambios jurisdiccionales eclesiásticos." García Martínez, *Pueblos de la sierra*.
30. Lawrence, *Plumed Serpent*.
31. Stewart, "Syncretism and Its Synonyms." Christian, *Local Religion*.
32. AHAM/MDR, c. 44/exp. 37, Rome to Mora, 5 Jun. 1927; c. 157/exp. 114, Mora to Paolo Morella, San Antonio, 10 Jun., 29 Jul. 1927.
33. AGN/TGC, c. 133/exp. 11, Garrido to José Ramírez, Villa Hermosa, 20 Jun. 1932.
34. Vaughan, *Cultural Politics in Revolution*; Bantjes, *As If Jesus Walked*. More nuanced studies include: De Giuseppe, *Messico 1900–1930*; Wright-Rios, *Revolutions in Mexican Catholicism*; Fallaw, *Religion and State Formation*; Morris, *Soldiers, Saints, and Shamans*.
35. Any consideration of which begins with Connaughton, esp. *Entre la voz* and *Ideología y sociedad*; Van Kley, *Religious Origins of the French Revolution*; Voekel, *Alone before God*.
36. As Francis Oakley, *Conciliarist Tradition*, 3, has it, naturalizing the ultramontane church required a major act of "ecclesiological forgetting." Cf. Cárdenas Ayala, *Roma*.
37. "A people of the book," surmises Knight, "Mentality and Modus Operandi"; Bantjes, "Mexican Revolutionary Anticlericalism"; and Fallaw, "Varieties of Mexican Revolutionary Anticlericalism": 467–80 and 481–509.
38. Falcón and García, *Semilla en el surco*, 32–33. Macías Richard, *Vida y temperamento*, 23, 27; Macías Richard, *Plutarco Elías Calles: pensamiento político y social*, 190–95.
39. Cannelli, *Nación católica*, 75.
40. Using Roberto Blancarte's definition of a secular state as having no religious legitimation, the regime was not secular: "Laicidad y secularización."
41. Smith, *Chosen Peoples*, 1–14. Dormady, *Primitive Revolution*, 19–62.
42. Johnson, Klassen, and Fallers Sullivan, *Ekklesia*, 1–32: "We see stateness and churchness as analytically distinct but as, in practice, also an interlocking series of documents, procedures, practices, discursive registers, buildings, uniforms, lawlike rules, sounds, and ways of seeing. Churchstateness designates partly isomorphic patterns of materials, practices, and procedures that join only apparently discrete domains." The paraphrasing of Scott (7) is originally Noah Shusterman's.
43. Clark and Kaiser, *Culture Wars*.
44. Crewe, *Mexican Mission*, 199–227.
45. Desan, *Reclaiming the Sacred*. It also behooves us to dispense with an essentialized view of indigenous pueblos, seeing them as relational and iterative, subject to multiple pressures, including those of church and state. López Caballero, *Indígenas de la nación*.
46. McNamara, *Sons of the Sierra*.
47. Andes, *Vatican and Catholic Activism*.
48. Other revolutionary-nationalist movements, such as Italian fascism or Argentine Peronismo, try to assimilate the church wholesale in an attempt to turn it into a ventriloquist's dummy. On France, Russia, Cuba, and Italy, see ahead in the notes. For the other cases, see Mariani, *Church Militant*; Conde Tudanca, "Incidente olvidado"; Rodríguez Iturbe, *Iglesia y Estado*, 140–55.

Though the case is not well known, the Cuban Revolution had its Pérez: Father Germán Lence González, cofounder in 1959 of Con la Cruz y con la Patria. Here, however, the idea of organizing Catholics within the revolution developed during the resistance to Batista, when Catholics began offering social services to victims of the dictatorship, following—one Spanish priest later recorded—Jacques Maritain's thesis that Catholics should forget the idea of Christian states and instead create good Christians who would catholicize their polities indirectly. The idea of an island revolutionary Church therefore owed more to 1930s Catholic integralism, Cuban nationalism, and the recurring element of Christian primitivism than it did to the Castroites' adopted Marxism.

After the revolution's rupture with the Church (ca. 1960), Lence was demonized in Roman Catholic circles as an immoral, alcoholic, and ultimately repentant schismatic, not to mention a failed life-insurance salesman and born-again fascist. Yet pastoral records from Lence's parish (Holguín, Santiago de Cuba), where this Galician-born priest alighted in 1938, reveal a different story: a man who from the early 1950s denounced his coadjutor's neglect of catechism and the young; who complained of the religious orders' preference for attending comfortable middle-class churches in the towns while impoverished seculars manned the countryside ("the friars make vows of poverty and we honor them"); and who was charged by his bishop with exploring the sexual peccadilloes of other clergy. The only documented prerevolutionary scandals unearthed by unsympathetic historians concern Lence's failure to use money sent by his bishop to buy new handles for the church doors and a stint as chaplain of the Cuban Falange. As with Pérez, the real crimes were ecclesiological: Lence's Maritainian belief that indirect christianization could be effected through the revolution and that parish clergy could not be bound by their bishops. When invited by two laypeople, Antonio Pruna de la Madrid and *Lula* Hortsman de Leyva, to join Con la Cruz y con la Patria, Lence did so, celebrating "revolutionary masses" in Santiago and Havana, commemorating revolutionary martyrdoms, presiding over "national-Catholic" liturgies before thousands of *fidelistas* to give thanks for Castro's health, and preaching to throngs of pilgrims on the anniversary (September 7) of the country's patroness, La Virgen de la Caridad del Cobre. Uría, *Iglesia y revolución en Cuba*, 103, 115–16, 314, 401, 407–8, 416–20, 417, 432–37, 447–48. Saludes, *Hilario Chaurrondo*, 57–60.

49. In 1926, ICAM's *Secretaría de Cámara y Gobierno* issued 4,562 correspondence items (*Restauración*, 1 Mar. 1927, "Informe General de la Secretaría de la Iglesia Ortodoxa, Católica, Apostólica, Mexicana, Presentado al Concilio de Obispos y Demás Autoridades Eclesiásticas de la Propia Iglesia"); "every letter received here is answered," claimed Secretary López y Sierra. This archive is lost (López y Sierra was alleged to have removed it himself). Other correspondence was intercepted by spies or stolen: priest claimed that letters were frequently opened by hostile postmasters; Eduardo Dávila's papers were lost in a mob attack outside Tenango (Méx.) in 1938 (AICAM, López y Sierra to Emeterio Valdéz, Mexico City, 21 Apr. and 6 Jun. 1927; García Gutiérrez, "Apuntamientos").
50. Van Young, "New Cultural History," 226.
51. Bernabéu Albert, "Vacío habitado"; Torres Puig, "Falso sobrino del papa."
52. Byrne, *Other Catholics*, 11.
53. *El Universal* (Venezuela), 2008, "CEV rechaza surgimiento de Iglesia Católica 'Chavista'" (27 Jun.); "Arzobispos Católicos critican a la Iglesia Reformada de

Venezuela" (28 Jun.); "Jerarcas religiosos denuncian que nueva Iglesia Reformada pretende dividir a los católicos" (30 Jun.); "Lo más grave es que tal Iglesia reformada puede ser una iniciativa del Gobierno" (13 Jul.). *El Día* (Bolivia), "Iglesia Católica teme cisma por 'iglesia paralela' impulsada por el Gobierno" (29 Jan. 2014). Ayorinde, *Afro-Cuban Religiosity*.
54. Barranco and Blancarte, *AMLO y la religión*.

CHAPTER ONE
1. Toussaint, *Catedral de México*, 121–23. AHAM/MDR, 121.61, "Lista de Misas y Celebrantes en el Altar del Perdón, 1925."
2. Peris, *Storming the Heavens*.
3. AHAM/MDR, 159.30, Pérez and López y Sierra to CROM, Mexico City, 26 Jan. 1925; Provisorato, 124.4, receipt, Tacubaya, 12 Feb. 1925.
4. Pérez denied the link: *Yo conozco al Sr. Sierra; pero no conozco á sus familiares* (AICAM, Pérez to José González, Mexico City, 9 Jan. 1929). Retinger, *Morones of Mexico*, 19–20.
5. Ortiz Petricioli, *Compañero Morones*; Sálazar, *Líderes y sindicatos*. Guadarrama, *Sindicatos y la política*, 52, 73–76, 105, 125–26; Rivera Castro, *Clase obrera*, 9–11, 29–30, 68–75; Barbosa Cano, *CROM de Luis N. Morones*, 30–36.
6. Mereles de Ogarrio, *Plutarco Elías Calles*; Buchenau, *Plutarco Elías Calles*; Cano Andaluz, *Gestión presidencial*; Macías Richard, *Vida y temperamento*, *Plutarco Elías Calles: correspondencia personal*, and *Plutarco Elías Calles: pensamiento político y social*; Loyola Díaz, *Crisis Obregón-Calles*; Krauze, *Historia de la revolución mexicana*; Meyer, *Historia de la revolución mexicana*; Puente, *Hombre de la revolución*; Solares, *Jefe máximo*; Elías Calles, *Yo fui Plutarco Elías Calles*.
7. Díaz Arciniega, *Querella por la cultura "revolucionaria"*; Díaz Arciniega, "Calles: el voluntarioso circunspecto"; Palacios, "Calles y la idea oficial."
8. Treviño, *Frente al ideal*, 3–4. AMPV, 100.720.6495, *The Tidings*, 9 Sep. 1927, "Mexican CROM Condemns Calles Policy."
9. Buford, "Biography of Luis N. Morones," 139–45, 259–60, 269, 271. Quote, Uroz, *Cuestión religiosa*, 246–66.
10. AHAM, Cisma, "Bases Fundamentales de la Iglesia Católica Apostólica Mexicana"; *El Sol*, 18 Feb. 1925, "La Iglesia Se Separó de Roma: Un Grupo de Sacerdotes Lanzó el Grito de Independencia contra el Vaticano."
11. Apostolic delegates: Ernesto Filippi (1918–1923), Serafin Cimino (1924–1925). "Lo que dice el Patriarca de la Iglesia Apostólica Mexicana," *El Demócrata*, 20 Feb. 1925.
12. AHAM, Cisma, Enrique Hernández to Mora, Mexico City, Manuel Monge to Saturnino Pinea, Tacubaya, both 20 Feb. 1925; Provisorato, 124.4, "Yo . . ."; "Telegrama. C. Presidente de la República. . . ."
13. AHAM/MDR, Santa Cruz y Soledad, "Bendición y Dedicación de la Iglesia de Sta. Cruz, 29 de octubre de 1731"; "Apuntes Históricos sobre el Origen de esta Parroquia de Santa Cruz y Soledad de Nuestra Señora, en México, y Razón de sus Curas Regulares y Seculares hasta 1832"; "Informe al Ilmo. Sr. Arzobispo de México dado por el propio cura, Dr. Maestro Gregorio Pérez Cancio," 3 Aug. 1766; "División de curatos," 8 Mar. 1772; "Informe de Contaduría de la Real Audiencia," 22 Feb. 1777. Pérez Cancio, *Libro de fábrica*. Florescano, *Bandera mexicana*, 58, 61. O'Hara, *Flock Divided*, 48–54, 111–20, 145–51. Truitt, *Sustaining the Divine*, 43, 54, 229.

14. Truitt, *Sustaining the Divine*, 43. Ben Smith, personal communication.
15. AHAM, Parroquias, exp. 22, letters to Mora, Mexico City, 1922, from: Amado Sandoval (9 Mar.); Alonso Apuleyo (6 Feb.); Salvador Puente (31 Mar.); Luis de la Vega (19 Mar.); S. Hernández (7 Apr.); Silva to Mora, Mexico City, 28, 29 Apr. 1924; Mora y del Río, 43.73, "Nombramientos," 1921–1926; 48.53, Mora to Silva, Mexico City, s/f; 24.51, questionnaire, Tenango, May 1913; 24.51, "Parroquia de Santa Cruz y Soledad de la Ciudad de México," 1913. AMPV, 61.467.144–81, "Juzgado 6° Correccional, Año de 1925. Partida No. 390. Querella Presentada por el Lic. Telésforo A. Ocampo como Apoderado del Presbítero Alejandro Silva contra Luis Monge y Socios. Atentados a las Garantías Individuales, Iniciada en 8 de Marzo de 1925."
16. AHAM, Parroquias, exp. 22, Alejandro Silva to Mora, Mexico City, 14 Dec. 1923. Revueltas, *Cuadrante de la Soledad*. La Soledad is now known for an *Ecce Homo* venerated by sex workers, addicts, and robbers, and for its soup kitchen for street people. Talanaz y Solórzano and Monterrosa Prado, *Devociones cristianas en México*, 102–5.
17. AHAM/MDR, 134.27, Ignacio García del Valle to Provisor, Mexico City, 11 Dec. 1913.
18. Zárate Toscano, "Tradición y Modernidad."
19. *El Demócrata*, 26 Feb. 1925, "El Patriarca Pérez Mandó Fusilar Curas e Imagenes"; *Omega*, 9 Apr. 1925, "¿Quién Es el Patriarca Pérez?"; *Excélsior*, 28 Apr. 1925.
20. AHAM/PDB, Díaz to Pablo Puigserver, Mexico City, 24 Sep. 1930.
21. familysearch.org/pal:/MM9.1.1/JMZW-DZQ; familysearch.org/ark:/61903/1:1:-JCPV-X54; familysearch.org/ark:/61903/1:1:JCPV-X5Q; familysearch.org/ark:/61903/1:1:JS84-GYZ. AGN/DGG, 2.340.99.10, Pérez to ayuntamiento, Mexico City, 24 Jan. 1927. AHAM, Provisorato, 124.4, Buenaventura Alamán to Pérez, Texcoco, 23 Aug. 1929. Hurtado, *Cisma mexicano*, 23.
22. Sedena, Cancelados, X1.111.8–14598, ff. 161–223: "El C. Macario González, Gral. de Brigada . . . ," Zaragoza, 2 Nov. 1876; reports, González, Mexico City, 22 Nov. 1877; Jesús Quiroz, Mexico City, 4 May 1904; Vital Escamilla, Izúcar de Morelos, 15 Jan. 1877; Juan Hernández, Ajalpam, 27 Jun. 1876; Albino Zertuche, Zaragoza, 21 Nov. 1876; Diego Trujillo, Izúcar de Matamoros, 1 Dec. 1876; "Juan C. Méndez, General de División, Jefe del Ejército y Línea de Oriente . . . ," Xochiapulco, 28 Sep. 1876; *acuerdo*, Porfirio Díaz, Mexico City, 21 Sep. 1877; Pérez to war ministry, Mexico City, 8 Sep., 13 Oct., 12, 23 Nov., 3 Dec. 1877; Dr. Manuel Domingo, Mexico City, 1877.
23. Chowning, "Catholic Church."
24. Hurtado, *Cisma mexicano*, 23. Medina Ruiz, *Calles*, 98. Martínez Cedillo, *Parroquia de Santiago Juxtlahuaca*, 28–30, 102–6, 144–45.
25. Archivo Porfirio Díaz (APD), Pérez to Díaz, Mexico City, 6 Apr. 1888 (10.3975); Darío Vasconcelos to Díaz, Bravos, 8 Apr. 1891 (10.4373); Díaz to Vasconcelos, Mexico City, 14 Apr. 1891 (10.4374). Sedena, Cancelados, X1.111.8–14598, ff. 195–206: Pérez to war ministry, Chilpancingo, 7 Apr. 1891, Mexico City, 15 Sep. 1894, Orizaba, 25 Jul. 1895.
26. AHAM, Cisma, "Citando al Pbro. D. Joaquín Pérez," 1892; Alarcón y Sánchez, 23.41, Pérez to Alarcón, Tacubaya, 15 Jan. 1893. Archivio Apostolico Vaticano, Archivio Visita Apostolica en Mexico (henceforth AAV), index 1139, busta IX, fasc. 26, ff. 218–19, Perfecto Amézquita to Nicolás Averardi, Puebla, 28 Aug. 1899.

27. Vera y Zuria, *Cartas a mis seminaristas*, 562–66.
28. AAV, index 1139, busta IX, fasc. 26, f. 216, "Presbítero J. Joaquín Pérez . . . ," Amecac, 23 May 1897; receipt, signed Lic. José C. Espíndola, 29 May 1897.
29. AAV, index 1139, busta IX, fasc. 26, f. 236, J. Pérez to Averardi, Puebla, 25 Jul. 1899.
30. AAV, index 1139, busta IX, fasc. 26, f. 239, Pérez to Averardi, Atlixco, 18 Nov. 1897. *Restauración*, 1 Dec. 1925, "Obra Redentora de un Buen Sacerdote"; 15 Aug. 1926, "Antecedentes y Fundamentos del Movimiento Evolutivo Religioso de México, para Establecer la Iglesia Ortodoxa, Católica, Apostólica, Mexicana."
31. AAV, index 1139, busta IX, fasc. 26, f. 239, Pérez to Averardi, Atlixco, 18 Nov. 1897.
32. AAV, index 1139, busta IX, fasc. 26, ff. 218–19, Amézquita to Averardi, Puebla, 28 Aug. 1899.
33. Mariano Rampolla del Tindaro (1843–1913), then Vatican Secretary of State.
34. AAV, index 1139, busta IX, fasc. 26, ff. 235–36, Pérez to Averardi, Puebla, 25 Jul., 13 Aug. 1899.
35. AAV, index 1139, busta IX, fasc. 26, f. 215, Amézquita to Averardi, Puebla, 6 Sep. 1899.
36. AAV, index 1139, busta IX, fasc. 26, f. 225, "Carta abierta al Señor Pbro. Don Joaquín Pérez," *El Amigo de la Verdad*, 30 Aug. 1899; f. 222, "Otra vez Averardi y el Presbítero J. Joaquín Pérez," *La Democracia*, 24 Aug. 1899.
37. Italian revolutionary (1871–1949), editor of *El Diario*. In *Díaz*, 108–9, De Fornaro wrote: "In 1901 a priest called Joachin Perez, 50 years old, wrote to Monsignor Averadi [sic], apostolic delegate, letters in which he begged for the modification of the high tariff for the administration of the sacraments. The petition was signed by thousands of Catholics. Monsignor Averadi diplomatically answered that he would consult the Pope. But instead of so doing, the archbishop of Puebla and the monsignor gave a private dinner to Mucio Martinez, Governor of Puebla, and convinced him that Pérez was hatching a political conspiracy. By order of the Governor the unfortunate priest was attacked in his parish, at Atlixco, at midnight, beaten and then taken to jail. All his property and chattels were confiscated and although suffering from rheumatism, he was kept in confinement for over fourteen months. Eventually through the efforts of his sister, who went to beg the intervention of her uncle, Ignacio Mariscal, Minister of foreign affairs, he was freed." At best, Mariscal can have been Pérez's relative in the second degree. Enríquez, *Religious Question*.
38. Sedena, Cancelados, X1.111.8–14598, ff. 82–238: Pérez to Guerra y Marina, Mexico City, 21 May, 14 Jul. 1904, 26 Sep. 1913; Nicolás Piñón to Guerra y Marina, Mexico City, 10, 11 Jun. 1904; acuerdo, 6 Jun. 1904; demob papers and oath, Mexico City, 21 Jun., 5 Oct. 1906; *hojas de servicio*, 1906–1913. AHAM/AS, 112.28, Federico Carpio to Alarcón, Mexico City, 23 Jan. 1903; AHAM/MDR, 59.12, "El Presbítero Dn. José Joaquín Pérez, con respecto al domicilio en este Arzobispado," 14 Aug. 1912; Pérez to Mora, Mexico City, 14 Aug. 1912; 92.46, Pérez to curia, Mexico City, 27 Apr. 1914. Trexler, *Reliving Golgotha*.
39. Butler, "¿Nuevo capítulo revolucionario?"
40. AHAM/MDR, Pérez to curia, Iztapalapa, 4 Oct. 1914, 26 Jan., 25 Jul. 1915 (99.11), and to Paredes, Iztapalapa, 17 Dec. 1914 (99.12); Provisorato, 124.4, León to Pérez, Mexico City, 2, 19 Jun. 1918.
41. Hurtado, *Cisma mexicano*, 25. AHAM, Provisorato, 124.4, curia to Pérez, Mexico City, 8 May 1923.

42. AHAM/MDR, 13.14, "Mayo 8 de 1924. Pérez, Joaquín, Sr. Pbro. Demanda que por pago de pesos le promueve la Sra. M. Larrazábal de Villafaña." "Lista de las cosas del Sr. Cura D. J. J. Pérez, que quedaron en la casa de su primo el Sr. D. Antonio Pérez Villafañe," 16 Feb. 1924; "Lista de los objetos que no ha entregado la Sra. María de Villafañe y precios muy bajos en que valuan los Sres. Pérez y Quiróz y dichos objetos en caso de que la Sra. antes mencionada insista en no devolverlos," 10 Jul. 1924.
43. Menéndez Rodríguez, *Iglesia y poder*, 279–301.
44. AICAM, Emeterio Valdéz sermon, Tlaola, 30 May 1931.
45. Newspapers, 1925: *El Universal*, "Pistola en Mano Se Ocupó La Soledad" (24 Feb.); "Pido a la Ley la Entrega del Templo, Dijo el Padre Silva" (10 Mar.); "Las Víctimas de la Soledad Declararon ante el Juez" (11 Mar.); *El Amigo de la Verdad*, "Primer Atentado de los Cismáticos de la Iglesia Apostólica Mexicana" (23 Feb.); *Excélsior*, "En Nombre del Verdadero Párroco de La Soledad, Se Pide la Entrega del Templo" (10 Mar.). AGN/IPS, 6.17, "Movimiento Cismático en el Templo de la Soledad. Asuntos Diversos"; agente #1 to Depto. Confidencial, Mexico City, 26 Feb. 1925. AGN/OC, 438-M-6, Monge to Calles, 21 Feb. 1925. AHAM/MDR: Ricardo Cox Méndez, "Cosas de México. El Gobierno de Calles y el Cisma Religioso" (148.85); Valdéz to Mora, 26 Feb. 1925, and Pedro Benavides, León, 11 Aug. 1919 (84.18). On Spanish clergy, see Sanz-Cerrada, *Catacumbas en Méjico*.
46. AHAM/MDR, 136.5, Mora to Valenzuela, Mexico City, 23 Feb. 1925.
47. On the hustings in 1929, Valenzuela attributed La Soledad to Calles's inability to resist Morones's desire to control Mexico's "vital forces." Valenzuela believed he had won the argument when Calles ordered Pérez's eviction; minutes later, Calles countermanded the order by telephone (Moctezuma, *Conflicto religioso de 1926*, 1:311–13). Newspapers, 1925: *El Universal*, "Formidable Tumulto Popular en el Templo de la Soledad," "Ningún Ataque o Limitación a la Libertad de Conciencia Será Tolerado" (24 Feb.); "Una Averiguación para Esclarecer los Hechos que Han Originado el Cisma en la Capital," "Se Pide un Informe al Sr. Arzobispo de México y Otro al Patriarca de los Disidentes" (25 Feb.). *Excélsior*, "Un Extranjero, que Antes Fue Sacerdote, Ocasionó un Gran Escándalo Ayer en un Templo," "El Gobierno No Tolerará que por la Fuerza Se Ocupen los Templos Católicos" (24 Feb.), "La Soledad Fue Cedida a los Cismáticos" (25 Feb.). AGN/OC, 438-M-6, M. F. Bárcenas to Calles, 23 Feb. 1925; Calles to Pérez, 24 Feb. 1925.
48. Various, 1925: *El Universal*, "Hubo Otro Escándalo en La Soledad," "Se Dijo Misa Privada para una Veintena de Cismáticos" (25 Feb.); *El Amigo de la Verdad*, "El Barrio de la Soledad Sigue Practicamente en Estado de Sitio" (25 Feb.); *Excélsior*, "Se Celebró una Misa en La Soledad" (25 Feb.); AGN/OC, 438-M-6, Pérez to Calles, 24 Feb.; AGN/IPS, 6.17, agent #1 to Depto. Confidencial, Mexico City, 24 Feb.
49. *El Universal*, "Hubo Ayer Ceremonias en la Iglesia de la Soledad, Dándose Ceniza a los Concurrentes" (26 Feb. 1925); *Excélsior*, "Los Sacerdotes Cismáticos Celebraron Dos Misas Durante la Mañana y Dieron la Ceniza a los Feligreses," "Fue Vitoreado S. S. el Papa en La Soledad" (26 Feb. 1925). *El Amigo de la Verdad*, 9 Mar. 1925, "En el Templo de La Soledad el Patriarca Cismático Está Consegrando con Berreteaga."
50. *El Universal*, "El Ex-capitán Pérez y el Sacerdote Manuel Monje Fueron Excomulgados Ayer" (24 Feb.), "El Sr. Arzobispo de México Declara que Están Excomulgados los Mtros. del Culto Cismático" (26 Feb.); *Excélsior*, "La Iglesia Decreta la Excomunión contra Todos los que Hagan Caso a los Sacerdotes

Cismáticos" (26 Feb.). AHAM, Parroquias, exp. 22, "Edicto," 25 Feb.; *Gaceta Oficial del Arzobispado de México*, 23, no. 3 (15 Mar.): 101–5, 125–32. CEHM, clxxxii.1.79, "La Iglesia Decreta la Excomunión contra Todos los que Hagan Caso a los Sacerdotes Cismáticos." AHAM/MDR, 69.68, "Circular a los Sres. Foráneos, Curas Párrocos, Vicarios Fijos, y Capellanes del Arzobispado," 10 Mar.
51. *El Universal*, 27 Feb. 1925, "Fue Golpeado el Patriarca." AGN/IPS, 6.17, agent #1 to Depto. Confidencial, Mexico City, 26 Feb. 1925.
52. Various, all 1925: AHAM, Cisma, "Carta Circular al Venerable Clero Circular y Regular de la Iglesia Católica Apostólica Romana"; *El Universal*, "Otro Escándalo en La Soledad" and Monge's retraction letter (28 Feb.), "Uno de los Sacerdotes Cismáticos Se Retracta" (2 Mar.), "Recibió Ya el Sr. Arzobispo Documentos del P. Monge" (6 Mar.); *Excélsior*, "Nuevo Escándalo frente a La Soledad" (28 Feb.), "Salió Rumbo a Roma el Padre Manuel Monje" (3 Mar. 1925); *El Gráfico*, "Dice el Llamado Patriarca que Ya No Ocuparán Más Templos" (27 Feb.).
53. Kloppe-Santamaría, *In the Vortex of Violence*.
54. Various, 1925: *El Universal*, "Otro Tumulto en la Iglesia de Santo Tomás de Palma," "En La Candelaria," "En la Iglesia de la Santísima" (all 27 Feb.), "La Agitación Causada por el Cisma Ha Continuado" (1 Mar.), "Una Falsa Alarma en la Villa" (2 Mar.), "Hubo Anoche en el Barrio de Loreto un Zafarrancho" (4 Mar.). *Excélsior*, "Alarma en Santo Tomás la Palma," "Fracasaron los Cismáticos al Intentar Apoderarse de un Templo Católico" (27 Feb.). *El Amigo de la Verdad*, "Magno Escándalo en los Alrededores del Templo de Santo Tomás de Palma" (27 Feb.). AGN/IPS, 6.17, Second Police Group to Servicios Confidenciales, Mexico City, 27 Feb.
55. *El Universal*, "Hubo Ayer Gran Alarma en Puebla," "El Movimiento Cismático en Guadalajara" (28 Feb.), "Italianos Confundidos con los Cismáticos," "En Guadalajara, No Prosperará" (6 Mar.), "Trabajos en la Ciudad de Orizaba" (10 Mar.), "Falsa Alarma en Chalco" (14. Mar.), "Los Católicos de Ozumba en Guardia," "Tumulto Popular Frente al Templo de La Santísima," "Alarma en Querétaro" (16 Mar.), "Un Grave Tumulto Se Registró en Querétaro: Creyeron los Católicos en un Ataque de los Cismáticos" (18 Mar.), "Enérgica Oposición a los Cismáticos en Huamantla" (20 Mar.), "Los Cismáticos Quieren Templos en Pachuca" (21. Mar.), "Actividades Cismáticas en Chalco" (23 Mar.), "Balazos y Mojicones en el Interior de un Templo en Oaxaca, Invadido por Rateros" (28 Mar.). *Excélsior*, "Alarma en La Santísima por Cuestión Religiosa" (16 Mar.), "Reina Alarma en Querétaro por el Cisma" (18 Mar.), "Los Católicos de Puebla Defendieron los Templos contra de los Cismáticos" (19 Mar.), "Están Alarmados los Católicos Romanos y Dicen Se Defenderán" (24 Mar.), "Campaña de Cismáticos en el Norte del País" (28 Apr.). *El Demócrata*, "Actividades de los Cismáticos en el Mineral de El Oro, Méx." (25 Apr.), "Los Cismáticos Hacen Propaganda en Durango" (6 May). AHAM/MDR, 125.25, "Club de Exploraciones de México" to Mora, Mexico City, 21 Apr.
56. *El Gráfico*, 2 Mar. 1925, "El Llamado Patriarca a Punto de Quedarse Solo con su Famoso Cisma."
57. See ch. 2, opening para.
58. Cano Andaluz, *Opinión pública*, 70 (Calles). Various, 1925: *El Universal*, "Envió su Informe el Señor Arzobispo" (27 Feb.), "El Sr. Presidente Hará el Estudio del Conflicto Religioso Surgido entre Católicos y Cismáticos" (5 Mar.), "La Política del Gobierno en la Cuestión de la Iglesia" (15 Mar.), "La Iglesia de la Soledad Será un Museo de Arte Popular" (17 Mar.); *Excélsior*, "Ni Católicos Ni Cismáticos

Ocuparán en lo Sucesivo el Templo de La Soledad y Santa Cruz" (14 Mar.), "El Criterio del Gobierno del País en Cuestiones Religiosos" (15 Mar.).

59. Various, 1925: *Excélsior*, "Los Bienes de La Soledad Se Han Asegurado" (18 Mar.), "Se Reclamará al Gobierno la Sagrada Imagen de la Virgen" (24 Mar.), "La Parroquia de la Soledad en el Pequeño Templo de San Jeronimito" (18 Apr.). AHAM, Parroquias, exp. 22, Valenzuela to Mora, Mexico City, 14 Mar.; circular, 27 Mar.; Nicasio Zepeda to Mora, Mexico City, 14 Apr.; Silva to Mora, Mexico City, 9 Oct., 10 Nov., and 24 Feb. 1926; microfilm 8.1230. AHAM/MDR, 43.73, "Nombramientos"; 30.31, accounts. AHAM/PDB, 61.18, *acta*; "Inventario de los Objetos Pertenecientes a la Parroquia de la 'Soledad de Santa Cruz,' de ésta ciudad, que se encontraban depositados en el Nacional Monte de Piedad y de los cuales hace entrega, según acta de fecha 10 de septiembre de 1930, a la que se anexa el presente inventario."

60. Various, 1925: AGN/OC, 438-M-6, Israel Limón to Calles, 31 Mar.; Rosario Mercadillo to Calles, Tacubaya, 24 Feb.; AHAM, Cisma, "El Clero Saltillense al Pueblo Católico"; bishop to Mora, Saltillo, 1 Mar.; "¡Alerta Católicos! ¡Los Herejes en Campaña!"; *El Universal*, "Defenderán los Templos los Católicos de Saltillo" (11 Mar.); "Los Sacerdotes de Saltillo, Publicamente Han Condenado el Movimiento Cismático" (16 Mar.). MacGregor Campuzano, "Informe confidencial."

61. AMPV, 61.467, ff. 182–88, "Informe sobre los Acontecimientos Verificados en el Templo de San Marcos de Aguascalientes, el Sábado 28 de Marzo de 1925," "Algunos Detalles de los Sucesos Acaecidos en Aguascalientes en los Días 28 y Siguiente del Pasado Mes de Marzo"; 80.9, f. 288, *Diario Nuevo*, 27 Mar. 1925, "Archivo de la Delincuencia." AHAM/MDR, 71.13, Valdespino to Mora, Encarnación, 2 Apr. 1925. *El Universal*, "Tremendo Motín Se Registró en Aguascalientes" (30 Mar.), "El Templo de San Marcos Ha Sido Cerrado al Culto" (31 Mar.); *Excélsior*, "Sangriento Motín por Cuestiones Religiosas" (30 Mar.), "El Gobierno Reprimirá con Mano de Hierro Toda Actuación Subversiva de los Católicos" (31 Mar.). ALNDLR, 34.161–2, "Lo Sucedido en Aguascalientes." AGN/IPS, 290.21, "Investigación de los hechos que tuvieron lugar en el templo de San Marcos, de la Ciudad de Aguascalientes, la noche del 28 de marzo último."

62. AGN/OC, 438-M-6, Pérez to Calles, 7, 13 Mar., Calles to Valenzuela, 14 Mar.; *El Universal*, "Un Obispo 'Cismático' para el Estado de Tabasco" (12 Mar.), "Trágico Zafarrancho entre Católicos y Cismáticos" (14 Mar.), "El Movimiento Cismático en Tabasco" (19 Mar.); *Excélsior*, "Separatistas de la Iglesia que Fracasan" (15 Apr.), "Separatistas que Nombran Obispo Rojo," "Aumenta el Cisma en Todo el Estado" (16 Apr.). AHAM/MDR, 43.73, "Nombramientos," 1921–1926; Provisorato, 124.4, Yárcilo Ruiz to Pérez, Villa Hermosa, 28 Feb. 1926. Correa, *Pascual Díaz*, 86–91. Kirshner, *Tomás Garrido Canabal*, 21–24; Martínez Assad, *Laboratorio de la revolución*, 32–33; Méndez Moreno, *Anticlericalismo en Tabasco*, 114–22, 185.

63. *El Universal*, "Los Protestantes y el Movimiento Cismático" (20 Mar.). AHAM, Cisma, Ramón Gaitán to Mora, 2 Mar. 1925; AHAM/MDR, 71.6, Ruiz y Flores to Mora, Morelia, 26 Feb.; 72.7, "Edicto," Papantla, 25 Mar.; AMPV, 61.467: "Oración para los Sacerdotes" (f. 133); "Urgentísima Circular No. 58" (f. 191).

64. CEHM, clxxxii.1.76, "C. Presidente de la República."

65. ASV, Sacra Congregazione degli Affari Ecclesiastici Straordinari, Messico, IV per., 1925–1946, 499.21: Antonio Guízar to Gasparri, Chihuahua, 22 Feb. (r. 3);

Crespi to Gasparri, 25 Feb., Mar. 4, Mar. 9, Mar. 11 (rr. 4–6, 10); *protesta*, 2 Mar. (rr. 8–9). AMPV, 61.467, ff. 209–13, bishops González Valencia and Mora de la Mora to Pius XI, Rome, 12 Nov.; *El Universal*, "Adhesión al Sr. Arzobispo Mora y del Río" (27 Feb.).

66. Various, 1925 unless stated: AHAM/MDR, 62.66, "Declaración Firme y Consciente," Guadalajara, 27 Feb.; 71.3, bishop of Puebla to Mora, Puebla, 1 Mar.; 71.9, bishop of Chilapa to Mora, Taxco, 5 Apr.; 35.12, minutes, Mexico City, 22–25 Apr.; 69.11, circular, 19 Apr.; 71.4, bishop of Zacatecas to Mora, Zacatecas, 2 Mar.; 134.7, Mora to episcopate, 14 Oct. AHAM, Secretaría, unnumbered box, circular, 7 Apr.; Mora to episcopate, Mexico City, 14 Oct.; José Velasco to Mora, Aguascalientes, 4 Jan. 1926. AHAM, Cisma, Nicolás Corona to Mora, Papantla, 7 Mar.; AHAM/PDB, c. 46, "Pastoral Colectiva del Episcopado Mexicano," Mexico City, 26 Apr.; *Excélsior*, "El Arzobispo de Guadalajara Dice que Jamás Ha Pretendido Ser Jefe de los Separatistas" (17 Mar.).
67. *El Universal*, "La Protección de los Cismáticos ante el Derecho" (22 Sep.), "El Eterno Pérez" and "El Llamado Cisma y las Violaciones Constitucionales" (6 Mar.).
68. *Excélsior*, "Todavía el 'Patriarca' Pérez" (29 Jul.), "La Imposible Iglesia Mexicana" (2 Mar.), "El Fracaso de los Cismas: La Religión Católica Apostólica Romana Tiene en México un Arraigo Secular y una Solidaridad que No Quebranta una Iniciativa Absurda" (8 Mar.).
69. *El Gráfico*, "Ni con los Caballeros de Colón, ni con los Caballeros de Guadalupe, ni con los Caballeros de Industria" (26 Feb.); *Omega*, "El Asalto al Templo de la Soledad y el Criterio del Señor Presidente" (26 Feb.), "La Jefatura de los Cismáticos Está en el Palacio Nacional" (28 Feb.).
70. *El Globo*, "¡Hombres de poca fe . . . !" (27 Feb.). AHAM/MDR, 71.4, bishop of Zacatecas to Mora, 3 Jul. 1925; *Gaceta Oficial*, Tomo 23, Núm. 3, 15 Mar., 125–32. Wernick, *Auguste Comte*.
71. AHAM/MDR, 136.5, Mora to Valenzuela, Mexico City, 23 Feb.; CEHM, clxxxii.1.76, "C. Presidente de la República." *El Universal*, "Una Diligencia en la Casa del Patriarca Pérez" (4 Mar.), "Si el Patriarca Pérez Ha Delinquido Será Llevado a la Cárcel" (9 Mar.), "Pido a la Ley la Entrega del Templo, Dijo el Padre Silva" (10 Mar.), "Una Nueva Cita para el Patriarca Pérez" (30 Jul.), "Comparecerá el Jueves a Declarar el Señor Pérez" (5 Aug.), "El Patriarca Pérez Ha Incurrido en Falsedad" (18 Aug.). *Excélsior*, "El 'Patriarca' de los Cismáticos Ha Sido Ya Consignado" (9 Mar.), "En Nombre del Verdadero Párroco de La Soledad, Se Pide la Entrega del Templo" (10 Mar.), "No Se Sabe el Domicilio del Patriarca Pérez, que Debe Acudir al Juzgado" (25 Mar.), "El Patriarca Pérez Llamado a Declarar" (11 Jul.). AMPV, 61.467, ff. 148–80, Telésforo Ocampo to Ministerio Público, Mexico City, 8 Mar. Letters to Juez Sexto Correccional from: Ricardo Treviño, Mexico City, 25 Mar.; J. Meza, Mexico City, 29 Apr.; Pérez, 7 Aug.; medical certificates, Mexico City, 18 Mar., 30 Jun., 7, 11 Aug.
72. *Excélsior*, "El Movimiento Cismático Ha Perjudicado a los Negocios" (13 Apr.); SD 812.404–256, Sheffield to Kellogg, Mexico City, 24 Feb.; SD 812.404–257, "Alleged Schismatic Movement in the Roman Catholic Church in Mexico and Anticlerical Manifestations in Mexico," 3 Mar.
73. Meyer, *Historia de la revolución mexicana*, 111.
74. Loyola Díaz, *Crisis Obregón-Calles*, 21, 31–34, 53, 61–63, 72–78, 85, 89. Moctezuma, *Conflicto religioso de 1926*, 2:309.

75. *El Universal*, "Carrancismo Religioso" (16 Mar.).
76. APEC, 5.13/13.608–611.4038, Obregón to Calles, Navojoa, 7 Apr., "Mis Puntos de Vista sobre el Aspecto que Reviste el Movimiento Cismático Religioso Recientemente Iniciado en Nuestro País." Macías Richard, *Plutarco Elías Calles: correspondencia personal*, 1:151–54. Buchenau, *Plutarco Elías Calles*, 137.
77. AGN/IPS, 6.17, "La CROM y la Cuestión del Cisma Religioso" (27 Feb.); CEHM, clxxxii.4.296, "A los Trabajadores Organizados y al Público en General"; AGN/OC, 438-M-6, Treviño to Calles, Mexico City, 8 Mar.; *El Universal*, "Pedirán que Sea Apoyada la Actitud de los Cismáticos" (6 Mar.), "Los Diputados que Apoyan al Cisma" (8 Mar.), "Bloque Estudiantil Cismático" (10 Mar.); *Excélsior*, "Los Diputados que Apoyan a los Cismáticos" (8 Mar.); *El Demócrata*, "Un Grupo de Senadores y Diputados Partidarios del Mov. Cismático" (8 Mar.).
78. AGN/OC, 438-M-6, Pérez to Calles, Mexico City, 14 Mar.; AHAM, Cisma, Circular 2, "Al Venerable Clero Secular y Regular de la Iglesia Católica Apostólica Mexicana." *El Universal*, "Dos Templos Pidieron los Sacerdotes Cismáticos" (17 Mar.), "El Templo de Corpus Christi Se Entregará a los Cismáticos" (25 Apr.), "El Templo Fue Entregado ya a los Cismáticos" (6 May); *Excélsior*, "Los Cismáticos Solo Piden Se Les Conceda un Templo" (4 Apr.), "Corpus Christi Será para los Cismáticos" (29 Apr.), "El Templo de Corpus Christi Es Cismático" (6 May); *El Amigo de la Verdad*, "Los Cismáticos No Podrán Poner en Servicio el Ruinoso Templo de Corpus Christi" (23 Apr.), "Fue Entregado Ayer el Templo de Corpus Christi" (3 May); *El Demócrata*, "Los Cismáticos Recibieron el Templo de Corpus" (29 Apr.), "Resolvió Gobernación Varios Asuntos sobre Cultos Religiosos" (6 May); *El Globo*, "Se Decretó el Entredicho para la Iglesia de Corpus Christi" (29 Jul.). Muriel, *Indias caciques*; Lavrín, "Indian Brides of Christ."
79. AGN/DGG, 2.342, 43.29, Cayetano Huerta to Calles, Veracruz, 24 Mar., 9 Apr.; Pilar García Ortiz to Gobernación, Veracruz, 5 Apr., and Obregón, 15 May; Migración to Gobernación, Veracruz, 4 May. AHAM, Provisorato, 124.4, Pérez to Huerta, Mexico City, 6 Sep.
80. AHAM, Cisma, "Protesta del Clero"; AGN/DGG, 2.340.28.29, "¡A los Católicos!"; *El Gráfico*, "Otra Vez las Funestas Actividades de los Cismáticos" (31 Aug.).
81. *Excélsior*, "El Informe que el Señor Presidente de la República Rindió Ayer ante el Congreso" (2 Sep.).
82. *El Demócrata*, "Los Cismáticos Están Impedidos de Tomar a Fuerza las Iglesias" (4 Dec.).
83. AHAM, Provisorato, 124.4, minutes, Mexico City, 12 Sep.; *Restauración*, "Resumen General Concreto de la Estabilidad de la ICAM" (15 Jul. 1927).
84. AHAM, Provisorato, 124.4, López y Sierra to Pérez, Iguala, 25 Feb.; Pérez to "hermanos en Jesucristo," Tacubaya, 18 Feb.; AGN/OC, 438-M-6, Efrén Osorio to Calles, Puebla, 11 Mar.; *El Universal*, "Otro Presbítero Cismático" (3 Mar.), "Propagandistas en Oaxaca" (11 Mar.), "Los Sucesos de Huichapan" (24 Mar.), "Diputados Cismáticos Pretenden Apoderarse de unos Templos" (10 May), "Piden un Templo Católico para el Culto Cismático" (11 Sep.); *Excélsior*, "Gran Escándalo por Asuntos de Orden Católico" (29 Mar.), "Dos Iglesias Van a Volver a los Cultos" (1 Apr.), "Un Atentado de los Cismáticos Católicos" (7 Jul.), "De Nuevo Intentan Hacer de las Suyas los Cismáticos" (11 Nov.), "Los Cismáticos No Ocuparán el Templo de San Agustín" (3 Sep.); *El Demócrata*, "Asaltaron los Cismáticos el Templo Parroquial de Huehueltan (Puebla) Dando Muerte a un Niño de Doce

Años" (8 May), "Un Movimiento Cismático Iba a Culminar en un Sangriento Choque en Tenango, Méx." (6 Nov.), "No Lograron en Tapachula Templo los Cismáticos" (7 Sep.); *El Gráfico*, "Intensa Agitación Reina entre los Católicos de la Villa" (7 Jul.), and "Otra Vez las Funestas Actividades de los Cismáticos" (31 Aug.); *Restauración*, "Interesantes Solicitudes de los Vecinos de Tenango de Doria, Hidalgo" (1 Dec.), "Un Nuevo Templo Adquirido" (15 Jan. 1926), "Clamoroso y Estupendo Triunfo en la C. de Tapachula, Chiapas, con Motivo de la Fundación de la Iglesia Ortodoxa Católica Apostólica Mexicana" (15 Sep.), "Nuestros Trabajos en Tapachula" (15 Nov.). *La Buena Lid*, tomo 2/no. 46, Nov. 1925, "El Padre Rivera." Hernández Enríquez, *Historia Moderna*, 226. AGN/DGG, 2.340.28.29, "¡A los Católicos!"

CHAPTER TWO
1. AGN/IPS, c. 6/exp. 17, agents #1/15 to Depto. Confidencial, Mexico City, 5 Mar. 1925.
2. BLAC, Herbert Gambrell Papers, "The New Catholic Church of Mexico," 1–2, 6.
3. AHAM, Cisma, and ADAM, *La Buena Lid*, tomo 2/nos. 43–46, Jul.–Nov. 1925, "Sermón Predicado en el Templo Patriarcal y Parroquia de Corpus Christi, Iglesia Católica Apostólica Mexicana, el Día 11 de Junio de 1925, Día de la Inauguración de Dicho Templo, por el Cura Párroco del Mismo, Presbítero Benigno Gómez R., México D.F."
4. BLAC, Herbert Gambrell Papers, "The Religious Ferment in Mexico," 3–4, 36.
5. The answer was no, just an excommunicate. AHAM/MDR, c. 148/exp. 85, Pedro Osorio to Mora, Mexico City, 21 Jul. 1926.
6. AHAM/DB, c. 59/exp. 15, anonymous priest to Mora, 1926.
7. AHAM, Cisma, Pbro. N. N. to Mora, Mexico City, 27 Feb. 1925.
8. AHAM/MDR, c. 148/exp. 85, Dudon, "Chaos."
9. James, *Varieties of Religious Experience*, 359. I thank Elizabeth Pritchard for this reference.
10. Byrne, *Other Catholics*, 11.
11. AHAM, Cisma, "La Carabina de Ambrosio y la Terrible Excomunión y Entredicho del Arzobispo José Mora y del Río."
12. Cárdenas, *Roma*. "Romanization" is a misnomer to Catholic historians for whom the church is ineffably Roman.
13. Matthew, 16:18. "Carta Abierta al Sr. Pbro. Don Encarnación Anaya, Ex-Vicario del Pueblo de Apam, Hidalgo," *Restauración*, 18 Feb., 1 Mar. 1927.
14. AHAM, Cisma, "Sermón . . ."
15. *Restauración*, 1 Aug. 1926 ("Rasgos Característicos de la Sucesión Papal"), 15 Dec. 1926 ("Los Católicos Romanos No Son los Católicos Mexicanos"), 15 May 1927 ("Es Ud. Católico Apostólico Cristiano").
16. *Restauración*, 15 Aug. 1926, "Antecedentes y Fundamentos del Movimiento Evolutivo Religioso de México, para Establecer la Iglesia Ortodoxa, Católica, Apostólica, Mexicana."
17. BLAC, Gambrell Papers, "New Catholic Church," 3.
18. Luke 10:1–20. Van Kley, *Origins of the French Revolution*, 337–58. Strayer, *Suffering Saints*, 3–56.
19. Trejo, *Límites de un discurso*, 357–74.
20. *Restauración*, 15 Jul. 1927, "La Segunda Independencia." AHAM, Cisma, "Mexicanos," ca. 1925.

21. Voekel, *Alone before God*, 1–9, 44–47, 58–59. Larkin, *Very Nature of God*.
22. AICAM, "Constitución General y Leyes Conexas de la Iglesia Ortodoxa Católica Apostólica Mexicana" (18 Jul. 1930). art. 9:37. Voekel, *Alone before God*, 44–50. Pelagius: fourth-century Celtic theologian and believer in human free will.
23. Carey, "Voluntaryism."
24. Byrnes, *Priests of the French Revolution*, 39, 61–65. Domínguez Michael, *Vida de Fray Servando*, 264. Tecuanhuey Sandoval, "Hermanos Troncoso."
25. Crook, "Citizen Bishops."
26. AHAM, Cisma, "Bases Fundamentales de la Iglesia Ortodoxa Católica Apostólica Mexicana," 18 Feb. 1925; *Restauración*, 1 Aug. 1926, "¿Por qué Nuestra Iglesia Se Denomina Ortodoxa, Católica, Apostólica, y Mexicana?"; AICAM, "Nuestra Profesión de Fe, Razonada" (1929); "Constitución General y Leyes Conexas de la Iglesia Ortodoxa Católica Apostólica Mexicana" (18 Jul. 1930).
27. *Restauración*, 15 Aug. 1926, "Antecedentes . . ."; 1 Aug. 1925, "Nuestro Programa."
28. AHAM, Cisma, "Carta Circular al Venerable Clero Circular y Regular de la Iglesia Católica Apostólica Romana," 26 Feb. 1925. *Restauración*, 1 Aug. 1925, "Nuestro Programa."
29. *Restauración*, 1 Aug. 1926, "¿Por qué Nuestra Iglesia . . . ?"
30. AHAM, Cisma, "Carta . . ."
31. AICAM, "Profesión de Fe," Zapotitlán, Jan. 1930; "Excitativa de la Santa Sede Episcopal del Estado de Veracruz a a Feligresía en Particular y a los Católicos en General," Dec. 1931 [n/d]."
32. AICAM, "Rúbrica para el Bautismo," Tacuba, 4 Jan. 1932; "Constitución," arts. 10:52, 55; "Misa de Requiem," s/f. *Restauración*, 15 Aug. 1926, "Las Conferencias Religiosas en Nuestro Templo de Corpus Christi."
33. AICAM, "Constitución," art. 10:49. AHAM, Cisma, *La Iglesia Romana Es Mistificadora, Fragmento del Libro* Las Cuatro Notas*, por Benigno Gómez R., Ex-Clérigo de la Iglesia Romana* (Mexico City: Tip. "Perla," s/f). Ben Fallaw, "Seduction of Revolution."
34. AICAM, "Constitución," arts. 10:46, 10:50, 10:51. *Restauración*, 15 Sep. 1925 ("¡Católicos Romanos!").
35. BLAC, Gambrell Papers, "Ferment," 3.
36. AICAM, "Constitución," arts. 2:4, 4:14, 10:43.
37. "Carta abierta . . . ," *Restauración*, 18 Feb., 1 Mar., 15 Mar., 1 Apr., 15 Apr. 1927.
38. AHAM, Cisma, "Bases," 1925.
39. AICAM, "Nuestra Profesión de Fe, Razonada," n/d.
40. *Restauración*, all 1927, "Programa de los Servicios Religiosos de Corpus Christi en Semana Santa" (1 Apr.), "La Semana Mayor en el Templo de Corpus Christi" (1 May), "Mes de María Santísima" and "Fiesta Titular en el Templo de Corpus Christi" (both 1 Jun.), "Festividades en Corpus Christi" (1 Jul.). AICAM, "Misa Pontifical," n/d. "Para el Domingo de Ramos," s/f (1925–30). AHAM, Cisma, "Invitación," 7 Jun. 1925.
41. Cressy, *Bonfires and Bells*.
42. AICAM, *carta pastoral*, Mexico City, 9 Sep. 1930. *Restauración*, "La Iglesia Católica Apostólica Mexicana, para Conmemorar de una Manera Digna el Glorioso Aniversario de la Proclamación de la Independencia" (15 Sep. 1926); "Glosario Religioso" (1 Jan. 1927); "La Iglesia Mexicana Celebra Hoy su Segundo Aniversario" (18 Feb. 1927); "Primero de Mayo" (1 May 1927); "Solemne

Invitación" (1 Oct. 1927). AHAM, Cisma, "Invitación," 27 Jun. 1925; "Edicto de la Inquisición Citando al Cura Hidalgo para que Se Presente a Contestar los Cargos de Herejía, Apostasía, etc."; "Opinión del Auditor de Guerra Pidiendo Pena de Muerte para el Generalísimo Morelos, de Acuerdo con el Arzobispo de México"; "Carta Abierta a su Ilustrísima el Señor José Mora y del Río, Arzobispo de la Arquidiócesis de Roma." SD 812.404-266, "Schismatic Movement in the Roman Catholic Church in Mexico," 7 Jul. 1925. *El Universal*, 11 Mar. 1925, "Misa de los Tres Poderes en la Iglesia de la Soledad." AGN/OC, 438-M-6, Pérez to Calles's private secretary, La Soledad, 6 Mar. 1925; "Aviso Religioso," Mexico City, 1925.

43. *Excélsior*, 25 Jul. 1925, "La Iglesia Cismática Celebró el 18 del Corriente una Fiesta Religiosa en Honor de Benito Juárez." *Restauración*, 1 Aug. 1926, "Oración Fúnebre al C. Benemérito de las Américas, Lic. D. Benito Juárez, en el Templo de Corpus Christi de la Iglesia Católica Mexicana." On Masonic symbolism and *juarismo*, Vázquez Mantecón, *Muerte y vida eterna*, 31, 45–52, 57–60, 69–76.
44. *Restauración*, "Sentida Difunción" (15 Sep. 1926), "Muere un Miembro de la Iglesia" (15 Oct. 1926), "Glosario Religioso" (1 Jan. 1927), "Pesame" (15 Jun. 1927). I cannot verify the Juárez genealogy. Some sources claim ICAM's treasurer was called Ángel Zesno.
45. Achútegui and Bernad, *Religious Revolution*, 1: 192–201, 270–71, 301, 381–409.
46. *Restauración*, 1 Aug. 1926, "¿Por qué Nuestra Iglesia . . . ?"
47. AMPV, c. 61/exp. 467/f. 385, *Orientación*, 4 Oct. 1926, "Dividir a la Iglesia." Condumex, clxxxii.4.373, "A los Católicos de Puebla y de México," Puebla, 15 Dec. 1926.
48. AHAM, Cisma, "Carta Circular . . . ," 26 Feb. 1925. Bailey, *¡Viva Cristo Rey!*, 52n14. Quirk, *Mexican Revolution*, 140–41. ADAM, *La Buena Lid*, tomo 2/no. 42, Jun. 1925, "El Nuevo Movimiento Religioso."
49. Gambrell Papers, "New Catholic Church," 5–6.
50. ADAM, *La Buena Lid*, tomo 2/no. 43, Jul. 1925, "Por qué Simpatizamos con el Nuevo Movimiento Religioso."
51. ADAM, *La Buena Lid*, tomo 2/nos. 39, 40, and 41 (Mar., Apr., May 1925), "El Nuevo Movimiento Religioso."
52. Touché-Porter, *Short History of Anglican Worship*, 18–25.
53. ADAM, ca. 1926, Hulse to Gómez Ruvalcaba, New York, 22 May 1925. BLAC, Gambrell papers, Gambrell to López y Sierra, 17 Dec. 1925; López Sierra to Gambrell, Mexico City, 3 Feb. 1926.
54. ADAM, *La Buena Lid*, tomo 2/no. 50, Feb. 1926, "La Iglesia Ortodoxa Mexicana."
55. ADAM, Gómez Ruvalcaba to Creighton, Mexico City, 19 May, 23 Aug. 1926; Creighton to Gómez Ruvalcaba, Mexico City, 19 Aug. 1926.
56. NAORC described itself as an apostolic, independent, Catholic church that was loyal to national (US) laws and ideals. Its liturgy was in English, its priests could marry, and it gave the sacraments to Catholics who had been "unchurched" by Rome. On Old Catholicism, see Howard, *Pope and the Professor*, 145, 178–90; C. B. Moss, *Old Catholic Movement*; Brandreth, *Episcopi Vagantes*; Prüter and Melton, *Old Catholic Sourcebook*; Anson, *Bishops at Large*; Neale, *History of the So-Called Jansenist Church*; Theriault, *René Vilatte*; Plummer, *Who Are the Independent Catholics?*
57. On Pérez's consecration, ADAM, *La Buena Lid*, tomo 2/no. 39, Mar. 1925, "El

Nuevo Movimiento Religioso." *Restauración*, all 1926, "Interesante Carta Remitida al Reverendísimo Señor Patriarca Pérez, por un Alto Prelado de Europa" (15 Aug.), "Importante Sínodo" (24 Sep.), "El Patriarca Pérez en el Extranjero" (15 Oct.), "El Patriarca Es Arzobispo Metropolitano" (1 Nov.), "A Quien Pueda Interesar" (1 Dec.). AHAM/MDR, unnumbered c./exp., Raymundo Chávez Triguero to M. M. Bustamante and Alfredo Arredondo, Mexico City, 12 Oct. 1926. AGN/DGG, 2.340.102.47, "*Instrumentum Consecrationis Reverendissimi Domini Antoni B. López y Sierra In Episcopum.*" AICAM, "Cuenta del Sr. Patriarca Dn. José Joaquín Pérez," n/d. Pérez's attire cost 330 pesos.

58. *Restauración*, 1 Nov. 1926, "Carta Pastoral del Ilmo. y Revmo. Señor Patriarca, Don José Joaquín Pérez, Arzobispado Metropolitano de la Ciudad de México, al Clero Secular y Regular y Fieles de la Iglesia Ortodoxa Católica Apostólica Mexicana en la República," 25 Oct. 1926. ICAM certainly commemorated its Jansenist-Gallican origins. See *Restauración*, 1 Dec. 1926, "Tabla Histórica de la Sucesión Episcopal Apostólica de la Iglesia de los Antiguos Católicos Romanos"; Schultz, *History of the Apostolic Succession*, 13–17.
59. AHAM/MDR, c. 44/exp. 37, Paolo Morera to Mora, 8 Aug. 1927 (Latin version, c. 157/exp. 114); c. 44/exp. 85, J. H. Suárez to C. Ordóñez, Chicago, 17 Jan. 1927.
60. ADAM, all 1926, Pérez to Creighton, Mexico City, 27 Oct.; ICAM to "Honorable Cuerpo Eclesiástico de la Misión de la Iglesia Episcopal Americana en México," Mexico City, 29 Oct.; Samuel Salinas to López y Sierra, Nopala, 5 Nov.; José F. Gómez to "Cuerpo Consejero del Distrito Misionero de México," Mexico City, 8 Nov.
61. ADAM, Patriarch Pérez to Bishop F. W. Creighton, Corpus Christi, 4 Dec. 1926.
62. *Restauración*, 1 Oct. 1925, "¡Escuchad Católicos Romanos!"
63. Matthew, 10: 8, 9–10. AICAM, "Nuestra Profesión . . ."
64. AHAM, Cisma, "Bases," 1925. AICAM, "Constitución General," art. 2:4.
65. *Restauración*, 1 Aug. 1925, "Limosnas."
66. *Restauración*, 1 Aug. 1926, "Detrás del Escándalo Religioso que Hace la Iglesia Romana, Obtiene un Negocio de Cientos de Miles de Pesos."
67. AICAM, "Nuestra Profesión . . ."
68. *Restauración*, 18 Feb. and 1 Mar. 1927, "Carta Abierta . . ."
69. AHAM, Cisma, "Mexicanos," ca. 1925.
70. AICAM, ICAM to municipality of Coyutla, Tacuba, 20 Nov. 1929.
71. AHAM, Cisma, "Alerta Católicos Mexicanos," ca. 1925.
72. AICAM, "Nuestra Profesión . . ."
73. Carey, "Voluntaryism."
74. For a fuller discussion, see the next chapter.
75. *Restauración*, 15 Jan. 1926, "Interesante Acuerdo Patriarcal."
76. AHAM, Cisma, "Bases," 1925. AICAM, "Nuestra Profesión . . ."
77. AHAM, Cisma, "Bases"; AICAM, "Nuestra Profesión . . ." Pérez to José González B., Mexico City, 9 Jan. 1929. Pérez occasionally married off his clergy, as in a "strange ceremony" reported in Corpus Christi in 1925: the marriage of Alberto Fernández de Haro (*El Gráfico*, 3 Dec. 1925, "Uno de los Cismáticos Va a Contraer Matrimonio").
78. AICAM, Macario López to municipio, Zapotitlán, 14 Aug. 1926 (quote). Other cases: López y Sierra to Valdéz, Mexico City, 14 Apr. 1928; Teódulo Alarcón to Valdéz, San Simón de Bravo, 18, 22 Oct. 1933.
79. AICAM, López Sierra to Emeterio Valdéz, Mexico City, 23 Apr. 1928.

80. AICAM, López y Sierra to J. E. Valdéz, Mexico City, 4 Mar., 9 Apr., 6, 29 Jun., 4, 23 Aug. 1927; 1, 14 Apr. 1928; *Alcance al No. 61 de Restauración*, 1 May 1928. Contrary to myth, ICAM was not flush with CROM funds. CROM donated the bell that hung in Corpus Christi in 1925, as Pérez later reminded Celestino Gasca, but seemingly little after that (AGN/DGG, 2.340.102.47, Pérez to Gobernación, Mexico City, 27 Sep. 1929).
81. AICAM, José F. Gómez to Adolfo Briones, Tlaola, 5 Sep. 1931.
82. AHAM, Provisorato, c. 124: Francisco Durán to ICAM, Tlaola, 4 Jun. 1930 (exp. 1); José Ramírez to Pérez, Tapachula, 21 Dec. 1926 (exp. 4); Zeferino R. Reyes to Pérez, Mexico City, 17 Feb. 1930 (exp. 2). AHAM/DB, c. 61/exp. 12, receipt, 3 Aug. 1930. AICAM, ICAM to Vicente Liñán, DF, 7 Jun. 1931.
83. AICAM, López y Sierra to Valdéz, Mexico, 23 Apr. 1928; to Teodoro Juárez, Mexico City, 6 Jul. 1928; and to Teodoro Juárez, Francisco Durán, and José de la Luz Coronado, Mexico City, 29 May 1928. Valdéz to López y Sierra, Mexico City, 28 May, 22 Jun. 1928, Coyutla, 28 May 1928. "Constitución," art. 5:5. AGN/DGG, 2.340.66.10, acta, Tetela de Ocampo, 23 Dec. 1926.
84. AICAM, "Lista de Asuntos que se Deben de Resolver por el Concilio, Presentada por el Diocesano de Veracruz," s/f [1929]. *Restauración*, 1 Mar. 1927, "Informe General de la Secretaría de la Iglesia Ortodoxa, Católica, Apostólica, Mexicana, Presentado al Concilio de Obispos y Demás Autoridades Eclesiásticas de la Propia Iglesia."
85. AHAM, Provisorato, c. 124: Pérez to López y Sierra, Mexico City, 8 Feb. 1928 (exp. 4); López y Sierra to Pérez, San Luis Potosí, 5 Mar. 1929 (exp. 1); "A los señores sacerdotes canónicamente relacionados con esta Sagrada Mitra," Mexico City, 7 Jan. 1929; Pérez to López y Sierra, Mexico City, 10 Feb. 1929; Circular, 6 Mar. 1929; Circular #2, 22 Jul. 1929; Pérez to Gobernación, Mexico City, 23 Aug. 1929 (all exp. 2). AICAM, "A los Ilmos. Señor Obispo D. Antonio López Sierra y Miembros del Juzgado Eclesiástico," 6 Feb. 1929. AGN/DGG, 2.340.102.47, Pérez to Gobernación, Mexico City, 27 Sep. 1929.
86. AHAM, Provisorato, c. 124: López y Sierra to Vicente Liñán, San Antonio, 4 Jul. 1929, and Pérez, San Antonio, 18 May 1929 (exp. 3); "Carta abierta del Ilmo. Señor Obispo Doctor Don Antonio B. López y Sierra al clero y miembros de la Iglesia Católica Apostólica Mexicana," Aug. 1929 (exp. 2).
87. AGN/DGG, 2.340.102.47, Pérez, Mexico City, 30 Dec. 1929. AHAM, Provisorato, c. 124/exp. 3, Zeferino R. Reyes to López y Sierra, Mexico City, 21 Jul. 1929.
88. APEC, 49.105.3294, José Melgoza to López y Sierra, Mexico City, 7 Jul. 1929.
89. AICAM, "Constitución," arts. 1:3, 3:82:4 (d), 5:5. Synods met annually. *Restauración*, 1 Mar. 1926, "Informe General . . ." (Synod of 15 Feb. 1926), 1 Mar. 1927, "Informe General . . ." (Synod of 18 Feb. 1927). Gómez Ruvalcaba was consecrated in Jan. 1927 before "anti-fanatical society" including General Roberto Cruz and SEP teachers (*Restauración*, 15 Jan. 1927, "Consagración del Nuevo Obispo, Muy Reverendo Eleuterio B. Gómez").
90. AICAM, circular núm. 10, DF, 4 Jun. 1931. Hurtado, *Cisma mexicano*, 40–1.
91. AGN/DGG, 2.340.105.17, agente #2, Mexico City, 2 Jun. 1931; 2.340.68.14, mayor, Tecamachalco, 6 May 1933. AHAM, Cisma, Macario López to J. Lazarini, Mexico City, 18 Oct. 1931. *Restauración*, 18 Oct. 1932, "Juan Crisóstomo Primero, Patriarca Arzobispo de la Santa Iglesia Ortodoxa Católica Mexicana." FPEC, 12.010086.68.628, *L'Osservatore Romano*, 6 Nov. 1932.
92. AHAM, Cisma, "Bases." AICAM, "Constitución," art. 2:4, and "Nuestra Profesión. . . ." (quoting Isaiah, 55:11); BLAC, Gambrell Papers, "New Catholic Church," 3.

231

93. BLAC Gambrell Papers, "New Catholic Church," 4: "When I asked how the retention of this modern miracle squared with the liberal tendency of the church, Father López explained that the belief in the Virgin had an excellent moral effect on the people and, inasmuch as the truth of the story could neither be proved nor disproved, it seemed well to allow those who find it helpful to continue to believe in it... The tendency of the new church is away from the veneration of saints and images, but that progress in that direction would be slow."
94. Byrne, *Other Catholics*, 126–31. In 1929, LCC was tainted by scandal when Jiddu Krishnamurti, a teenaged Indian prophet groomed as a Liberal Catholic world guru (and allegedly Leadbeter's catamite) denounced his messianic/sexual role. The syphilitic Wedgwood had resigned as bishop in 1923.
95. *The Liberal Catholic Church: General Constitution, as Revised by the Second General Episcopal Synod* (Los Angeles: St. Alban Press, 1927), 3–8; *The Liberal Catholic Church: Statement of Principle, Summary of Doctrine, and Table of the Apostolic Succession* (Los Angeles: St. Alban Press, 1926), 5–8, 11–12; F. W. Pigott, *The Parting of the Ways: The Teachings of the Liberal Catholic Church Compared and Contrasted with Traditional Catholic Teachings* (London: Liberal Catholic Church, 1927), 53–63.
96. AMPV, c. 61/exp. 467/f. 117, *Iglesia Católica Liberal: Información General* (1925).
97. Urias Horcasitas, "Poder de los símbolos." Rugeley, *Of Wonders and Wise Men*, 199–200.
98. AHAM, Provisorato, c. 124/exp. 4, Juan Félix Hernández to Pérez, Jalapa, 22 Jun. 1925.
99. AHAM, Provisorato, c. 124/exp. 1, *Mensaje esotérico*, 3 Dec. 1926, others n/d.
100. Irving S. Cooper (1882–1935), LCC bishop and Theosophist (misspelled "Youviuz de Cooper"). AHAM, Provisorato, c. 124/exp. 4, "La Iglesia Católica Mexicana," 6 Jan. 1925.
101. Levitt, "Religion on the Move."
102. AHAM, Cisma, "Asistencia a Corpus Christi Xti. el Domingo 28 de P.P.," dated 1 Jul. 1925. *Restauración*, 1 Mar. 1926, "Informe General Concreto de los Trabajos de la Iglesia Ortodoxa Católica Mexicana."
103. *Restauración*, "Venid Católicos" and "Los Servicios Religiosos en Corpus Christi" (15 Sep. 1926); "La Semana Mayor en el Templo de Corpus Christi" (1 May 1927).
104. Tackett, *Religion, Revolution*.
105. AHAM, Cisma, "Asunto Muy Importante," 1925. *Restauración*, 1 Feb. 1927, "Una Carta que Acusa la Ignorancia Religiosa del Clero."
106. Respectively: Deuteronomy, 6:5; Romans, 12:14; Matthew, 5:44.
107. ADAM, *La Buena Lid*, tomo 2/no. 40, Apr. 1925, "Iglesia Católica Apostólica Mexicana: Sermón Predicado por el Pbro. B. Gómez R., en la Parroquia de la Soledad y Santa Cruz, el Domingo 8 de Marzo de 1925 ante una Escogida y Numerosa Concurrencia."
108. "Carta abierta...," *Restauración*, 18 Feb., 1 Mar., 15 Mar., 1 Apr., 15 Apr. 1927.
109. *Restauración*, 1 Mar. 1927, "Informe General..."; 1 Feb. 1927, "Lo que Dicen y lo que Hacen los Sacerdotes de la Iglesia Romana."
110. *Restauración*, 1926, "Solamente los Ricos Tienen Derecho a la Religión de los Romanistas" (1 Dec.), "Engaño al Público y una Violación a la Ley" (1 Sep.), "En

la Ciudad de los Mártires Oficia un Sacerdotista" (15 Nov.), and "El Romanismo Continúa Oficiando Clandestinamente" (15 Nov.).
111. AICAM, Emeterio Valdéz to Francisco Durán, Mexico City, 11 May 1928. "Constitución," arts. 10:45, 10:53, 11:58.

CHAPTER THREE
1. Patulli Trythall, "Edmund A. Walsh." AHAM/MDR 31.43, Gasparri to Mora, Rome, 16 Nov. 1927. Anon., *Estudio sobre el actual conflicto religioso por un obispo católico mexicano sobre*, 1:85–102, 3:52–53.
2. Olimón Nolasco, *Paz a medias*, 14.
3. Kertzer, *Pope and Mussolini*.
4. AHAM, Provisorato, c. 124/exp. 4, Pérez to Raymundo Young, Beaumont, 29 May 1926.
5. Cantor, *Church, Kingship*.
6. Gruzinski, "'Segunda aculturación.'"
7. Lanz Duret, "Estado y la Iglesia." Martí, "Separación Iglesia-estado," 121–65.
8. Carey, *People, Priests*. Beal, "It's Déjà Vu."
9. *Diario de los debates del Congreso Constituyente*, 2:703–6.
10. Leo XIII's order to French Catholics to support the Third Republic electorally (1892).
11. *Vous, Église*, Jaurès challenged, why do you not embrace democracy internally? If you did, the Church would be a "perpetual force of creation, revelation, and revolution," not reaction, achieving "a burning fusion of hearts, pouring life into an incomparable humanity." Poulat, *Scruter la loi*, 197–98.
12. *Respecter les règles d'organisation générale du culte dont il propose d'assurer l'exercice*.
13. Larkin, *Church and State*. Coquet, *Albert de Mun*. Mayeur, *Séparation de l'Église*; Mayeur, "Religion et Politique." Appolis, "En Marge."
14. Carey, *People, Priests*, 1–5, 70–127, 140–89. Beal, "It's Déjà-Vu."
15. The debate (27 Jan. 1917) was tediously doctrinaire. Only Félix Palavicini considered the technicalities of juntas. *Diario*, 754–67.
16. *Ley reformando el código penal para el Distrito Federal y Territorios Federales sobre delitos del fuero común y delitos contra la Federación en materia de culto religioso y disciplina externa* (Mexico City: Talleres Gráficos de la Nación, 1926), 8, 10.
17. The Calles Law appeared in the *Diario Oficial* on 2 Jul. 1926.
18. *Excélsior*, 1 Aug. 1926, "Los Sacerdotes No Serán Molestados Si No Violan la Ley, Dice el Sr. Presidente."
19. "Ley Reglamentaria del Artículo 130 de la Constitución Federal," *Diario Oficial*, 18 Jan. 1927, 1–4.
20. AHAM, Provisorato, c. 124: Pérez to Calles, 10 Jul. 1925 (exp. 1), 29 Jul. 1926 (exp. 4); Garrido Canabal, 24 Sep. 1926; Gasca, 11 Mar. 1927; Treviño, 15 Jan. 1927 (exp. 4). AICAM, Pérez to Gasca, 20 Oct. 1929 (all Mexico City).
21. AHAM, Provisorato, c. 124: Tejeda to Pérez, Jalapa, 11 Jan. 1930 (exp. 2), 6 Aug. 1929 (exp. 4); Miguel Hernández to Pérez, Juchitán, 16 Jul. 1928, 6 Jul. 1929 (exp. 1); Adolfo Briones to Tejeda, Acayucan, 18 Jul. 1929 (exp. 3); Briones to Pérez, Acayucan, 18 Feb. 1930 (exp. 2); Francisco Durán to Pérez, Mecatlán, 30 Jan. 1931 (exp. 3).

Notes to Pages 75–81

22. AICAM, Pbro. Pedro Infante to Patriarch Pérez, Mexico City, 22 Sep. 1931.
23. CEHM, clxxxii.2.105, "Tercera Carta Pastoral del Episcopado Mexicano con Motivo de la Actual Persecución Religiosa," 12 Sep. 1926; 2.130, "Católicos."
24. *Restauración*, 1 Oct. 1926 ("Carta Abierta al Sr. Arzobispo de la Diócesis de Puebla, D. Pedro Vera"); 1 Aug. 1926 ("Detrás del Escándalo Religioso que Hace la Iglesia Romana, Obtiene un Negocio de Cientos de Miles de Pesos"); 15 Aug. 1926 ("La Huelga del Clero Romano y el Sueño del Papa").
25. Ezekiel, 12:13; Daniel, 5:1–31. AHAM, Provisorato, c. 124/exp. 1, López y Sierra to Pérez, Ixtepec, 26 Feb. 1928.
26. Peña Espinosa, "Catedral Angelipolitana." Zúñiga Trujillo, "Conflicto Religioso," 39–80.
27. *Restauración*, 1 Mar. 1926 ("Informe General Concreto de los Trabajos de la Iglesia Ortodoxa Católica Mexicana"); 1 Mar. 1927 ("Informe General de la Secretaría de la Iglesia Ortodoxa, Católica, Apostólica, Mexicana, Presentado al Concilio de Obispos y Demás Autoridades Eclesiásticas de la Propia Iglesia"); 15 Jul. 1927 ("Resumen General Concreto de la Estabilidad de la Iglesia Ortodoxa, Católica, Apostólica, Mexicana"); 15 Oct. 1927 ("Interesante Cuestionario Presentado a la Iglesia Mexicana"); *Alcance al No. 61 de Restauración, Organo de la Iglesia Católica Mexicana*; "Refutación," 1929.
28. Alfonseca Giner de los Ríos, "El conflicto religioso."
29. Parish numbers: Pue. (168), Oax. (148), Ver. (98). Bravo Ugarte, *Diócesis y obispos*, 26.
30. AHAM, Provisorato, c. 124/exp. 4, Pérez to Miguel Castro, Mexico City, 9 Dec. 1926.
31. AICAM, Emeterio Valdéz to mayoralty, Tenoxtitlán, 20 Feb. 1928. AGN/DGG, letters: mayor, Acatzingo, 5 Dec. 1929 (2.340.67.1); inhabitants, Amanalco, 22 Jan. 1929; Ildefonso Velázquez, Mexico City, 24 Jan. 1929 (2.340.50.16); Gregorio Méndez, Yehualtepec, 8 Apr., 9 Apr., 13 Apr. 1928 (2.340.66.35); G. Pérez, Mexico City, 13 Sep. 1929 (2.340.66.35).
32. Byrne, *Other Catholics*, 58.
33. Ramírez Rancaño, *Patriarca Pérez*, 214–15. Bastian, *Disidentes*, 320. *Restauración*, 15 Dec. 1926 ("Nuestra Iglesia Se Establece en Apam, Hidalgo"), 1 Jan. 1927 ("La Iglesia Mexicana en Pachuca"); 1 Mar. 1926 ("Informe . . ."); 1 Jan. 1927, ("Tiro de Hoy, 10,000 Ejemplares"); 1 Mar. 1927 ("Informe General . . .").
34. AICAM, Teodoro Juárez, Zozocolco, 16 May 1934. *Restauración*, 1 Oct. 1927, "La Iglesia Mexicana en Diferentes Partes del País."
35. Purnell, *Popular Movements*, 95. Ricard, *Conquista espiritual*, 146.
36. Thomson with LaFrance, *Patriotism, Politics*. Brewster, *Militarism, Ethnicity*. *Restauración*, 15 Mar. 1927, "Adquisición del Templo de Tuzamapa, Puebla." AHAM, Provisorato, c. 124/exp. 4, Pérez to Miguel Castro, Mexico City, 9 Dec. 1926.
37. Pace Friedlander, "Secularization of the *Cargo* System."
38. Lockhart, *Nahuas after the Conquest*, 211–15; Taylor, *Magistrates*, 234–40; Yannakakis, *Art of Being In-Between*, 65–95. Ricard, *Conquista espiritual*, 182–83.
39. Knight, *Mexican Revolution*, 1:115–27.
40. AHAM, Provisorato, c. 124: Leonardo de Régules to Pérez, Mexico City, 3 Nov. 1926; Ysmael Limón to Pérez, Mexico City, 8 Apr. 1929; Castro to Pérez, Puebla, 13 Oct. 1928 (exp. 1); Pérez to Ramón Iturbe, Mexico City, 29 Oct. 1926. (exp. 4).
41. Carey, *People, Priests*, 1–5, 70–72, 90–91, 117–27, 140–89. Yox, "Parochial Context of Trusteeism"; Galush, "Trusteeism Revived"; Regan, "Irish Catholics"; Di Gioacchino, "Ecclesiastical Participation."

42. Carey, *People, Priests*, 118–20.
43. AHAM, Provisorato, c. 124, letters to Pérez: José Emeterio Valdéz, Coyutla, Oct. 1928, n/d (exp. 3); Teodoro Juárez, Zozocolco, 7 Jun. 1930; Francisco Durán, Tlaola, 27 Dec. 1929; José Varela, Coxquihuí, 31 Jan. 1931 (exp. 2).
44. AHAM, Provisorato, c. 124/exp. 2, Francisco Durán to Pérez, Tlaola, 25 Jan. 1930.
45. AHAM, Provisorato, c. 124/exp. 4, Florentino Guzmán to Pérez, Tuxtla, 6 Nov. 1926. Covarrubias, *Mexico South*.
46. Smith, *Roots of Conservatism in Mexico*. Ulloa, *Predicadores divididos*; Álvarez, *Hábitos blancos*; Esparza, *Gillow durante*, 24–27.
47. AHAM, Provisorato, c. 124/exp. 2, García to Pérez, Puebla, 22 Jan. 1929.
48. AGN/DGG: actas, Tetela, 23 Dec. 1926 (2.340.66.10), Xochitlán, 13 Oct. 1928 (2.340.66.49); Guillermo de la Peña, Xochitlán, 14 Oct. 1928 (2.340.66.49).
49. AICAM: José M. López to municipal president, Tapayula, 14 Jul. 1926; López y Sierra to Emeterio Valdéz, Mexico City, 6 Jun., 26 Jul., and 4 Aug. 1927; ICAM to municipal president, Coyutla, 8 Nov. 1927. AHAM: Provisorato, c. 124/exp. 3, Agapito Vázquez to Pérez, Tepetlaoxtoc, 20 Jun. 1925; exp. 1, Pérez to Adrián Abad, Mexico City, 29 Jan. 1929. AGN/DGG, 2.340.66.11, municipio, Hueyapan, 1 Dec. 1926.
50. AICAM, inhabitants, Santo Domingo, 24 Dec. 1927. AGN/DGG, 2.340.66.10, Arredondo López, Zapotitlán, 15 Nov. 1926; 2.340.67.13, Mariano García, Zongozotla, 21 Nov. 1929.
51. Duffy, *Stripping of the Altars*.
52. AICAM: actas/inventories, Tapayula, 14 Jul. 1926; Zongozotla, 15 Jul. 1926; Nanacatlán, 19 Jul. 1926; Ahuacatlán, 6 Aug. 1927; José M. López to municipios of Nanacatlán, 19 Jul. 1926, and Tuxtla, 19 Jul. 1926; municipio to López, Nanacatlán, 21 Jul. 1926. AGN/DGG, 2.340.50.8, inventory, Jocotlán, 24 Feb. 1928.
53. Peña Espinosa, "Catedral Angelipolitana."
54. AICAM, Ramón Rico to Emeterio Valdez, Zapotitlán, 5 and 14 Feb. 1927. AGN/DGG: Rutilio Carrera to Gobernación, Tecamachalco, 15 Dec. 1928 (2.340.66.49); municipio to Gobierno, Villa Juárez, 30 May 1928 (2.340.66.32).
55. Letters to Gobernación (AGN/DGG): mayor, Tlaixpan, 17 Dec. 1928 (2.340.66.50); Palemón Jiménez, Tezoyuca, 15 Sep. 1926 (2.340.50.4); Joaquín Castro, Tepexpam, 12 May 1928 (2.340.50.13); Joaquín Sánchez, Ixtápan, 25 Dec. 1927, 10 Feb. 1928 (2.340–50–7).
56. AHAM, Provisorato, c. 124/exp. 3, Macario López to Pérez, Los Angeles, 12 Apr. 1929. Vera y Zuria, *Cartas a mis seminaristas*, 588. Esparza, *Gillow durante*, 62–64. Kloppe-Santamaría, *In the Vortex of Violence*.
57. AGN/DGG: José María López, Zacapoaxtla, 21 Jun. 1926 (2.340.66.16), Ahuacatlán, 6 Sep. 1926 (2.340.66.8); municipio, Hueyapan, 1 Dec. 1926; Pedro Infante, Jaunahuac, 28 Dec. 1926 (2.340.66.11); municipio to Montes, Zoquiapan, 14 Dec. 1926; Montes, Puebla, 10 Jan. 1927 (2.340.66.32); Arredondo, Zapotitlán, 15 Nov. 1926, and municipio, Tetela, 23 Dec. 1926 (2.340.66.10). AICAM: acta, Zongozotla, 15 Jul. 1926; José María López to municipio, Tapayula, 14 Jul. 1926; Roberto Vázquez to Arredondo, Ozelonacaxtla, 11 Aug. 1926; Macario López to Emeterio Valdéz, Mexico City, 1 Dec. 1926. *Restauración*, 1 Oct. 1926 ("Carta Abierta . . ."), 1 Nov. 1926 ("Glosario Religioso"), and 15 Jan. 1927 ("La Iglesia Mexicana Toma Posesión de Otro Templo").
58. AGN/DGG: Heriberto Jara to Tejeda, Xalapa, 13 and 16 Aug. 1926 (2.340.81.10); actas, Mecatlán, 26 Sep. 1926 (2.340.81.2), Santo Domingo, n/d. (2.340.81.2).

AICAM, José María López to municipio and actas, Nanacatlán, Tuxtla, 19 Jul. 1926. *Restauración*, 15 Oct. 1926, "El Triunfo de Nuestra Iglesia en Veracruz." AHAM/MDR, Veracruz, "Habla el Señor Obispo de Veracruz a los Católicos de la Parroquia de Jalancingo," 10 Aug. 1926.

59. AICAM: Ramón Rico to Valdez, Zapotitlán, 14 Feb. 1927; Valdéz to municipio, Yaquihuacan, 9 Aug. 1927, Coyutla, 8 Nov. 1927; Filiberto Rodríguez to Valdéz, Jopala, 18 Apr. 1928; Miguel Medina to Valdéz, Patla, 19 Apr. 1928; Luciano Andrade to Valdéz and Coronado, Chicontla, 20 Apr. 1928. AGN/DGG: Hacienda, Mexico City, 22 Jun. 1927; *oficial mayor*, Ecatlán, 11 May 1927 (2.340.66.32); municipio, Xochitlán, 23 Sep. 1927 (2.340.66.11); Cruz Campos to municipio, Tehuizotla, 31 Jan. 1928 (2.340.66.34).

60. AICAM, Federico Rodríguez to Durán, Huehuetla, 19 Mar. 1928; López y Sierra to Valdéz, Mexico City, 19, 23 Aug. 1927. Letters to Gobernación (AGN/DGG): Gregorio Méndez, Yehualtepec, 8 Apr. 1928 (2.340.66.35); Juan Castillo, Alquizapan, 16 May 1928; Vicente Liñán, Alquizapan, 21 Jul. 1928 (2.340.66.40); Luis Merino, Xochitlán, 14 Oct. 1928; Jesús Vázquez, San Simón del Bravo, 5 Dec. 1928 (2.340.66.49); Facundo de Jesús, Portezuelo, 25 Jan. 1929; José Espíndola, General Felipe Ángeles, 3 Feb. 1929 (2.340.67.3); 2.340.67.1, ejidatarios, Actipan, 10 Jan. 1929; mayor, Actipan, 12 Feb. 1929 (2.340.67.1).

61. *Restauración*, 15 Jul. 1927, "Un Templo Más para la Iglesia Mexicana"; 1 Oct. 1927, "La Iglesia Mexicana en Diferentes Partes del País." AGN/DGG: acta, Jalostoc, 2 Jul. 1927 (2.340.50.2); mayor [Otumba], Toluca, 24 Aug. 1927 (2.340.50.2); ecclesiastical register, Toluca, 14 Mar. 1930 (2.340.50.17); Joaquín Sánchez, Ixtápan, 25 Dec. 1927, 10 Feb. 1928 (2.340.50.7); mayor, Tenoxtitlán, 7 Mar. 1928; acta, 22 Feb. 1928 (2.340.66.32); Guadalupe Flores, Atenco, April 30, 1928; "special agent 3," Atenco, May 15, 1928 (2.340–50–11); municipio, Amecameca, 9 May 1928 (2.340.50.12); Ildefonso Velázquez, Mexico City, 24 Jan. 19292 (340–50–16). AICAM: Nicacio and Maximino Pérez to Pérez, Tenoxtitlán 18 Feb. 1928; junta vecinal, Tenoxtitlán, 20 Feb. 1928; Valdéz, Coyotepec, 21 Jul. 1928. Hurtado, *Cisma mexicano*, 61.

62. AGN/DGG, 2.340.43.22, Pedro Yáñez, Tenango, 16 Dec. 1926. Fallaw, *Religion and State Formation*, 91.

63. AGN/DGG, 2.340.50.8, inventory, Jocotlán, 24 Feb. 1928.

64. *Restauración*, 15 Dec. 1926 ("Nuestra Iglesia Se Establece en Apam, Hidalgo"), 1 Jan. 1927 ("La Iglesia Mexicana en Pachuca"). AGN/DGG: Calles to Tejeda, Mexico City, 14 Aug. 1926 (2.340.49.89); governor, Tlaxcala, 17 Jan. 1927; Pascual Luciano García, Tenancingo, 21 Dec. 1926 (2.340.80.3); acta, Jocotitlán, 24 Feb. 1928 (2.340.50.8); Ricardo González to municipio, El Oro, 31 Aug. 1928 (2.340.50.14); governor, Toluca, 16 Aug. 1926 (2.340.49.84); Juez de 1ª Instancia, 7 Aug. 1926 (2.340.49.86).

65. AGN/DGG, letters: Porfirio Castañeda, La Unión, 2 Aug. 1926 (2.340.41.2); mayor, Zacualpan, 31 Aug., 28 Sep. 1926 (2.340.49.83); Arredondo, Tepecoacuilco, 22 Feb. 1927 (2.340.41.6); mayor, La Unión, 4 Jul. 1927 (2.340.41.2). *Restauración*, 1 Feb. 1927 ("La Iglesia Mexicana Avanza en Diferentes Estados"), 1 Mar. 1927 ("En Guerrero Ha Triunfado la Iglesia Mexicana"), 1 Apr. ("La Iglesia Mexicana Está de Duelo"), 15 Apr. 1927 ("Relación del Asesinato del Rev. Padre Alfredo Arredondo López en Manayalán"), 1 Oct. 1927 ("La Iglesia Mexicana en Diferentes Partes del País"). Fallaw, *Religion and State Formation*, 109. Guardino, *Peasants, Politics*, 21–23.

66. *Restauración*, 15 Sep. 1926, "La Matanza de los Cismáticos"; 15 Apr. 1927, "Excequias en Memoria del Primer Mártir de la Iglesia Católica Mexicana." AGN/DGG, 2.340.41.6, Pedro Infante, Tepecoacuilco, 29 Mar. 1927. AICAM, López y Sierra, Mexico City, 21 Apr., 11, 19 Aug. 1927. *La Opinión*, 27 Oct. 1928, "Tres Enmascarados lo Sacaron de su Templo, en Guadalajara, y lo Cosieron a Puñaladas." *El Heraldo Mexicano*, 2 Dec. 1928, "En Memoria del Reverendo Padre Felipe de Jesús Ochoa." AHAM/MDR c. 157/exp. 114, Mora to Paolo Marella, San Antonio, 10 Jun. 1927. Interview with Antonio Celis (Mexico City, Mar. 2006). Hurtado, *Cisma mexicano*, 59.
67. AHAM, Provisorato, c. 124/exp. 4, Pérez to Ondilón Sánchez, Mexico City, 14 Jan. 1927.
68. AGN/DGG, 2.340.61.32, Genaro Vázquez to Tejeda, Oaxaca, 11 Aug. 1926. AHAM, Provisorato, c. 124: Pérez to Treviño, Mexico City, 3 Oct. 1926 (exp. 3); Pérez to Pérez Villafañe, Mexico City, 10 Nov. 1926; Pérez to Agapito Pérez, Mexico City, 17, 21 Sep. 1926, 1, 10 Nov. 1926, 11 Dec., 1926, 7, 14 Jan. 1927; Méndez to Pérez, Calihualá, 21 Nov. 1926, 21 Jun. 1927; Pérez to Méndez, Atzcapotzalco, 7 Oct. 1927; Margarita Morales to Pérez, Calihualá, 27 Dec. 1926; Pérez to Morales, Mexico City, 7 Jan. 1927. Agapito Pérez to Pérez, Tlapancingo, 27 Dec. 1926, Mexico City, 22 Sep. 1927 (exp. 4).
69. AGN/DGG, Velasco to Calles, Concepción Pápalo, 6 Oct. 1926 (2.340.61.16); Genaro Vázquez to Tejeda, Oaxaca, 1 Nov. 1926 (2.340.61.19); Amador, Pochutla, 19 Apr. 1928; acta, Pochutla, 14 Oct. 1928 (2.340.61.34); Castellanos, Teotepec, 10 Sep. 1927 (2.340.61.33). AHAO, diocese to Amador, Oaxaca, 31 Mar. 1928; Elpidio Beltrán, Teotepec, 5 Jul. 1927; Gobierno to ayuntamiento, Oaxaca, 14 Jul. 1927; acta, Teotepec, 27 Jul. 1927. Wright-Rios, *Revolutions in Mexican Catholicism*, 229–30, 264.
70. AHAO, Canseco to Carlos Gracida, Juquila, 15 Jan. 1928; diocese to Castellanos, Oaxaca, 31 Mar. 1928; Canseco to Agustín Espinoza, Juquila, 17, 19 Apr. 1928; Abraham Jiménez to Apolinar Palacios, Teotepec, 1 Nov. 1929.
71. AGN/DGG, 2.340.61.18, letters: Mexican Catholics, Ixtepec, 18 Aug., 31 Dec. 1929; "Miguelito" Fernández, Ixtepec, 10 Sep. 1926, 7 Mar. 1930; Roman Catholics, Ixtepec, 26 Aug. 1929, 14 Feb. 1930; Ruiz y Flores, Mexico City, 22 Feb. 1930. AHAM, Provisorato, c. 124: López y Sierra to Pérez, Ixtepec, 26 Feb. 1928 (exp. 1); "Miguelito" to Pérez, Ixtepec, 3 Mar. 1930 (exp. 2). *Restauración*, 1 Aug. 1927, "La Iglesia Mexicana en el Istmo."
72. AGN/DGG: acta, Acayucan, 9 Nov. 1926 (2.340.81.5), and letters: Heriberto Jara, Xalapa, 4 Nov. 1926 (2.340.81.14); Juan Pablo, Pajapam, 5 Feb. 1927 (2.340.81.9); junta, Jaltipan, 26 Aug. 1927 (2.340.82.16); Gobierno, Xalapa, 11 Feb. 1928 (2.340.81.5); Briones, Acayucan, 7 Dec. 1928 (2.340.83.12); Tejeda, Xalapa, 16 Jan. 1929 (2.340.83.2); Mexican Catholics, Acayucan, 6 Oct. 1929 (2.340.83.12). AHAM/MDR c. 141/exp. 45, F. Gutiérrez to Mora, Puerto México, 30 Nov., 12 Dec. 1926. SD, 812.404.640, William Myers, Veracruz, 1 Sep. 1926.
73. AGN/DGG, 2.340.83.22, Mexican Catholics, Tuxtla, 15 Aug. 1929; Emeterio Román, Tampico-Alto, 11 Feb. 1929.
74. AGN/DGG: Calles to Tejeda, Mexico City, 3, 18 Aug. 1926; Tejeda to A. Hermida Figueroa, Mexico City, 5 Aug. 1926, and Gómez, Mexico City, 26 Aug. 1926; Figueroa to Tejeda, Alvarado, 6 Aug. 1926; Anguiano to Tejeda, Veracruz, 5 Mar. 1927; Tejeda to Anguiano, Mexico City, 2 Apr. 1927; Jara to Tejeda, Veracruz, 5

Notes to Pages 93–96

Apr. and 21 Jul. 1927; Anguiano to Tejeda, Cardel, 5 Nov. 1927; Gobernación to Anguiano, Mexico City, 22 Nov. 1927 (all 2.344.18.8). AHAM/MDR, Veracruz, "Declaración que Hace el Ilustrísimo Señor Obispo de Veracruz Doctor Don Rafael Guízar Valencia a sus Diocesanos, Refiriéndose al Sacerdote Cismático Dimás Anguiano, quien Se Encuentra Actualmente en el Pueblo de Alvarado, Estado de Veracruz," 4 Aug. 1926.

75. All 1926, AGN/DGG, 2.340.28.29, Elías de la Cruz, Tapachula, 2 Aug., 4 Sep., 16 Oct.; Carmen Rodas, Tapachula, 7 Sep.; José Ramírez, Tapachua, 3 Aug., 1 Oct. *Restauración*, 15 Oct., "La Iglesia Ortodoxa Triunfante en el Estado de Chiapas." Lurtz, *From the Grounds Up*, 87–115.

76. AGN/DGG, 2.340.78.38, governor, Ciudad Victoria, 8 Apr. 1929. *El Heraldo Mexicano*, 2 Jun. 1929, "La Iglesia Católica Apostólica Mexicana Triunfa en los Estados de Nuevo León y Tamaulipas." AHAM, Provisorato, c. 124: Guerrero to Pérez, Reynosa, 6 Apr., 10 Jul., 26 Aug. 1929 (exp. 1), Los Aldamas, 2 Feb. 1930 (exp. 2); Pérez to Guerrero, Mexico City, 26 Jun., 30 Oct. 1929; Guerrero to Pérez, Los Aldamas, 24 May 1930, Hunter, 8 Dec. 1930 (exp. 3). AHAM, circulars #8 (23 Feb. 1929), #3 (Mar. 1930, n/d), Libro de gobierno (arzobispado) #20, 1914–1952, fs. 230, 241–42; "A los católicos del Arzobispado," *Boletín Eclesiástico* Año VII, Nos. 3–4, Mar.–Apr. 1929, 40–43.

77. Butler and Powell, "Father, Where Art Thou?"

78. La Soledad was received by a Roman cura in Jan. 1930. AHAM/DB, c. 51/exp. 29, Pascual Díaz to Marcos Tovar, Mexico City, 27 Jan. 1930; c. 61/exp. 17, Alberto María Carreño to Díaz, Mexico City, 12 Aug. 1930.

79. AHAM, Provisorato, c. 124: Felip Indá to Hacienda, Mexico City, 2 Jun. 1930; Adolfo Santibáñez to Hacienda, Mexico City, 8 Jul. 1930 (exp. 1); Félix Escalante to ICAM, Mexico City, 27 Sep., 24 Oct., 11 Nov. 1929, Salubridad to ICAM, Mexico City, 30 Sep. 1929 (exp. 2); Pérez to José Ramírez, Mexico City, 28 Jul. 1929 (exp. 3).

80. AHAM/DB, c. 61/exp. 56, circular #29, 13 Jul. 1929; "Circular número 33 por la cual se recuerdan las disposiciones legales que deben observarse para la entrega de templos a los sacerdotes," *Diario Oficial*, 14 Sep. 1929, 1–3.

81. *El Heraldo Mexicano*, 14 Jul. 1929 ("La Autoridad Eclesiástica Romana Trató de Imponerse en la H. Matamoros, Pidiendo se le Entregara el Templo"), 21 Jul. 1929 ("La Autoridad Eclesiástica Romana Fue Favorecida en la H. Matamoros, donde Se Le Entregó la Parroquia que Deseaba").

82. Negrete, *Relaciones entre la Iglesia*, 129. AHAM/DB, c. 9: circulars, 14 Mar. 1930 (exp. 3), and 6 Dec. 1930 (exp. 21). *La Opinión*, 28 Jun. 1929, "Templos Cismáticos."

83. AHAM, Provisorato, c. 124: E. Medina to Pérez, Mexico City, 23 Jul. 1929 (exp. 4); Pérez to Portes Gil, Mexico City, 21 Jun. 1929 (exp. 3).

84. *La Lucha*, 30 Jun. 1929, "Los Sacerdotes Cismáticos Defenderán los Templos." AICAM, "Refutación," 1929.

85. AHAM, Provisorato, c. 124: Pérez to Gamez Flores, Mexico City, n/d (exp. 2) and José Ramírez, Mexico City, 28 Jul. 1929 (exp. 3); Cisma, c. 65/exp. 15, circular, 29 Aug. 1929.

86. AHAM, Provisorato, c. 124, exp. 2: Luisa Reboulen to Pérez, Puerto México, 25 Jun. 1929.

87. AICAM, Rafael Huerta to Emeterio Valdéz, Progreso de Zaragoza, n/d.

88. Brewster, *Militarism, Ethnicity*, 154–57. Blumenkron and Campomanes, *Puebla bajo*.

89. AGN/DGG, letters: Francisco Durán, Tlaola, 5 Aug. 1929; mayor, Tlaola, 6 Jan. 1931; Camilo Cruz, Xaltepuxtla, 20 Aug. 1931; José Cortés, Tlaola, 26 Dec. 1933 (2.340.67.4); Mariano García, Zongozotla, 21 Nov. 1929 (2.340.67.13). AICAM, Durán to Valdéz, Tlaola, 22 Aug. 1929. AHAM, Provisorato, c. 124: Durán to Pérez, Tlaola, 14 Jan. 1930 (exp. 2), Mecatlán, 29, 30 Jan. 1931 (exp. 3).
90. AGN/DGG, 2.340.66.35, memo, Mexico City, 13 Sep. 1929. AMPV, c. 106/exp. 745/f. 8502, *Diario de El Paso*, 23 Aug. 1929, "Cismáticos Tienen que Dejar los Templos."
91. AHAM/DB, c. 61/exp. 12, ICAM to Gómez, Mexico City, 22 Aug. 1930. AGN/DGG: governor to Gobernación, Tlaxcala, 16 Feb. 19332 (340.80.3); Felipe Canales to Fernando Badillo, Mexico City, 7 Aug. 1929 (2.340.52.7); registry, Toluca, 14 Mar. 1932 (340.50.17).
92. AGN/DGG, letters: governor, Toluca, 6 Oct. 1932, Eduardo Vasconcelos, Mexico City, 20 Oct. 1932 (2.340.51.10); Felipe de Jesús Vázquez Aguirre, Tepexoxuca, 25 Jul. 1938 (2.340.52.32), Juan Serrano, Maxtleca, 31 Jul. 1938, Feliciano Aguirre, San Miguelito, 4 Aug. 1938, Tiburcio Coronado, Toluca, 23 Dec. 1938 (2.340.52.7). García Gutiérrez, "Apuntamientos."
93. AHAM, Cisma, "Circular a los Sres. Curas de la Foránea de Amecameca," 25 Jun. 1937, M. Gómez to ICAM, Ozumba, 21 Jun. 1937. Hurtado, *Cisma mexicano*, 60–63.
94. AMPV, c. 106/exp. 745/ff. 8451, 8456, 8459, 8486, *La Opinión*, 1929: 5 Aug. ("Protesta de los Vecinos"); 6 Aug. ("Iba a Ser Linchado: Los Católicos de S. Andrés Tuxtla Lapidaron la Casa del Cura Cismático"); 7 Aug. ("Las Fuerzas Federales Intervienen en San Andrés"); 16 Aug. ("Se Queja un Sacerdote Cismático"). AGN/DGG: A. Mirarete, Tuxtla, 10 Aug. 1929; Roman Catholics, Tuxtla, 10 Aug. 1929; junta vecinal, Tuxtla, 30 Aug. 1929 (340.83.22); Gobernación, Mexico City, 20 Sep. 1929 (2.340.83.19). AHAM, Provisorato, c. 124: Briones to Pérez, Tuxtla, 2 Aug. 1929, Acayucan, 29 Aug. 1929 (exp. 1). Winfield Capitaine, "Cofradía de Cristo Negro."
95. AMPV, c. 106/exp. 745/f. 8480, *La Opinión*, 14 Aug. 1929, "Templos a los Cismáticos de Acayucan, Ver."; AHAM/DB, c. 61/exp. 9, Damas Católicas to Portes Gil, Acayucan, 12 Aug. 1929. AGN/DGG, 2.340.83.12: Genaro Méndez to Tejeda, Tehuantepec, 13 Sep. 1929, and letters to Gobernación: acayuqueños, 12 Aug. 1929; Briones, Acayucan, 5 Feb. 1930, 28 Apr. 1931; SHCP, Mexico City, 4 Oct. 1930; Pedro Olivera, Olutla, 11 May 1931. *Diario Oficial*, 4 Mar. 1933.
96. AGN/DGG, 2.340.83.42, junta vecinal, Tuxpan, 24 Jul. 1929. AHAM, Provisorato, c. 124, letters to ICAM from: Varela, Mecatlán, 1 Aug. 1930; junta vecinal, Mecatlán, 30 Jul. 1930; exp. 2, Juárez, Zozocolco, 19 Jul. 1930 (exp. 1); Durán, Mecatlán, 23 Feb. 1931; Juárez, Zozocolco, 24 Aug. 1930 (exp. 3). SD 812.404.1829, C. E. Macy, Tampico, 10 Dec. 1935; "Memorandum Concerning Religious Situation in Tampico Consular District"; "Memorandum Regarding Religious Situation in Northern Veracruz."
97. AGN/DGG: Anguiano, Veracruz, 26 Jun. 1929, Jalapa, 18 Sep. 1929; Hacienda, Veracruz, 1 Jul. 1929; Ignacio García Téllez to Anguiano, Mexico City, 6 Jul. 1929; Guízar y Valencia, Córdoba, 8 Oct. 1929; Ruiz y Flores, Mexico City, 25 Oct. 1929; Logia "Manuel Verdad," Veracruz, 10 Apr. 1930; Hacienda, Mexico City, 12 Feb. 19322 (all 344.18.8). SD 812.404.2053, Josephus Daniels, Mexico City, 11 Jul. 1939.
98. AICAM, mayor to governor, Filomeno Mata, 4 Apr. 1933; governor to Miguel García, Jalapa, 13 Jul. 1933; Juárez to ICAM, Chicontepec (22 Jan. 1938), Zacamixtla (25 Apr. 1938)

239

99. AGN/DGG, 2.340.61.18, Portes Gil to Gobernación, Mexico City, 3 Jul. 1929. FPEC, 12.010086.37. 617, E. Balmoreji to Genaro Méndez del Río, Coatzacoalcos, 4 Nov. 1932.
100. AHAM, Provisorato, c. 124, all 1929: "Católicos," 8 Aug. (exp. 2); Gobernación to Ramírez, Mexico City, 24 Jun. (exp. 3); Pérez to Ramírez, Mexico City, 18 Aug.; Ramírez to Pérez, Tapachula, 2 Jul., 12 19 Aug.; "A los fieles católicos," 6 Aug. (exp. 4). AGN/DGG: José Ramírez, Tapachula, 29 Jun., 7 Sep.; romanos, Tapachula, 22 Aug. (2.340.28.29); Urbano Gómez, Motozintla, 4 Nov. 1931 (2.340.30.2).
101. AGN/DGG: José Ramírez, Tapachula, 27 Jan. 1932; governor, Tuxtla, 4 Feb. 1932 (2.340.28.29); Ernesto Lavariega to National Property Directorate, Tapachula, 26 Feb. 1932 (2.340.29.1).
102. AGN/DGG, 2.340.29.1, Lorenzo Bravo, Tapachula, 5 Feb., 9 Mar. 1932. AHSEP, Chiapas, c. 45/ IV.161(IV-14).1495, *informes*, Huixtla, Feb. 1930; Álvaro Obregón, Aug. 1930.
103. AGN/DGG: Gobierno, Tuxtla, 4 Mar. 1932; "Catholic *Pueblo* Committee," Tapachula, 9 Mar. 1932; Enríquez, Tapachula, 19 Mar. 1932; Ramírez, Tapachula, 22 Mar. 1932; decree, Mexico City, 13 Jun. 1932; *Diario Oficial*, 20 Jun., 22 Aug. 1932. (2.340.28.29).
104. Decree 40, *Periódico Oficial del Gobierno del Estado de Chiapas*, 14 Feb. 1934; Congregación de la Iglesia Mexicana to Cárdenas, Tapachula, 10 Dec. 1934.
105. Lanz Duret, "Estado y la Iglesia," 393.
106. Elías Calles, *Méjico ante el mundo*.
107. Crewe, *Mexican Mission*, 200–208.

CHAPTER FOUR

1. *Address Delivered by Hon. Engineer Luis L. León, Secretary of Agriculture and Promotion and President of the National Agrarian Commission, at the Town of San Juan Ixtayopan, Federal District, Mexico, on the Thirtieth Day of October 1926, when the International Workingmen Delegates Were Present* (Tacubaya: Dirección de Estudios Geográficos y Climatológicos, 1927), 25–26. León, *Crónica del poder*.
2. Valenzuela, "Viaje de Plutarco Elías Calles"; Ramos Torres, "México callista."
3. On which, see Herrera Serna, "Plutarco Elías Calles"; Fujigaki Cruz and Olvera López, "Ideas Agrarias y Cooperativismo"; Rivera Castro, "Política Agraria"; Carton de Grammont, "Calles y el agrarismo."
4. AHAM/MDR, c. 82/exp. 19, *Lo que dice el Ilmo. Sr. Arzobispo sobre las cuestiones de actualidad* (Mexico City: Escuela Tipográfica Salesiana, 1925). McIntyre, *Protestantism and State Formation*. Dormady, *Primitive Revolution*, 63–101.
5. Herrera Serna, "Plutarco Elías Calles," 63.
6. Acts 2:42–47, 4:32–37. AICAM, "Nuestra Profesión de Fe, Razonada."
7. AGN/DGG, 2.340.66.34, Cruz Campos to Gobernación, Tehuizotla, 31 Jan., 31 Jul. 1928.
8. 2 Thessalonians 3:10. Mendoza López Schwerdtfeger, *¡Tierra Libre!*, 19, 24–29, 65–69. Valles Medina, *Del anarquismo a la utopía*.
9. Spenser, *En combate*, 71–74.
10. Matthew, 5:4, 6–10, 14.
11. *El reparto de tierras a los pobres no se opone a las enseñanzas de Nuestro Señor Jesucristo y de la Santa Madre Iglesia* (Mexico City: GSMO, 1923), in Lombardo

Toledano, *Obra Histórica-Cronológica*, 1:1, 1, 117–21. Krauze, *Caudillos culturales*, 121–22. Ogaz Pierce, "Pensamiento agrícola."
12. Peal, "Self-Help and the State."
13. Pamphlets, Mexico City, 1925: *Resumen histórico del desenvolvimiento de las cooperativas en varias naciones* (SEP), 5, 8–10, 51–52; *El aspecto económico, el estado actual de las cooperativas en varias naciones y los factores económicos* (SEP); *La historia de las sociedades cooperativas* (Talleres Gráficos de la Nación), 13; *La organización "Raiffeisen," editada por la Unión Central de las Asociaciones Alemanas "Raiffeisen," en Berlín* (SEP), 5–9, 13, 22–24, 28; *Las sociedades cooperativas en la escuela rural, iniciativa del Departamento de Escuelas Rurales e Incorporación Indígena, a cargo de Ignacio Ramírez* (SEP); *Resultados económicos y morales de la cooperación: ¿pensamos seguir en la explotación y expoliación del prójimo?* (Talleres Gráficos de la Nación), 43. *Estatutos de la organización "Raiffeisen"* (SEP); *La "Producción" en Hamburgo: historia de una sociedad de consumo desde su fundación hasta el fin de su XXV año fiscal* (SEP); *Estatutos de la sociedad de consumo, construcción, y ahorros "Producción," sociedad registrada con responsabilidad limitada, en Hamburgo, según acuerdo de la asamblea general de 11 de mayo de 1923* (SEP); *Extractos de la crónica de la Unión Central de Sociedades Alemanas de Consumo del año de 1924* (SEP); *Descripción de la película "Una visita a los establecimientos 'Producción' de Hamburgo"* (SEP).
14. *Ley de crédito agrícola* (Mexico City: Secretaría de Hacienda, 1926), 15–36. Méndez Reyes, *Capitalizar el campo*, 105–50. Gómez Mont, *Manuel Gómez Morín*, 246–52.
15. *Ley de 19 de diciembre de 1925 sobre repartición de tierras y constitución del patrimonio parcelario ejidal, y su reglamento de 4 de marzo de 1926* (Mexico City: Comisión Nacional Agraria, 1926).
16. León, *Address*, 19–25.
17. AICAM, "Conoce la Verdad y Serás Libre."
18. *Restauración*, 1 Aug. 1925, "Carta Pastoral del Patriarca de la Iglesia Ortodoxa Apostólica Mexicana, A Nuestros Muy Amados Hermanos Campesinos."
19. *Restauración*, 15 Jul. 1926.
20. *Restauración*, 1 Sep. 1926, "El Agrarismo en México."
21. *Controversia celebrada en el Teatro Iris, de la capital de la República, el día 4 de agosto de 1926: bajo los auspicios de la Federación de Sindicatos Obreros del Distrito Federal, pertenecientes a la Confederación Regional Obrera Mexicana, entre el Sr. Ing. Luis L. León, por parte de las organizaciones obreras, y el Sr. Lic. Manuel Herrera Lasso, por parte de la Liga de Defensa de la Libertad Religiosa en Mexico, sobre el tema "El movimiento revolucionario y el clericalismo mexicano"* (Tacubaya: Dirección de Estudios Geográficos y Climatológicos, 1926), 10, 21.
22. Barbosa Guzmán, *Caja rural católica*, 107–15. AHAM/MDR, c. 71/exp. 13, Ignacio Valdespino to episcopate [1926].
23. Ramírez Rodríguez, *Querella por el pulque*, 366–90.
24. Ortiz Petricioli, *Compañero Morones*, flyleaf bio.
25. FAPECFT, Fondo Elías Calles, 8.42.493.¾, "Informe del Departamento de Crédito Agrícola del BNCA S.A., 15 mar. 1932." Rivera, "Política," 48. Méndez, *Capitalizar*, 154–55.
26. *Excélsior*, "Un Atentado de los Cismáticos Católicos"; *El Gráfico*, "Intensa Agitación Reina entre los Católicos de la Villa"; AHAM, Provisorato, c. 124/exp. 4, "Sr. Director. . . ." (all 7 Jul. 1925). *Sol de México*, 11 Jul. 1925, "Con

los Romanos Quedó el Templo de Coatepec." AGN/IPS, c. 6/exp. 17, agente de 1ª, Mexico City, 10 Jul. 1925. AGA, Dotación, 23.895.13, "Censo de Jefes de Familia y Varones Solteros Mayores de 18 Años que Residen en el Pueblo de Coatepec," 30 Oct. 1927; "Acta de Posesión y Deslinde de la Posesión Definitiva de Ampliación de Ejidos," 18 May 1929.
27. AGA, Dotación, 23.2434.1, petition, 12 Jun. 1920; acta, 5 Sep. 1925; CLA *dictamen*, Toluca, 20 Dec. 1926. Ortiz Petricioli to Isaías Romero, Toluca, 4 Mar. 1927, and CNA, Toluca, 29 Mar. 1927; acta, Xalostoc, 11 Dec. 1928; "Censo Pecuario del Pueblo de San Pedro Xalostoc," 14 Oct. 1927. *Restauración*, 15 Jul. 1927, "Un Templo Más para la Iglesia Mexicana."
28. AGA, *Dotación*, 23.2313.4, Ignacio Solís to CNA, Mexico City, 20 May 1925; Federación Social Campesina to León, Melchor Ocampo, 9 Aug. 1925; Macario Pallares to CNA, Ixtacalco, 11 Feb. 1926; resolution, 26 Aug. 1926; Lorenzo Barberi to CNA, Mexico City, 30 Nov. 1926; B. Vargas to Sebastián Cano, Mexico City, 19 Feb. 1927.
29. AGN/DGG, 2.340.50.3, agraristas, Ixtacalco, 11 Aug. 1927; Pallares, Ixtacalco, 6 Oct. 1927, and Calles, Ixtacalco, 12 Oct. 1927.
30. AGN/DGG, 2.340.50.3, acta, Ixtacalco, 30 Dec. 1927; López y Sierra to CNA, Ixtacalco, 25 Mar. 1928; Jesús Domínguez, Ixtacalco, 19 Dec. 1929. AGA, Dotación, 23.2313.5, Pallares to León, Ixtacalco, 30 May 1927; Mario Hoyo to Pallares, Mexico City, 24 Jun. 1927; Sebastián Cano to Agricultura, Ixtacalco, 22 Apr. 1929; 23.2323.3, petition, 22 Apr. 1928; 23.2323.2, Manuel Vilchis to CLA, Mexico City, 25 Jul. 1931.
31. AGA, Dotación, 23.1548.2, CNA memo, 22 Oct. 1925; CLA to CNA, Pachuca, 2 Jun. 1922; Gobernación to CLA, Mexico City, 28 Sep. 1922; CNA to CLA, Mexico City, 9 Nov. 1922. 23.1548.2, 23.1548.1, G. Sánchez to CNA, Pachuca, 18 Dec. 1922; George Summerlin to Pani, Mexico City, 9 Jan. 1923; "Informe Rendido ante la C. N. Agraria Referente a la Aprehensión del C. J. Guadalupe Juárez del Mpio. de Tepejí del Río, Dto. De Tula, Edo. De Hidalgo," 29 Jul. 1923; Samuel Rico Córdova to CNA, Pachuca, 24 Jun. 1924, 6 Jan. 1925, 15 Dec. 1926; Miguel Servín to CNA, Tepejí, 6 Jun. 1925, 19 Apr. 1927; Mario López to procurador de pueblos, Pachuca, 14 Aug. 1927; "Acta de Elección de Comisarios Ejidales e Inspectores de Vigilancia," Tepejí, 28 Aug. 1927; petition, *ampliación de ejidos*, 30 Nov. 1926. AHAM, Mora y del Río, c. 86/exp. 121, Carlos Salgado to Mora, Guadalupe Hidalgo, 6 May 1924.
32. AGA, Dotación, 23.1576.6, CNA dictamen, 12 Jan. 1925; resolution, 4 Mar. 1926; agraristas to CNA, Apan, 15 Jan. 1926; reply, Mexico City, 13 Mar. 1926. León, "Address," 21–24. Ramírez Rodríguez, *Querella por el pulque*, 232–38.
33. AGA, Dotación, 23.1576.6, decree, 12 Sep. 1921; letters to CNA, Apan, Juan Sánchez (2 Sep. 1923), Emilio Coca (30 Mar. 1925).
34. *Restauración*, 15 Dec. 1926, "Nuestra Iglesia Se Establece en Apam, Hidalgo."
35. *Restauración*, 1 Jun. 1927, "Carta Abierta de los Ejidatarios de Almoloya, Municipio y Distrito de Apan, Hidalgo."
36. AGN/DGG, 2.340.49.89, Calles to Tejeda, Mexico City, 14 Aug. 1926; petition, Aug. 1926; Hernández, Ajoloapan, 22, 29 Aug., 16 Oct. (1926), 18 Aug. 1929; Tejeda, Mexico City, 27 Oct. 1926; Joaquín Juárez, Ajoloapan, 15 Jan. 1927; A. Galván, Mexico City, 19 Aug. 1929; inventory, 13 Aug. 1929.
37. AGA, Dotación, 23.2203.1, memo, Toluca, 3 Aug. 1917; provisional resolution, 15 Mar. 1922; 23.2203.3, presidential resolution, 25 Oct. 1923. Letters, Coyote-

pec, 1926, Gerónimo de las Casas to CNA, 26 Nov. (23.2203.13); José Galván to Obregón, 16 Apr. 1926, Tiburcio Cortés to CNA, 21 Feb. (23.2203.2).
38. AGN, 2.340.50.1, mayor to Gobernación, Coyotepec, 11 Jun. 1927, 12 Jul. 1930; Carlos Riva Palacio to Gobernación, Toluca, 15 Aug. 1927. AGA, Dotación, 23.2203.3, dictamen, 30 Aug. 1927; 23.2203.5, José Galván and Hilario Castillo to CLA, Coyotepec, 10 Sep. 1928; decree, Toluca, 19 Mar. 19292; 3.2203.8, actas, Coyotepec, 28 Apr., 19 May, 22 Jun. 1929, 10 Jul. 1930.
39. AGN, 2.340.50.1, letters, Coyotepc, to Gobernación, from: A. Ortega, 2 Aug. 1929; Pomposo Martínez, 31 Jul. 1929; Roman Catholics, 17 Aug., 19 Nov.; Pedro Díaz, 6 Nov. 1929.
40. AGN, 2.340.50.1, letters, Coyotepec, to Gobernación, from: Mexican Catholics, 19 Nov. 1929; mayor, 12 Jul. 1930; Felipe Pineda, 15 Feb. 1930; Pomposo Martínez, 15 Jun. 1930. "Memorial que elevan á la Secretaría de Gobernación los vecinos del pueblo de San Cristóbal Coyotepec del Estado de México," 10 Dec. 1929.
41. AGN/DGG, 2.340.50.1: Ruiz y Flores to Carlos Riva Palacio, Mexico City, 16 Jun. 1930; Pascual Díaz to same, Mexico City, 1 Oct. 1930. Letters, Coyotepec, from: mayor to Gobierno (27 Oct. 1930); Hilario Castillo to Riva Palacio (22 Sep. 1930); *campesinos liberales* to governor (6 Mar. 1934); José Sánchez to Abelardo Rodríguez (10 Mar. 1934); J. Abad to Gobernación, Coyotepec (12 Mar. 1934). Letters to Gobernación, Mexico City, from: Rafael Mancera (19 Jun. 1931), CNC (19 Jun. 1934).
42. Castellanos Suárez, *Empeño por una expectativa agraria*. Mendoza García, "Oposición al reparto agrario."
43. AGA, Dotación, 23.2233.2, dictamen, 19 Jan. 1921, and letters from: CNA delegate, Toluca, 19 Jul. 1922; *revisor*, Mexico City, 14 Aug. 1922; Ismael Juárez, Xometla, 16 Nov. 1922, 26 May, 31 Aug. 1923; Liga de C. Agrarias, Tezoyuca, 10 Jun. 1923; representative, Acolman, 26 Jun. 1923.
44. AGA, Dotación, 23.2233.2, letters to CNA, Mexico City, from: Ángel Arratia (12 Sep. 1923); 2° ingeniero (23 Sep. 1923); Gobernación (17 Oct. 1923); resolution, 8 May 1924. Letters to CNA, Xometla, from: Ismael Juárez, 4, 17 Jun., 15 Jul. 1924; 1er Ingeniero to CNA, Oaxaca, 31 Jul. 1925.
45. AGA, Dotación, 23.2233.2, letters, 1925: CNA to ejidal committee, Mexico City, 17 Feb.; procurador de pueblos to CNA, Mexico City, Feb. (n/d); Brigadier Subjefe to CNA, Mexico City, 12 Jun.; Ismael Juárez to procurador de pueblos, Xometla, 2 Dec. AGN/DGG, 2.340.52.7, Camerino García Mota to mayor, Xometla, 6 Aug. 1927; Juan Juárez to Gobernación Xometla, 25 Jul. 1929.
46. AGN/DGG, 2.340.52.7, Juan Juárez to Gobernación, Xometla, 25 Jul. 1929. AGA, Dotación, 23.2233.2, Gabino Onofre to CNA, Xometla, 1 Feb. 1929; "Cosecheros de Trigo" to BNCA, Mexico City, 31 Oct. 1929.
47. AGN/DGG, 2.340.52.7, letters, 1929: Catalino Juárez (Teotihuacán, 9 Aug., Texcoco, 20 Aug.); Nicolás Juárez (Belém prison, 12 Aug.); Joaquín Lozano (Acolman, 12 Aug.).
48. The brothers claimed that Acolman's caciques broke into their sister Romana's house "to rape her" and beat their mother. Others accused Acolman officials of "abusing their wives." AGN/DGG, 2.340.52.7, Catalino Juárez, Texcoco, 17 Sep. 1929. Letters, Mexico City, 1929, from J. Estrada (16 Aug.), LNC (23 Aug.).
49. AGN/DGG, 2.340.52.7, letters, 1929: Joaquín Lozano (Acolman, 24 Aug.), Catalino Juárez (Texcoco jail, 17 Sep.), Francisco Galicia (Xometla, 8 Oct.), José Ramírez (Xometla, 11 Nov.); Juan Juárez (Mexico City, 25 Nov.); state government (Toluca, 14 Nov., and 11 Jun. 1930). Trinidad and Catalino Juárez to Gobernación,

Xometla, Apr. 1930 (n/d). AHAM, Provisorato, c. 124/exp. 3, letters to Pérez, 1929, from María Galindo, Xometla, 27 Oct.; Juan, Marcos, Antonio, and Catalino Juárez, Texcoco jail, 1 Nov.
50. AGN/DGG, 2.340.52.7, letters, 1931: Pérez (Mexico City, 17 Jun.); Ismael Juárez (Xometla, 21 May); Agustín Juárez (Xometla, 23 Aug.); Gobierno (Toluca, 17 Oct.); municipal president (Acolman, 25 Sep.). Subsequent letters: Marcos Juárez, "Presidente del Comité Pro-Educación" (Xometla, 14 Jan.); Marcos Juárez (Xometla, 16 Oct. 1934); Gobierno (Toluca, 7 Dec.). Dávila to Cárdenas, Mexico City, 28 Mar. 1936.
51. Williman, *Iglesia y el estado*, 85–86, 106, 134–35.
52. Falcón, *Agrarismo en Veracruz*; Fowler Salamini, *Agrarian Radicalism in Veracruz*, 4–11; Skerritt, "Papel de Adalberto Tejeda"; Falcón and García, *Semilla en el surco*, quote, 209; Corzo Ramírez, *Nunca un desleal*; Domínguez Pérez, *Agraristas y agrarismo*; Ginzberg, "State Agrarianism; Ginzberg, "Formación de la infraestructura política."
53. Kourí, *A Pueblo Divided*. Velázquez Hernández, *Territorios fragmentados*. Velázquez et al., *Istmo mexicano*. Ramírez Lavoignet, *Problema agrario*.
54. Falcón, *Agrarismo en Veracruz*, 49. Léonard and Velázquez, "Reparto agrario." Buckles and Chevalier, "Ejido *versus* bienes comunales," 231–47. Velázquez, *Territorios*, 241–58, 283–308.
55. Falcón, *Agrarismo en Veracruz*, 64–69. Falcón and García, *Semilla en el surco*, 123–25, 194–96. Ginzberg, "Formación de la infraestructura política," 685, 704.
56. Léonard and Velázquez, "Reparto agrario," 405–7. AMPV, c. 106/exp. 745/ff. 8451, 8456, 8459, 8515, *La Opinión*, 1929: 5 Aug. ("Protesta de los Vecinos"), 6 Aug. ("Iba a Ser Linchado: Los Católicos de S. Andrés Tuxtla Lapidaron la Casa del Cura Cismático"), 7 Aug. ("Fuerzas Federales Intervienen en San Andrés"), 31 Aug. ("Los Sacerdotes Católicos los Recibieron Ayer: Huyen Deportados los Cismáticos"). AGN/DGG, 2.340.83.22, letters to Gobernación, Tuxtla, 1929, from: A. Mirarete (10 Aug.); Roman Catholics (10 Aug.); Civil Administration Junta (30 Aug.).
57. AHAM, Provisorato, c. 124/exp. 1, López y Sierra to Pérez, Jaltipan, 16 Feb. 1928. Jiménez Arce, "Reforma Agraria."
58. García de León, *Tierra adentro*, 205–57, 271–98, 343–96, 402–9.
59. Ramírez Lavoignet, *Problema agrario*, 45–53, 65–108, 130–35, 164–93.
60. AGEV/CAM, Tierras, exp. 35, PLM to Tejeda, Acayucan, 15, 31 May 1922; Gobierno to CLA, Xalapa, 15 Jun. 1922; CLA dictamen, 15 Aug. 1923.
61. AGEV/CAM, Tierras, exp. 35, letters to Tejeda, Acayucan, from: Rafael Subaran (10 Aug. 1923); J. Alcantara (26 Mar. 1924); Sindicato "Hilario C. Salas" (13 Dec. 1928).
62. Various, 1929: AHAM/PDB, c. 61/exp. 9, Damas Católicas to Portes Gil, Acayucan (12 Aug.); AGN/DGG, 2.340.83.12, petition, Acayucan, (12 Aug.); Genaro Méndez to Tejeda, Tehuantepec, (13 Sep.). AMPV, c. 106/exp. 745/f. 8480, *La Opinión*, 14 Aug., "Templos a los Cismáticos de Acayucan, Ver."
63. AGN/DGG, 2.340.83.12, campesinos, Acayucan, 6 Oct. 1929; 2.340.83.12, Huguet to Fernando Noriega, Oluta, 18 Nov. 1929. Fonseca, *Danza de los arrieros*.
64. AGN/DGG, 2.340.83.12, letters, Briones, Acayucan, 5 Feb. 1930, 28 Apr. 1931; Hacienda, Mexico City, 4 Oct. 1930; Pedro Olivera, Oluta, 11 May 1931; *Diario Oficial*, 4 Mar. 1933.

65. AGEV/CAM, exp. 1487, *censo agrario*, 1918. AGN/DGG, 2.340.81.14, Evaristo Torres to Pérez, Chinameca, 26 Jun. 1928; *comité particular administrativo* to Portes Gil, Jaltipan, 29 Oct. 1928.
66. AGN/DGG, 2.340.81.14, letters: Bibiana Ortiz, Jaltipan, 9 Sep. 1929, Chinameca, 10 Sep., 16, 19 Oct. 1929; Nemesio Fernández, Chinameca, 15 May 1930; Mexican Catholics, Chinameca, 12 Aug. 1935; Rubén Darío Cano Ballesteros, Mexico City, 19 Aug. 1935.
67. Tepehua, once considered a Totonac dialect, is actually a separate language. See Roberto Williams García's important fieldwork, *Tepehuas*, 32–66; *Mitos tepehuas*. García Valencia, "Religión, política," and García Valencia, "Sistemas Normativos." David Lagunas, *Hablar de otros: miradas y voces del mundo tepehua* (Mexico City: Plaza y Valdés, 2004); Heiras Rodríguez, *San Pedro Tziltzicuapan*.
68. *Restauración*, 15 Oct. 1926, "El triunfo de nuestra Iglesia en Veracruz."
69. Williams García, *Tepehuas*, 67, 77–78, 92–94.
70. Williams García, 94–96.
71. See ch. 6.
72. Celestino Barradas, *Historia de la Iglesia en Veracruz* (Xalapa: Ediciones San José, 1990), 258, cited in García Valencia, "Sistemas Normativos," 189. García Valencia, "Religión, política," 160–61, 169–75. Williams García, *Tepehuas*, 22.

CHAPTER FIVE
1. SD 812.404.871 (Harold Wood, Veracruz, 13 Mar. 1928), 812.404.1829 ("Memorandum Regarding Religious Situation in Northern Veracruz," 10 Dec. 1935). Corzo Ramírez, *Curato de Papantla*.
2. AHAM, Provisorato, c. 124/exp. 1, de la Peña to Pérez, Xochitlán, 20 Dec. 1928.
3. AICAM, Lazarini to Pérez, Actipan, 18 Oct. 1929. Cervantes, *Don Quijote*, 888: "salió el regimiento del pueblo a recibirle, tocaron las campanas y todos los vecinos dieron muestras de general alegría y con mucha pompa le llevaron a la iglesia mayor a dar gracias a Dios."
4. Bantjes, *As If Jesus Walked*, 6–21. Fallaw, *Religion and State Formation*, 35–62.
5. Lisbona Guillén, *Persecución religiosa*; Ríos Figueroa, *Siglo XX*. Williman, *Iglesia y el estado*.
6. AHAM, Provisorato, c. 124: Francisco Durán, Tlaola, 29 Jan. 1930 (exp. 2); José Varela, Coxquihuí, 14 Feb. 1931, Francisco Fernández, Coyotepec, 2 Jun. 1930 (exp. 3); María Jesús Palacios, Tapachula, 30 Apr. 1929 (exp. 4).
7. Diocesan bishop Manríquez y Zárate (Huejutla) was exiled.
8. Aguilera González, *Cardenal Miguel*, 307–8.
9. Miranda's 1950s Indigenous Pastoral was feted, even in *Life* magazine.
10. AHAM, Provisorato, c. 124: Florentino Guzmán to Pérez, Tuxtla, 6 Nov. 1926 (exp. 4); Pedro Infante to ICAM, Tepetlixpa, 9 Jun. 1929 (exp. 2); and 17 Apr. 1929, 19 Jan. 1930 (exp. 3).
11. López Caballero, *Indígenas de la nación*.
12. León Portilla and Johansson, *Ángel María Garibay K.*
13. AHAM, Provisorato, c. 124/exp. 1, Manuel Caballero to Pérez, Lagunillas, 20 Apr. 1928.
14. *Restauración*, 15 Dec. 1926, "Los Católicos Romanos No Son los Católicos Mexicanos."
15. AICAM, "Nuevo Prelado para la Diócesis de Veracruz y Puebla."
16. Gamio, *Población del Valle*, 5:208.

17. Gamio, 5:134–36, 208, 209.
18. Planchet, *Derecho canónico*, 21. AHAM, Secretaría, circulars, 2 Mar., 23 May 1925. Trexler, *Reliving Golgotha*, 88–98. Peñalosa, *Rafael Guízar*, 140. Velasco Toro, "Indigenismo y rebelión totonaca"; González de la Lama, "Papeles de Díaz Manfort." Flores, *Revolución de Olarte en Papantla*; Masferrer Kan, "Totonacos y sus relaciones," and "Factores étnicos."
19. AHAM/MDR, c. 90/exp. 85, Trinidad Juárez, Xometla, 17 Jul. 1926. c. 141; exp. 45, Francisco Gutiérrez, Puerto México, 30 Nov., 12 Dec. 1926; Provisorato, c. 124/exp. 1, Julio Urbina to ICAM, Tenoxtitlán, 18 Mar. 1928. AICAM, Junta Vecinal, Tenoxtitlán, 20 Feb. 1928. Nicacio Pérez, Tenoxtitlán, 18 Feb. 1928. Pedro Pérez, Tenoxtitlán, 23 Feb. 1928. *Restauración*, 15 Oct. 1926, "El Obispo Romanista de Querétaro y Nuestra Actuación Religiosa." Vera y Zuria, *Cartas a mis seminaristas*, 196–97.
20. Two hundred and fifteen patron saints were identified from www.oficinaparroquial.com; Vera y Zuria, *Cartas a mis seminaristas*; Vera, *Itinerario parroquial*. Chauvet, *Culto a la Asunción*, 64–71, 157–68; Leyva-Gutiérrez, "Conflict and Imagery"; Ontiveros Valdés, "Andanzas de Santiago."
21. AGN/DGG, 2.340.81.9, mayor, Pajapam, 5 Feb. 1927; 2.340.83.15, Emeterio Román, Tampico-Alto, 11 Feb. 1929. AICAM, Miguel García, Santo Domingo, 1 Apr. 1929. AHAM, Provisorato, c. 124/exp. 4, Juan José Guzmán, Tenancingo, 6 Mar. 1928; c. 124/exp. 2, *junta parroquial*, Ixhuatlán, 18 May 1929. *Restauración*, 15 Jul. 1927, "Un Templo Más para la Iglesia Mexicana."
22. AICAM, López y Sierra, Mexico City, 4 Aug. 1927; inhabitants, Santo Domingo, 24 Dec. 1927. AGN/DGG, 2.2340.61.18, Fernández, Ixtepec, 13 Oct. 1926. *Restauración*: "Glosario Religioso," "El Triunfo de Nuestra Iglesia en Veracruz" (15 Oct. 1926); "Glosario Religioso" (15 Dec. 1926), "En Guerrero Ha Triunfado la Iglesia Mexicana" (1 Mar. 1927), "La Semana Mayor en Nuestros Templos" (1 May 1927), "La Visita del Ilmo. Señor Obispo de Hidalgo, al Estado de Tlaxcala" (15 Jun. 1927), "La Iglesia Mexicana en Diferentes Partes del País" (1 Oct. 1927).
23. AICAM, "Totonaca-Español," ca. 1929.
24. AHAM, Provisorato, c. 124, letters to ICAM, Almoloya, 1930, from: José Varela, 22 May; Antonio Ramírez, 5 Feb., 22 Jul., Agustín Mójica 25 Aug. (exp. 1); Agustín Mójica, Actipan, 18 Jan. 1930; Teodoro Juárez, Huitzilan, 31 Jan. 1930 (exp. 3). *Restauración*, 1 Mar. 1927, "El Revmo. Obispo de Hidalgo Visita su Diócesis."
25. AGN/DGG, 2.340.67.4, José de Jesús Gómez, Tlaola, 31 Mar., 22 Aug. 1931.
26. AHAM, Provisorato, c. 124: Francisco Fernández, Coyotepec, 13 Feb. (exp. 2), 18 Feb., 1930 (exp. 3).
27. Nutini and Isaac, *Pueblos de habla Náhuatl*, 358–60. Provisorato, c. 124, letters to ICAM from: Agustín Mójica, Almoloya, 25 Aug. 1930; Evaristo Torres, Chinameca, 20 Jun. 1928; Salvador Arámbula, Actipan, 25 May 1929 (exp. 1); Teodoro Juárez, 7 Jun. 1930; José Varela, Zozocolco, 19 Sep. 1930 (exp. 2); Isauro Flores, San Simón de Bravo, 15 Mar. 1931 (exp. 3). AICAM, José Luis Lazarini, Actipan, 18 Oct. 1929.
28. AICAM, "Sacramentos Registrados durante el Mes de Junio de 1928," Huehuetla, 5 Jul. 1928; José Gómez, Tlaola, 5 Sep. 1931; partidas, Zapotitlán, 23 Aug. 1927, Huehuetla, 15 Nov. 1927; "Lista de los Trabajos Efectuados en Sosocolco de Hgo., Ver.," 1928. AHAM, Provisorato, c. 124: *cortes de caja*, Xochitlán, 31 Mar., 30 Apr., 1929; "Almoloya, Dominica," 17 Feb. 1930 (exp. 1); Ricardo

González, Mexico City, s/f; José Ramírez, Tapachula, 27 Feb., 31 Mar., 11 May 1929; "Quadrante que manifiesta los ingresos y egresos habidos en la Parroquia de San Miguel Zozocalco de Hgo., Ver." Mar.–Apr. 1930; *corte de caja*, Xochitlán, 20 Jul. 1929 (exp. 4).
29. AHAM, Provisorato, c. 124: José Ramírez, Tapachula, 21 Dec. 1926 (exp. 4); López y Sierra, Jaltipan, 16 Feb. 1928 (exp. 1); Francisco Durán, Actipan, 17 Dec. 1929; Pérez to Dolores Coronado Picón, Mexico City, n/d. (exp. 2); *Restauración*, 1 Mar. 1927, "Informe General . . ."
30. AICAM, Francisco Durán to ICAM, Tlaola, 22 Aug. 1929.
31. AHAM, Provisorato, c. 124/exp. 3, Emeterio Valdéz, Mexico City, 11 Jun. 1929. AICAM, José Gómez, Tlaola, 5 Sep. 1931, and letters, 1929, Francisco Durán, Tlaola, 22 Aug.; Félix Hernández, Chumatlán, 31 Dec.; Emilio Torres, Ahuacatlán, 28 Dec.
32. AICAM, Francisco Durán, Tlaola, 22 Aug. 1929; Pedro Infante, Mexico City, 22 Sep. 1931.
33. AICAM, all 1929: Luisa Reboulen, Puerto México, 21 May; ICAM to Coyutla's mayor, Tacuba, 20 Nov.; Félix Hernández, Chumatlán, 31 Dec.; Emilio Torres, Ahuacatlán, 28 Dec.
34. AHAM, Provisorato, c. 124/exp. 3, Ricardo V. González, Mexico City, s/f [Jul./Aug. 1929].
35. Chance and Taylor, "*Cofradías* and *Cargos*."
36. Gamio, *Población del Valle*, 4:214–16.
37. AGN/DGG, 2.340.66.32, mayor, Zoquiapan, 14 Dec. 1926; acta, 13 Dec. 1926. AICAM, Constancia Vázquez, Santo Domingo, 28 Nov. 1928. AHAM, Provisorato, c. 124: Pedro Infante, Tepetlixpa, 10 Dec. 1929 (exp. 1); Emigdio Gabino, Luis Abad (separate letters), Coyotepec, 28 Mar. 1929 (exp. 2). *Restauración*, 15 Mar. 1927, "Adquisición del Templo de Tuzamapa, Puebla." García, "Apuntamientos," 419–24. Hurtado, *Cisma mexicano*, 55.
38. AHAM, Provisorato, c. 124, letters to Pérez, 1929, from: Francisco Fernández, Coyotepec, 21 Dec. (exp. 4); Marcos Castillo, Xochitlán, 30 Jul., 11 Aug. (exp. 1).
39. AHAM, Provisorato, c. 124/exp. 4, Lazarini, Xochitlán, 29 Jul., 2, 3 Aug. 1929; AHAM/PDB, c. 60/exp. 46, *La Razón*, 18 Nov. 1928, "El Sanguinario Callismo Convertido en Hipócrita Cisma Llorón. Sacrilegio Abominable a Base de Mujeres."
40. *Restauración*, 15 Oct. 1926, "Glosario Religioso." AHAM, Provisorato, c. 124: Varela, Mecatlán, 12 Aug. 1930 (exp. 1); García, Tapachula, 10 Dec. 1928 (exp. 2).
41. AHAM, Provisorato, c. 124, letters to Pérez from: Juan Allende, San Simón de Bravo, 25 Sep. 1930 (exp. 2), 19 Feb. 1931 (exp. 3); Agustín Mójica, Yehualtepec, n/d (exp. 2).
42. AICAM, José Gómez, Tlaola, 5 Sep. 1931. AHAM, Provisorato, c. 124, letters to ICAM, 1930, from: Teodoro Juárez, Zapotitlán, 12 Aug., José Varela, Zozocolco, 29 Aug., Vicente Pérez, Tepetlixpa, 11 Feb., 23 Mar., 1 Apr. (exp. 2); Agustín Mójica, Almoloya, 25 Aug. (exp. 1).
43. AHAM, Provisorato, c. 124, letters to ICAM from: Jorge Celis Casillas, San Simón de Bravo, 8 Apr. 1930 (exp. 2); Guillermo de la Peña, Xochitlán, 15 Jan., 19 Dec. 1929 (exp. 1); Maximino Pino, Coyotepec, 14 Jul. 1929; Román Enríquez, Xalostoc, 27 Jan. 1930 (exp. 3); Pérez to Lazarini, Mexico City, 19 Jul. 1929 (exp. 3). AGN/DGG, 2.340.67.1, Mexican Catholics, Actipan, 17 Jul. 1931. AICAM, Miguel García, Santo Domingo, 1 Apr. 1929.

44. AHAM, Provisorato, c. 124, letters to ICAM, 1930, from: Locadio Acalco, Actipan, 24 Mar.; Pascual Luciano García, Actipan, 20 Jun. (exp. 3); Teodoro Juárez, Zozocolco, 3 Jul. (exp. 2). AICAM, Valdéz to Francisco Torres, Mexico City, 30 May 1931, 31 Sep. 1935; López y Sierra to Fernando Melo, Mexico City, 10 Jan. 1928. Interview, Lola Torres to Antonio Celis, Tlaola, 1 May 2006.
45. AGN/DGG, 2.340.50.3, "special agent #3," Atenco, 15 May 1928. AHAM, Provisorato, c. 124/exp. 3, Gómez Ruvalcaba, Jaltipan, 31 Jan. 1928. AICAM, Lazarini, Actipan, 18 Oct. 1929.
46. AHAM, Cisma, "Aviso Religioso." *Restauración*, "Preparativos para las Fiestas en Xometla" (15 Sep. 1927); "Solemne Festividad en San Miguel Xometla" (15 Oct. 1927). Ichon, *Religión de los totonacos*, 392–408. Stresser-Péan, *Sun God and the Savior*, 327–30. AHAM, Provisorato, c. 124, letters to Pérez, 1928, from: de la Peña, Xochitlán, 19 Dec. (exp. 1); Gómez Ruvalcaba, Jaltipan, 31 Jan. (exp. 3). AICAM, *Alcance al No. 61 de Restauración*, May 1928, 1–8.
47. Vera y Zuria, *Cartas a mis seminaristas*, 570.
48. Johnson, *Pueblos within Pueblos*. Dehouve, "'Secession' of Villages." Perkins, "Macehuales and the Corporate Solution."
49. Acevedo-Rodrigo, "Paying for Progress."
50. *Quinto censo de población, 15 de mayo de 1930* (8 vols. Mexico City: Dirección General de Estadística, 1932–1936).
51. Letters to Gobernación: Marcos Juárez, Xometla, 27 Aug. 1930 (AHAM, Provisorato, c. 124/exp. 1); Junta Vecinal, Tenoxtitlán, 20 Feb. 1928 (AICAM); Juan Castillo and Vicente Liñán, Alquizapan, 16 May, 21 Jul. 1928 respectively (AGN/DGG, 2.340.66.40).
52. AGN/DGG, 2.340.67.1, ejidatarios to Gobernación, Actipan, 10 Jan.; auxiliary president, Actipan, 12 Feb.; José Varela, Actipan, 30 Jun.; Gregorio López, Acatzingo, 28 Aug.; Lorenzo Bautista, Actipan, 9 Aug.; Marciano Pérez, Actipan, 7 Aug. (all 1929).
53. AHAM, Provisorato, c. 124/exp. 1, Arámbula to Lazarini, Actipan, 6 Aug. 1929.
54. AGN/DGG, 2.340.67.1, "Toma y Lee" (17 Nov. 1929); Juan Sandoval, 17 Sep. 1929; auxiliary president, 22 Nov. 1929; Mexican Catholics, 22 Nov. 1929, 17 Jul. 1931; Antonio Muníve, 3 Feb. 1930; Pascual Luciano García, 27 Jul. 1931; *junta auxiliar*, 5 Jan. 1932 (all Actipan); mayor, Acatzingo, 5 Dec. 1929; Pérez, 2 Dec. 1929; Heraclio Ortiz, 19 Jan. 1934; Eduardo Dávila, 20 Jul. 1934 (all Mexico City). AICAM (all 1931), Emeterio Valdéz, Mexico City, 21 Sep.; Rafael Méndez, Actipan, 28 Sep.; acta, Actipan, 22 Sep.; Macario López, Mexico City, 1 Oct.; Manuel García Téllez, Actipan, 3 Oct.; *Diario Oficial*, 30 Oct.
55. AGN/DGG, 2.340.66.34, letters, Tehuizotla, 1928: Cruz Campos to Molcaxac's ayuntamiento (31 Jan.), state governor (27 Feb.), Gobernación (31 Jul.); 2.340.65.35, Tomás Flores to governor, Tecamachalco, 24 Sep. 1929.
56. AHAM, Provisorato, c. 124/exp. 4, Juan José Guzmán, Florentino Guzmán, Justo Marabilla to ICAM, Tenancingo, 6 Mar. 1928. *Restauración*, 1927, "La Semana Mayor en Nuestros Templos" (1 May), "La Visita del Ilmo. Señor Obispo de Hidalgo, al Estado de Tlaxcala" (15 Jun.), "La Iglesia Mexicana en Diferentes Partes del País" (1 Oct.). Nutini and Isaac, *Pueblos de habla Náhuatl*, 67–78. Ramírez Rancaño, *Patriarca Pérez*, 250–54, asserts that Heredia and García were the same; this is not certain.
57. AHAM, Provisorato, c. 124/exp. 1, Gumersindo Castro, Ponciano Rojas, Yehualtepec, 6 Aug., 8 Sep. 1930.

58. AGN/DIPS, c. 292/exp. 42, Pío R. Lara, Mata Cabestro, 10 Dec. 1927; *agente primero substituto*, Mexico City, 20 Jan. 1928; Anguiano, Veracruz, 20 Dec. 1927. AHAM, Provisorato, c. 124/exp. 1, López y Sierra, Jaltipan, 16 Feb. 1928. García de León, *Tierra adentro*, 201 (incl. 201n205), 344, 351, 362n3; Hamnett, "Obstáculos a la política agraria," esp. 63–66. Santoyo, *Mano negra*.
59. AGN, Gobierno, 2.344.18.8, Hernández to Jara, San Cristóbal de la Llave, 5, 7 Nov. 1928; Anguiano, Veracruz, 6 Nov., 1 Dec. 1928, 11 Jan. 1929; Jara, Veracruz, 4 Dec. 1928.
60. AICAM, Durán to ICAM, Santo Domingo, 7 Sep. 1928.
61. AGN/DGG, 2.340.66.45, Cancino, Ixcaquixtla, 13 Nov., 8 Dec. 1928, and Puebla, 26 Jun. 1929; 2.340.66.47, ayuntamiento, Ixcaquixtla, 7 Dec. 1928; Cancino, Ixcaquixtla, 18 Jun. 1929; Nicolás Simón, Puebla, 26 Jun. 1929; Portes Gil, Mexico City, 27 Jun. 1929.
62. Vera y Zuria, *Cartas a mis seminaristas*, 197. Reck, "Goodbye Ixoxolotl," 71–77. Pace Stresser-Péan, *Sun God and the Savior*, 134–35.
63. Reck, "Goodbye Ixoxolotl," 26, 39, 60, 71–78, 80. AGN, 2.340.66.32, mayor, Jonotla, 29 Jul. 1927. AICAM, Valdéz, Jonotla, 27 Apr. 1927; "Movimiento havido hasta hoy en los Templos religiosos administrados por el suscrito ministro de la Iglesia Ortodoxa Católica Apostólica Mexicana."
64. Stresser-Péan, *Sun God and the Savior*, 352–53; Ichon, *Religión de los totonacos*, 363–64.
65. Kelly and Palerm, *Tajin Totonac*, 70, 110, 112, 115, 173, 223–25. Stresser-Péan, *Sun God and the Savior*, 130–47. Ichon, *Religión de los totonacos*, 37–47, 71–73, 92, 104–5, 123–25, 224–27, 282–302, 363–67.
66. Gallop, *Mexican Mosaic*, 258–82. Covarrubias, *Mexico South*, 42. AICAM, Federico Rodríguez, Huehuetla, 19 Mar. 1928.
67. García Valencia, "Sistemas Normativos," and García Valencia, "Religión, política," 169–77; Williams García, *Tepehuas*, 189–242; Bower, "Notes on Shamanism."
68. García de León, *Tierra adentro*, 231–36, 404–9. Williman, *Iglesia y el estado*, 62–63. AHAM, Provisorato, c. 124: Mexican Catholics, Jaltipan, n/d (exp. 4); Macario López, Los Angeles, 8 Apr. 1930 (exp. 3). AICAM, López y Sierra, Mexico City, 21 Apr. 1927. *Restauración*, "Una Nueva Parroquia de Nuestra Iglesia en Jaltipan, Veracruz" (15 Sep. 1927), "Alcance . . ." (1 May 1928). AGN/DGG, 2.340.82.16, ayuntamiento, Jaltipan, 30 Sep. 1927; junta, Jaltipan, 26 Aug. 1927; García, Puerto México, 8 Aug. 1929.
69. AGN/DGG, 2.340.82.16, junta Jaltipan, 12 Dec. 1927; Manuel Aragón, Jaltipan, 16 Dec. 1927; García, Puerto México, 18 Jun. 1928; Gobierno, Xalapa, 4 Sep. 1928. AHAM, Provisorato, c. 124, 1928: García to López y Sierra, Jaltipan, 24 Jan.; Melquíades García to Pérez, Jaltipan, 2 Sep. (exp. 4); García to Pérez, Jaltipan, 10 Jul., Puebla, 2, 12 Nov. (exp. 2); Muníve to Pérez, Puerto México, 3 Sep.; Tejeda to ayuntamientos, Jalapa, 13 Dec. (exp. 1).
70. See ch. 2.
71. AHAM, Provisorato, c. 124: García to Pérez, Puerto México, 20 Feb. 1929 (exp. 4); *presidente parroquial* Florentino Aguilar to Pérez, Jaltipan, 28 Jan. 1929 (exp. 3). AGN/DGG, 2.340.82.16, civil administration president to Gobernación, Jaltipan, 4 Apr. 1929.
72. AHAM, Provisorato, c. 124: García to Pérez, Puerto México, 31 Jan. 1929, and Puebla, 26 May, 14 Jun. 1929; ICAM, Mexico City, 19 Apr. 1929 (exp. 2); Games Flores, Puerto México, 29 Apr. 1929. exp. 4,

73. AHAM, Provisorato, c. 124/exp. 1, Manuel Aragón, Jaltipan, 4 Sep., 15 Nov. 1929. AGN/DGG, 2.340.82.16, letters García, Puerto México, 8 Aug.; Mexican Catholics, Jaltipan, 30 Sep., 2 Nov. (all 1929).
74. AICAM, Muníve, Jaltipan, 28 Nov. 1929.
75. AHAM, Provisorato, c. 124: Mexican Catholics, Jaltipan, n/d. (exp. 4); García, Jalitpan, 10 Jul. 1928 (exp. 2). AGN/DGG, 2.340.82.16, García, Puerto México, 18 Jun. 1928, 8 Aug. 1929; Sandra González, Jaltipan, 13 Dec. 1927; Victoriano Martínez, Jaltipan, 14 Dec. 1927. AICAM, Luisa Reboulen, Puerto México, 8 May 1929.
76. AICAM, Reboulen, Puerto México, 8, 15, 21, 31 May 1929. AGN/DGG, 2.340.82.16, 25 Roman Catholics, Jaltipan, 13 Jan. 1930. FPEC, 12.010086.37.617, E. Balmoreji, Puerto México, 4 Nov. 1932.
77. Rugely, *Of Wonders and Wise Men*, 212–18.
78. AHAM, Cisma, José María Rincón, Tapachula, 4 Sep. 1925.
79. AGN/DGG, 2.340.28.29, Ramírez, Tapachula, 3 Nov. 1926. *Restauración*, "Clamoroso y Estupendo Triunfo en la C. de Tapachula, Chiapas, con Motivo de la Fundación de la Iglesia Ortodoxa Católica Apostólica Mexicana" (15 Sep. 1925); "Glosario Religioso" (1 Nov., 15 Dec., 1926, 1 Feb. 1927); "Nuestros Trabajos Religiosos en Tapachula, Chiapas" (1 Dec. 1926); "La Iglesia Mexicana en Diferentes Partes del País" (1 Oct. 1927).
80. AGN/DGG, 2.340.28.29, Ramírez, Tapachula, 24 Jan. 1927; PGR, Mexico City, 9 Mar. 1927. Simona R. de Martínez, Tapachula, 31 Jan. 1931. *Restauración*, 1 May 1927, "La Semana Mayor en Nuestros Templos."
81. *Restauración*, "La Iglesia Ortodoxa Triunfante en el Estado de Chiapas" (15 Oct. 1926), "Un Notable Bautizo" (15 Mar. 1927), "Un Rebautizo y un Acto de Barbarie Romanista" (15 Nov. 1925), "Glosario Religioso" (15 Nov. 1926). AGN/DGG, 2.340.28.29, Gobierno, Tuxtla Gutiérrez, 2 Jul. 1927; Alejo Villareal, Mazatán, 16 Sep. 1930. AHAM, Provisorato, c. 124/exp. 4, petitions, 1929, from: Rosa, Carmen, Juana, Emilia, and Encarnación Santeliz, Tuxtla Chico, n/d; Marcelo Velázquez, Talquián, 20 Apr.; Natividad de León, San Fernando, n/d.
82. AGN/DGG, 2.340.29.1, letters, Tapachula, 1932, from, Lorenzo Bravo, 23 Mar.; Vicente López, 20 Apr. Nolan-Ferrell, *Constructing Citizenship*, 43–45, 75–96.
83. AGN/DGG, 2.340.30.16, Tapachula, 1935: Vidal Becerra, 24 Dec.; acta, "Congregación Católica Apostólica Mexicana," 5 Dec.

CHAPTER SIX
1. SD 812.404.1040, "The Religious Crisis in Mexico," 18 Sep. 1926, 18–21.
2. AGN/DGG: "Edicto Diocesano," 12 Oct. 1929 (2.340.61.18); Ignacio Merino Burgos, Tuxtla Gutiérrez, 27 Sep. 1929 (2.340.83.30); Arturo Huguet, Olutla, 18 Nov. 1929 (2.340.83.12); A. de Cuenca, Mexico City, 1 Jun. 1932 (2.340.29.1). AICAM, Enrique Lomarroy Flores, Jaltipan, 15 Oct. 1929. AHAM/DB, c. 60/exp. 46, *La Razón*, 1928, "El Cisma Callista . . ." (7 Sep.), "La Fiereza del Cisma Callista" (14 Oct.), "Los Léperos del Cisma" (25 Nov.). AMPV, 103.735.7621, *Revista Católica*, 2 Dec. 1928, "Escándalo en una Iglesia Cismática Mexicana." CEHM, 1926, "Católicos: Alerta" (clxxxii.4.362), "¡Alerta! ¡No Os Dejéis Engañar!" (clxxxii.2.132).
3. SD 812.404.1040, "Religious Crisis," 3–4.
4. Scott, *Domination and the Arts of Resistance*.

5. Meyer, *Cristiada*, 2:287.
6. Butler and Powell, "Father, Where Art Thou?"
7. 60 percent of French *curés* took the 1791 constitutional oath; 70 percent of Russian Orthodox parishes pledged themselves to the Bolsheviks' Renovationist Church. Byrnes, *Priests of the French Revolution*, xiii, 259. Roslof, *Red Priests*, 125. Menegus and Aguirre, *Los indios, el sacerdocio*, 117–39.
8. SD 812.404.1040, "Religious Crisis," 19.
9. Meyer, *Samuel Ruiz*.
10. Byrne, *Priests of the French Revolution*, xvi.
11. *Gaceta Oficial del Arzobispado de México*, 23, no. 4, 15 Apr. 1925, "El Pretendido Cisma: Juicio contra los Asaltantes." Meyer, *Cristiada*, 2:195. Guadarrama Gómez, *Notas eclesiásticas*, 275.
12. Morones, *Capítulos sueltos*, 64–72.
13. APEC, 49.105.3294, José Melgosa to López y Sierra, Mexico City, 7 Jul. 1929. *Excélsior*, 13 Mar. 1925, "El Ejército de Salvación No Apoya al Patriarca." AGN/OC, 438-M-6, "Los Protestantes y el Movimiento Cismático: Declaraciones al Público," 12 Mar. 1925.
14. *Alcance al No. 61 de Restauración*, 1 May 1928, "Personal Eclesiástico." *El Amigo de la Verdad*, 19 May 1925, "El Primer Concilio Cismático." Hurtado (*Cisma mexicano*, 22–75), counts 20 priests, Meyer, 12 (*Cristiada*, 2:151), and Ramírez Rancaño, 65 (*Patriarca Pérez*, 220–22).
15. RC = Roman Catholic (incl. minor) orders; MC = Mexican Catholic; P = Protestant (Episcopalian). Presumptively Mexican orders = *MC*. I make no judgment concerning orders' validity. Sources: AICAM, AHAO, ADAM, FPEC; AHAM Cisma ("Cismáticos," exp. s/n), AHAM/MDR ("Lista de los Sacerdotes Cismáticos . . . ," 31 Jul. 1929, exp. s/n; c. 31/exp. 27, c. 43/exps. 43, 73, c. 72/exp. 19, c. 197/exp. 45), AHAM/DB ("Lista de los Sacerdotes que se han registrado como Sacerdotes Católicos Apostólicos Mexicanos y cuyo registro consta en el Registro General de Sacerdotes," Mexico City, 31 Jul. 1929, exp. s/n; c. 2/exp. 49, c. 3/exp. 73, c. 60/exp. 46, c. 61/exp. 9, c. 61/exp. 12, c. 63/exp. 97, c. 65/exp. 15); AHAM/MDM (c. 67/exp. 121). AGN/DGG, Gobierno, 2.340, exps. 30.2, 41.2, 49.85, 49.89, 50.1, 50.8, 50.17, 51.10, 52.32, 61.16, 61.19, 61.32, 61.33, 61.34, 66.10, 66.11, 66.40, 66.49, 67.1, 67.3, 67.4, 67.13, 80.3, 81.10, 81.2/6, 81.14, 82.14, 83.12, and 2.343.12.4. AGN/IPS, c. 6/exp. 17; *Restauración*, 1925–1932; *El Amigo de la Verdad*, 1925; *El Globo*, 1925; *El Universal*, 1925; *Excélsior*, 1925; *La Opinión*, 1928; *La Buena Lid*, 1925–1927; Hurtado, *Cisma mexicano*; Ramírez, *Patriarca Pérez*; Schulz, *History*; Bastian, *Disidentes*; Méndez, *Anticlericalismo*. Interviews, Mexico City: F. Antonio Celis, Mar. 2006–Jun. 2007; Bishop Carlos Touché-Porter, Jun. 2007; Bishop Martiniano García, Jun. 2007.
16. AHAM/MDR, Jacobo y Calvo, Mexico City, 31 Jul., 27 Sep. 1926 (c. 32/exp. 59); *La Controversia*, Mexico City, 27 Sep. 1926 (c. 91/exp. 74). Sánchez, *Episodios eclesiásticos*, 476–79.
17. ADAM, *La Buena Lid* 2, no. 46, Nov. 1925, "El Padre Rivera." AGN/DGG: José Velasco, Concepción Pápalo, 6 Oct. 1926 (2.340.61.16); Maximiano Amador, Pochutla, 14 Oct. 1928 (2.340.61.34); Genaro Vázquez, Oaxaca, 11 Aug. 1926 (2.340.61.32).
18. *Restauración*, "Carta Abierta . . . ," 18 Feb. and 1 Mar. 1927.
19. AHAM/MDR, c. 147/exp. 31, Guízar to Mora and Agustín de la Cueva, Orizaba, 19, 15 Aug. 1926; Obispos, Veracruz, "Habla el Señor Obispo de Veracruz a los

Católicos de la Parroquia de Jalancingo," Altotonga, 10 Aug. 1926. *Restauración*, 1 Sep. 1926, "El Obispo de Veracruz y la Actitud del Sacerdote D. Rafael Morfín." Byrnes, *Priests of the French Revolution*, 65 (Jansenism).

20. AGN/DGG: mayor, Zacualpan, 31 Aug. 1926 (2.340.49.83); Urbano Gómez, Motozintla, 4 Nov. 1931 (2.340.30.2)."
21. *El Globo*, 1 Mar. 1925, "Presbíteros Episcopales Se Unen a la Nueva Iglesia." AGN/DGG, 2.340.49.85, Carrión, Tecámac, 30 Aug. 1926. Bastian, *Disidentes*, 336.
22. Spicer, *Hitler's Priests*, 239.
23. O'Dogherty, "Ascenso de una jerarquía," 179–98. Ramírez Mercado, *Seminario de Guadalajara*.
24. Treviño, *Frente al ideal*, 48. Macías, *Vida*, 44–69, 80, 305. Hurtado, *Cisma mexicano*, 42. AHAM, Cisma, López y Sierra to Mójica, San Antonio, 20 Jun. 1930.
25. AGN/DGG, 2.340.99.12, Gobierno del D.F., Mexico City, 14 Feb., 26 Sep. 1927. AHAM, Cisma, Pedro Benavides to Pablo Puigserver, Mexico City, s/f; Mora y del Río, c. 148/exp. 92, press release, Mexico City, s/f. ADAM, *La Buena Lid* 1, no. 4, 15 Jun. 1919, "Gratas Visitas," and 3, no. 18, Aug.–Sep. 1928, "Un Obispo de la Iglesia Ortodoxa Católica Mexicana."
26. AGN/DGG, 2.340.105.17, agente #2, Mexico City, 2 Jun. 1931; AGN/IPS, c. 6/exp. 17, agents #1 and #15 to Depto. Confidencial, Mexico City, 5 Mar. 1925. AICAM, Valdéz to Pérez, Mexico City, 15 Nov. 1928; "Nota," 16 Nov. 1928. AHAM, Cisma, López y Sierra to Mójica, San Antonio, 20 Jun. 1930; Benavides to Puigserver, Mexico City, s/f. *Restauración*, 18 Oct. 1932, "Juan Crisóstomo Primero, Patriarca Arzobispo de la Santa Iglesia Ortodoxa Católica Mexicana."
27. AGN/DGG, agente #2, Mexico City, 2 Jun. 1931 (2.340.105.17); mayor, Tapachula, 28 Dec. 1926 (2.340.29.2). Hurtado, *Cisma mexicano*, 37–41. AHAM, Provisorato, c. 124/exp. 3, López Valdéz to Pérez, Los Angeles, 11 Jul. 1929.
28. AHAM, Provisorato, c. 124/exp. 2, López Valdéz to Pérez, Los Angeles, 17 May 1929.
29. ADAM, *La Buena Lid* 2, nos. 24 (Nov. 1923, "Mi '*Alma Mater*'") and 37 (Jan. 1925, "Nuestro Compañero Gómez"). AHAM, Díaz Barreto, c. 63/exp. 99, "Algunos Datos sobre el Pseudo-Obispo Eleuterio Benigno G. Ruvalcaba," 24 Sep. 1930.
30. AEC, Board of Missions and National Council, "GÓMEZ, Mr. Benigno R.," 1914–1925; "Foreign, Mexico. Subject: Transfer of Salary of M. F. Rueda, Item 21, Schedule 1913–1914, to Benigno Gómez R." (3 Feb. 1914); "Advancement to Priesthood of Rev. Benigno Gómez R." (17 May 1921); "Estimate from Mexico District for the Fiscal Year from January 1, 1921 to December 31, 1921"; "Estimate from Mexico District for the Fiscal Year from January 1, 1922 to December 31, 1922"; "Medical Expenses for the Rev. B. Gómez R.," 22 Nov., 14 Dec. 1920. ADAM, *La Buena Lid* 2, no. 37, Jan. 1925, "Fiesta de Navidad en Tecalco, Estado de México."
31. AEC, "The Domestic and Foreign Missionary Society of the Protestant Episcopal Church in the United States of America. Original Minutes, Meeting of the National Council, October 6, 1925"; "Latin America, Mexico. Subject: Resignation of the Rev. Benigio [sic] Gómez R.," 3 Jul. 1925; *Journal of the General Convention of the Protestant Episcopal Church in the United States of America. Held in the City of New Orleans from October Seventeenth to October Twenty-Fourth, Inclusive, in the Year of Our Lord 1925* (New York: Abott Press, 1926), 59–60.

32. AGN/DGG, 2.340.101.2, *oficial mayor*, Mexico City, 7 Sep. 1929; Vicente Gutiérrez, Mexico City, 10 Aug. 1929. *El Amigo de la Verdad*, 9 Mar. 1925. ADAM, *La Buena Lid* 1, no. 3, 15 May 1919 ("La Convención en Nopala, Hgo.") and 1, no. 20, Nov. 1920 ("Sermón Bacalario Predicado en 'San José de Gracia,' México, en la Clausura del Año Escolar, 7 de noviembre de 1920. Por el Diac. B. R. Gómez").
33. ADAM, *La Buena Lid* 1, no. 4, 15 Jun. 1919 ("Las Facultades en la Vida Religiosa"). On sentiment, see the Christmas and Easter reveries: *La Buena Lid* 1, no. 10, 15 Dec. 1919 ("Visiones Sagradas"); 1, no. 23, Apr. 1921 ("Semana Santa: Diario Sagrado"); and 2, no. 38, Feb. 1925 ("Miserere").
34. ADAM, *La Buena Lid* 1, no. 27, Aug. 1921, "La Educación de los Futuros Ministros"; 2, no. 2, Dec. 1921, "¡Tengo Hambre!"
35. ADAM, *La Buena Lid* 2, nos. 4, Feb. 1922 ("La Santa Unción"), 33, Sep. 1924 ("Sermón sobre el Matrimonio Cristiano"), 35–7, Nov. 1924–Jan. 1925 ("Las Aclamaciones e Invocaciones Litúrgicas," parts i–iii, "Tolerancia").
36. Sedena, Cancelados, 662.D-111.4–7802, boleta, 11 Jan. 1917 (f. 6); Siurob to Juan Sánchez, Querétaro, 9 Dec. 1916 (f. 24); Valdéz to Cuerpo de Defensores de Oficio de Justicia Militar, Mexico City, 27 Nov. 1916 (f. 29); "Determinación," 12 Jul. 1918 (ff. 39–42). AICAM, Siurob to Enrique Colunga, Mexico City, 18 Sep. 1920.
37. AICAM, Valdéz, Mexico City, 16 May 1929, 3 Jan. 1932; Gobernación, Mexico City, 20 May 1929; López y Sierra to Valdéz, Mexico City, 9 Apr., 21 Apr., 6 Jun., 11 Aug. 1927.
38. AICAM, Pérez to Valdéz, Corpus Christi, 17 Oct. 1929; comité ejecutivo, Cebanco, 20 Sep. 1943. Valdéz to Gobernación, Mexico City, 26 Aug. 1954; reply, 19 Oct. 1954; acta, Mexico City, 22 Jan. 1953; cuadrante parroquia, Mexico City, 29 May 1953.
39. AGN/DGG, 2.340.105.17, Monte de Honor, Mexico City, 2, 16 Dec. 1929; José Lara Camarena, Mexico City, 16 Dec. 1929; agente #2, Mexico City, 2 Jun. 1931. AHAM, Provisorato, c. 124/exp. 2, Monte de Honor to ICAM, Mexico City, 1 Aug. 1930. Ramírez Rancaño, *Patriarca Pérez*, 271–78, 380–83. AICAM, declaration, Monte de Honor, D.F., 19 Feb. 1984. On his naturalization, revoked during the arreglos, *Diario Oficial*, 14 Sep. 1929. Priest Jorge Higinio Hank was a carbon copy: purported German émigré, veteran, Old Catholic priest, etc. His real distinction, apparently, was as biological father of PRI *capo de tutti capo* Carlos Hank González (Ramírez Rancaño, *Patriarca Pérez*, 278–94, 329–31; Hurtado, *Cisma mexicano*, 64–65).
40. AHAM, Provisorato, c. 124/exp. 2, Monte de Honor to ICAM, Mexico City, 1 Aug. 1930. Ramírez Rancaño, *Patriarca Pérez*, 335–61. Hurtado, *Cisma mexicano*, 50–61. Camargo Melo, *América, No Debe Importar*, 753–57. García, "Apuntamientos," 423–24; https://familysearch.org/ark:/61903/1:1:23GG-4GX, 21 Sep. 1985; defunciones, Cuauhtémoc, D.F., Mexico, Archivo de Registro Civil de Distrito Federal; FHL microfilm 2,383,192.
41. AGN/DGG, José Mijares Palencia, Puebla, 29 Dec. 1922 (2.340.68.19); AGN/DGG, acta, Xochistlán, 14 Oct. 1927 (2.340.66.49); Ricardo González, El Oro, 31 Aug. 1928 (2.340.50.14); José de Jesús Gómez, Tlaola, 31 Dec. 1930 (2.340.67.4). AHAM, Cisma, "Cismáticos," s/f, and Pedro Benavides to Pablo Puigserver, Mexico City, Sep. 1931; AHAM/MDR, c. 191, *Libro de asuntos comunes*, 1919; AHAM/DB, c. 63/exp. 101, report for Puigserver, Sep. 1931; Hurtado, *Cisma mexicano*, 75.

Notes to Pages 188–192

42. AGN/DGG, Francisco Durán, Mexico City, 18 May 1929 (2.340.104.27), Tlaola, 5 Aug. 1929 (2.340.67.4); Depto. del DDF, Mexico City, 8 Apr. 1929 (2.340.104.21); Antonio Muníve, Acatzingo, 3 Feb. 1930 (2.340.67.1); Tejeda, Xalapa, 16 Jan. 1929 (2.340.83.2); acta, Ixtepec, 24 Sep. 1926 (2.340.61.18); civil junta, Jaltipan, 26 Aug. 1927 (2.340.82.16); Adolfo Briones, Acayucan, 11 Apr. 1930 (2.340.83.12); Alfredo Arredondo López, Coyoacán, 9 Feb. 1927 (2.340.66.10).
43. AGN/DGG, Pedro Infante, Mexico City, 14 Feb. 1927 (2.340.66.11); municipality of Hueypoxtla, 6 Oct. 1926 (2.340.49.89); DDF Oficial Mayor, Mexico City, 20 Mar. 1929 (2.340.104.4). AICAM, José Reyes to Gobernación, Tacuba, 4 Jan. 1932. Hurtado, *Cisma mexicano*, 62–63.
44. AHAM/MDR, c. 114/exp. 35, hoja de servicios, Mexico City, 30 Oct. 1913; Aguilera Robles, Mexico City, 10 May 1919. AICAM, "Nos, el Dr. D. Martín Tritschler, por la gracia de Dios y de la Sta. Sede Apostólica Arzobispo de Yucatán, por sí y a nombre del Ilmo. Obispo Dr. D. Carlos de Jesús Mejía, al Ilmo. y Rmo. Sr. Dr. y Maestro D. José Mora y del Río, Digmo. Arzobispo de México, Salud y Paz en Nuestro Señor Jesucristo," Mérida, 22 Mar. 1923; Carrillo y Ancona, Mérida, 11 Sep. 1896.
45. AHAM/MDR, c. 13/exp. 6, Aguilera to Mora, Mexico City, 9 May, 10 Jun., 1924, and Benavides, Mexico City, 8 May 1924; "Aguilera, Francisco, Sr. Pbro. Sobre que Se Averigüen los Antecedentes de la Pena de Suspensión que en su contra Se Ha Fulminado," 14 Jun. 1924; Cisma, Pérez to Aguilera, Mexico City, 3 Mar. 1925; AHAM/DB, c. 28/exp. 17, *licencias*, 4 May 1926, 7 May 1928, 6 May 1930; Aguilera to curia, Mexico City, 4 May 1932.
46. AICAM, Melgosa to Valdéz, Mexico City, 28 Oct. 1929. Ríos, *Siglo*, 123.
47. Condumex, clxxxii.4.322, *El Fuego*, 16 Oct. 1926, "Antes que Romano, Declara Ser Mexicano." AGN/DGG, 2.340.61.18, Fernández, Ixtepec, 15 Oct. 1927; Juchitán, 11 Dec. 1927, 17, 28 Jul. 1929.
48. AHAM/MDR, Veracruz, "Habla el Señor Obispo de Veracruz a los Católicos de la Parroquia de Jalancingo," 10 Aug. 1926; AHAM/DB, c. 1, Rafael Guízar to Díaz, 5 Oct. 1929. APEC, 010702.19.12321, *El Dictamen*, 3 Aug. 1926, "El Cura de Alvarado Dimás Anguiano Protesta su Adhesión a la Política del P. Calles en el Asunto Religioso."
49. AHAM, Provisorato, c. 124/exp. 2, de la Peña to López y Sierra, Tlacotepec, 7 Apr. 1929; José Varela to Pérez, San Simón de Bravo, 3 Jan. 1929.
50. AHAM, Provisorato, c. 124/exp. 3, Lazarini to Pérez, Mexico City, 9 Mar. 1929; AHAM/DB, c. 64/exp. 15, Pérez to Lazarini, Mexico City, 12 Jun., 22, 29 Aug. 1929. AICAM, Varela to ICAM, San Simón de Bravo, 21 Oct. 1929; Lazarini to Ruiz y Flores, Mexico City, 20 Jun. 1930. Dávila to Lazarini, Mexico City, 10 Oct. 1932; Francisco Carbajal to Lazarini, Toluca, 26 Oct. 1932.
51. Hurtado, *Cisma mexicano*, 75–6.
52. AGN/DGG, 2.340.51.10, Aniceto Trujillo, Mexico City, 24 Sep. 1932. FPEC, 12.010086.37.617, E. Balmoreji to Genaro Méndez, Puerto México, 4 Nov. 1932. Hurtado, *Cisma mexicano*, 44–48.
53. AHAM, Provisorato, c. 124/exp. 2, Alarcón to ICAM, Puebla, 16 Jan. 1931. AICAM, Alarcón to Valdéz, San Simón de Bravo, 22 Oct. 1933. SD 812.404–270, C. Van H. Engert, San Salvador, 23 Sep. 1925. Hurtado, *Cisma mexicano*, 74–75.
54. AGN/DGG, Ricardo González, El Oro, 31 Aug., 3 Oct.1928 (2.340.50.14); municipal president, Yehualtepec, 10 Aug. 1928 (2.340.66.35). AHAM/DB, c. 61/exp. 9, "Comité de Damas Católicas," Acayucan, 12 Aug. 1929; c. 12/exp. 49,

"Ricardo V. González, Sr. Pbro. Abjuración que hace, *ad cautelam*, de los errores en que había incurrido," 13 Jan. 1930; Provisorato, c. 124/exp. 2, Francisco Durán to Pérez, Tlaola, 25 Jan. 1930.
55. AHAM/DB, c. 12/exp. 49, González to Pascual Díaz, Mexico City, 28 Dec. 1929. AGN/IPS, c. 292/exp. 13, González to Tejeda, Mexico City, n/d; Tejeda to José Ponce, Mexico City, 23 Feb. 1927; Ponce to Francisco Delgado, Guadalajara, 8 Mar. 1927.
56. AHAM/MDR: c. 112/exp. 27, service record, 30 Oct. 1913; c. 51/exp. 29, "Pbro. José Uribe, Demanda que sobre Devolución de Varios Objetos Pertenecientes a la Asociación del Sagrado Corazón de Jesús de la Vicaría de La Magdalena . . . ," 17 Oct. 1918. Letters, 1924: c. 72/exp. 19, curia to Uribe, Pachuca, 24 Mar.; Gabriel Arroyo to Uribe, Tulancingo, 26 Sep. 1924; letters to Mora, Mexico City, from Uribe, 20 Jun.; Luis G. Sepúlveda, 25 Jul., 30 Sep., 14, 27 Oct.; Apolinar Jorge, 24 Oct.; Pablo Ortiz, 9 Jun.; c. 86/exp. 26, Andrés Rodríguez, 4 Jul.; c. 117/exp. 121, Uribe, 14 Nov.
57. *Restauración*, "Nueva Admisión de un Sacerdote a la Iglesia Mexicana, quien Dirige a su Ex-Obispo la Siguiente Carta Abierta" (1 Oct. 1925), "Carta Abierta" (1 Nov. 1925).
58. AHAM/MDR, c. 72/exp. 19, letters to Mora, all Mexico City, from: Uribe, 27 May, 27 Jul. 1926; Luis Benítez, 28 May, 28 Jul. 1926; licenses, 28 Jul. 1926; Luis G. Sepúlveda, 14 Dec. 1937. Provisorato, c. 124/exp. 4, Uribe to Pérez, Mexico City, 21 Jan. 1926.
59. AHAM/DB, c. 63/exp. 97, Cano to Díaz, Mexico City, 18 Sep. 1935; Mora y del Río, c. 99/exp. 12, Rebollar to vicar general, Mexico City, 18 Jun. 1918; c. 43/exp. 73, "Nombramientos."
60. AHAMTY, Libro de Gobierno 20, 1914–1952, circulars 8 ("A los católicos del Arzobispado," 23 Feb. 1929, f. 230) and 3 (Mar. 1930, n/d, ff. 241–42). *Boletín Eclesiástico* VII, nos. 1–2 and 3–4, Mar.–Apr. 1929; VIII, no. 3, Mar. 1930. Correspondencia, 1932: Leopoldo Alejandro to Guadalupe Ortíz y López, Camarón, 8 Jul.; Antonio Rábago to Ortiz, Lampazos, 13 Jul.
61. AHAM/MDR, c. 31/exp. 27, Monge to Mora, Otumba, 12 Jan., 1 Feb., 22 Feb. 1912, and Mexico City, 5 Jan. 1912; to Rafael Favila Vargas, Mexico City, 11 Jul. 1911; Sebastián Fonseca to Mora, Zinacantepec, 21 Feb. 1910. Hurtado, *Cisma mexicano*, 36.
62. AHAM/MDR, c. 31/exp. 27, all 1912: Monge to Mora, Otumba, 9, 19 Feb.; Mexico City, 25 Sep., 25 Oct., 9, 12 Nov.; Morelia, 30 Nov.
63. All 1925: AGN/IPS, c. 6/exp. 17, agent #1 to Depto. Confidencial, Mexico City, 26 Feb., 5 Mar.; Calles to Valenzuela, 4 Mar. AGN/OC, 438-M-6, Magdalena Mercado to Calles, Coyoacán, 3 Mar. *El Globo*, 5 Mar. ("El Padre Monge Está Escondido Voluntariamente en Tacubaya: No Es Exacto que Lo Hayan Secuestrado los Romanos"), 7 Mar. ("El Secretario de la Iglesia Católica Cismática en los EEUU"). *El Demócrata*, 6 Mar., "El Paradero del Presbitero Monge Sigue en el Misterio." AHAM/MDR, c. 139/exp. 75, Plácido Angel to Mora, Lugo, 19 Jun.
64. Mójica, *Yo Pecador*.
65. ADAM, *La Buena Lid* 2, nos. 48, Dec. 1925 ("Un Eminente Orador Sagrado") and 49, Jan. 1926 ("Magnífico Sermón"). AHAM/MDR, c. 43/exp. 43, "Fórmula de la Abjuración, Profesión de Fé, y Absolución que ha de darse a los que habiendo caido en Herejía de Protestantismo u otras sectas, vuelven al seno de la Santa Madre Iglesia Católica," 9 Jul. 1926; and Mójica to Mora, Mexico City, 23 Jun.; c. 197/exp. 45, letters, all to curia, 1926, from: Mójica, Tlalpan, 5 Jul. and Tacubaya,

26 Oct.; Maximino Ruiz, n/d; Antonio Gómez, Mexico City, 6 Jul., and San Luis Potosí, 13 Jul.
66. AHAM/MDR, c. 43/exp. 43, Mójica to curia, Tacubaya, 15 Mar. 1927, Mexico City, 10 Dec. 1928; circular no. 26, 2 Jul. 1931; AHAM/DB, c. 61/exp. 12, Santibáñez to ICAM, Mexico City, 22 Aug. 1930; c. 24/exp. 11, Mójica to Díaz, Guadalupe Hidalgo, 24 Feb. 1931; AGN/DGG, 2.340.67.15, Pérez, Corpus Christi, 27 Nov. 1929.
67. AHAM, Provisorato, c. 124: Pedro Infante to ICAM, Coyotepec, 5 Feb. 1929 (exp. 1); Adolfo Briones to Pérez, Acayucan, 20 Jan. and 7 Feb. 1930 (exp. 2).
68. Hurtado, *Cisma mexicano*, 64. AICAM, Durán to ICAM, Santo Domingo, 7 Sep. 1928, Tlaola, 22 Aug. 1929; "Vicario Apostólico" to Agente Municipal, Coyutla, 6 Dec. 1928. AHAM/MDR, c. 43/exp. 73, "Nombramientos." AGN/DGG, 2.340.67.4, Durán to mayor, Tlaola, 5 Aug. 1929.
69. AGN/DGG, 2.340.67.4, Durán to Plácido Angeles, Papatlatla, 26 Aug. 1929, Tlaola, 22 Aug. 1930; and Gobernación, Tlaola, 12 Jul. 1930.
70. AHAM, Provisorato, c. 124: Varela to ICAM, Mecatlán, 29 Jul. 1930 (exp. 1), Zozocolco, 29 Aug. 1930 (exp. 2).
71. AHAM, Provisorato, c. 124: Torres to ICAM, Tlaola, 23 Jul. 1930; Juárez to ICAM, Zozocolco, 23 Jul. 1930 (exp. 2); Pérez to Gobernación, Mexico City, 6 Mar. 1930 (exp. 1).
72. AHAM, Provisorato, c. 124/exp. 1, Durán to ICAM, Tlaola, 29 Aug. 1930. AGN/DGG, 2.340.67.4, Catholics of Chicahuaxtla, 14 Nov. 1930. AICAM, edict, Coxquihuí, 2 Dec. 1933; Teodoro Juárez to J. de la Luz Coronado, Chicontepec, 22 Jan. 1938, Zacamixtla, 25 Apr. 1938.
73. AGN/DGG, 2.340.82.16, Muníve to Tejeda, Jaltipan, 17 Jan. 1929. AHAM, Provisorato, c. 124/exp. 1, Muníve to Pérez, Mexico City, 10 Oct. 1928, Panzacola, 25, 27 May, 16 Jun., 31 Jul. 1929, Jun. 6 1930, Jaltipan, 2 Mar., 1, 7, 20 Apr. 1929; Salas to ICAM, Yehualtepec, 9 Apr. 1930.
74. AHAM, Provisorato, c. 124/exp. 1, Salas (Yehualtepec, 1930) to municipio (26 Aug.), Muníve (1 Sep.), and ICAM (5 Sep.).
75. AHAM, Provisorato, c. 124/exp. 2, all 1930: Muníve to ICAM, Panzacola, 27 May, 14 Jul., and Portezuelo, 3, 20 Jul., 26 Sep.; José Enríquez to ICAM, Portezuelo, 22 Jul., 12 Sep., 7 Oct.; Eleuterio Santos to ICAM, Portezuelo, 11 Sep.; Gobernación to Muníve, Mexico City, 15 Aug.
76. AHAM, Provisorato, c. 124/exp. 2, José Varela to ICAM, Zozocolco, 19 Sep. 1930. AICAM, Mexico City, 1931, Valdéz to ICAM (21 Sep.), Francisco Torres, (30 May).
77. AGN/DGG, 2.340.83.12, Briones to Gobernación, Acayucan, 30 Sep. 1929, 11 Apr. 1930. AICAM, Enrique Lomarroy Flores to Pérez, Jaltipan, 15 Oct. 1929. AHAM, Provisorato, c. 124/exp. 3, Ricardo González to Pérez, Mexico City, n/d; Cisma, Elías Rojas Vargas to curia, Mexico City, 11 May 1937.
78. *Restauración*, 15 Dec. 1926, "Glosario Religioso." AHAM, Provisorato, c. 124/exp. 2, Pérez to Adolfo Briones, Mexico City, 3 Sep. 1929.
79. AHAM, Provisorato, c. 124/exp. 3, Ángel Herrera, Torreón, 14 Jul. and 1 Aug. 1929. Rodrigo Amadeo Sequeiros, Mexico City, n/d; Arturo Gómez, Mexico City, 18 Jul. 1925.
80. AHAM, Provisorato, c. 124/exp. 3, Ricardo González to Pérez, Acayucan, 5 Aug. 1929, Mexico City, n/d.
81. AICAM, López y Sierra to Valdéz, Mexico City, 6 Jun. 1927.

82. AHAM, Provisorato, c. 124/exp. 2, Teodoro Juárez to Adolfo Santibáñez, Zozocolco, 7 Jun. 1930.
83. AICAM, Luisa Reboulen to Pérez, Puerto México, 31 May 1929.
84. AICAM, Macario López to Valdéz, Mexico City, 1 Dec. 1926; Teódulo Alarcón to Valdéz, San Simón de Bravo, 22 Oct. 1933.
85. Corporales: altar linen on which the celebrant places the chalice and host.
86. AICAM, Valdéz to to López y Sierra, 6 Aug. 1928.
87. AHAM, Provisorato, c. 124: Fernández to Pérez, Coyotepec, 13, 18 Feb. 1930 (exps. 2, 3 respectively), 21 Dec. 1929 (exp. 4). AICAM, Gómez to ICAM, Tlaola, 5 Sep. 1931.
88. AHAM/DB, c. 3/exp. 73, "Celis, Jorge O.—Sobre su abjuración de los errores en que incurrió por haber pertenecido a la Iglesia Católica Mexicana, actuando como Sacerdote de la misma," 31 Oct. 1929.
89. APEC, 49.105.3294, José Melgosa to ICAM, Mexico City, 7 Jul. 1929. AHAM/DB, Provisorato, c. 124/exp. 1, letters to Pérez, 1930, from: Agustín Mójica, Tlaola, 23 Feb.; Manuel Salas, Yehualtepec, 10 Mar., 23 Apr.
90. AICAM, José Gómez to ICAM, Tlaola, 5 Sep. 1931. AHAM, Provisorato, c. 124/exp. 3, Luisa Reboulen to Pérez, Puerto México, 23 Jul. 1929, Patricio Cinta to Pérez, Santa Lucrecia, 7 May 1929. Isauro Flores to ICAM, San Simón de Bravo, 15 Mar. 1931.
91. AHAM, Provisorato, c. 124/exp. 2, Teodoro Juárez to ICAM, Zozocolco, 7 Jun. 1930.
92. AGN/DGG, 2.34082.16, Mexican Catholics to Portes Gil, Puerto México, 24 Sep. 1929.

CONCLUSION

1. Dormady, *Primitive Revolution*, 5.
2. Aguilera González, *Cardenal Miguel*, 209–11.
3. AHAM, Provisorato, c. 124, exps. 2–3: N. R. Fuentes to Pérez, Calexico, 28 Apr., 12 Feb. 1929. AICAM, López y Sierra to Valdéz, Mexico City, 14 Apr. 1928. *La Prensa*, 9 Oct. 1931, "El Patriarca Pérez *In Articulo Mortis* Volvió al Seno de la Iglesia Católica Apostólica Romana," "Se Retracta el Patriarca Pérez."
4. AHAM, Cisma, circular, Mexico City, 9 Oct. 1931. "*Mors Schismatici Sacerdotis Mexici*," *Memorabilia Societatis Iesu*, IV: 205, 31 Dec. 1931.
5. AHAM, Cisma, anon. to Pedro Benavides, Mexico City, 18 Jun. 1928.
6. AICAM, Pérez to Lupita Yepez, Mexico City, 8 Jun. 1931.
7. *El Universal*, 10 Oct. 1931, "Murió el Patriarca de la Iglesia Cismática."
8. *Diario Oficial*, 73, 14, 16 Jul. 1932. It now houses the capital's notarial archive.
9. APEC, 76.133.5901, Salvador Vieyra to Calles, Corpus Christi, 9 Oct. 1931.
10. AHAM/DB, c. 63/exp. 93, Amado Pardavé to Díaz, Mexico City, 7 Oct. 1931. "Notaría Pública Número 24 A Cargo de Federico Ignacio Velázquez —. Testimonio de la Escritura de Protocolización. El Señor Mariano Navarro ante el Juzgado Cuarto de lo Civil de Esta Capital. México, 23 de Diciembre de 1931."
11. Luke, 15:10. AHAM/DB, c. 63/exp. 101, Santibáñez to Díaz, Mexico City, 13 Apr. 1936; c. 61/exp. 12, absolution, Mexico City, 12 Sep. 1930; Cisma, Miter to Juan Buitrón, Mexico City, 26 Jun. 1937.
12. AHAM/MDM, c. 67/exp. 121, Fidel Ruben Mayorga Sánchez to Miranda, Tlanalapa, 5 Jun. 1960.

13. AGN, 2.343.27.20, Eleuterio Guzmán to Gobn., Tenancingo, 28 Dec. 1951. Nutini and Isaac, *Pueblos de habla Náhuatl*, 67–75.
14. AGN/IPS, 1989-B/2–1/57–75, IPS-9 to IPS, Mexico City, 18 May 1957. AHAM/MDM, c. 200/exp. 91, Eduardo Dávila to Humberto Moreno, Mexico City, 26 Apr. 1960.
15. AGN/IPS, 1989-B/2–1/57–75, IPS-9 to IPS, Mexico City, 18, 20 May 1957.
16. AGN/DGG, 2.343.10.21, Eduardo Dávila, Mexico City, 16 Mar. 1944; Jesús Merino Fernández, Mexico City, 13 Mar. 1945.
17. AHAM/MDM, c. 328/exp. 31, Guillermo Ledesma to curia, Huauchinango, 5 Nov. 1944.
18. AGN/DGG, 2.343, c. 28/exp. 45, Anastasio Jiménez, Tebanco, 10 Oct. 1943; Valdéz, Mexico City, 22 Oct. 1943. AGN/IPS, 89.9, P8–23 to IPS, Mexico City, 27 Jun. 1941. AICAM, Comité Ejecutivo, Tebanco, 20 Sep. 1943.
19. AGN/IPS, 428.16, "Investigación sobre el conflicto por la posesión del Templo Católico 'Margarita-Concepción' de Mazatán, Chis.," 7 Dec. 1965.
20. Rivera Farfán, García Aguilar, Lisbona Guillén, Sánchez Franco, and Meza, *Diversidad religiosa en Chiapas*, 65–73; López Meza, *Sistema religioso-político*; Meyer, *Samuel Ruiz*, 159–62; Rus, "Struggle against Indigenous Caciques."
21. Anon., *Testimonio de un sacerdote*, 31–36. See also introduction, note 48.
22. Navarrete, *San Pascualito Rey*, 15–52.
23. AGN/DGG, 2.343.12.4, Cortés Olmos, Mexico City, 16 Nov. 1962; "Nos, Hieronymus María . . . ," Mexico City, 15 Nov. 1962. AHAM/MDM, c. 306/exp. 38, Circular, 6 Aug. 1976. AHAM/Cancillería, c. 140/exp. 3, Jorge Durán Piñeyro, 7 Nov. 1979; José Candia Unda to Corripio Ahumada, Mexico City, 18 Oct. 1980.
24. AHAM/MDM, c. 233/exp. 6, "Notificación," 27 Feb. 1983; AHAM/Cancillería, c. 147/exp. 24, Camargo Melo to Corripio Ahumada, Mexico City, 4 Oct. 1978. *Una hostia sangrante en México Distrito Federal: lo que dijo la Mitra y hechos y pruebas científicas* (Mexico City, 1979); *Una hostia sangrante en México, D.F.: testimonios de hechos extraordinarios* (Mexico City, 1980).
25. Various, 1991: *Excélsior*, 25 Apr. ("Responsabilidad de Corripio, cualquier agresión en mi contra"), 19 Jun. ("Realizó el sacerdote José Camargo Melo diligencia de careo en sus denunciantes"); *El Universal*, 25 Apr. ("Camargo Melo dice que no abandonará su misión ni permitirá intervenciones"); *Uno Más Uno*, 25 Apr. ("Negó Camargo Melo culpas de amenazas y usurpación") and 26 Apr. ("Llamado de la Iglesia católica para no dejarse engañar por falsos sacerdotes"); *La Jornada*, 25 Apr. ("Liberan bajo fianza al sacerdote José Camargo Melo"), 26 Apr. ("Fue excomulgado hace nueve años el sacerdote acusado de despojo").
26. García Valencia, "Sistemas Normativos," 179. AHAM, s/n, Corripio Ahumada to Arturo Vélez Martínez, Mexico City, June 24, 1985. AHAM/MDM, c. 67/exp. 121, Ruben Mayorga to Miranda, Tlanalapa, 5 Jun. 1960.

BIBLIOGRAPHY

MEXICAN ARCHIVES

Ecclesiastical
Archivo de la Diócesis Anglicana de México (ADAM), Mexico City
Archivo de la Iglesia Católica Apostólica Mexicana (AICAM), Mexico City
Archivo Histórico de la Arquidiócesis de México (AHAM), Mexico City, Fondos:
    Cancillería/Provisorato
    Cisma
    Conflicto Religioso
    Episcopado Nacional
    Sacerdotes
    José Mora y del Río (MDR)
    Miguel Darío Miranda (MDM)
    Pascual Díaz y Barreto (DB)
    Pelagio Antonio Labastida y Dávalos (LD)
    Próspero María Alarcón y Sánchez (AS)
    Siglo XIX
Archivo Histórico de la Arquidiócesis de Morelia, Morelia (AAM)
Archivo Histórico de la Arquidiócesis de Oaxaca, Oaxaca (AHAO), Fondo:
    Diocesano, Gobierno, Autoridades Civiles
Archivo Histórico del Arzobispado de Monterrey, Monterrey (AHAMTY)
Archivo del Obispado de Tacámbaro (AOT)

State and Public
Archivo General de la Nación (AGN), Mexico City, Fondos:
    Dirección General de Gobierno (DGG)
    Investigaciones Políticas y Sociales (IPS)
    Particulares, Archivo Tomás Garrido Canabal (TGC)
    Presidentes, Ramo Emilio Portes Gil (EPG)
    Presidentes, Ramo Obregón-Calles (OC)
Archivo General Agrario (AGA), Mexico City
Archivo General del Estado de Veracruz (AGEV), Xalapa, Veracruz:
    Fondo Comisión Agraria Mixta
Archivo Histórico de la Secretaría de Educación Pública (AHSEP), Mexico City
Archivo Liga Nacional Defensora de la Libertad Religiosa (ALNDLR), Mexico City
Archivo Miguel Palomar y Vizcarra (AMPV), Mexico City
Archivo Plutarco Elías Calles (APEC), Mexico City

Private
Archivo Cristero, Centro de Estudios de Historia de México Fundación Carlos Slim,
    Mexico City
Biblioteca Palafoxiana, Puebla

Bibliography

INTERNATIONAL ARCHIVES
Archivio Apostolico Vaticano (AAV), Vatican City
  Archivio Visita Apostolica en Mexico
Department of State Records Regarding Internal Affairs of Mexico (SD), USA
Episcopal Church Archive, Austin, Texas
Nettie Lee Benson Latin American Collection (BLAC), Austin, Texas:
  El Heraldo Mexicano: Seminario Popular Independiente
  Herbert Gambrell Papers

NEWSPAPERS
Hemeroteca Nacional, Mexico City
  El Amigo de la Verdad
  CROM
  El Demócrata
  Excélsior
  El Globo
  El Monitor Republicano
  Omega
  La Prensa
  Restauración
  El Sol
  El Universal

PUBLISHED WORKS
Acevedo-Rodrigo, Ariadna. "Paying for Progress: School Taxes, Municipal Government, and Liberal State-Building, Cuetzalan and Huehuetla, Mexico, 1876–1930." *Hispanic American Historical Review* 99, no. 4 (2019): 649–80.
Achútegui, Pedro S. de, and Miguel A. Bernad. *Religious Revolution in the Philippines: The Life and Church of Gregorio Aglipay, 1860–1960*. 4 vols. Manila: Ateneo de Manila, 1961.
Aguilera González, Francisco María. *Cardenal Miguel Darío Miranda. El hombre, el cristiano, el obispo*. Mexico City: IMDOSOC, 2005.
Alfonseca Giner de los Ríos, Juan B. "El conflicto religioso en las escuelas rurales de Texcoco y Chalco, 1923–1933." *Secuencia* 94 (2016): 148–80.
Álvarez, Jesús. *Hábitos blancos sobre tierras de México*. Mexico City, 1948.
Andes, Stephen J. C. *The Vatican and Catholic Activism in Mexico and Chile: The Politics of Transnational Catholicism, 1920–1940*. Oxford: Oxford University Press, 2014.
Anon. *Estudio sobre el actual conflicto religioso por un obispo católico mexicano*. 3 vols. "En el destierro," 1928.
Anon. *Testimonio de un sacerdote sobre la Pasión de Cristo en Cuba*. Santiago: Departamento de Publicaciones del Secretariado de Difusión, 1962.
Anson, Peter. *Bishops at Large* Berkeley, CA: Apocryphile Press, 2006.
Appolis, Émile. "En Marge de la Séparation: les Associations Cultuelles Schismatiques," *Revue de l'Histoire de l'Église de France* 146 (1963): 47–88.
Ayorinde, Christine. *Afro-Cuban Religiosity, Revolution, and National Identity*. Gainesville: University of Florida Press, 2004.

Baldwin, Deborah. *Protestants and the Mexican Revolution: Missionaries, Ministers, and Social Change.* Urbana: University of Illinois Press, 1990.

Bantjes, Adrian. *As If Jesus Walked on Earth: Cardenismo, Sonora, and the Mexican Revolution.* Wilmington, DE: Scholarly Resources, 1998.

———. "Idolatry and Iconoclasm in Revolutionary Mexico: The Dechristianization Campaigns, 1929–1940." *Mexican Studies/Estudios Mexicanos* 13, no. 1 (1997): 87–120.

———. "Mexican Revolutionary Anticlericalism: Concepts and Typologies." *Americas* 65, no. 4 (2009): 467–80.

Barbosa Cano, Fabio. *La CROM de Luis N. Morones a Antonio J. Hernández.* Puebla: BUAP, 1980.

Barbosa Guzmán, Francisco. *La caja rural católica de préstamos y ahorros en Jalisco (1910–1914 y 1920–1924).* Mexico City: Instituto Mexicano de Doctrina Social Cristiana, 1996.

Barranco, Bernardo, and Roberto Blancarte. *AMLO y la religión: el Estado laico bajo amenaza.* Mexico City: Grijalbo, 2019.

Bastian, Jean-Pierre. *Los disidentes: sociedades protestantes y revolución social en México, 1872–1911.* Mexico City: El Colegio de México, 1989.

Beal, John P. "It's Déjà Vu All Over Again: Lay Trusteeism Rides Again," *Jurist* 68 (2008): 497–568.

Bernabéu Albert, Salvador. "El vacío habitado. Jesuitas reales y simulados en México durante los años de la supresión (1767–1816)." *Historia Mexicana* 58, no. 4 (2009): 1261–1303.

Blancarte, Roberto. "Laicidad y secularización en México." *Revista de Estudios Sociológicos* 19, no. 57 (2001): 843–55.

Blissett, Luther (pseud.). *Q.* London: Arrow, 2004.

Blumenkron, Daniel, and Luis Campomanes. *Puebla bajo el terror almazanista: el libro rojo de un mal gobierno.* Puebla, 1933.

Bower, Bethel. "Notes on Shamanism among the Tepehua Indians." *American Anthropologist* 48, no. 4 (1946): 680–83.

Boyer, Christopher. *Becoming Campesinos: Politics, Identity, and Agrarian Struggle in Postrevolutionary Michoacán, 1920–1935.* Stanford, CA: Stanford University Press, 2003.

Brading, David. *The First America: The Spanish Monarchy, Creole Patriots, and the Liberal State, 1492–1867.* Cambridge: Cambridge University Press, 1991.

Brandreth, Henry R. T. *Episcopi Vagantes and the Anglican Church.* London: SPCK, 1947.

Bravo Ugarte, José. *Diócesis y obispos de la Iglesia mexicana, 1519–1939.* Mexico City: Buena Prensa, 1941.

Brewster, Keith. *Militarism, Ethnicity, and Politics in the Sierra Norte de Puebla, 1917–1930.* Tucson: University of Arizona Press, 2003.

Buchenau, Jürgen. *Plutarco Elías Calles and the Mexican Revolution.* Lanham, MD: Rowman & Littlefield, 2007.

Buckles, Daniel, and Jacques Chevalier. "Ejido *versus* bienes comunales: historia política de Pajapan." In *Agraristas y agrarismo: la Liga de Comunidades Agrarias del Estado de Veracuz*, edited by Olivia Domínguez Pérez, 231–47. Xalapa: Gobierno del Estado de Veracruz, 1992.

Buford, Nick. "A Biography of Luis N. Morones, Mexican Labor and Political Leader." PhD diss., Louisiana State University, 1971.

Bibliography

Butler, Matthew. "Christ Stopped at Cementville: Mexican Revolutionary Catholicism in the U.S. Southwest, 1925–1935." In *Beyond Rome: The New Global Catholicism*, edited by Elizabeth Pritchard and Peter-Ben Smit, ms. in progress.

———. "God's *Campesinos*? Mexico's Revolutionary Church in the Countryside." *Bulletin of Latin American Research* 28, no. 2 (2009): 165–84.

———. "*Misa a la mexicana*: los ritos de la religión revolucionaria." In *México a la luz de sus revoluciones*, 2 vols., edited by Laura Rojas and Susan Deeds, 2:425–57. Mexico City: El Colegio de México, 2014.

———. "¿Nuevo capítulo revolucionario? Antonio de Jesús Paredes, el cabildo metropolitano, y el resurgimiento de un catolicismo 'constitucional' en la Arquidiócesis de México, 1914–1920." In *México católico: proyectos y trayectorias eclesiales mexicanos, siglos XIX y XX*, edited by Marta Eugenia García Ugarte, Pablo Serrano Álvarez, and Matthew Butler, 420–68. Mexico City: Universidad Intercultural del Estado de Hidalgo, Colegio de Hidalgo, Consejo Estatal para la Cultura y las Artes de Hidalgo, 2016.

———. *Popular Piety and Political Identity in Mexico's Cristero Rebellion: Michoacán, 1927–1929*. Oxford: Published for The British Academy by Oxford University Press, 2004.

———. "*Sotanas Rojinegras*: Catholic Anticlericalism and Mexico's Revolutionary Schism." *Americas* 65, no. 4 (2009): 531–54.

Butler, Matthew, and Kevin Powell. "Father, Where Art Thou? Catholic Priests and Mexico's 1929 *Relación de Sacerdotes*." *Hispanic American Historical Review* 98, no 4. (2018): 635–67.

Byrne, Julie. *The Other Catholics: Remaking America's Largest Religion*. New York: Columbia University Press, 2016.

Byrnes, Joseph. *Priests of the French Revolution: Saints and Renegades in a New Political Era*. University Park: Pennsylvania State University Press, 2014.

Camargo Melo, José. *América, No Debe Importar Más la Fe: Santa Iglesia Católica Apostólica Mexicana*. Mexico City, 1992.

Cannelli, Riccardo. *Nación católica y estado laico: el conflicto político-religioso en México desde la Independencia hasta la Revolución (1821–1914)*. Mexico City: INEHRM, 2012.

Cano Andaluz, Aurora. *La opinión pública sobre el régimen de Plutarco Elías Calles (1924–1928)*. Mexico City: UNAM, 2007.

———. *La gestión presidencial de Plutarco Elías Calles: bibliografía y notas para su estudio*. Mexico City: UNAM, 2006.

Cantor, Norman. *Church, Kingship, and Lay Investiture in England, 1089–1135*. Princeton, NJ: Princeton University Press, 1958.

Cárdenas Ayala, Elisa. *Roma: el descubrimiento de América*. Mexico City: El Colegio de México, 2018.

Carey, Patrick W. "John F. O. Fernández: Enlightened Lay Catholic Reformer, 1815–1820." *Review of Politics* 43, no. 1 (1981): 112–29.

———. "The Laity's Understanding of the Trustee System, 1785–1855." *Catholic Historical Review* 64, no. 3 (1978): 357–76.

———. *People, Priests, and Prelates: Ecclesiastical Democracy and the Tensions of Trusteeism*. Notre Dame, IN: University of Notre Dame Press, 1987.

———. "Republicanism within Catholicism, 1785–1860." *Journal of the Early Republic* 3, no. 4 (1983): 413–37.

———. "Voluntaryism: An Irish Catholic Tradition." *Church History* 48, no. 1 (1979): 49–62.

Carton de Grammont, Hubert. "Calles y el agrarismo mexicano a principios de los 30: organización gremial de los pequeños propietarios." *Caravelle: Cahiers du Monde Hispanique et Luso-brasilien* 56 (1991): 37–52.

Castellanos Suárez, José Alfredo. *Empeño por una expectativa agraria: experiencia ejidal en el municipio de Acolman, 1915–1940.* Mexico City: INEHRM, 1998.

Celis García, Antonio. *¡Aquí estamos resistiendo! Relación histórica y doctrinaria del surgimiento del movimiento religioso de la Iglesia Ortodoxa Católica Apostólica Mexicana, Iglesia de los mexicanos, por el obispo metropolitano Antonio Celis García.* Mexico City: Ediciones Janus, 2014.

Cervantes, Miguel de. *Don Quijote de la Mancha.* Mexico City: Real Academia Española, 2004.

Chance, John K., and William Taylor. "*Cofradías* and *Cargos*: An Historical Perspective on the Mesoamerican Civil-Religious Hierarchy." *American Ethnologist* 12, no. 1 (1985): 1–26.

Chauvet, Fidel de Jesús. *El culto a la Asunción de Nuestra Señora en México.* Mexico City: Editorial Fr. Junípero Serra, 1951.

Chowning, Margaret. "The Catholic Church and the Ladies of the Vela Perpetua: Gender and Devotional Change in Nineteenth-Century Mexico." *Past and Present* 221, no. 1 (2013): 197–237.

Christian, William. *Local Religion in Sixteenth-Century Spain.* Princeton, NJ: Princeton University Press, 1981.

Clark, Christopher, and Wolfram Kaiser, eds., *Culture Wars: Secular Catholic Conflict in Nineteenth-Century Europe.* Cambridge: Cambridge University Press, 2003.

Conde Tudanca, Rodrigo. "Un incidente olvidado del trienio adeco: la creación de la Iglesia Católica, Apostólica, Venezolana." *Boletín de la Academia Nacional de la Historia (Venezuela)* 77, no. 32 (1993): 87–117.

[Congreso Constituyente]. *Diario de los debates del Congreso Constituyente, Querétaro, 1916–1917.* 2 vols. Mexico City: Camara de Diputados, 1989. First published in 1922.

Connaughton, Brian. *Entre la voz de Dios y el llamado de la patria: religión, identidad, y ciudadanía en México, siglo XIX.* Mexico City: Fondo de Cultura Económica, 2010.

———. *Ideología y sociedad en Guadalajara (1788–1853).* Mexico City: Conaculta, 1992.

Coquet, Édouard. *Albert de Mun et la séparation de l'Église et de l'État, 1904–1907: «soldat vaincu d'un cause invincible.»* Paris: Cerf, 2019.

Correa, Eduardo. *Pascual Díaz, S.J.: el arzobispo mártir.* Mexico City: Minerva, 1945.

Corzo Ramírez, Ricardo. *El curato de Papantla: Corpus Christi y otros festejos, 1864–1868.* Veracruz: Instituto Veracruzano de Cultura, 1995.

———. *Nunca un desleal: Cándido Aguilar, 1889–1960.* Mexico City: El Colegio de México, 1986.

Covarrubias, Miguel. *Mexico South: The Isthmus of Tehuantepec.* New York: Knopf, 1946.

Cressy, David. *Bonfires and Bells: National Memory and the Protestant Calendar in Elizabethan and Stuart England.* Woodbridge, UK: Sutton, 2004.

Crewe, Ryan Dominic. *The Mexican Mission: Indigenous Reconstruction and Mendicant Enterprise in New Spain, 1521–1600.* Cambridge: Cambridge University Press, 2019.

Crook, Malcolm. "Citizen Bishops: Episcopal Elections in the French Revolution." *Historical Journal* 43, no. 4 (2000): 955–76.

Bibliography

Curley, Robert. *Citizens and Believers: Religion and Politics in Revolutionary Jalisco, 1900–1930*. Albuquerque: University of New Mexico Press, 2018.
De Fornaro, Carlo. *Díaz, Czar of Mexico: An Arraignment*. New York, 1909.
De Giuseppe, Massimo. *Messico 1900–1930: stato, Chiesa, y popoli indigeni*. Brescia, Italy: Morcelliana, 2007.
Dehouve, Danièle. "The 'Secession' of Villages in the Jurisdiction of Tlapa (Eighteenth Century)." In *The Indian Community of Colonial Mexico: Fifteen Essays on Land Tenure, Corporate Organization, Ideology, and Village Politics*, edited by Arij Ouweneel and Simon Miller, 162–82. Amsterdam: CEDLA, 1990.
Desan, Susan. *Reclaiming the Sacred: Lay Religion and Popular Politics in Revolutionary France*. Ithaca, NY: Cornell University Press, 1990.
Díaz Arciniega, Víctor. *Querella por la cultura "revolucionaria" (1925)*. Mexico City: Fondo de Cultura Económica, 2010. First published in 1985.
———. "Calles: el voluntarioso circunspecto." *Historia Mexicana* 34, no. 3 (1985): 460–505.
di Gioacchino, Massimo. "Ecclesiastical Participation of the Catholic Laity in the Late Modern Period: The Case of Italian Immigrants in the United States." *Catholic Historical Review* 106, no. 4 (2020): 625–53.
Domínguez Michael, Christopher. *Vida de Fray Servando*. Mexico City: Editorial Era, 2004.
Domínguez Pérez, Olivia, ed. *Agraristas y agrarismo: la Liga de Comunidades Agrarias del Estado de Veracuz*. Xalapa: Gobierno del Estado de Veracruz, 1992.
———. "Del sueño regional a la experiencia nacional: la Liga de Comunidades Agrarias del Estado de Veracruz." In *Agraristas y agrarismo: la Liga de Comunidades Agrarias del Estado de Veracuz*, edited by Olivia Domínguez Pérez, 19–37. Xalapa: Gobierno del Estado de Veracruz, 1992.
Dormady, Jason. *Primitive Revolution: Restorationist Religion and the Idea of the Mexican Revolution, 1940–1968*. Albuquerque: University of New Mexico Press, 2011.
Duffy, Eamon. *The Stripping of the Altars: Traditional Religion in England, 1400–1580*. New Haven, CT: Yale University Press, 1992.
Elías Calles, Alfredo. *Yo fui Plutarco Elías Calles: la versión jamás contada*. Mexico City: Santillana, 2011.
Elías Calles, Plutarco. *Méjico ante el mundo*. Barcelona: Editorial Cervantes, 1927.
Enríquez, Ignacio C. *The Religious Question in Mexico, by a Mexican Catholic, I. C. Enriques*. New York, 1915.
Esparza, Manuel. *Gillow durante el Porfiriato y la Revolución en Oaxaca (1887–1922)*. Oaxaca, 1985.
Falcón, Romana. *El agrarismo en Veracruz: la etapa radical (1928–1934)*. Mexico City: El Colegio de México, 1977.
Falcón, Romana, and Soledad García. *La semilla en el surco: Adalberto Tejeda y el radicalismo en Veracruz, 1883–1960*. Mexico City: El Colegio de México, 1986.
Fallaw, Ben. *Religion and State Formation in Postrevolutionary Mexico*. Durham, NC: Duke University Press, 2013.
———. "The Seduction of Revolution: Anticlerical Campaigns against Confession in Mexico, 1914–1935." *Journal of Latin American Studies* 45, no 1. (2013): 91–120.
———. "Varieties of Mexican Revolutionary Anticlericalism: Radicalism, Iconoclasm, and Otherwise, 1914–1935." *Americas* 65, no. 4 (2009): 481–509.

Bibliography

Flores, Jorge. *La revolución de Olarte en Papantla (1836–1838)*. Mexico City: Imprenta Mundial, 1938.
Florescano, Enrique. *La bandera mexicana: breve historia de su formación y simbolismo*. Mexico City: FCE, 1998.
Fonseca, Román. *La danza de los arrieros y morenos en Acayucan*. Acayucan: Dirección General de Culturas Populares/SEP, 1991.
Fowler Salamini, Heather. *Agrarian Radicalism in Veracruz, 1920–38*. Lincoln: University of Nebraska Press, 1978.
Friedlander, Judith. "The Secularization of the *Cargo* System: An Example from Postrevolutionary Central Mexico." *Latin American Research Review* 16, no. 2 (1981): 132–43.
Fujigaki Cruz, Esperanza, and Adriana Olvera López. "Ideas Agrarias y Cooperativismo Agrícola en los Años Veinte." In *Personajes, cuestión agraria, y revolución mexicana*, edited by Mónica Blanco and Esperanza Fujigaki, 199–253. Mexico City: INEHRM, 2004.
Gallop, Rodney. *Mexican Mosaic*. London: Faber &Faber, 1939.
Galush, William. "Trusteeism Revived: The Federation of Polish Catholic Laymen," *American Catholic Studies* 125, no. 2 (2014): 45–61.
Gamio, Manuel. *La población del Valle de Teotihuacán, representativa de las que habitan las regiones rurales del Distrito Federal, y de los estados de Hidalgo, Puebla, México, y Tlaxcala*. 2nd ed. 5 vols. Mexico City: Instituto Nacional Indigenista, 1979. First published in 1922.
García de León, Antonio. *Tierra adentro, mar en fuera: el puerto de Veracruz y su litoral a Sotavento, 1519–1821*. Mexico City: Fondo de Cultura Económica, 2011.
García Martínez, Bernardo. *Los pueblos de la sierra: el poder y el espacio entre los indios del norte de Puebla hasta 1700*. Mexico City: El Colegio de México, 1986.
García Valencia, Enrique Hugo. "Religión, política, y brujería." *Dimensión Antropológica* 13, no. 7 (2006): 151–80.
García Valencia, Enrique Hugo. "Sistemas Normativos y Nuevas Tendencias Religiosas en Veracruz." In *Los dioses, el evangelio, y el costumbre: ensayos de pluralidad religiosa en las regiones indígenas de México*, edited by Ella F. Quintal, Aída Castilleja, Elio Masferrer, 147–230. Mexico City: INAH, 2010.
Ginzberg, Eitan. "Formación de la infraestructura política para una reforma agraria radical: Adalberto Tejeda y la cuestión municipal en Veracruz, 1928–1932." *Historia Mexicana* 49, no. 4 (2000): 673–727.
———. "State Agrarianism versus Democratic Agrarianism: Adalberto Tejeda's Experiment in Veracruz, 1928–32." *Journal of Latin American Studies* 30, no. 2 (1998): 341–72.
Gómez Mont, María Teresa. *Manuel Gómez Morín, 1915–1939: la raíz y la simiente de un proyecto nacional*. Mexico City: FCE, 2008.
González de la Lama, Renée. "Los papeles de Días Manfort: una revuelta popular en Misantla (Veracruz), 1885–1886." *Historia Mexicana* 39, no 2 (1989): 475–521.
Gruzinski, Serge. "La 'segunda aculturación': el estado ilustrado y la religiosidad indígena en Nueva España (1775–1800)." *Estudios de Historia Novohispana* 8, no. 8 (1985): 175–201.
Guadarrama, Rocío. *Los sindicatos y la política en México: la CROM (1918–1928)*. Mexico City: Era, Mexico, 1981.

Bibliography

Guadarrama Gómez, Juan. *Notas eclesiásticas del estado de Guerrero*. Mexico City, 1992.
Guardino, Peter. *Peasants, Politics, and the Formation of Mexico's National State: Guerrero, 1800–1857*. Stanford, CA: Stanford University Press, 1996.
Gutiérrez García, Jesús. "Apuntamientos para la Historia del Cisma Mejicano." *Christus* 21 (1956): 419–24.
Hamnett, Brian. "Obstáculos a la política agraria del despotismo ilustrado." *Historia Mexicana* 20, no. 1 (1970): 55–75.
Heiras Rodríguez, Carlos Guadalupe. *San Pedro Tziltzacuapan: el año ritual en una comunidad tepehua*. Veracruz: Gobierno del Estado de Veracruz, 2014.
Hernández Enríquez, Gustavo Abel. *Historia Moderna de Puebla, 1925–1926: la contrarrevolución en Puebla*. Puebla, 1988.
Herrera Serna, Laura. "Plutarco Elías Calles y su Política Agraria." *Secuencia* 4 (1986), 42–65.
Howard, Thomas Albert. *The Pope and the Professor: Pius IX, Ignaz von Döllinger, and the Quandary of the Modern Age*. Oxford: Oxford University Press, 2017.
Hurtado, Arnulfo. *El cisma mexicano*. Mexico City: Buena Prensa, 1956.
Ibarra, Gabriela, and Hernán Gutiérrez, eds. *Plutarco Elías Calles y la prensa norteamericana, 1924–1929*. Mexico City: Miguel Ángel Porrúa, 1982.
Ichon, Alain. *La religión de los totonacos de la sierra*. Mexico City: Conaculta, 1990. First published in 1969.
James, William. *The Varieties of Religious Experience*. New York: Macmillan, 1961.
Jiménez Abollado, Francisco Luis. "Los cambios jurisdiccionales eclesiásticos en la Provincia de Tabasco durante el siglo XVI y principios del XVII." *Estudios de Historia Novohispana* 36 (2007): 83–99.
Jiménez Arce, Rogelio. "Reforma Agraria y Violencia Campesina en Catemaco, Veracruz (México), 1921–1958." *Anuario de Historia Regional y de las Fronteras* 20, no. 2 (2015): 71–99.
Joseph, Gilbert, and Daniel Nugent, eds. *Everyday Forms of State Formation: Revolution and The Negotiation of Rule in Modern Mexico*. Durham, NC: Duke University Press, 1994.
Johnson, Benjamin. *Pueblos within Pueblos: Tlaxilacalli Communities in Acolhuacan, Mexico, ca. 1272–1692*. Boulder: University of Colorado Press, 2017.
Johnson, Paul Christopher, Pamela Klassen, and Winnifred Fallers Sullivan. *Ekklesia: Three Enquiries into Church and State*. Chicago: University of Chicago Press, 2018.
Kelly, Isabel, and Angel Palerm. *The Tajin Totonac*. Pt. 1, *History, Subsistence, Shelter, and Technology*. Washington, DC: United States Government Printing Office, 1952.
Kertzer, David. *The Pope and Mussolini: The Secret History of Pius XI and the Rise of Fascism in Europe*. New York: Random House, 2015.
Kirshner, Alan. *Tomás Garrido Canabal y el movimiento de los Camisas Rojas*. Mexico City: SepSetentas, 1976.
Kloppe-Santamaría, Gema. *In the Vortex of Violence: Lynching, Extralegal Justice, and the State in Postrevolutionary Mexico*. Berkeley, CA: University of California Press, 2020.
Knight, Alan. "The Mentality and Modus Operandi of Mexican Revolutionary Anticlericalism." In *Faith and Impiety in Revolutionary Mexico*, edited by Matthew Butler, 21–58. New York: Palgrave, 2007.

———. *The Mexican Revolution*. 2 vols. Lincoln: University of Nebraska, 1990.
Kourí, Emilio. *A Pueblo Divided: Business, Property, and Community in Papantla, Mexico*. Stanford, CA: Stanford University Press, 2004.
Krauze, Enrique. *Caudillos culturales en la revolución mexicana*. Mexico City: Siglo XXI, 1985.
———. *Historia de la revolución mexicana, 1924–1928: la reconstrucción económica*. Mexico City: Colegio de México, 1977.
Lanz Duret, Miguel. "El Estado y la Iglesia: intervención de los poderes federales en materia de culto religioso." In *Derecho constitucional mexicano y consideraciones sobre la realidad política de nuestro regimen*, 389–99. Mexico City: Norgis Editores, 1959. Essay first published in 1931.
Larkin, Brian. *The Very Nature of God: Baroque Catholicism and Religious Reform in Bourbon Mexico City*. Albuquerque: University of New Mexico Press, 2010.
Larkin, Maurice. *Church and State after the Dreyfus Affair*. London: Macmillan, 1974.
Lavrín, Asunción. "Indian Brides of Christ: Creating New Spaces for Indigenous Women in New Spain." *Mexican Studies/Estudios Mexicanos* 15, no. 2 (1999): 225–60.
Lawrence, D. H. *The Plumed Serpent*. London: Penguin, 1995. First published in 1926.
León, Luis L. *Crónica del poder en los recuerdos de un político en el México revolucionario*. Mexico City: Fondo de Cultura Económica, 1987.
Léonard, Éric, and Emilia Velázquez. "El reparto agrario y el fraccionamiento de los territorios comunitarios en el Sotavento veracruzano: construcción local del Estado e impugnación del proyecto comunal." In *El istmo mexicano: una región inasequible. Estado, poderes locales, y dinámicas espaciales (siglos XVI–XXI)*, edited by Emilia Velázquez, Éric Léonard, Odile Hoffmann, and M.-F. Prévôt-Schapira, 399–454. Mexico City: CIESAS, 2009.
León Portilla, Miguel, and Patrick Johansson. *Ángel María Garibay K.: la rueda y el río*. Mexico City: UNAM, 2013.
Le Roy Ladurie, Emmanuel. *Carnival in Romans*. New York: George Braziller, 1979.
Levitt, Peggy. "Religion on the Move: Mapping Global Cultural Production and Consumption." In *Religion on the Edge: De-centering and Re-centering the Sociology of Religion*, edited by Courtney Bender, Wendy Cadge, Peggy Levitt, and David Smilde, 159–178. Oxford: Oxford University Press, 2013.
Leyva-Gutiérrez, Niria E. "Conflict and Imagery: Saint Michael and Ecclesiastical Power in New Spain." *Hispanic Research Journal* 15, no. 5 (2014): 422–44.
Lisbona Guillén, Miguel. *Persecución religiosa en Chiapas (1910–1940): Iglesia, estado, y feligresía en el periodo revolucionario*. Mexico City: UNAM, 2008.
———. "La Iglesia Católica Apostólica Mexicana en Chiapas, 1925–1934," *Relaciones* 30 (2009): 263–308.
Lockhart, James. *The Nahuas after the Conquest: A Social and Cultural History of the Indians of Central Mexico, Sixteenth through Eighteenth Centuries*. Stanford, CA: Stanford University Press, 1992.
Lombardo Toledano, Vicente. *Obra Histórica-Cronológica*. 9 vols. Mexico City: Centro de Estudios Filosóficos, Políticos, y Sociales "Vicente Lombardo Toledano," 1994.
López Caballero, Paola. *Indígenas de la nación: etnografía histórica de la alteridad en México (Milpa Alta, siglos XVII–XXI)*. Mexico City: Fondo de Cultura Económica, 2017.
López Meza, Antonio. *Sistema religioso-político y las expulsiones en Chamula*. Tuxtla Gutiérrez: Gobierno del Estado de Chiapas, 2002.

Bibliography

Loyola Díaz, Rafael. *La crisis Obregón-Calles y el estado mexicano*. Mexico City: Siglo XXI, 1980.
Lurtz, Casey Marina. *From the Grounds Up: Building an Export Economy in Southern Mexico*. Stanford, CA: Stanford University Press, 2019.
McCullagh, Francis. *Red Mexico*. London: Brentano's, 1928.
McIntyre, Kathleen. *Protestantism and State Formation in Postrevolutionary Oaxaca*. Albuquerque: University of New Mexico Press, 2019.
McNamara, Patrick. *Sons of the Sierra: Juárez, Díaz, and the People of Ixtlán, Oaxaca, 1880–1920*. Chapel Hill: University of North Carolina Press, 2007.
MacGregor Campuzano, Javier. "Un informe confidencial: las elecciones municipales de 1925," *Signos Históricos* 26 (2011): 154–79.
Macías Richard, Carlos, ed. *Plutarco Elías Calles: correspondencia personal (1919–1945)*. 2 vols. Mexico City: FCE, 1996.
———, ed. *Plutarco Elías Calles: pensamiento político y social. Antología (1913–1936)*. Mexico City: Fondo de Cultura Económica, 1991.
———. *Vida y temperamento: Plutarco Elías Calles, 1877–1920*. Mexico City: Fondo de Cultura Económica, 1995.
Mariani, Paul P. *Church Militant: Bishop Kung and Catholic Resistance in Communist Shanghai* Cambridge, MA: Harvard University Press, 2011.
Martí, José María. "La separación Iglesia-estado en Francia: precedentes y consecuencias." In *La autonomía de las entidades religiosas en el derecho*, edited by José María Martí and María del Mar Moreno, 121–65. Madrid: Dykinson, 2017.
Martínez Assad, Carlos. *El laboratorio de la revolución: el Tabasco garridista*. Mexico City: Siglo XXI, 1991.
Martínez Cedillo, Margarito. *La parroquia de Santiago Juxtlahuaca y sus templos*. Oaxaca: Carteles Editores, 2003.
Masferrer Kan, Elio. "Los factores étnicos en la rebelión de Olarte en Papantla (1836–1838)." *Cuicuilco* 14–15 (1984): 24–31.
———. "Los totonacos y sus relaciones con el clero católico (siglo XIX)." In eds. *El anticlericalismo en México*, edited by Franco Savarino and Andrea Mutolo, 399–415. Mexico City: Miguel Ángel Porrúa, 2008.
Mayeur, Jean-Marie. "Religion et Politique: Géographie de la Résistance aux Inventaires (Février-Mars 1906)." *Annales: Histoire, Sciences Sociales* 21, no. 6 (1966): 1259–72.
———. *La séparation de l'Église et de l'État (1905)*. Paris: Juillard, 1966. First published in 1905.
Medin, Tzvi. *El minimato presidencial: historia política del maximato (1928–1935)*. Mexico City: Era, 1982.
Medina Ruiz, Fernando. *Calles, un destino melancólico*. Mexico City: Jus, 1960).
Méndez Moreno, Carlos Domingo. *El anticlericalismo en Tabasco: entre prácticas, símbolos, y representaciones*. Morelia: UMSNH, 2016.
Méndez Reyes, Jesús. *Capitalizar el campo. Financiamiento y organización rural en México: los inicios del Banco Nacional de Crédito Agrícola*. Mexico City: El Colegio de México, 2017.
Mendoza García, Édgar. "Oposición al reparto agrario: los hacendados de Otumba y Teotihuacán, 1917–1930." *Contribuciones desde Coatepec* 19 (2010): 61–88.
Mendoza López Schwerdtfeger, Miguel *¡Tierra Libre!* Mexico City: Secretaría de Fomento, 1915.

Menegus, Margarita, and Rodolfo Aguirre. *Los indios, el sacerdocio, y la Universidad en Nueva España, siglos XVI–XVIII*. Mexico City: Plaza y Valdés, 2006.

Menéndez Rodríguez, Hernán. *Iglesia y poder: proyectos sociales, alianzas políticas y económicas en Yucatán, 1857–1917*. Mexico City: Conaculta, 1995.

Mereles de Ogarrio, Norma, ed. *Plutarco Elías Calles y Fernando Torreblanca: un ejemplo de la importancia de los archivos privados en la historiografía de México*. Mexico City: Miguel Ángel Porrúa, 2009.

Meyer, Jean. *La cristiada*. 3 vols. Mexico City: Siglo XXI, 1973–1974.

———. *Historia de la revolución mexicana, 1924–1928: estado y sociedad con Calles*. Mexico City: Colegio de México, 1977.

———. *Samuel Ruiz en San Cristóbal, 1960–2000*. Mexico City: Tusquets, 2000.

Miguélez Domínguez, Lorenzo, Sabino Alonso Morán, and Marcelino Cabreros de Anta. *Código de derecho canónico y legislación complementaria*. Madrid: Biblioteca de Autores Cristianos, 1951.

Miller, Kristin Cheasty. "Una Iglesia Más Mexicana: Catholics, Schismatics, and the Mexican Revolution in Texas." *U.S. Catholic Historian* 26, no. 4 (2008): 45–69.

Moctezuma, Aquiles P. *El conflicto religioso de 1926. Sus orígenes. Su desarrollo. Su solución*. 2 vols. Mexico City: Jus, 1960.

Mójica, José Francisco de Guadalupe. *Yo Pecador*. Mexico City: Jus, 1957.

Morones, Felipe. *Capítulos sueltos o apuntes sobre la persecución religiosa en Aguascalientes*. Aguascalientes, 1955.

Morris, Nathaniel. *Soldiers, Saints, and Shamans: Indigenous Communities and the Revolutionary State in the Gran Nayar, 1919–1940*. Tucson: University of Arizona Press, 2021.

Moss, C. B. *The Old Catholic Movement: Its Origins and History*. London: SPCK, 1964.

Muriel, Josefina. *Las indias caciques de Corpus Christi*. Mexico City: UNAM, 1963.

Navarrete, Carlos. *San Pascualito Rey y el culto a la muerte en Chiapas*. Mexico City: UNAM, 1982.

Neale, John. *A History of the So-Called Jansenist Church of Holland*. Berkeley, CA: Apocryphile Press, 2005.

Negrete, Martaelena. *Relaciones entre la Iglesia y el estado en México, 1930–1940*. Mexico City: Colegio de México, 1988.

Nolan-Ferrell, Catherine. *Constructing Citizenship: Transnational Workers and Revolution on the Mexico-Guatemalan Border, 1880–1950*. Tucson: University of Arizona Press, 2012.

Nutini, Hugo, and Barry Isaac. *Los pueblos de habla Náhuatl de la región Tlaxcala y Puebla*. Mexico City: Conaculta/INI, 1989.

Oakley, Francis. *The Conciliarist Tradition: Constitutionalism in the Catholic Church, 1300–1870*. Oxford: Oxford University Press, 2003.

O'Dogherty, Laura. "El ascenso de una jerarquía eclesial intransigente, 1890–1914." In *Historia de la Iglesia en el siglo XIX*, edited by Manuel Ramos Medina, 179–98. Mexico City: Condumex, 1998.

Ogaz Pierce, José Abel. "El pensamiento agrícola del joven Vicente Lombardo Toledano." In *Personajes, cuestión agraria, y revolución mexicana*, edited by Mónica Blanco and Esperanza Fujigaki, 311–43. Mexico City: INEHRM, 2004.

O'Hara, Matthew. *A Flock Divided: Race, Religion, and Politics in Mexico, 1749–1857*. Durham, NC: Duke University Press, 2009.

Olimón Nolasco, Manuel. *Paz a medias. El "modus vivendi" entre la Iglesia y el Estado y su crisis (1929–1931)*. Mexico City: IMDOSOC, 2008.

Ontiveros Valdés, Constanza. "Las andanzas de Santiago en la Nueva España y la imagen del indio: Santa María Chiconautla." *Ad Limina* 4, no. 4 (2013): 177–217.

Ortiz Petricioli, José. *El compañero Morones: biografía de un gran líder*. Mexico City: Costa- Amic, 1968.

Pachecho María, Martha, ed. *Religión y sociedad en México durante el siglo XX*. Mexico City: INEHRM, 2007.

Palacios, Guillermo. "Calles y la idea oficial de la Revolución Mexicana." *Historia Mexicana* 22, no. 3 (1973): 261–78.

Parsons, Wilfrid. *Mexican Martyrdom*. New York: Macmillan, 1936.

Peal, David. "Self-Help and the State: Rural Cooperatives in Imperial Germany." *Central European History* 21, no. 3 (1988): 244–66.

Peña Espinosa, Jesús Joel. "La Catedral Angelipolitana: sus Autoridades y Administradores durante el Conflicto Religioso, 1927–1929." In *Clérigos, políticos, y política: las relaciones Iglesia y estado en Puebla, siglos XIX y XX*, edited by Alicia Tecuanhuey Sandoval, 123–47. Puebla: BUAP, 2012.

Peñalosa, Joaquín Antonio. *Rafael Guízar a sus órdenes*. Xalapa: Ediciones Rafael Guízar y Valencia, 1995.

Pérez Cancio, Gregorio. *Libro de fábrica del templo parroquial de la Santa Cruz y Soledad de Nuestra Señora. Años de 1773–1784*. Mexico City: INAH, 1970.

Pérez Montfort, Ricardo. "La Iglesia Cismática de 1925, o las Pugnas del Nacionalismo." In *XIII Jornadas de Historia de Occidente. Religión, Iglesia, y Estado*, 217–32. Jiquilpan: CERMLC, 1990.

———. "La Iglesia Cismática Mexicana del Patriarca Joaquín Pérez." *Eslabones* 1 (1991): 105–12. Reprinted in In *A Dios lo que es de Dios*, edited by Carlos Martínez Assad, 379–94. Mexico City: Aguilar, 1994.

Peris, Daniel. *Storming the Heavens: The Soviet League of the Militant Godless*. Ithaca, NY: Cornell University Press, 1998.

Perkins, Stephen. "Macehuales and the Corporate Solution: Colonial Secessions in Nahua Central Mexico." *Mexican Studies/Estudios Mexicanos* 21, no. 2 (2005): 277–306.

Planchet, Régis. *El derecho canónico y el clero mexicano ó sea anotaciones al concilio V mexicano*. Mexico City, 1900.

Plummer, John. *Who Are the Independent Catholics?* Berkeley, CA: Apocryphile Press, 2006.

Poulat, Émile. *Scruter la loi de 1905: la République française et la religion*. Paris: Fayard, 2010.

Prüter, Karl, and J. Gordon Melton. *The Old Catholic Sourcebook*. New York: Garland, 1983.

Puente, Ramón. *Hombre de la revolución: Calles*. Mexico City: FCE, 1994. First published in 1933.

Purnell, Jennie. *Popular Movements and State Formation in Revolutionary Mexico: the Agraristas and Cristeros of Michoacán*. Durham: Duke University Press, 1999.

Quirk, Robert. *The Mexican Revolution and the Catholic Church, 1910–1929*. Bloomington: University of Indiana Press, 1973.

Ramírez González, Beatriz. *En la pobreza y en la riqueza: biografía de doña Natalia Chacón de Elías Calles, primera dama de 1924 a 1927*. Mexico City: Demac, 2008.

Bibliography

Ramírez Lavoignet, David. *El problema agrario en Acayucan*. Xalapa: Universidad Veracruzana, 1997.

Ramírez Mercado, José. *El seminario de Guadalajara y el liberalismo en Jalisco*. Guadalajara: Instituto Cultural Ignacio Dávila Garibi, 1999.

Ramírez Rancaño, Mario. *El patriarca Pérez: la Iglesia Católica Apostólica Mexicana*. Mexico City: UNAM, 2006.

———. "La Ruptura con el Vaticano: José Joaquín Pérez y la Iglesia Católica Apostólica Mexicana, 1925–1931." *Estudios de Historia Moderna y Contemporánea de México* 24 (2002): 103–42.

Ramírez Rodríguez, Rodolfo. *La querella por el pulque: auge y ocaso de una industria mexicana, 1890–1930*. Zamora: Colegio de Michoacán, 2018.

Ramos Torres, Rogelio Josué. "El México callista y la Italia fascista, sus relaciones," *Tzintzun* 64 (2016): 195–222.

Reck, Gregory. "Goodbye Ixoxolotl: Acculturation in a Mestizo-Indio Village in Mexico." PhD diss., Catholic University of America, 1972.

Regan, Joe. "Irish Catholics and the Marguillier Controversies of New Orleans, 1805–1844." *Catholic Historical Review* 105, no. 1 (2019): 91–115.

Retinger, J. H. *Morones of Mexico: A History of the Labour Movement in That Country*. London: Labour Publishing, 1926.

Revueltas, José. *El cuadrante de la Soledad*. Mexico City: Novaro, 1971. First published in 1953.

Reyes de la Maza, Luis. *Juan Xóchitl I (el pontífice mexicano)*. Mexico City: Ediciones de Ermitaño, 1999.

Ricard, Robert. *La conquista espiritual de México: ensayo sobre el apostolado y los métodos misioneros de las órdenes mendicantes en la Nueva España de 1523–1524 a 1572*. Mexico City: FCE, 2001.

Ríos Figueroa, Julio. *Siglo XX: muerte y resurección de la Iglesia católica en Chiapas. Dos estudios históricos*. Mexico City: UNAM, 2002.

Riva Palacio, Vicente. *Martín Garratuza*. 2 vols. Mexico City: Porrúa, 2005. First published in 1868.

Rivera Castro, José. *La clase obrera en la historia de México en la presidencia de Plutarco Elías Calles (1924–1928)*. Mexico City: Siglo XXI, 1983.

———. "Política Agraria, Organizaciones, Luchas, y Resistencias Campesinas entre 1920 y 1928." In *Historia de la cuestión agraria mexicana: modernización, lucha agraria, y poder político, 1920–1934*, edited by Enrique Montalvo Ortega, José Rivera Castro, and Óscar Betanzos Piñón, 21–149. Mexico City: Siglo XXI, 1988.

Rivera Farfán, Carolina, María del Carmen García Aguilar, Miguel Lisbona Guillén, Irene Sánchez Franco, and Salvador Meza. *Diversidad religiosa en Chiapas: intereses, utopías, y realidades*. Mexico City: CIESAS, 2011.

Rodríguez Iturbe, José. *Iglesia y Estado en Venezuela (1824–1964)*. Caracas: Universidad Central de Venezuela, 1968.

Romero, José Rubén. *La vida inútil de Pito Pérez*. Mexico City: Porrúa, 2007. First published in 1938.

Roslof, Edward. *Red Priests: Renovationism, Russian Orthodoxy, and Revolution, 1905–1946*. Bloomington: Indiana University Press, 2002.

Rugely, Terry. *Of Wonders and Wise Men: Religion and Popular Cultures in Southeast México, 1800–1876*. Austin: University of Texas Press, 2001.

Ruiz-Gálvez Priego, Estrella. "La conquista espiritual de México: Robert Ricard (1900–1983) y los comienzos del hispanismo americanista francés en su relación

con la crisis del modernismo teológico." *Investigaciones Históricas, época moderna y contemporánea* 39 (2019): 357–412.
Rus, Jan. "The Struggle against Indigenous Caciques in Highland Chiapas: Dissent, Religion, and Exile in Chamula, 1965–1977." In *Caciquismo in Twentieth-Century Mexico*, edited by Alan Knight and Wil Pansters, 169–200. London: Institute for the Study of the Americas, 2005.
Sálazar, Rosendo. *Líderes y sindicatos*. Mexico City: T. C. Modelo, 1953.
Saludes, Miguel. *Hilario Chaurrondo entre Iglesia y Revolucion. Apuntes de un sacerdote paúl español en Cuba*. Miami: Alexandria Library, 2014.
Sánchez, Pedro. *Episodios eclesiásticos de México (contribución a nuestra historia)*. Mexico City: Barrié, 1948.
Santoyo, Antonio. *La mano negra: poder regional y estado en México (Veracruz, 1928–1943)*. Mexico City: Conaculta, 1995.
Sanz-Cerrada, Antonio Ma. *Las catacumbas en Méjico o la tiranía bolchevique*. Los Angeles: Vincent Printing, 1926.
Schultz, Paul. *A History of the Apostolic Succession of Archbishop Emile F. Rodríguez-Fairfield from the Mexican National Catholic Church, Iglesia Ortodoxa Católica Apostólica Mexicana*. Glendale, 1985.
Scott, James. *Domination and the Arts of Resistance: Hidden Transcripts*. New Haven, CT: Yale University Press, 1992.
Sicilia, Javier. *Concepción Cabrera de Armida: la amante de Cristo*. Mexico City: Fondo de Cultura Económica, 2001.
Silva Herzog, Jesús. *El agrarismo mexicano y la reforma agraria: exposición y crítica*. Mexico City: FCE, 1959.
Simmons, Merle Edwin. *The Mexican Corrido as a Source for Interpretive Study of Modern Mexico, 1870–1950*. Bloomington: Indiana University Press, 1957.
Skerritt, David A. "El papel de Adalberto Tejeda en la cuestión agraria." *La Palabra y el Hombre* 32 (1979): 15–24.
Smith, Anthony D. *Chosen Peoples: Sacred Sources of National Identity*. Oxford: Oxford University Press, 2003.
Smith, Benjamin. *The Roots of Conservatism in Mexico: Catholicism, Society, and Politics in the Mixteca Baja, 1750–1963*. Albuquerque: University of New Mexico Press, 2012.
Solares, Ignacio. *El jefe máximo*. Mexico City: Alfaguara, 2011.
Spenser, Daniela. *En combate: la vida de Lombardo Toledano*. Mexico City: Debate, 2018.
Spicer, Kevin. *Hitler's Priests: Catholic Clergy and National Socialism*. DeKalb: Northern Illinois University Press, 2008.
Stewart, Charles. "Syncretism and Its Synonyms: Reflections on Cultural Mixture." *Diacritics* 29, no. 3 (1999): 40–62.
Strayer, Brian. *Suffering Saints: Jansenists and the Convulsionnaires in France, 1640–1799*. Brighton, UK: Sussex Academic Press, 2008.
Stresser-Péan, Guy. *The Sun God and the Savior: The Christianization of the Nahua and Totonac in the Sierra Norte de Puebla, Mexico*. Boulder: University Press of Colorado, 2009.
Tackett, Timothy. *Religion, Revolution, and Regional Culture in Eighteenth-Century France: The Ecclesiastical Oath of 1791*. Princeton, NJ: Princeton University Press, 1986.
Talanaz y Solórzano, Leticia, and Mariano Monterrosa Prado *Las devociones cristianas en México en el cambio del milenio*. Mexico City: INAH, 2002.

Bibliography

Taylor, William. *Magistrates of the Sacred: Priests and Parishioners in Eighteenth-Century Mexico*. Stanford: Stanford University Press, 1996.
Tecuanhuey Sandoval, Alicia. "Los hermanos Troncoso. La vocación de dos curas por reformar la Iglesia mexicana." In *Religión, política, e identidad en la Independencia de México*, edited by Brian Connaughton, 351–87. Mexico City: UAM/BUAP, 2010.
Theriault, Serge, Msgr. *René Vilatte: Community Organizer of Religion (1854–1929)*. Berkeley, CA: Apocryphile Press, 2006.
Thomson, Guy, with David LaFrance. *Patriotism, Politics, and Popular Liberalism in Nineteenth-Century Mexico: Juan Francisco Lucas and the Puebla Sierra*. Wilmington, DE: SR Books, 1999.
Torres Puig, Gabriel. "El falso sobrino del papa: un plan contra el obispo de Puebla durante la expulsión de los jesuitas." *Historia Mexicana* 65, no. 3 (2016): 987–1043.
Touché-Porter, Carlos. *A Short History of Anglican Worship in Mexico*. Mexico City, 1996.
Toussaint, Manuel. *La catedral de México y el Sagrario Metropolitano: su historia, su tesoro, su arte*. Mexico City: Porrúa, 1948.
Trejo, Evelia. *Los límites de un discurso: Lorenzo de Zavala, su 'Ensayo Histórico,' y la cuestión religiosa en México*. Mexico City: Fondo de Cultura Económica, 2001.
Treviño, Ricardo. *Frente al ideal, mis memorias*. Mexico City: Casa del Obrero Mundial, 1974.
Trexler, Richard. *Reliving Golgotha: The Passion Play of Iztapalapa*. Cambridge, MA: Harvard University Press, 2003.
Truitt, Jonathan. *Sustaining the Divine in Mexico Tenochtitlan: Nahuas and Catholicism, 1523–1700*. Norman: University of Oklahoma Press, 2018.
Trythall, Marissa Patulli. "Edmund A. Walsh S.J. and the Settlement of the Religious Question in Mexico, 1929." *Archivum Historicum Societatis Iesu* 80 (2011): 3–44.
Ulloa, Daniel. *Los predicadores divididos: los dominicos en Nueva España, siglo XVI*. Mexico City: El Colegio de México, 1977.
Uría, Ignacio. *Iglesia y revolución en Cuba: Enrique Pérez Serantes (1883–1968), el obispo que salvó a Fidel Castro*. Madrid: Ediciones Encuentro, 2011.
Urias Horcasitas, Beatriz. "El poder de los símbolos/los símbolos en el poder: teosofía y 'mayanismo' en Yucatán (1922–1923)." *Relaciones* 29 (2008): 179–212.
Uroz, Antonio. *La cuestión religiosa en México*. Mexico City, 1926.
Valenzuela, Georgette José. *La campaña presidencial de 1923–1924 en México*. Mexico City: INEHRM, 1998.
———. "El viaje de Plutarco Elías Calles como presidente electo por Europa y Estados Unidos." *Revista Mexicana de Sociología* 57, no. 3 (1995): 191–210.
Valles Medina, Patricia. *Del anarquismo a la utopía: la visión revolucionaria de Miguel Mendoza López Schwerdtfeger*. Guadalajara: Universidad de Guadalajara, 1996.
Van Kley, Dale. *The Religious Origins of the French Revolution: From Calvin to the Civil Constitution, 1560–1791*. New Haven, CT: Yale University Press, 1996.
Van Young, Eric. "The New Cultural History Comes to Old Mexico." *Hispanic American Historical Review* 79, no. 2 (1999): 212–47.
Vasconcelos, José. *El Desastre*. Mexico City: Trillas, 2000. First published in 1938.
Vaughan, Mary Kay. *Cultural Politics in Revolution: Teachers, Peasants, and Schools in Mexico, 1930–1940*. Tucson: University of Arizona Press, 1997.

Vázquez Mantecón, María del Carmen. *Muerte y vida eterna de Benito Juárez: el deceso, sus rituales, y su memoria*. Mexico City: UNAM, 2006.
Velasco Toro, José. "Indigenismo y rebelión totonaca de Papantla, 1885–1886." *América Indígena* 39, no. 1 (1979): 81–105.
Velázquez Hernández, Emilia. "Las comunidades indígenas del Istmo veracruzano frente al proyecto liberal de fines del siglo XIX" In *El istmo mexicano: una región inasequible. Estado, poderes locales, y dinámicas espaciales (siglos XVI–XXI)*, edited by Emilia Velázquez, Éric Léonard, Odile Hoffmann, and M.-F. Prévôt-Schapira, 291–352. Mexico City: CIESAS, 2009.
———. *Territorios fragmentados: estado y comunidad indígena en el Istmo veracruzano*. Mexico City: CIESAS, 2006.
Velázquez, Emilia, Éric Léonard, Odile Hoffmann, and M.-F. Prévôt-Schapira, eds. *El istmo mexicano: una región inasequible. Estado, poderes locales, y dinámicas espaciales (siglos XVI–XXI)*. Mexico City: CIESAS, 2009.
Vera, Fortino Hipólito. *Itinerario parroquial del Arzobispado de México y reseña histórica, geográfica y estadística de las parroquias del mismo Arzobispado: apéndices, erecciones parroquiales de México y Puebla y Santuario del Sacromonte*. Mexico City: Biblioteca Enciclopédica del Estado de México, 1981. First published in 1880.
Vera y Zuria, Pedro. *Cartas a mis seminaristas en la primera visita pastoral de la arquidiócesis*. Barcelona: Librería Católica Internacional, 1929.
Voekel, Pamela. *Alone before God: The Religious Origins of Modernity in Mexico*. Durham, NC: Duke University Press, 2002.
Weis, Robert. *For Christ and Country: Militant Catholic Youth in Postrevolutionary Mexico*. Cambridge: Cambridge University Press, 2019.
Wernick, Andrew. *Auguste Comte and the Religion of Humanity: The Post-Theistic Program of French Social Theory*. Cambridge: Cambridge University Press, 2001.
Williams García, Roberto. *Mitos tepehuas*. Mexico City: SepSetentas, 1972.
———. *Los tepehuas*. Xalapa: Universidad Veracruzana, 2004. First published in 1963.
Williman, John B. *La Iglesia y el estado en Veracruz, 1840–1940*. Mexico City: SepSetentas, 1976.
Winfield Capitaine, Fernando. "La cofradía de Cristo Negro de Otatitlán en el siglo XVIII." *La Palabra y el Hombre* 89 (1994): 43–54.
Wright-Rios, Edward. *Revolutions in Mexican Catholicism: Reform and Revelation in Oaxaca, 1887–1934*. Durham, NC: Duke University Press, 2008.
Yannakakis, Yanna. *The Art of Being In-Between: Native Intermediaries, Indian Identity, and Local Rule in Colonial Oaxaca*. Durham, NC: Duke University Press, 2008.
Yox, Andrew. "The Parochial Context of Trusteeism: Buffalo's St. Louis Church, 1828–1855." *Catholic Historical Review* 76, no. 4 (1990): 712–33.
Zalpa, Genaro. *Enciclopedia de las religiones en México*. Aguascalientes: Universidad Autónoma de Aguascalientes, 2014.
Zárate Toscano, Verónica. "Tradición y Modernidad: La Orden Imperial de Guadalupe. Su Organización y sus Rituales." *Historia Mexicana* 45, no. 2 (1995): 191–220.
Zúñiga Trujillo, Julio César. "El Conflicto Religioso en Orizaba: de la Ley Calles a la Ley Tejeda." BA thesis, Universidad Veracruzana, 2015.

INDEX

Acatzingo (Pue.), 79
Acayucan (Ver.), 92, 98, 147, 151; agrarian conflicts, 134–36
Actipan (Pue.), 79, 88, 142, 150, 156; religious hatred of Acatzingo, 159–60
Actopan (Hgo.), 38
Aglipay, Gregorio (*filipino* indie Catholic leader), 50–51
Agrarismo: affinity with ICAM, 113, 117–18, 120–40; Christian cooperativist roots of, 112, 114–18; Raiffeisenism, 115–16, 117; sectarian politics, 120–30, 159–60; targeting *pulque* estates, 119
Agraristas: core supporters of ICAM, 79; regional support in México and Veracruz, 112–40; religious devotion and ideas, 88–89, 123–24, 128; violence and ICAM, 98, 159–60, 164
Aguascalientes: San Marcos tragedy, 31
Aguilera Robles, Francisco (ICAM priest): biography, 188; accusations of Jacobinism, 189–90
Ahuacatlán (Pue.), 85, 87, 152, 163
Ajoloapan (Hgo.), 124–25
Alarcón, Próspero María (archbishop of Mexico), 21
Alarcón, Teodoro (ICAM priest), 137, 192, 209
Almazán, Leonides Andreu (governor of Puebla): persecutes ICAM, 96, 97
Almoloya (Hgo.), 97, 124, 149–50, 151, 156
Altaplanicie pulquera: agrarian reform in, 113, 118–30
Altar del perdón (Mexico City cathedral): Pérez as celebrant, 14, 25
Alva, Pedro de (congressman): opposes ICAM, 51
Alvarado (Ver.), 92
Amador, Maximino (juring Oaxacan priest), 90
Amecac (Pue.): 1890s secessionist revolt led by Pérez, 21–22
Amecameca (Méx.), 88
Amézquita, Perfecto (bishop of Puebla): problems with Pérez, 21, 22, 23

Anaya, Encarnación (Hidalgo priest): theological dispute with Pérez, 43, 66, 67
Anguiano, Dimás (ICAM priest), 76, 92–93, 99, 162–63, 180, 190
Anticlericalism, 14, 70–72. *See also* Calles Law
Apan (Hgo.), 43, 79, 89, 122–24
Apostolicity and ICAM, 50–55
Arámbula, Salvador (ICAM priest), 159–60, 191
Arancel (parish schedule). *See* sacramental fees
Araujo, Abraham (CROM governor), 37
Arías, Alfonso María (ICAM priest), 124–25, 171
Arredondo López, Alfredo (ICAM priest): parish appointments and work, 61, 81, 84, 85, 87, 157–58; martyrdom, 89–90
Arreglos (1929 religious truce), history and implications of, 10, 69, 94–96, 128, 132, 145
Atenco (Méx.), 88
Associations cultuelles (French lay corporations): 71, 73–74
Averardi, Nicolá (apostolic visitor): 1890s controversy with Pérez, 21–22, 23
Aves, Henry (Episcopalian bishop), 52, 184
Azamar, Manuel (Veracruz boss), 132–33

Baltimore Council (1829), 74
Bárcenas, Victoriano (*cristero*): attacks ICAM, 89
Barrios, Gabriel (Puebla *cacique*): supports ICAM, 81, 96
Basilica of Guadalupe: almost falls into ICAM's hands, 180; overpriced sacraments, 120
Becerra Acosta, Manuel, 30
Bell, Ricardo (clown), 155
Bellringing: assembly and alarm, 27, 31, 97, 128; celebratory, 98, 111 (to end Cristero War), 161; CROM foundry, 231n80; liturgical uses, 85, 171, 200; religious-political battles over, 129, 144, 167
Blavatsky, Helena (Theosophist), 64

275

Index

BNCA. *See* National Bank of Agrarian Credit
Braceros, 5, 61
Bravo, Lorenzo (PNR), 100
Briand, Aristide, 73
Briones, Adolfo (ICAM priest), 92, 98, 133, 136, 199
"Brown priests" (pro-Nazi), 181
Burial fights, 159–60

Cabeceras and *sujetos* (head and subject towns parishes): secessionist struggles involving, 21–22, 97, 143, 158–67; secessions encouraged by Bourbons, 158; tlalixacalli, 158
Cabrera de Armida, Concepción, 1
Cahíta indigenes (Sin.), 183
California, 5, 6
Calles, Plutarco Elías: agrarianism of, 118–19; closes Soledad y Santa Cruz, 30; presidency of, 3, 14; press attacks on, 32–34; religious views of, 8; reprimanded by Obregón, 34–35; support for ICAM, 27, 37; U-turn after La Soledad, 36, 38. *See also* Calles Law
Calles Law: accepted by some priests, 180; religious Bourbonism, 101; social meaning and religious implications of, 70–72, 74, 76, 153
Callismo: Christian influences over, 112, 241n13; religion and nationalism, 14, 15–16. See also *agrarismo*, Calles Law
Camargo Melo, José (ICAM priest), 212–13
Campillo Seyde, Arturo (Veracruz boss), 132
Cano, José (ICAM priest), 194
Cantores, ordination of, 202
Cárdenas, Lázaro, 136
Carfora, Carmel Henry (NAORC bishop), 53–55
Carnival, 3, 27, 132
Carrión, Ernesto (Protestant divine), 54
Casaponsa, José (ICAM priest), 31
Cassocks: allegations of *jorongo* used as, 1; burning of, 101; made by CROM, 173; primitive Christian emblem, 182
Castellanos, Salvador (ICAM priest), 100
Castellanos López, Aureo (juring priest), 91
Castillo, Hilario, 125
Castro, Miguel, 81

Cather, Willa (novelist), 4
Catholic clergy: autonomy of, 82, 91; lower clergy and class antagonisms, 6, 7, 26, 29, 44, 47, 174, 187–88, 192, 193–96. *See also* Mexican Catholic priests
Celis, Father Antonio (ICAM priest), 12
Celis Casillas, Jorge (ICAM priest), 156, 201
Cervantes Castro, Melecio (ICAM priest), 138
Cessatio a divinis. *See* suspension of public worship (July 31, 1926)
Chacón, Manuel (lay sponsor of ICAM), 170
Chacón, Natalia (Calles's wife): ICAM exequies, 50
Chalco (Méx.), 29
Chamula (Chis.) and ICAM, 210–11
Chicontepec (Ver.), 99, 143–44
Chinameca (Ver.), 92, 136–37
Chinese Patriotic Catholic Association, 11
"Churchstateness," 9, 217n42
Church-state separation: history of in Mexico, 3, 9. *See also* French Church-State Separation Law (1905)
Circular 33 (1929 edict ousting Mexican clergy), 95
Cismáticos. *See* schism
Ciudad Hidalgo (Mich.), 1
Coatepec (D.F.), 117, 120
Coatzacoalcos, colonial Catholic diocese of, 7
Communalism, 130–40
Condueñazgos, 131, 139
Confederación Regional Obrera Mexicana (CROM): 3, 14, 15–17, 30–31, 35, 37; Grupo Solidario del Movimiento Obrero, 115; religious action, 115, 173. *See also* Lombardo Toledano, Vicente; Morones, Luis; Treviño, Ricardo
Con la Cruz y con la Patria (Cuban revolutionary church), 11, 211, 217–18n48
Concepción Pápalo (Oax.), 90
Constitution of 1917, 3, 32, 70, 72, 74. *See also* Calles Law
Constitutionalist fathers (*padres constitucionalistas*), 43
Contreras, Romualdo, 121
Cooper, Irving (LCC bishop), 64
Coronado, José de la Luz (ICAM priest), 151
Coronel, Eduardo (ICAM priest), 31

Index

Corpus Christi (ICAM's cathedral): as seminary, 199–200; Pérez's funeral in, 207; political wrangling, 95; services, 2, 35, 39–40, 65

Corripio Ahumada, Ernesto (archbishop of Mexico): pastoral problems with ICAM, 213, 214

Cortés, José F. Xavier (ICAM vicar general), 211

Cosoloeacaque (Ver.), 166

Costumbre, religious, 164–66, 172, 211

Covarrubias, Miguel, 95, 166

Coxquihui (Ver.), 82, 85, 99, 149

Coyotepec (Méx.): agrarian-religious conflict with Teoloyucan, 125–26; ICAM priests in, 85, 88, 151–52

Coyutla (Ver.), 56, 81, 85, 99

Creighton, Frank (Episcopalian bishop), 52, 55

Cristeros, 89

Cristero War: ICAM as proximate cause of, 4; views and interpretations of, 9, 11, 70, 204

Crownation Day (English Protestant ritual), 49

Cruz, Roberto, 50

Cuatotalapan hacienda (Ver.), 134–35

Cuevas, Mariano (S.J.): kidnapping of ICAM priest, 29, 195

Culture wars, intra-Catholic, 11, 204

Cuyucuenda estata (Ver.), 162–63

Dávila Garza y Pardo, Eduardo (ICAM priest): churches claimed, 130, 212; "papal" pretensions, 62, 97; revolutionary career and death, 187

De la Peña, Guillermo (ICAM priest), 84–85, 88, 142, 156

De la Cruz, Elías (Knight of Guadalupe and sacristan), 170

De la Garza Treviño, Santiago (ICAM priest), 197

Díaz, Porfirio, 19, 20–21

Díaz y Barreto, Pascual (archbishop of Mexico), 95

Des Houx, Henri (supporter of *cultuelles*), 74

Dominicans: affinity with ICAM, 18, 20, 25, 82, 85

Drums, ceremonial, 165–66

Durán, Francisco (ICAM priest): charges of homosexuality and pederasty, 157, 196–97; criticizes Pérez, 163; parish work, 88, 96, 139, 151

Ecclesiastical oaths, 84–85. *See also* Mexican Catholic priests, village registrations of

Église *constitutionnelle*. *See* French revolutionary church

Eisenstein, Sergei, 122

Elizalde, José María (CROM governor), 31

El Oro (Méx.), 89

Enríquez, Ignacio (*carrancista*), 24

Enríquez, Raymundo (governor of Chiapas), 100

Episcopalian Church: relations with ICAM, 51–52, 182; priests in ICAM, 181, 183–85

Fernández, Álvaro (agronomist), 135

Fernández, Miguel Guillermo (Father "Miguelito," ICAM priest), 91–92, 99, 149, 190

Fernández de Haro, Alberto (ICAM priest), 61, 97, 208

Fiestas: Candlemas, 158; communalism, 132; Corpus Christi, 141, 150; *danza de arrieros y morenos*, 136; driver of ICAM support, 80; festive commissions and ICAM, 56–57; ICAM priests and, 146–58; legitimation of indigenous elite, 141–42; San Pascualito Bailón, 211–12; Santigueros (Moors and Christians), 157. See also *fiscales, mayordomos*

Fiscales, 81, 85, 151, 161–62

Flores, Isauro (ICAM priest), 155, 202

Fornaro, Carlo de, 24

Franciscans, 181, 183, 191, 194, 195

Fray Servando. *See* Mier, Fray Servando Teresa de

French Church-State Separation Law (1905): enactment and significance, 71, 72, 73–74; precedent for Mexico's Calles Law, 72–73

French revolutionary church, 8, 11, 21, 40, 45, 91, 174, 251n7

Galván, Úrsulo, 131

Gambrell, Herbert Pickens (Baptist professor), 39–40, 43, 51, 52, 62, 63

Games Flores, Luis (ICAM priest), 152, 199

277

Index

Gamio, Manuel, 146–47, 153
García, Pascual Luciano (ICAM priest): biography and indigeneity, 167; cares for religious images, 169; internal ICAM politics, 61; parish efforts, 92, 167–69; successful indigenous proselytism, 82–84, 155, 156, 161
García de la Cruz, Agustín (ICAM priest), 209, 212
García Mota, Camerino (ICAM priest), 88, 128
Garibay, Ángel María, 145
Garrido Canabal, Tomás: hostility to ICAM, 7–8, 75, 100-1; support for ICAM, 31
Gasca, Celestino (CROM), 16, 75
Gasparri, Pietro (Vatican Secretary of State), 69
Gente de razón, clashes with indigenous people, 158, 163–66. See also *cabeceras* and *sujetos*
Gide, Charles (economist), 116
Gillow, Eulogio (bishop of Oaxaca), 19, 20, 24, 82, 181
Gómez, José de Jesús (ICAM priest), 150
Gómez, José Filogonio (ICAM priest), 55, 201
Gómez, Urbano (ICAM priest), 100, 181
Gómez Morín, Manuel, 112, 116–17
Gómez Ruvalcaba, Benigno (Episcopalian and ICAM priest): attacks sacrament of confession, 48; biography and Episcopalian career, 52, 183–85; mixes primitive religion and psychology, 184–85; pastoral and parish visits, 61, 149–50; sacred orator, 43, 49–50, 66–67
González, Ricardo V. (ICAM priest), 89, 136, 151, 199; liberalism, 192; offer to Tejeda, 192–93
González Púnaro, Manuel, 31
Grajales, Victórico (governor of Chiapas), 101
Gravissimo Officii (encyclical on French *cultuelles*), 73
Guadalajara seminary, alleged liberalism of, 181, 182, 183
Guatemalannesss, and Mexican citizenship, 93, 100, 171–72
Guerrero, Melesio (ICAM priest), 94, 95
Guízar y Valencia, Rafael (bishop of Veracruz), 99, 147, 180–81

Gunpowder Plot, 49
Guzmán, Florentino, 82

Hernández, Silvestre, 18
Higinio Hank, Jorge (ICAM priest, assumed father of Carlos Hank González), 253n59
Hostia Sangrante (Mexico City Bleeding Christ devotion), 212–13
Huehuetla (Hgo.), 138
Huehuetla (Pue.), 38, 88, 138, 151, 166
Huetxoyuca (Pue.): 1950s defection to ICAM, 209–10
Huguet, Arturo, 136
Hurtado, Arnulfo (Jesuit historian), 26

Iglesia Católica Apostólica Mexicana (ICAM): agrarianism of, 117–18; allegations of consecrations using *mezcal* and *tortillas*, 1, 28, 215n10; almsgiving, 40–41, 58–59; anti-Romanism, 17, 42–43, 47, 56–57; apostolic succession, 50–55; auricular confession, 62; Bible-reading, 62; Catholic primitivism, 39–40, 46–50; creation of new dioceses, 60–61; ecclesiology, 40–41, 44, 47, 75–76; finances and parish remittances, 58–60, 75; geography, 76–79, 80; *guadalupanismo*, 40, 46, 188, 232n93; historiography, 4, 5, 142–43, 156, 172, 204–06; indigeneity, 5, 6, 7, 84–94, 145; *indigenismo*, 146; internal conflicts, 60–62; lay oversight, 57–58; manifesto, 17, 40, 46; mediation of local religion, 60, 145; missionary quality of, 6, 94; numerical strength of, 6, 76, 79; orders, 44; pastoral visits by bishops, 151; patriotic cult, 49; plans for parish redistribution, 29, 17, 47; religious calendar, 148; religious pluralism and, 11; rurality, 4–5, 7, 37–38; sacraments, 48, 62; sources and archives, 12, 178–79, 218n49; state formation role, 6, 7, 11; supported by CROM and PLM, 14–17, 35, 39; theological innovations, 62–63; transnational networking, 65; vernacular liturgy, 46, 47, 48–49; women's support for, 28, 29, 30, 65, 144, 156. See also Mexican Catholic priests
Iglesia Católica Apostólica Renovada del Estado Plurinacional de Bolivia (ICARBOL), 13

Index

Iglesia Católica Reformada de Venezuela (ICARVEN), 13
Independente Filipino Church (IFI), 51
Indigenous elites. See *principales*
Indigenous priesthood, 174, 198–202, 205. See also García, Pascual Luciano; Mexican Catholic priests
Infante, Pedro (ICAM priest), 75, 87–88
Ixcaquistla (Pue.), 37, 163–64
Ixhuatlán (Ver.), 138, 149
Ixtacalco (Méx.), 121–22
Ixtayopan (D.F.), 112
Ixtepec (Pue.), 151
Iztapalapa (D.F.), 24–25

Jacobo y Calvo, Mauricio (archpriest of Basilica of Guadalupe), 180
Jacobinism, 189
Jaltipan (Ver.), 92, 167–69
Jansenism, 8, 43, 44–45, 53, 66–67
Jara, Heriberto (governor of Veracruz): religious policy, 93, 167; rivalry with Adalberto Tejeda, 167
Jaurès, Jean (French socialist), 73, 233n11
Jesuits, 13, 16, 206
Jiménez Juárez, Ángel (ICAM official), 15, 50
Jonotla (Pue.), 87, 164–66
Juanco, Rufino (Spiritist), 64
Juárez, Benito: separates Church and state, 3; ICAM veneration of, 49–50
Juárez, Teodoro (ICAM priest), 80, 81, 99, 151
Juárez clan (Xometla *agraristas*), 127–30, 147
Juchitán (Oax.), 37, 75, 91
Juntas de administración civil (Ver.), 132, 133
Juntas vecinales, 57–58, 71, 72, 74–75, 86, 137
Juring priests, 90, 91, 180
Juxtlahuaca (Oax.), 19, 20, 90

Keys to churches, battles over, 86, 88, 163
Knights of Guadalupe (CROM religious order), 18–19, 26–27, 36, 170

Lagarde, Ernest (French ambassador), 173, 174
Landas Berghes de Rache, prince (Old Catholic), 53

Lanz Duret, Miguel (jurist), 71, 101
Lárrazabal de Villafañe, María, 25
La Soledad. See Santa Cruz y Soledad, parish of; Virgin of Solitude
Law of Agricultural Credit (1926), 116–17. See also *agrarismo*
Law of Ejidal Patrimony (1925), 117. See also *agrarismo*
Lawrence, D. H. (novelist), vi, 7
Lay patronage of churches, 45, 57–58, 70–71, 72, 74–75
Lazarini, José Luis (ICAM priest), 142, 154–55, 156, 157, 191
LCAEV. See League of Agrarian Communities of Veracruz State
Leadbeter, Charles (LCC founder), 63
League of Agrarian Communities of Veracruz State (LCAEV), 98, 113, 130–40
Lence, Germán ("the Cuban Pérez"), 211, 217–18n48
León, Luis L. (Calles's agriculture minister), 8, 112, 117, 118
León Toral, José de, 1
Liberal Catholic Church (LCC), 46, 63–64
Liberal clergy, 4, 8, 47, 63, 181, 188
Liga Nacional Campesina (LNC), 130–31
Liga Nacional Defensora de la Libertad Religiosa (LNDLR), 4, 14
Liñán, Vicente (ICAM priest), 79, 88, 151, 154–55, 201
Local Agricultural Credit Society (SLCA), 117, 119, 123, 125, 128
Lombardo Toledano, Vicente, 16, 112–13, 115
López, José María, Dr. (ICAM priest), 87
López Guerra, Alfonso, 145
López Obrador, Andrés Manuel, 13
López Sierra, Benigno (Porfirian pedagogue and Calles's mentor), 182
López y Sierra, Antonio Benigno (ICAM vicar general, brother of Benigno López Sierra): administration, 218n49; attacks *cessatio a divinis*, 76; biography, 181–83; constitutionalizes ICAM, 57; CROM connections, 15, 181–82; episcopal consecration, 54; knight of Guadalupe, 36; liturgical martinet, 200; power struggle with Pérez, 61–62, 182; remittance collector, 59
López Valdéz, Macario (ICAM priest), 54, 61, 62, 85, 86, 151, 182–83

279

Index

Los Mixtecos (colonial parish), 18
Los Tuxtlas (Ver.), 98, 132–34
Lozano, Joaquín, 128–29

Mano Negra (Veracruz gang), 163
Martínez, Eudaldo (infamous priest), 170–71
Matamoros (Tamps.), 93, 95
Mathew, Arnold Harris (Old Catholic), 53
Mayorga, Rubén Fidel (ICAM priest), 208, 214
Mayordomos, 56, 81, 85, 93, 150, 151, 154–56 (and Calles Law, 153), 161–62, 167–69
Mazatán (Chis.), 155, 210
Melgosa, José (ICAM priest), 190
Melo, Fernando (tax collector and ICAM patron), 85, 157, 163
Méndez, Juan M., 20, 80
Méndez, Ruperto, 21
Mendoza López Schwerdtfeger, Miguel (Catholic Zapatista), 114
Meyer, Jean, 4
Mexican Catholics: affiliation dismissed as indigenous "ignorance," 143–44, 146–47, 171; agrarian participation, 114, 120–40; animosity towards, 2; attitudes and attachments to Catholic priests and sacraments, 143, 149, 150–51, 156–57; identity, 13; indigeneity of, 5, 141, 145, 149; Marianism and apparitions, 148, 165–66; migration, 5; saintly devotions, 153; sectarianism and religious intolerance, 120–30, 159–61; women, 28, 29, 30, 65, 144, 156. See also *agraristas, fiestas, cabeceras* and *sujetos, costumbre*, Iglesia Católica Apostólica Mexicana (ICAM)
Mexican Catholic priests: *arreglos*, responses to, 190; beatings, lynchings, and killings of, 31, 86, 89, 97; biographies, 187–202; bishops, 181–87; celibacy and marriage, 58, 182, 183, 185, 193, 194–96; defined by sacramental ministry not obedience, 65–68, 76; dislike of *indios*, 157; ecclesiastical tribunal, 198; *fiestas*, 141–42, 145, 146–58; financial improprieties, 152, 155–56, 173, 199, 193; geographical origins of, 181–84, 188; homosexuality, 156–57, 197–98; *cantores*, ordination of, 202; indigenous languages, 149, 154, 188; views on indigenous politics, 144–45; martyrdom, 89–90; numbers and distribution, 174, 176–79; parish livings, 58–59; parish ministry, 173–203; poverty and professional occupations, 58, 183, 191, 193–96; recantations, 194, 196, 207–08; recruitment and training, 90, 199–201, 208; relations with *mayordomos*, 154–56; resurgence with PRI, 1950s–1960s, 208–12; sacraments and record-keeping, 59, 151, 141, 165; stipends and remittances, 58–60, 142; synods, 54, 58, 62, 64, 68, 156; village registrations of, 84-94. See also Iglesia Católica Apostólica Mexicana (ICAM)
Mexican revolutionaries, personal religiosity of, 8–9, 16
Mexican Spiritist Federation, 64
Mier, Fray Servando Teresa de, 8, 33, 43
Miranda, Miguel Darío (bishop of Tulancingo), 143–44, 205
Mójica, José Agustín (ICAM priest): parish complaints, 150; biography, 195–96
Moneda, Eduardo (CROM), 16
Monge, Manuel (ICAM priest): La Soledad, 17, 26, 27; kidnapping and retraction, 29; biography, 194–95
Monte de Honor, Hieronymus von (ICAM priest): in Huasteca, 139–40, 166; biography, 186–87
Mora y Daza, José María (bishop of Veracruz), 20
Mora y del Río, José (archbishop of Mexico), 26–27, 28, 32, 33, 40, 147
Morfín, Rafael (juring priest), 87, 180–81
Morones, Felipe (canon), apostatizes at gunpoint, 175–76
Morones, Luis (CROM), 4, 14, 16, 17, 37. See also Confederación Regional Obrera Mexicana (CROM)
Motozintla (Chis.), 100, 181
Muníve, José Antonio Toribio (ICAM priest): parish activities, 92, 137, 168, 202; homosexuality, 156–57, 197–98
Mussolini, Benito, 70

Nahuas, 92, 132, 134–36, 143–44, 167–69
Napoleonic Concordat (1801), 11

National Bank of Agrarian Credit, 115–16
Nopalucan (Tlax.), ICAM and 1950s Niño Dios cult, 209
North American Old Roman Catholic Church (NAORC), 54

Oaxaca (Oax.), 18, 20, 30, 90, 91, 180
Obregón, Álvaro: agrarian views, 118, 122, 127; martial law, 185: rivalry with Calles, 14, 34; reprimands Calles for La Soledad, 34–35;
Ochoa, Felipe de Jesús (ICAM priest), 90
Old Catholic churches, 51, 52–55
Orozco y Jiménez, Francisco (archbishop of Guadalajara), 32
Ortiz, Eulogio, 175
Ortiz, Heraclio (ICAM priest), 99
Ortiz Petricioli, José (CROM), 119
Ortiz Rubio, Pascual, uses church squabbles as secularization pretext, 160, 207
Ortiz y Rodríguez, José de Jesús (archbishop of Guadalajara), 181

Páez, Alberto (Veracruz boss), 162
Pajapan (Ver.), 132
Palavicini, Félix, positivistic support for ICAM, 33, 233n15
Pallares, Eduardo (jurist), 32
Pallares, Macario (ICAM priest), 121
Palomar y Vizcarra, Miguel, 118
Papantla (Ver.), 141
Papantla, diocese of, 80
Paredes, Antonio de Jesús (revolutionary priest), 24
Parish inventories, 85–86
Partido Laborista Mexicano (1920s PLM), 15, 30, 35, 36, 39, 135. *See also* Confederación Regional Obrera Mexicana (CROM)
Partido Liberal Mexicano (*magonista* PLM), 135
Partido Nacional Revolucionario (PNR), 16, 100, 132
Partido Revolucionario Institucional (PRI), relations with ICAM, 208–13
Partido Rojo Sanandrescano (Ver.), 132
"Patriarca Pérez" ("Patriarch Pérez"). *See* Pérez Budar, José Joaquín
Patron saints and ICAM, 148–49
Peralvillo, 193

Pérez, Agapito (Pérez's nephew and general), 90
Pérez, Jesús L. (ICAM priest), 51
Pérez Budar, Eustaquio (brother of José Joaquín), 19–20
Pérez Budar, Dionisia (sister of José Joaquín), 23
Pérez Budar, José Joaquín ("Patriarch"): alleged apostasy of, 1; alleged recantation, 206–7; Amecac revolt, 21–22; army career, 19–20, 21, 24, 80; *arreglos* and, 96; assassination target, 1; campaigns against sacramental fees, 21–24, 25; communication with Calles, 27; communication with Morones, 15; death, 62, 206–7; friends and relatives of, 19–20, 25, 81, 90; emulates Hidalgo, 3, 17, 26, 49; governance of ICAM, 60–61; holy and episcopal orders, 20, 44, 50, 51, 54–55; indigeneity and prestige, 4, 145–46; jail, 22; myths surrounding, 1, 19, 28; nationalism of, 1, 17, 25, 47; personal and devotional life, 19–20, 25–26, 70; popular animosity towards, 1, 4; *pueblo* visits, 120; relationship with Porfirio Díaz, 20–21; revolutionary views of, 7–8, 113; Roman Catholic ministry, 14, 19–20, 24–26; Soledad y Santa Cruz occupation, 26, 27; views on Protestantism, 22, 51; Spiritism and Theosophy, 63–64. *Passim*.
Pérez Serantes, Enrique (Cuban bishop), 211
Pérez Treviño, Manuel, 37
Pérez Villafañe, Antonio (Pérez's cousin), 25
Pérez Villafañe, Pedro (Pérez's nephew), 90
Pérez Villafañe, Manuel (Pérez's cousin), 90
Pisa Flores (Ver.): Tepehuas' agrarian struggle, 138–39; religion, 166–67, 214
Pistoia Synod, 45
"Pito" Pérez (fictional character): Patriarch Pérez compared to, 1, 215n10
Pius X, 73–74
Pius XI, 7, 32
Plumed Serpent, The. *See* Lawrence, D. H.
Pochutla (Oax.), 90
Polish National Catholic Church, 53

Index

Portes Gil, Emilio, 10, 69, 70, 94, 95, 96, 98, 129
Presenssé, Francis de (French socialist), 73, 74
Priests, registration of: laws and meaning, 9, 15, 69, 71, 72, 74; local reactions and enactment, 85–86, 92, 94, 96, 159, 164, 209. *See also* Calles Law
Principales (indigenous elites), 6, 10, 81, 85, 141, 146, 157, 161–62, 163, 171, 197. See also *fiscales, mayordomos*
Protestantism: 6, 16, 22, 39, 49, 57, 86, 174, 185, 197
Protestants: connections real and imagined to ICAM, 51, 54, 61, 84, 91, 176
Puerto México (Ver., today Coatzacoalcos), 92, 141, 149, 150
Pulque estates, 113, 118–30

Quemasantos, 101
Querétaro, 30

Raiffeisen, Friedrich Wilhelm (Christian cooperativist), 115–16
Ramírez, José (ICAM priest), 36, 93, 99–101, 169–72, 190
Reboulen, Luisa (ICAM benefactress), 96, 167–68, 200, 202
"Red priests" (pro-Soviet), 251n7
Regulez, Dr. (Knight of Guadalupe), 36, 81
Reinoso, José Laurencio (ICAM priest), 93
Religious pluralism, ICAM and roots of, 11, 205
Religious revivalism, indigenous, 164–66
Rerum Novarum (encyclical), 115
Restauración (ICAM newspaper), publication and circulation, 12, 80, 90
Retinger, Joseph (Polish-British militant), 15
Revueltas, José (author), 18
Reyes, Zeferino, Ing. (ICAM official), 60, 61
Reyes Heroles, Jesús, and official support for ICAM, 212
Reynosa (Tamps.), 94
Ricard, Robert, views on ICAM, 6, 216n27
Rioting, 27, 29–31, 100, 127–28
Riva Palacio, Carlos (governor of México), 182
Rivera, Agustín (liberal priest), 181

Rivera, Diego, 30
Rodarte, Fernando (CROM governor), 37
Rodríguez, Tiburcio, 125
Rojas Vargas, Elías (ICAM priest), 199
Roman Catholic Church, views of Pérez, 1, 4, 7, 32, 54
Roman Catholic priests and laity: *arreglos*, 95, 135–36; curiosity about ICAM, 40–41; forced to join ICAM, 175–76; hostility to ICAM, 32, 76, 86; opposition to *agrarismo*, 122; priests' indiscretions, 170, 173; relations with indigenous Catholics, 147
"Romanization," 3, 7, 41, 205
Ruiz, Manuel (Knight of Guadalupe), 27
Ruiz, Samuel (bishop of San Cristóbal Las Casas), 211
Ruiz Cortines, Adolfo, and 1950s revival of ICAM, 208, 209
Ruiz y Flores, Leopoldo (Archbishop of Morelia and Apostolic Delegate), 4, 92, 126

Sacramental fees: controversies surrounding, 21–24, 56–57. *See also* voluntarism, Mexican Catholic priests
Sáenz, Moisés, 16
Salas Vidal, Manuel (ICAM priest), 60, 88, 155, 208
Salinas de Gortari, Carlos, and ICAM, 213
Saltillo (Coah.), 31
Sánchez Camacho, Eduardo (dissident bishop of Tamaulipas): performs special ordination for Pérez, 44, 51; seminary teaching, 181
San Marcos church (Aguas.), 31
San Simón de Bravo (Pue.), 79, 155, 156
San Pascualito Bailón, Chiapanecan cult of and ICAM, 211–12
Santa Cruz y Soledad, parish of: attack on, 3, 14, 26-30; history of, 17–18; interdiction, 28; reactions to occupation by ICAM, 32–37, 39–40; reopening, 95, 111
Santa María Magdalena (Qro.), 147
Santería, 13
Santo Domingo (Ver.), 85, 149
Schism: conceptual problems of term, 13; theological offense and canon law concept, 4, 28, 216n19; confused with rebellion, 180

Schismatics. *See* schism
Schultz-Delitsch, Hermann (German cooperativist), 116
Scio de San Miguel, Felipe, Spanish bible of, 46
Secretaría de Educación Pública (SEP), 6, 49, 82, 144, 184
Secularization: theory and practice, 7, 9, 205; eighteenth-century style, 10; sectarian tensions as pretext for, 160. *See also* "Churchstateness"
Sermons, 43, 66–67, 82–84; importance to ICAM's indigenous congregations, 154–56, 161, 169
Sexuality: indigenous views on, 197; pederasty, 196–97; priests' homosexuality, 156–57, 197–98; priests' sexual incontinence, 173, 194–96; sexual abuse, 170; sexual violence as political weapon, 129. *See also* Mexican Catholic priests
Sierra Norte (Pue.), 80, 82, 86, 142
Silva, Alejandro (priest of Santa Cruz y Soledad), 18, 26, 33
Simony. *See* sacramental fees; voluntarism
Sindicato "Hilario C. Salas" (Ver.), 135
Siurob, José (revolutionary), 185
Sociedad Local de Crédito Agrícola. *See* Local Agricultural Credit Society (SLCA)
Soconusco (Chis.), 6, 7, 82, 93, 169
Soriano, Manuel, 37
Spanish clergy, 18, 26, 47, 164, 191–92, 194–95
Spiritism, 49–50, 63
Stresser-Péan, Guy (anthropologist), 12, 157, 165
Sujetos. See *cabeceras* and *sujetos*
Suspension of public worship (July 31, 1926–June 21, 1929): concepts of priesthood in relation to, 65–68, 180; meanings and implications of, 10, 69, 76, 80, 146–47. *See also* Calles Law
Syncretism, 7, 157

Tabasco, 7–8
Tacuba (D.F.), 30
Tamaulipas, 92–93
Tapachula (Chis.), 36, 60, 82, 93, 169–72
Tapayula (Pue.), 85

Tecamachalco (Pue.), 86, 88, 97
Tehuantepec isthmus, 91–92
Tehuantepec, diocese of, 80
Tehuizotla (Pue.): theological reasons for backing ICAM, 88, 114; violent rivalry with Molcaxac, 160–61
Tejeda, Adalberto: agrarian leasing policy, 130; governor of Veracruz, 93, 98, 130–40; interior minister, 10, 34, 74–75; interviews putative schismatics, 180; relationship with Pérez, 10, 19, 75; religious views of, 8; rivalry with Jara, 167; support for ICAM and agrarian politics, 130–40
Tejeda, Miguel (priest and uncle of Adalberto Tejeda), 8
Tenango (Hgo.), 38, 89–99
Tenango (Méx.), 97
Tenancingo (Tlax.): ICAM and parish self-determination, 161; invitations to ICAM, 89, 149; PRI and 1950s sectarian clashes, 208–09
Tenoxtitlán (Méx.): agrarian-religious conflict with Jocotitlán, 158–59; petitions to Pérez, 37, 79, 88, 147
Teotepec (Oax.), 91
Tepecoacuilco (Gro.), 89–90
Tepehuas, 138–40, 166–67, 214
Tepejí (Hgo.), 122
Tepetlaoxtoc (Méx.): Pérez as *cura*, 25; Pérez's relations with *principales*, 85
Tepetlixpa (Méx.), 145, 156
Tetela (Pue.), 84
Texas, 5, 6, 61, 62, 182
Theosophy, 46, 63–64
¡Tierra Libre!, 114
Tinocos (Coatepec *agraristas*), 120
Tirado, Claudio (governor of Puebla), 81
Tlachinola (Pue.), 20
Tlaola (Pue.), ICAM stronghold, 59, 82, 96, 150, 151, 155, 157, 187, 197
Torres, Francisco (lay patron of ICAM), 157, 197
Torres, Juan Jacobo, 133
Totonacs, 85, 87, 88, 132, 138, 141, 147, 148, 149, 164–66
Treviño, Ricardo (PLM deputy and CROM general secretary), 15, 16, 17, 26, 33, 50, 75, 182
Trujillo, Aniceto (ICAM priest), 97, 191

Index

Trusteeism (practice of religious incorporation in U.S.), 71, 74, 81
Tuxtepec revolt, 19
Tuxtla Gutiérrez (Chis.), 144, 211–12
Tziltzacuapan (Ver.), 138–39

Uribe, José (ICAM priest), 38, 193
U.S. responses to ICAM, 34, 69
Utrecht, Jansenist Dutch see of, 53, 54

Valdéz, Emeterio (ICAM priest and ex-revolutionary), 59, 60, 87, 90, 185–86
Valdéz, Laureano, 26
Varlet, Dominique Marie (French Jansenist bishop), 53
Vasconcelos, José, 2, 34
Valenzuela Galindo, Gilberto (Calles's interior minister), 26–27, 30, 34
Varela, José (ICAM priest), 150, 155
Vatican Council, 42, 51
Vázquez Aguirre, Felipe (ICAM priest), 97
Vehementer Nos (encyclical on French *cultuelles*), 73
Veracruz, diocese of, 80
Veracruz (Ver.): ICAM in, 36, 92–93, 99; state elections of 1929, 132, 136, 137
Vera y Zuria, Pedro (archbishop of Puebla), 51, 86, 87, 147, 158
Villahermosa (Tab.), 31
Virgen de la Aparecida ("Virgen de la O"), 162
Virgen de la Soledad. *See* Virgin of Solitude
Virgen del Peñón, 164–65
Virgin of Solitude: image of, 1, 18, 27, 40–41
Viveros, María Guadalupe (Pérez's wife), 19

Voladores, 132
Voluntarism, religious, 45, 55–58, 151–52, 169

Wallace, Henry Agard (LCC supporter), 64
Walsh, Edmund, S.J. (author of the *arreglos*), 69
Wedgwood, James Inglewood (LCC founder), 63
Williams García, Roberto (anthropologist), 12, 138, 140
"With the Cross and the Fatherland." *See* Con la Cruz y con la Patria

Xalapa (Ver.), 20
Xalostoc (Méx.), 88, 120–21, 156
Xilitla (Ver.), 140
Xochiapulco (Pue.), 20
Xochitlán (Pue.), 84–85, 151, 154–55, 156
Xometla (Méx.): agrarian-religious conflict with Acolman, 127–30, 158; religious petitions to ICAM and Mora y del Río, 79, 147; Santiagueros, 157

Yehualtepec (Pue.), 79, 88, 96, 155, 158, 161–62

Zacatelco (Tlax.), 82–83
Zacatlán (Pue.), 86
Zacapoaxtla (Pue.), 87
Zapotecs, 90–91
Zapotitlán (Pue.), 59, 85, 86, 87, 151, 157–58
Zavala, Lorenzo de, 44
Zavala, Mauricio (agrarian priest), 26
Zongozotla (Ver.), 85, 87
Zoques, 170, 211, 212
Zozocolco (Ver.), 151

www.ingramcontent.com/pod-product-compliance
Lightning Source LLC
Chambersburg PA
CBHW020943230426
43666CB00005B/139